# FORBIDDEN MEMORIES

# FORBIDDEN MEMORIES

*Women's experiences of 1965 in Eastern Indonesia*

Edited by Mery Kolimon, Liliya Wetangterah
and Karen Campbell-Nelson

*Translated by Jennifer Lindsay*

**Originally published as**
*Memori-Memori Terlarang:*
*Perempuan Korban & Penyintas Tragedi '65 di Nusa Tenggara Timur.*
NTT: Yayasan Bonet Pinggupir, 2012 (ISBN: 978-602-99955-1-0)

Authors:
Mery Kolimon, Dorkas Sir, Adriania Tiluata, Erna Hinadang, Petronela Loy Bhoga, Martha Bire, Golda M. E. Sooai, Welys Hawu Haba- TaEdini, Elfrantin J. de Haan, Fransina Rissi, Paoina Bara Pa, Dorkas Nyake Wiwi, Yetty Leyloh, Irene Umbu Lolo, Dina Penpada, Ivonne Peka, Anna Salukhfeto and Liliya Wetangterah

*Forbidden Memories: Women's experiences of 1965 in Eastern Indonesia*
   Edited by Mery Kolimon, Liliya Wetangterah and Karen Campbell-Nelson
   Translated by Jennifer Lindsay

© Copyright 2015
All rights reserved. Apart from any uses permitted by Australia's Copyright Act 1968, no part of this book may be reproduced by any process without prior written permission from the copyright owners. Inquiries should be directed to the publisher.

Monash University Publishing
Matheson Library and Information Services Building
40 Exhibition Walk
Monash University
Clayton, Victoria 3800, Australia
www.publishing.monash.edu

Monash University Publishing brings to the world publications which advance the best traditions of humane and enlightened thought. Monash University Publishing titles pass through a rigorous process of independent peer review.

www.publishing.monash.edu/books/fm-9781922235909.html

Design: Les Thomas

Cover photograph: © Indah Pascalia Radja. The photograph was taken at Getsemany Sikumana Church building, near Kupang, on 3 November 2013.

Series: Herb Feith Translation Series

**National Library of Australia Cataloguing-in-Publication entry:**

| | |
|---|---|
| Title: | Forbidden memories : women's experiences of 1965 in Eastern Indonesia / Mery Kolimon, Liliya Wetangterah and Karen Campbell-Nelson, editors ; Jennifer Lindsay, translator. |
| ISBN: | 9781922235909 (paperback) |
| Subjects: | War victims--Abuse of--Indonesia--Personal narratives. |
| | Women--Abuse of--Indonesia. |
| | Women--Crimes against--Indonesia. |
| | Indonesia--History--Coup d'état, 1965--Personal narratives. |
| Other Creators/Contributors: | |
| | Kolimon, Mery, editor. |
| | Wetangterah, Liliya, editor. |
| | Campbell-Nelson, Karen, editor. |
| | Lindsay, Jennifer, 1951- translator. |
| Dewey Number: | 959.8036 |

Printed in Australia by Griffin Press an Accredited ISO AS/NZS 14001:2004 Environmental Management System printer.

The paper this book is printed on is certified against the Forest Stewardship Council ® Standards. Griffin Press holds FSC chain of custody certification SGS-COC-005088. FSC promotes environmentally responsible, socially beneficial and economically viable management of the world's forests.

# Contents

List of Illustrations . . . . . . . . . . . . . . . . . . . . . . . . . . . . . . . . . . . . . .viii
Acknowledgements. . . . . . . . . . . . . . . . . . . . . . . . . . . . . . . . . . . . . . .ix
About the Herb Feith Translation Series . . . . . . . . . . . . . . . . . . . . . . xii
About the Editors. . . . . . . . . . . . . . . . . . . . . . . . . . . . . . . . . . . . . . .xiii
Foreword. . . . . . . . . . . . . . . . . . . . . . . . . . . . . . . . . . . . . . . . . . . . . . xv
    *Rev. Dr. Andreas A. Yewangoe*
Foreword. . . . . . . . . . . . . . . . . . . . . . . . . . . . . . . . . . . . . . . . . . . . . . xx
    *Rev. Elga Sarapung*

**Introduction**
Forbidden Memories: Women Victims and Survivors
of the 1965 Tragedy in Eastern Indonesia. . . . . . . . . . . . . . . . . . . . . . 1
    *Mery Kolimon*

PART I. . . . . . . . . . . . . . . . . . . . . . . . . . . . . . . . . . . . . . . . . . . . . . . 21

**Chapter 1**
State Destruction of Sabu-Raijua Women Teachers. . . . . . . . . . . . . . . 25
    *Paoina Bara Pa and Dorkas Nyake Wiwi*

**Chapter 2**
The 1965 Incident and Female Activists in the City of Kupang. . . . . . . . 74
    *Nela Loy Bhoga, Martha Bire, and Golda Sooai*

**Chapter 3**
There is a Gulf Between Us: The 1965 Events, the Destruction
of Family Relationships and the Pastoral Role of the Church in
East Kupang . . . . . . . . . . . . . . . . . . . . . . . . . . . . . . . . . . . . . . . . . . 92
    *Welys Hawuhaba-TaEdini, Elfrantin de Haan, and Fransina Rissi*

**Chapter 4**
The 1965 Incident and the Women of South Central Timor's
Fight for Identity..........................................111
 *Dina Penpada, Ivonne Peka, and Anna Salukhfeto*

**Chapter 5**
Widows Fight Against Injustice in Alor.....................150
 *Dorkas Sir, Erna Hinadang, and Ina Tiluata*

**PART II**..................................................175

**Chapter 6**
Victims of the 1965 Tragedy: Sinners?......................179
 *Yetty Leyloh*

**Chapter 7**
The 1965 Tragedy in East Sumba: History from Victims'
Perspectives...............................................213
 *Irene Umbu Lolo*

**Chapter 8**
The 1965 Incidents through the Eyes of GKS Missionaries....231
 *Liliya Wetangterah*

**Epilogue**
Start with the Victims: The Meaning of the 1965 Tragedy for Contextual
Theology and Pastoral Action in NTT........................244
 *Mery Kolimon*

Glossary................................................. 275

# Appendices ............................................ 279

**Appendix 1**
Chronology of Events in Selected Areas of NTT.................. 279

**Appendix 2**
Chronology of Two Cases..................................... 288

**Appendix 3**
List of Human Rights Abuses................................. 299

**Appendix 4**
Efforts to Source Secondary Data............................. 329

**Appendix 5**
Tools for 1965 Victims' Advocacy............................. 337

**Appendix 6**
Biodata of Research Team Members ........................... 339

Bibliography .............................................. 347

# List of Illustrations

1. Map of Nusa Tenggara Timur province . . . . . . . . . . . . . . . . . . . . . . . xxiv
2. Hanga Loko Pedae, Mab'ba (Seba): Massacre site . . . . . . . . . . . . . . . . 24
3. Map of Sabu-Raijua . . . . . . . . . . . . . . . . . . . . . . . . . . . . . . . . . . . . . . . . 27
4. Former home of a Communist Party leader in the village of Rae Loro used as a detention centre for Gerwani women and women accused of being Gerwani. . . . . . . . . . . . . . . . . . . . . . . . . . . . . . . . . . . . . . . . . . . 44
5. The yard of a house beside the Seba police station where on the night of the massacre of 29 March 1966, the people were ordered to watch a film about development . . . . . . . . . . . . . . . . . . . . . . . . . . . . . . . . . . 60
6. Tegid'a, the women's house in a customary village in Sabu . . . . . . . . . . 65
7. Merdeka Stadium (Freedom Stadium), Kupang City. Female detention centre. . . . . . . . . . . . . . . . . . . . . . . . . . . . . . . . . . . . . . . . . . 73
8. Old Prison, Kupang. Male detention centre. . . . . . . . . . . . . . . . . . . . . 83
9. Document. On 29 October, 1966, the Military Resort Command 161 decided that Pak Nyongki Ndili and other colleagues should be freed from detention and from suspicion . . . . . . . . . . . . . . . . . . . . . . . . . . 87
10. Behind Oesao Market: Execution and mass burial site . . . . . . . . . . . . 91
11. One of at least seven known graves for the 1965 massacre victims in Tanah Putih, East Kupang. . . . . . . . . . . . . . . . . . . . . . . . . . . . . . . 100
12. The old East Kupang Sub District Head's office, where Nona Asmi was interrogated . . . . . . . . . . . . . . . . . . . . . . . . . . . . . . . . . . . . . . . . 104
13. Naismetan Forest, subdistrict of Mollo Tengah: Massacre site . . . . . . 110
14. Barrcks where victims from various places were detained and tortured . . . . . . . . . . . . . . . . . . . . . . . . . . . . . . . . . . . . . . . . . . . . . . . 129
15. The Imanuel Congregation worship hall in the village of Kombaki, subdsitrict of Polen, which was used as a place of torture. . . . . . . . . . 137
16. One of the execution sites in Kolbebe, village of Bena, subdistrict of South Amanuban . . . . . . . . . . . . . . . . . . . . . . . . . . . . . . . . . . . . . 139
17. Tanjung Sembilan, sub district of Teluk Mutiara (in 1965 the sub district name was Alor Barat Laut, or North West Alor): Execution site. . . . . 149
18. Isolated forest in Alor Kecil where, in February 1966, the army killed around 200 people. . . . . . . . . . . . . . . . . . . . . . . . . . . . . . . . . 159
19. Army (Puterpra) office building in Kalabahi, Alor where women were detained, forced to work and were sexually abused . . . . . . . . . . 163
20. Rua Beach, West Sumba: Massacre site . . . . . . . . . . . . . . . . . . . . . . 177
21. Mananga Beach, Mamboro, where seven people were Executed on 5 May 1966. . . . . . . . . . . . . . . . . . . . . . . . . . . . . . . . . . . . . . . . . 189
22. Notes from Synod XXI meeting of GKS in Ede, 1967 . . . . . . . . . . . 202
23. Torture site. The old prison in Melolo, District of Rindi Umalulu, East Sumba. . . . . . . . . . . . . . . . . . . . . . . . . . . . . . . . . . . . . . . . . . . 217
24. The old wharf. One of the execution sites in East Sumba. . . . . . . . . . 226

# Acknowledgements

Firstly, and most important of all, we wish to express our sincere thanks to the informants who agreed to share their stories with us, and even agreed for them to be published so they could be shared with a wide public. The church and the nation are in their debt. If Indonesia wishes to be cured, if the churches want to be healed from the collective trauma that still hinders the path of this nation moving towards the future, then one way is to listen and respond to the valuable stories of women and their children.

When members of our research team were wrestling with understanding this sensitive issue, and seeking ways to better prepare themselves with appropriate research methods, we received valuable input from our friends: namely Pak Putu Oka from the Institute for Human Creativity (LKK) in Jakarta, Th. J. Erlijna from the Indonesian Institute for Social history (ISSI) in Jakarta, and Galuh Wandita from the International Center for Transitional Justice, Indonesia (ICTJ). They helped us with training, workshops, focus groups discussions, and informal conversations. For this collaboration and support we offer our sincere thanks.

Some other parties helped us with secondary data that we needed in order to understand within a broader context the stories we collected. Father John Prior and Father Hubert Thomas from the Candraditya Research Centre in Maumere, Flores were of great assistance here. Also the Netherlands Protestant Church Archives in Utrecht, Holland gave us support by copying some material we needed. Through this, inter-church ecumenical relations gained meaning through the joint struggle for truth and justice.

Further, we also received valuable response and assistance from former missionaries of the Dutch and German churches and their families, who worked during the period 1960–70 with the Christian Church of Sumba (GKS). They were: Pastor Hendrik and Mrs Willemien Olde in Zwolle (Holland); the children of Pastor H.J. van Oostrum, namely Mr Jaap van Oostrum in Assen and his sister Mme Jeanette van Oostrum in Amsterdam; and Pastor Heinrich Baarlink in Germany. They even agreed to give us photocopies of notes from their ministries in Sumba. We also wish to give special thanks to Miss Liliya (Lia) Wetangterah who agreed to help us by interviewing the former missionaries and their families when she visited the Netherlands for a church seminar in November 2011. Further, we thank Mme Corrie van der Venn who facilitated Lia's journey and accommodation when she was in Holland. We also wish to thank Pastor M.G. Baldee, a former Dutch missionary who worked for the Christian Evangelical Church in Timor (GMIT) over this period, and who corresponded with us by email.

Many of our friends, especially our husbands and boyfriends when we were doing field research, supported us in various ways: driving team members to meet informants; facilitating communication; pointing out massacre and burial sites; helping type up notes; translating interview transcripts from local languages into Indonesian, and helping in many other ways. We remember the kindness of our friends: Marconi Gorang Mau in Alor; Aleks Hoti and Willem Siubelan in Sumba; Arifin Betty in South Central Timor; Talen Ngefak, Dian Nenometa, and Yustus Maro in Kupang. Pastor Messakh Dethan helped us translate the material in German we received from Pastor Baarlink. Dany Wetangterah helped us with the layout of the original Indonesian version of this book. Our friend Mrs Karen Campbell-Nelson, with extraordinary seriousness and commitment, worked alongside us during the research and publication process. We learned a lot through our friendship with her. Apart from the names above, there are still many other friends who, in their various ways, supported this work. May God bless them for their kindness.

We wish to particularly thank the Faculty of Theology at the Artha Wacana Christian University (UKAW) that provided institutional support for us to carry out this collective research. The faculty gave leave to the female lecturers involved in this research project to enable them to go into the field to gather the stories collected here in this book. This was a valuable contribution to attempts to further theology in the specific context of the fight for truth and justice in the church and the nation. We also especially want to mention Rev. Ari Kalemudji as head of the Research and Development Unit of the alumni of the Faculty of Theology at UKAW who supported us by translating some of the interviews from the Sabunese language into Indonesian.

Before publishing this book, we asked some friends to read the manuscript and make comments, both on specific sections and on the book as a whole. We thank them for giving their time to do this and for offering valuable suggestions. The final responsibility for the text of course remains with us, as the writing team.

During the research and the publishing of this book, we received support from other parties. Our colleagues in the *Kerk in Actie,* namely the Protestant Church in the Netherlands, as well as the Center for Transitional Justice in Indonesia supported us with funding for research and publication. Without that support and their kindness, our efforts would have remained ideals. For their help, we offer our sincere thanks.

For the publication of this English language version of the book we have some special thankyous. First to Dr. Kate McGregor from the School of Historical and Philosophical Studies at the University of Melbourne who initiated the publication effort. Kate's special interest in studies about memory and history opened the way for the voices of the women victims and survivors of the 1965 tragedy to be heard by a wide international audience. We also offer our sincere thanks to Jemma Purdey and colleagues from the Herb Feith Foundation and Monash University Publishing who have made this English translation possible. We express our respect and love to Jennifer Lindsay who worked so hard on translating this thick book full of Eastern Indonesian dialect which was often difficult to translate. For all your hard work, thank you Jenny!

We hope that the publication of this book in the English language will be another contribution to the international understanding of the humanitarian evil that happened half a century ago in Indonesia, information about which was stifled, in all kinds of ways. At least, in learning from this cruel history, together we will have the commitment to build a world civilization with more love of peace and justice.

Kupang, December 2014

**Mery Kolimon**

# About the Herb Feith Translation Series

The Herb Feith Translation Series publishes high-quality non-fiction manuscripts not yet available in English, which enhance scholarship and teaching about Indonesia. Published by the Herb Feith Foundation in conjunction with Monash University, the books are available 'open access' or for free download.

The Herb Feith Foundation was established in 2003 to commemorate the life and work of Herb Feith (1930–2001), volunteer, scholar, teacher and peace activist. Its mission is to promote and support work of the kind to which Herb Feith devoted his life, including the study of Indonesia, through a range of educational activities including research and teaching and in the publication and promotion of such work.

## Series Board

Professor Greg Barton
Assoc. Prof. Charles. A. Coppel
Dr Jemma Purdey
Dr Djin Siauw
Mr Pat Walsh OA

## Translating accounts of the 1965–66 mass violence in Indonesia

Series co-ordinated by Dr Kate McGregor and Dr Jemma Purdey

Until recently there have been very few accounts available in Indonesian or English of the 1965–66 mass violence as told by witnesses, survivors or perpetrators. Today an increasing number of memoirs and short testimony collections are available in Indonesian, however, very few are yet available in English language. This has prevented a greater understanding outside Indonesia of how this violence continues to impact on Indonesians and of how they now understand this traumatic period of their nation's history.

These translated works are valuable resources for all who seek to understand Indonesia today, and especially for undergraduate students of Asian history and the history of mass violence and genocide. This book is the second in this series of translated accounts of the 1965–66 mass violence in Indonesia.

# About the Editors

***Mery Kolimon*** was born in SoE, South Central Timor. She began serving as a pastor with the congregation in Bijeli, East Mollo Presbytery, South Central Timor (1997–99). After completing her doctoral studies at the Protestant Theological University in Holland in 2008, she worked as a lecturer at her alma mater, the Faculty of Theology at Artha Wacana Christian University (UKAW) Kupang. Apart from acting as Director of the Postgraduate program at UKAW, Mery is also coordinator of the Women's Network of East Indonesia (Jaringan Perempuan Indonesia Timur, JPIT). Mery wrote the story of her father's role as a perpetrator in the book *Memecah Pembisuan*, ed. Putu Oka Sukanta (2011), published in English as *Breaking the Silence* (Melbourne: Monash University Publishing 2014).

***Liliya Wetangterah*** was born in Kupang. She completed her theological studies at the Faculty of Theology at UKAW in 2007 and served with the Ebenhezer-Oeba Congregation in Kupang. The following year, she began further study of church law at the Jakarta Theology College (Sekolah Tinggi Teologi/STT Jakarta), and graduated in March 2011. In November 2011, Lia joined the JPIT research team, assisting in particular with editing. In the same month she had the opportunity to attend a conference on church law in Holland. While she was there she carried out some interviews to assist the report of the Sumba research team, and also managed to gather some relevant documentation. Now Lia is teaching at Sekolah Tinggi Agama Negeri (STAKN) Kupang.

***Karen Campbell-Nelson***, Ed.D., works as a professor on the Theology Faculty and with the Graduate Program of Artha Wacana Christian University (UKAW) in Kupang, NTT, Indonesia. She has experience with human rights documentation and gender issues, including gender- and sexual-based violence, at local, national, and international levels. She served as a consultant with the Commission for Reception, Truth, and Reconciliaion of Timor-Leste (CAVR), the American Bar Association Rule of Law Initiative, UNIFEM (now UN Women), and the International Center for Transitional Justice in Indonesia. Besides teaching, she joins others in the Women's Network of Eastern Indonesia (JPIT), Asian Justice and Rights (AJAR), and the Alliance Against Human Trafficking (AMPERA) in research, training, and advocacy efforts on behalf of gender justice.

***The Women's Network of East Indonesia*** for the Study of Women in Religion and Culture (Jaringan Perempuan Indonesia Timur, JPIT) comprises more than forty women from different religions across eastern Indonesia (NTT, Kalimantan, Sulawesi, Maluku, Halmahera and Papua). Formed in August 2009, the network, agreed to focus its activities on research and publication in three areas: women, religion, and culture. In their meeting in March 2010, the organising committee agreed to make the 1965 tragedy one focus of study. JPIT began its research into the 1965 tragedy by taking NTT as a pilot project. It was hoped that the research would soon spread to other areas in Eastern Indonesia, taking lessons learned from the first stage in NTT.

# Foreword

### Rev. Dr. Andreas A. Yewangoe,
### Head of the Communion of Churches in Indonesia (PGI)

There is an episode in the history of our nation which to this day remains dark. Many interpretations have arisen around it. This is what came to be labeled the 'G30S/PKI Incident', or more usually 'Gestapu', a word that reminds us of Gestapo, Hitler's kind of secret police during World War II. The event was preceded by the kidnapping of six generals and one high-ranking officer, who later came to be called 'Heroes of the Revolution'. They were taken from their homes on the night of 30 September-1 October 1965. They were taken – alive or dead – to a place within the Halim Perdama Kusuma airport precincts where their bodies were later found in a well called the Crocodile Hole. The situation was extremely tense and confusing on that day. Nothing was clear. I myself was in Jakarta at the time as a third-year student at Jakarta Theological Seminary. I witnessed the unusual movement of the army. Army convoys were going here and there. Some soldiers wore red armbands on their right arms. Some did not. We did not know what was going on because communications were extremely limited. The only source of information was the national radio, RRI, which not everyone could listen to, as not everyone owned a radio.

Early in the afternoon things became a little 'clearer'. It began with the declaration by Lieutenant Colonel Untung representing the group calling itself the Revolutionary Council. He dismissed the Dwikora Cabinet under President Sukarno. He proclaimed that the highest military rank was Lieutenant Colonel, so those with the rank of General had to accommodate themselves to this. Then he formed the 'Revolutionary Council', which was headed by Lieutenant Colonel Untung himself. But who was Untung? No one had heard of him before this. Where did he stand in terms of national direction and ideology? And what was the fate of the revolution that Bung Karno had always said was 'unfinished'? And where was Bung Karno? Had he been murdered, even though it was said that he was in a safe place? It was all very confusing.

Things became even more confused later in the afternoon after an announcement by Major General Soeharto that Untung's *coup d'état* had been broken. The national radio station's studio was retaken. Then the names of the generals and the high-ranking officers who were missing were announced. The Indonesian Communist Party (PKI) was alleged to have been the mastermind of everything that had happened. But where was Bung Karno? It was a mystery. Towards midnight, at last Bung Karno's voice was heard. He sounded tired. He said that he was well. The reins of the state were in his hands. For the meantime, he had taken control of the army. And so forth. But the even more confusing days were yet to come.

We got to know the story as it continued because it is written in books. But not everything written tells things as they really happened. There still remain so many questions. Was this really the treacherous deed of the Communist Party, as the official version has always claimed? Or was there an internal struggle within the army, as many foreign scholars have said? We remember, for instance, the different version presented in what came to be called the 'Cornell Paper'. And the statements of Prof. Utrecht in the Netherlands make it clear that the Communist Party was the 'scapegoat' for everything that happened.

We do not want to go into that complicated discussion now. Nor is this the place for it. What we want to say is that so many people became victims in that turmoil. The period after the 30<sup>th</sup> September Movement saw the deaths of thousands, even millions of people who were alleged to have been part of the Communist Party or affiliated with it. After the party was banned throughout Indonesia, hunts and massacres happened everywhere. Only God knows the exact numbers. The people arrested were given no due legal process. Many of them had no idea why they were arrested, because no fair trial was ever carried out. What we know is that these unfortunate people were grouped into three categories: Group A was the most serious. They were usually summarily executed. Group B were those who had to regularly report to the authorities. Those in group C were released, but with certain qualifications that led to them living under constant suspicion. The stigma placed upon them became a life-long burden, not only for themselves, but also for their children and grandchildren. This stigma has still not completely disappeared today.

Our nation has still not been able to emerge from this oppressive burden of history. Recently, there have been a number of publications that explain what really happened. Books like *Aku Bangga Menjadi Anak PKI* (I am proud to be the child of a communist), for instance, show how injustice and obliteration of our humanitarian dignity occurred and will continue to do so as long as we do not have the courage to free our nation from this burden of the past.[1] The writings of Pramoedya Ananta Toer from Buru Island (where he was held as a political prisoner from from c.1969 to 1979) are another example of an effort to free our nation from this burden. The issue is this; does our nation have the courage to go down that path, and to truly strive for healing?

\* \* \*

In the midst of this struggle to make peace with the past, the writing collected by a group of women from the Theology Faculty at Artha Wacana Christian University in Kupang is extremely significant. Thus far, we have heard only stories passed orally about all the things that happened in East Nusa Tenggara after the 30th September Movement. I myself heard various stories about what happened in Sumba and Timor from various informants. But what was heard was never published, and can be easily lost. This documentation invites us not only to look at the past and learn from it, but also to dare to enter our history and strive to carry out healing. These are *memoria passionis*, memories of suffering, which, as many other nations have experienced, can give the strength to continue to move forward. But its conditions are not easy. There must be a confession of sin. Only with confession is true forgiveness possible, and only then can our nation be healed. If not, we will remain burdened by the heavy past.

We deeply sympathize with the victims, who largely had no idea of what wrong they were supposed to have done. We especially feel for the women and children who had to carry the burden from their husbands and fathers. When I was staying in the Netherlands, my friend Pastor H.J. van Oostrum told me about what he did in Sumba to help those accused of being Communist Party members. He accompanied them to the execution site. When they were executed on Mamboru Beach, Pastor H.J. van Oostrum knelt behind the firing squad, begging them not to prolong the victims 'suffering'. Evidently, when he talked to the victims, he fortified them by saying, 'Be calm, it will feel like being bitten by an ant, and then it will end.' End? Certainly not. He strengthened their faith as followers of Christ, and publicly declared that they were members of the Christian Church of

---

1   *Aku Bangga Menjadi Anak PKI* Ribka Tjiptaning Proletariyati. Jakarta: Cipta Lestari 2002.

Sumba. In those last moments, Pastor van Oostrum gave them communion as a sign of their union in Christ.

It makes us deeply sad when apparently the church also participated in judging them. But we should not then judge the church here. We also know that in that critical time of confusion, even the church needed courage to truly state that it must not neglect its pastoral role. The resolutions of the GKS Synod in Tenggaba (1957), for instance, were the church's effort to prevent its members from being easily influenced by various Communist Party 'propaganda and campaigns' that were indeed extraordinary at that time. The heat of the propaganda and campaigns was felt all over Indonesia. The incident at the Bandara Betsy plantation in North Sumatra in the 1960s, when an army lieutenant was killed over a land dispute, was a huge issue at the time. It was not strange that the Communist Party was alleged to be the provocateur, firing up the people to carry out 'revolutionary' acts. Not long before the 30 September Movement, the Communist Party celebrated its 40th anniversary in Jakarta. The capital city looked like an ocean of red. The hammer and sickle was in every corner of the city. This memory is still vivid to most people.

But this does not mean that the Communist Party can be blamed without any open legal process for its leaders to defend themselves. After all, the Communist Party was at the time a legal organization under the protection of the law. Sadly, no open trials were ever held, so to this day the whole thing remains a burden of history.

The church did indeed have difficulty with statements denying the existence of God, as in Communist Party propaganda, although to understand Marxist teaching, proper philosophical training is needed to really understand the intention of Marx's statement, 'religion is the opium of the people'. This statement cannot be separated from its historical context, when the church paid no heed to the dreadful conditions of the workers in Europe, even giving the impression of turning religion into an opiate. When this statement is taken out of its context and casually applied to a society that has, in historical terms, not experienced similar conditions, misunderstanding is likely. This is why, when what was called 'liberation theology' took off in Latin America in the 1990s, it was seen as the church's fulfillment of an obligation that had been long ignored in Europe. The churches in Latin America (at least in their theology) were considered to have rediscovered that obligation. Those who had been marginalized by poverty because of a social structure of oppression (the oppressor-oppressed axis) were returned to their place as subjects of history. When this happened the church could overcome its stagnation by returning its diaconal function to its rightful place. The church participates in, and even pioneers change to social structure to make it more fair and prosperous.

Statements of concern about atheist propaganda should therefore be made alongside the church's true role of improving society. In saying this, I am not belittling the situation back in the 1960s, which was indeed extremely difficult for society and the church, and not only in East Nusa Tenggara. However, today when we face the future, our churches can make those past events a valuable lesson for the true performance of ministry to our society.

This book, even though it is somewhat incomplete because it omits Flores [and Rote, ed.], is now in your hands, dear reader. Various living narratives are presented here. Suffering and misery. But also hope and optimism. I am sure that readers will take away many useful things from this book. With God's blessing.

**Jakarta 13 March, 2012**

# Foreword

### Rev. Elga Sarapung, Director Interfidei

*They have taken away my Lord,
and I know not where they have laid him.*
(John 20:13)

*Sir, if thou have borne him hence, tell me where thou hast laid him,
and I will take him away.*
(John 20:15)

The two Biblical quotes above are the expressions of a woman named Mary Magdalene in a state of grief and confusion when she found the tomb of Jesus empty. Mary was one of a few women who witnessed – although from a distance – the events of Jesus's arrest, crucifixion and burial, with no opportunity for defence. After all, the actors in that scene were men who were submissive to an unjust government that was preoccupied with the political interests of power, both in the state and religion. The deception between 'religion and state' in the interest of power is truly evident in this incident.

This profound expression of grief and confusion, when carried into the 'time frame' of 1965 to the present – with the arrest, kidnapping, imprisonment, torture and murder of thousands of Indonesian people without any due process of the law, and with their families, wives, children, relatives having no knowledge of where their husbands, brothers, fathers or sons had been taken never to return – is deeply meaningful when listening to the victims' grievances and hopes. Where was truth and justice? Is there still truth and justice in Indonesia? Is there any sympathy, attention and demand for justice among people, among officials of this Republic of Indonesia, for the victims of injustice and deviation from truth?

The hymn 'Berserah kepada Tuhan' (Surrender to God) which one family sang at a church service, was not an expression of despair, nor was it merely for consolation, but it was a heartfelt cry about the injustice inflicted by the state and the church that was felt then and continues to be felt, and at the same time a lament of hope. They no longer believed in other people, and did not even believe in themselves. Their husbands were dead, but the memory of injustice gave them the valuable lesson that this experience was not the end of their lives, not the end of their hopes, but was an expression of their faith that God would surely declare His justice and truth.

> On the night before the killing, I met my husband at the door of the Seba prison. We knelt together, prayed and sang the hymn, 'Surrender to Jesus, my body, spirit and soul.' That was the last night we met. Gad'i. (Report from Sabu)

Ironically, religions become weak when faced with problems like this – weak because the 'prophetic voice about truth and justice' is virtually silent. There are a whole range of humanitarian tragedies that get virtually no attention from religions, including those linked with violence and murder. There are two reasons: first, religions in Indonesia are afraid of authorities/the state/the government, and secondly, the religious institutions are so strong they are unable to carry out the critical, deep theological reflection needed to confront problems like these. They are more afraid of the authorities and the state that carry out injustice and falsify truth, than of justice and truth that God clearly mandates to people and religions, including the church. Both these reasons weaken the church's resolve and power to act in the name of truth and justice.

When we enter into the space and time of this book, into the stories, that is – the living witness of eyes, consciences, reflections presented here – various questions arise for the church. Where was the church's defence of the victims? Where did the church carry out truth and justice? Did the church raise its voice or do any anything on behalf of the victims? And why the church? Because it turns out that the church also participated in this 'scene', directly or indirectly, and continues to do so today. The church, in particular the Christian Church of Sumba (GKS) and the Timor Evangelical Christian Church (GMIT), as the research in this book shows, has still not undertaken any significant change in its position on the 1965 humanitarian tragedy. Victims are still not completely received in the church, because they have 'sinned'.

This reminds me of what the Buddhist monk Thich Nhat Hanh once said in his book *Going Home, Jesus and Buddha as Brothers*, when talking about love, forgiveness and reconciliation:

> ... unless you know how to love your neighbor, you cannot love God. Before placing an offering on the altar of God, you have to reconcile with your neighbor, because reconciling with your neighbor is to reconcile with God. It means that you will never touch and be close to God if you can't love your neighbor, you can't forgive your neighbor and you can't reconcile with your neighbor... [1]

When we link Thich Nhat Than's words to what Kyai Abdurrahman Wahid (Gus Dur) said and practiced, they become more rounded. Thirty-five years after the tragedy occurred, Gus Dur, as head of the Indonesian Islamic organization Nahdlatul Ulama (NU, Revival of Islamic Scholars), apologised to the people, to former political prisoners and to those who suffered because they were accused of being involved with what came to be labeled G30S-PKI. I think that Gus Dur was aware that the 1965 conflict was a complex problem. There was state involvement, but there was also the involvement of ordinary people. At the latter level, Gus Dur pushed for 'reconciliation' to occur first at the social level. As the head of NU, Gus Dur himself began by asking forgiveness with the implicit understanding that the NU or NU members were probably involved in the tragedy as perpetrators.

Asking forgiveness is a confession of wrong. There is a very strong foundation for this in our culture. Gus Dur proceeded from the moral principle he held. This moral principle is extremely simple, namely humility. To quote him:

> Humility is needed to see everything that happened from a humanitarian perspective, not ideologically. If we have only an ideological point of view, then it is extremely easy for us to consider ourselves right and others wrong.[2]

The question is whether religion, and here the church (GKS and GMIT), is prepared to love, ask forgiveness, forgive, carry out reconciliation, and change various regulations and church liturgy that perpetuate the injustice and falsehood that has gone on since the 1965 tragedy. Is the church prepared to itself confess because it participated in actions that are contrary to justice and truth, and are inhumane?

---

1 *Going Home, Jesus and Buddha as Brothers*. New York: The Penguin Group, 1999:160. Thich Nhat Hanh is a Buddhist monk from Vietnam who experienced bitter times during the Vietnam War. He then moved to France, while there, he often went on pilgrimages and studied the insights of other religions, including Christianity.
2 Writing on an email list on 16 February 2004. https://www.mail-archive.com/mencintai-islam@yahoogroups.com/msg07725.html

The experience in South Africa shows us how the church can spearhead openness and the asking of forgiveness, and carry out deeply meaningful reconciliation with the government that implemented apartheid. This is concrete proof that forgiveness, reconciliation, improvement and change can take place, as long as there is political will (including church politics) grounded in morality and strong conscience from the church.

To end, I wish to quote Gregory Baum and Harold Wells:

> Churches should be trusting enough in the reconciling grace of God to admit their own failings and in ways of working toward reconciliation... Reconciliation could become one way of defining its mission in the world today.[3]

It is hoped that the Christian Church of Sumba and the Timor Evangelical Christian Church are prepared to pioneer reconciliation among their faithful, and also together with their faithful, for humanity. In this way, they will show how the role of religion and the church for justice, truth and peace can become manifest to society, to humanity. This reconciliation has been announced from Nusa Tenggara Timur. We welcome this book with the belief and hope that it will bring about change; change from the church and in the church for the world and mankind.

---

3  Gregory Baum and Harold Wells (eds.), *The Reconciliation of Peoples: Challenge to the Churches* (Geneva: WCC Publications, 1997), pp.129–30.

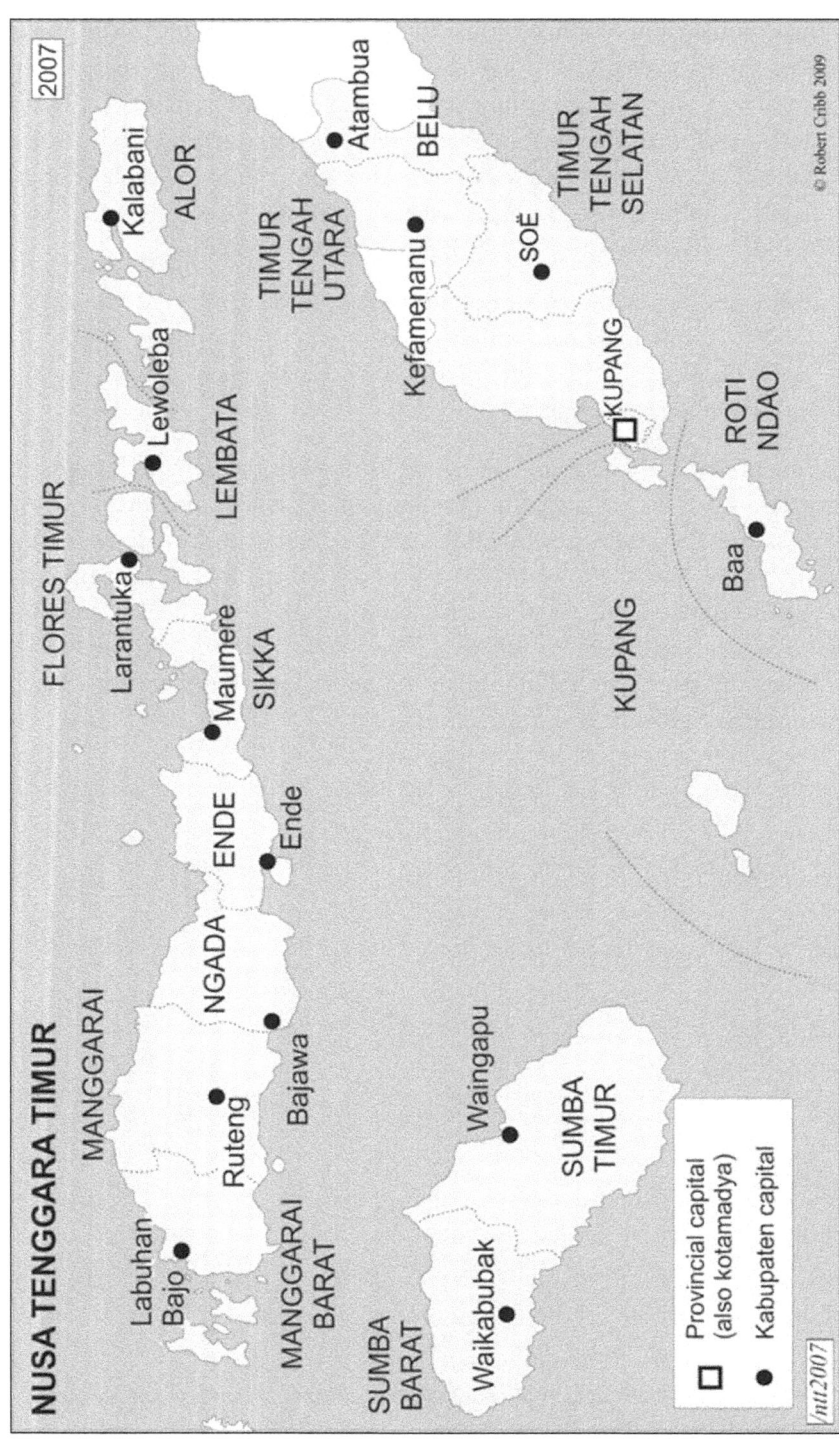

Source: Robert Cribb, *Digital Atlas of Indonesian History* (Copenhagen: NIAS Press, 2010), reproduced with permission.

# Introduction

Forbidden Memories: Women Victims and Survivors of the 1965 Tragedy in Eastern Indonesia

Mery Kolimon

The anti-communist violence surrounding the '1965 Incident' in Indonesia was a humanitarian tragedy that created a dark shadow over various aspects of the life of this nation. The murder of hundreds of thousands of people, and the shackling of freedom left a serious collective trauma in the life of the Indonesian people. The victims of the 1965 violence include not only individuals and families, but the entire nation. The event created terror and paralysed the people's courage to be critical towards power. The political dynamics of the nation following this humanitarian tragedy cannot be understood without understanding its effects. Yet sadly, there is still little motivation from many quarters, including the church, to review the humanitarian tragedy that occurred as a consequence of political interests.

Today, many questions still remain about what actually happened. Why were so many people killed? Who should take responsibility for the evil that engulfed my fellow countrymen? Thankfully, some awareness of the need to express the truth has now begun to emerge. The fall of the Soeharto regime has allowed the emergence of research, writing and publications that set out to contribute to the expression of truth through understanding what really happened.

## Motivation for research

To date there has been no writing about the 1965 events seen from the viewpoint of victims in the Eastern Indonesia province of Nusa Tenggara Timur (NTT). All the existing writing from the viewpoint of the victims has focused on Java and Bali.[1] There has been some writing about the Indonesian

---

1   See, for instance, Ita Nadia *Suara Perempuan Korban Tragedi '65* (Yogyakarta: Galang Press 2009) and Fransisca Ria Susanti, *Kembang-kembang Genjer* (Yogyakarta: Jejak 2007)

Communist Party movement in Eastern Indonesia, but this has not given much attention to the perspective of the victims.[2]

The majority of the population of NTT province is Christian (both Catholic and Protestant).[3] One consequence of the 1965 tragedy was to fan the phobia of the Protestant churches of NTT, particularly the Christian Evangelical Church in Timor (Gereja Masehi Injil di Timor, GMIT) and the Christian Church of Sumba (Gereja Kristen Sumba, GKS), towards people's political education and the fight for justice. Although the church claims it has a prophetic social role to fight for justice and uphold truth, in fact, as part of this nation the church is itself wounded and not entirely free of collective trauma. As a result, the church has never reached its potential in the fight for justice in this country.

The church in Indonesia today is concerned with pursuing a contextual theology that springs from the rich social and cultural heritage of local congregations. In the global context, awareness has arisen that for a local theology, a post-colonial critique is needed to explain and affirm the self-identity of previously colonised peoples. In the Indonesian context, apart from this post-colonial context, the development of local theology also needs a critique of the post 1965 violence, particularly to develop contextual theological-political reflection.

In the particular case of the development of local theology after the violence of 1965, it is essential to recognise that the anti-Communist Party violence of 1965 helped to destroy local cultures and religions. This is related to the presidential edict no. 1/PNPS of 1965 about religious tolerance. The Sukarno government, in pursuit of the national revolutionary ideal of a just and prosperous society, regulated against misuse and abuse of religion. The presidential edict mentioned above stipulated that the six official religions of the Indonesian people were Islam, Protestant Christianity, Catholicism, Hinduism, Buddhism, and Confucianism. Other religions 'for instance

---

2   See R.A.F. Paul Webb and Steven Farram *Di-PKI-kan. Tragedi 1965 dan Kaum Nasrani di Indonesia Timur*, (Syarikat 2005). This is a translation by Chandra Utara, of two articles: (1) 'The Sickle and the Cross: Christians and communists in Bali, Flores, Sumba and Timor, 1965–1967', R.A.F. Paul Webb in *Journal of Southeast Asian Studies* XVII: 1 (March 1986) 94–112; and (2) 'Revolution, religion and magic: the PKI in West Timor, 1924–1966', Steven Farram in *Bijdragen tot de taal-, land-en volkenkunde*, 158 (2002) 21–48. Also see John Prior, 'The Silent Scream of a Silenced History: The Maumere Massacre of 1966,' *Exchange* 40 (2011), 117–43, 311–21.

3   According to the Indonesian Ministry of Religion's website, in 2008 the composition of the population of NTT in terms of religion was as follows: Islam 8.8%; Christian (Catholic and Protestant) 90.9%, Buddhist 0,034%, and Hindu 0.082%. Accessed 13 October 2011, http://www.depdagri.go.id/pages/ profil-daerah/provinsi/detail/53/nusa-tenggara-timur.

Judaism, Zoroastrianism, Shintoism and Taoism' were not forbidden. During the Soeharto regime, this presidential edict became law, through the edict UU no. 5 of 1966, and various other edicts and regulations. It was only in 1978 that the Minister of Internal Affairs issued the Regulation no. 477/74054 1978 on the guidelines for filling in identity cards. According to these guidelines, unofficial religions were now forbidden, and the official religions were reduced to five, with Confucianism now withdrawn.[4]

Even though Sukarno established six official religions initially to safeguard against the abuse and defamation of religion in the name of attaining national revolutionary ideals, it transpired that the later interpretation and narrowing of definition in the New Order period resulted in violence in the name of the destruction of 'the communist movement'.[5] During the crushing of the communist movement in Indonesia, people who did not embrace one of the six official religions of the time were declared to be atheist, and therefore communist. As a result, local religions that were tightly linked to local cultures were destroyed. This is why, in striving for contextual theology today, it is absolutely imperative that we strive for a design to build a perspective of local cultures that were also victims of the state violence in 1965.

Retelling the 1965 Tragedy is not an easy thing. Attempts to revisit the past are extremely difficult and risky. The 1965 period is still a dark period in the history of this nation. This period has become a forbidden memory in Indonesian history. There is no open conversation about it. The voices of victims are muzzled; their names are blackened; even in the church they are threatened. Actually, everyone in this nation has been struck by the impact of the 1965 Incident, whether as victims, as relatives of victims including their descendants, as perpetrators, or as people who have been deliberately

---

4   See the presidential edict: 1 PNPS 1965 Tentang Penodaan Agama and the UU no. 5 1969 tentang Pernyataan Berbagai Penetapan Presiden dan Peraturan Presiden Sebagai Undang-Undang, on the website www.hukumonline.com, accessed 23 August 2011. See also Danielle Samsoeri's 'Judicial Review UU Penodaan Agama', unpublished paper accessed 8 March 2012 from www.komnasperempuan.or.id/wp-content/uploads/2010/03/JR-UU-No.1-Tahun-1965. On the stipulation from the Minister of Internal Affairs about completing identity cards, see Moh. Mahfud MD, *Kebebasan Beragama dalam Perspektif Konstitusi*, 2, footnote 3, accessed 10 January 2012 from the website http://law.uii.ac.id/dokumentasi/task.doc_download/gid,62/
5   Even though article 29 clause 2 of the National Constitution of 1945 guarantees freedom of religion for the people of Indonesia, at the level of implementation, regulations such as UU No 1/PNPS/1965 actually limit the freedom of religion. For example, the local Towani Tolotang religion in South Sulawesi had to become Hindu. See further J Hasse 'Kebijakan Negara terhadap Agama Lokal "Towani Tolotang" di Kabupaten Sidrap, Sulawesi Selatan' in *Jurnal Studi Pemerintahan* 1:1 (August 2010).

duped. We tend to think that peace will come as long as we leave things alone. But the opposite is true – for then we will never be resolved within ourselves. We will continue to be haunted by ghosts of the past. This is why, difficult as it is, we must attempt to heal this collective trauma. We are learning from the process of gathering the stories in this book that this is the price we must pay if this nation wants to move forward and not continue to be haunted by those ghosts. The process of healing from collective trauma can only take place when this nation is courageous enough to talk once more about what took place.

In the context of NTT, the church's concern to realise its full prophetic role will be met only when the church is brave enough to do a few things: First, to listen to the voices of victims and to acknowledge the evils done to them in the past; second, to openly acknowledge the silence and complicity of the church – including its complicity in acts of violence – which gave support to the mass evil when these things occurred. Further, to strive for restoration and reparation of the rights of victims which have thus far been ignored or deliberately transgressed. One hopes that these measures would contribute to the Indonesian nation so that it could be more at peace with itself and step forward to become more just and civilised. This process should involve reparations to victims and their descendants, reconciliation in society, and should lead to the reformation of state and social institutions, including the reformation of religious institutions.

We therefore offer this book to the Protestant church in Indonesia, especially the GMIT and GKS. However, we also hope that other communities in Indonesia can benefit from this book. Proceeding from the findings of our research, one inevitable agenda is institutional reformation together with renewal of theology and church ecclesiology, for it is clear the church is deeply wounded and needs to be healed, while healing itself.

## Listening to victims' perspectives so as to uphold justice and truth

Theology and politics are inextricably connected. Faith communities' reflections on the Divine as Creator and Eternal Regulator determine an attitude towards the regulation of communal life within a society. Politics is in essence the ordering of a society for the welfare of all its members. When politics no longer serves the noble aim of justice and welfare of all citizens, but instead, for various reasons, becomes a tool of oppression of one group of citizens, then religious language about God, man, and the world must respond to this deviation. Religions that lay claim to truth, love, justice and equality as their foremost values should be at the front line in challenging justice and human rights abuses.

A good example of the involvement of religions in upholding human rights is the transitional process of justice that took place in South Africa over the second half of the 1990s.[6] In the struggle to ensure the end of apartheid, and for there to be change towards permanent democracy, the Truth and Reconciliation Commission (TRC) was formed to find the facts and the context of severe human rights abuses that had occurred. The TRC was unique in that it was led by the church leader in South Africa, Bishop Desmond Tutu.[7] Further, the TRC also summoned the Church and other faith communities for questioning about their complicity, in both supporting and opposing the system of apartheid that was imposed by the state and which caused severe human rights abuse. The questions asked by the TRC of the faith communities included:

25. Did the theology and the actions of the organisations or faith communities contribute to the individuals, institutions and organisations responsible for human rights abuses, in perpetuating or opposing the system of apartheid?

26. How did the organisations of faith communities contribute to the creation of the situation or the justification of human rights abuses that occurred?

27. In what way, through actions either right or wrong, did religious organisations and communities support the past conflict?

28. How did faith and religious communities fail to uphold the principles of their faith that oppose human rights abuse?

---

6 Transitional justice is in itself a process of upholding justice and truth in a society that is undergoing transition from a dark period brought about by conflict or an authoritarian regime, towards a better future. It sets out to express and acknowledge the human rights abuses that have occurred, to try the perpetrators most responsible, to restore and rehabilitate victims, and to carry out institutional reform, particularly reform of security institutions. A deeper explanation about the framework of transitional justice in Indonesia can be found in *Keluar Jalur: Keadilan Transisi di Indonesia Setelah Jatuhnya Soeharto*, Jakarta: ICTJ and KontraS, 2011; and also on line at kontras.org/buku/Indonesia%20report-derailed-Indo.pdf. Also see 'What is Transitional Justice?', on http://ictj.org/about/transitional-justice, accessed 6 December, 2011.

7 On Desmond Tutu, see *Tiada Masa Depan Tanpa Pengampunan* (Jakarta: CISCORE, 2010).

29. In what ways did the religious and faith communities and organisations actively reject the human rights abuses that occurred?[8]

What is interesting in this process is the fact that religions, and particularly the church, were given the opportunity to examine their positions and to determine internal institutional reform both in their theological interpretation and in their political actions. In their statements before the TRC, it was clear that religions were at once victims, perpetrators, and opponents of the oppressive system of apartheid. In particular, the church in South Africa was a victim because the majority of its Black congregations were victims. Because of this, the church was a suffering church. But at the same time, the church perpetrated human rights abuse. In its declaration before the TRC, the church made a public apology for playing a particular role, whether directly or indirectly, in the evil of the past. In fact, when the church chose a position of neutrality, it actually supported the perpetuation of the climate of human rights abuse. The stance of neutrality was easily exploited to support the oppressive state. In this way, many church denominations in South Africa admitted that they did not do enough to oppose state violence. Only a tiny proportion of faith communities openly and whole-heartedly opposed the state policies that produced these human rights abuses.[9]

In the case of the 1965 tragedy in Indonesia, we need to ask: What position did religions in Indonesia, and in particular the church in NTT, take at the time of this humanitarian tragedy? Just as the churches in South Africa were trapped in the fear created by authorities for what was called 'the red danger' (communist danger),[10] churches in Indonesia in 1965 were trapped in the same fear. And just as churches in South Africa have been

---

8   See *Faith Communities and Apartheid*, The Research Institute on Christianity in South Africa, Report Prepared for the Truth and Reconciliation Commission, March 1990, 26, http://web.uct.ac.za/depts/ricsa/commiss/trc/trcout.htm accessed 30 November, 2011.

9   See Stephen William Martin, 'Civic Sacrament and Social Imaginaries in Transition: The Case of South African Churches and the Truth and Reconciliation Commission', *Political Theology* 12:3 (2011), accessed on 6 December 2011 at http://www.politicaltheology.com/PT/article/view/6399.

10  One group at the front line of resistance to the system of apartheid in South Africa was the African National Congress (ANC) with Nelson Mandela as one of its leaders. As a political party, the ANC openly accommodated Marxist ideology in its struggle for justice and democracy in South Africa. It called itself a socialist democrat party. And precisely because of this, the White community accused the anti-apartheid movement of being a communist movement. See 'African National Congress' at https://en.wikipedia.org/wiki/African_National_Congress, and 'Internal resistance to South African apartheid' at http://en.wikipedia.org/wiki/Internal_resistance_to-South_African_apartheid, both accessed on 25 January, 2012.

open to self-criticism, so too should churches in Indonesia, particularly in NTT, examine their past positions and strive for a revision of theology and their attitudes in the struggle for justice in the present and the future.

We hope that this research will contribute towards healing in the church, both as the broken and wounded body of Christ, and as a civil social institution that was once coopted by the state, and has still not recovered enough to be fully involved in the struggle for democratisation in Indonesia.

The primary aim of this research is to commence the reform of religious institutions, particularly the GMIT and GKS. For this reason, the research prioritises victims who are or were members of these two churches. Consequently, we acknowledge that we have not yet paid due attention to the effect of the 1965 events on other religious communities in NTT.[11] This remains a task for the future.

## Researchers

The Network of Women of Eastern Indonesia for the Study of Women in Religion and Culture (JPIT SPAB) comprises more than forty women from different religions across eastern Indonesia (NTT, Kalimantan, Sulawesi, Maluku, Halmahera and Papua). Formed in August 2009, the network, agreed to focus its activities on research and publication in three areas: women, religion, and culture. In their meeting in March 2010, the organising committee agreed to make the 1965 tragedy one focus of study.

JPIT began its research into the 1965 tragedy by taking NTT as a pilot project. It was hoped that the research would soon spread to other areas in Eastern Indonesia, taking lessons learned from the first stage in NTT.

In the case of the current research, JPIT collaborated with the Faculty of Theology at the Christian University of Artha Wacana (UKAW) in Kupang. This collaboration was based on the fact that a large number of the motivators of the research were lecturers and alumni of this Faculty. The research is inseparable from the need for theology in the NTT context. All theology should commence from a thorough familiarity with the context

---

11  See further the efforts of the youth from Nahdlatul Ulama (NU) who call themselves the Masyarakat Santri untuk Advokasi Rakyat Indonesia (Syarikat Indonesia). The results of their research and publications include: Singgih Nugroho, *Melintas dan Menyeberang. Perpindahan Massal Keagamaan Pasca 65 di Pedesaan Jawa*, (Yogyakarta: Syarikat, 2008) and Katharine E McGregor, *History in Uniform: Military Ideology and the Construction of Indonesia's Past*, NUS Press, 2007. (Indonesian translation published as *Ketika Sejarah Berseragam. Membongkar Ideologi Militer dalam Nenyusun Sejarah Indonesia* Yogyakarta: Syarikat, 2008).

where the theology is being carried out. This research is part of such theological development.

The researchers in this project together with the supporting secretariat were all members of the Kupang branch of JPIT, together with a few other friends who were interested in participating. Apart from a few female lecturers from the Faculty of Theology at UKAW in Kupang, some other researchers were lecturers at the Theological College (STT) of the GKS at Lewa, Sumba. The research team also included women pastors and recently graduated theology students intending to become candidates for ordination as pastors in both GMIT and GKS.

The process of forming the team made us even more aware of just how strong the collective trauma of this nation remains today. In the initial stage of research, some trainee pastors were extremely enthusiastic about joining, but they later withdrew. The reason they gave was that their parents did not allow their children to be involved in seeking information about things that might put them in danger. When these colleagues withdrew, this made the rest of us more determined than ever to know what exactly had happened.

## Method

The structure of this book reflects the case study method we used overall to manage a wide range of experiences of female victims; beginning with the descriptions from the victims and their families, then analysis of those experiences, followed by theological reflection. This analysis and reflection led to some pastoral action.[12] Each of the regional reports in the following chapters contains description and analysis, and sometimes also theological reflection linked to prominent themes of the relevant area. The epilogue of theological reflection and recommendations for pastoral action is more broadly based on findings from all the areas.

This theological method stresses God's presence and involvement in human history, including the history of suffering and oppression. God, in

---

12   On case study method, see Mary Elizabeth Moore, *Teaching from the Heart: Theology and Educational Method* (Harrisburg PA: Trinity Press International, 1998) 31-32; also John Campbell-Nelson and Corrie van der Ven, *Pedoman Penggunaan Metode Studi Kasus* at http://www.oaseonline.org/artikel/corrie-johnMSK.htm accessed on 18 February 21012; also SEAGST Institute of Advanced Pastoral Studies, *Seri Studi Kasus Pastoral I-III*, especially 'Metode Studi Kasus dalam Theologi [sic] Pastoral' in *Studi Kasus Pastoral I: Sumut* (Jakarta: BPK, 1985) and 'Metode Studi Kasus Sebagai Alat Kontekstualisasi Teologi Pastoral' in *Studi Kasus Pastoral II: Nusa Tenggara Timur* (Jakarta: BPK, 1990).

His involvement, sides with the oppressed. He defends and frees them. Faith in God who sides with the oppressed should definitely not be interpreted as passivity in confronting evil and justice, with the pretext that God's partiality is declared only after a person's death. On the contrary, belief in God's partiality towards the oppressed encourages people to believe in challenging structures and to oppose oppressive behaviour, and to fight for social change in society. In the context of the church and Indonesian society wounded by the effects of the 1965 humanitarian tragedy, contextual theology leads to acts of liberation from falsified history, and to healing. Theology is not merely talking about what is right (ortho-doxy), but it leads to action that is right (ortho-praxy).[13] In the context of society still suffering collective trauma, healing efforts must begin by listening to victims tell their stories, and striving for healing for them, their families, church communities, and society as a whole.

One technique we used to find informants was snowballing – information about an informant is obtained from someone else's prior story. At the description stage, we combined two methods of gathering information in the field, namely oral history, and in-depth interviews to get information from victims, their families, perpetrators, and others. The data gathered with these two methods is qualitative, namely the resource person tells his or her story, expressing what he or she experienced and witnessed, and the effect this had or is still having on them.[14]

We found the oral history method extremely good for expressing the victims' perspectives about the 1965 tragedy. Whereas to date, history has been written from the perspective of those in power while muzzling victims' voices, oral history created the space to hear their voices, and respect for their perspectives. It also provided the opportunity to re-map what had really happened, from the victims' point of view and experience. Using oral history, we attempted to record a person's whole life. In this way, the biographical frame allowed us to interpret how they gave meaning to the state-sponsored violence perpetrated against them. Further, oral history is in spirit fitting for the oral culture of NTT.

---

13  The term 'orthodoxy', which is also used in Indonesian, as *ortodoksi*, is from two Greek words, *ortho*, meaning true and *doxy* meaning praise. Literally, orthodoxy means true praise, but is understood as true belief. Orthopraxy thus means true *praxis* or action.

14  These experiences were explored in in-depth interviews, whereas with the oral history approach, the 1965 experiences were part of a broader story about their entire lives, from birth to the present.

Finding and meeting female victims turned out to be no easy thing. Most of them are elderly, and many have died. Some agreed to talk, but many still refused. Those who agreed to talk were motivated by their belief that their families and the church, and indeed this nation, should know what really happened to them. Apart from that, the openness of some of the informants was influenced by the fact that the researchers were pastors or trainee pastors, representatives of institutions they wanted to trust, but also institutions some of them knew as the perpetrators of violence. Those who refused to talk always gave the same short answer to the team's question: 'I don't know', even though the people around them knew full well that they were victims of the 1965 violence. Others agreed to tell their stories, but refused to allow them to be published. They wanted to keep their stories to themselves out of consideration for their families' security. Although we were disappointed, we could appreciate their objections.

For reasons of security, we have changed all names of informants and respondents, while the names of those people not linked to the 1965 events have not been changed. We have tried to still convey original ethnic identity with our choice of pseudonyms. If there are cases in this book where a pseudonym used is someone's true name, then this is just a coincidence and the research team apologises.

We conducted interviews with victims' families and with people beyond their families who knew about the violence, in order to encourage the victims families and surrounding people to recall what took place – who the perpetrators, victims, and witnesses were, along with times and locations. We found that in this way the families and people we interviewed would return to the 'forbidden memories' of this period of Indonesian history. Memories that had been long buried because they were thought dangerous were prized open and reflected upon. Informants who were not victims themselves spoke more openly. Even so, it was clear that the violence of 1965 was still an extremely taboo subject. Many people, when speaking of it, used hushed voices. Trauma remains. Our team found that those who dared to speak about the 1965 events took this opportunity to question whether the blackening of the names of victims and their families was right. In their retelling, people were able to take a distance from the claims that blackened the names of victims, and to criticise the arbitrary violence inflicted upon them.

Although the informants' stories are extremely rich in terms of personal experience and in the way they reflect on the context of the events, there is still a shortcoming, namely that the macro context of the tragedy tends to be ignored. We noticed that not many of the informants were able to link their personal experiences to the spread of systematic violence that occurred in NTT and other areas of Indonesia, or to the national and even international social, political and economic dynamics that had such an influence on to their suffering. At this stage, our research group was also not yet able to produce a full picture of the trend of violence in the 1965 period in NTT. Our focus on oral history methods meant that we tended to ignore the wider picture. We hope that our team of researchers and others will pursue further research to contribute to a more complete macro picture of the 1965 tragedy in NTT, including the political and security actors.

In our effort to better understand the stories here and obtain a picture of the macro context, we tried to find secondary data from various sources including church and government institutions. But this turned out to be extremely difficult. We got the strong impression that the period 1960–70, and particularly 1965–67 is a 'black hole' in the history of NTT. There are various causes. First, certain parties have vested interest in controlling information about this historical period, in order to hide the human rights abuse committed by perpetrators. It could be that all the data about this period has been deliberately 'lost'. Other reasons why some parties still keep information about this period but do not want to share it include fear, expectations of some kind of payment, or because they want to publish it themselves. Thirdly, we have the impression that Indonesia in general, and particularly the heads of civil and religious institutions, have not yet learnt to value archives and archiving. When we asked various formal institutions responsible for important community and state archives (such as the NTT regional library, the NTT Office for Provincial Development and the GMIT Synod Council) they said they no longer held archives of this period (see Appendix 4: Efforts to Source Secondary Data).

In our analysis of the data we gathered, we used an inductive approach. Each team formulated questions for the analysis based on the stories told by the victims, their families, perpetrators, and others interviewed. The victims' stories about their experience of violence, the way they gave meaning to that experience, their determination to survive when their very humanity was threated with destruction, and the attitude of the church and society towards this humanitarian tragedy, encouraged us to formulate analytical questions linked to all those things.

Our analysis along these lines helped us to then determine theological themes that arose from the stories. Here we are indebted to Liberation Theology's framework of the hermeneutical circle, which we mentioned earlier.[15] Based on the victims' life stories and reflections on their faith, we found rich theological themes to explore as part of the efforts for theology in the context of oppression leading to liberation of self, society and the church. We therefore did not take Biblical texts as our point of departure, but rather real human life experience, particularly the experience of oppression and marginalisation of female victims and survivors of 1965. This way of conducting theology in turn contributes to attempts to transform the life of the church and the nation, particularly in the struggle for truth and justice.

## Women narrate history

Victims are not a single category, but are diverse; so too their experiences. We need to distinguish experience of violence based on gender, to see what men and women experience. In patriarchal societies, insensitivity to this fact means that history is always written from the male perspective, as his-story, and neglects female perspectives and experience, her-story. As a result, history is usually equated with male experience and perspective. In this current research, we attempted to write the history of the 1965 tragedy from the perspective of its female victims. Listening to their voices helped us learn from their experience and strength as well as sources of spirituality that gave them resilience and allowed them to move forward. Our choice of prioritising female experience and perspectives also provided us with rich material to develop valuable analysis and NTT feminist theological reflection.

---

15   The hermeneutic circle was first developed by the German philosophers Heidegger and Gadamer to describe the process of understanding a text. The circle refers to the idea that a person's understanding of a text as a whole is built by referring to an understanding of parts of that text, while on the other hand, a person's understanding of each part is built with reference to the whole text. The whole text and its parts cannot be understood without referring one to the other, and because of this, they are always in a circle. In this way, the meaning of a text must be understood in it cultural, historical and literary context. In third world theology, Juan Luis Segundo, a liberation theologian from Latin America, developed the hermeneutic circle for theological purposes. He defined the hermeneutic circle as continuous change in our interpretation of the Bible, which is determined by changes that occur continuously in our present reality, as individuals and society. To him, this circle of interpretation comes from the reality that every new reality demands that we interpret the Word of God anew, to change reality according to that interpretation, and then to return to interpreting the Word of God, and so on. See 'Juan Luis Segundo (1925–1996)', *Boston Collective Encyclopedia of Western Theology*, http://people.bu.edu/wwildman/bce/segundo.htm accessed on 13 October, 2011.

## When elephants fight, ants are trampled

At the beginning of this research, the team focused its attention on listening to and documenting the voices of the victims/survivors in NTT. In the final stages, when the manuscript draft was given to peer reviewers, some encouraged us to supplement the text with information about the wider context, both on a national scale as well as regional (Asia/Southeast Asia) and global. This wider picture helped us better understand the meaning of the women's stories as well as the church's attitude at the time. We can say that they were victims of a global conspiracy and of particular national forces, namely between the power of capitalism and international anti-communism with the right-wing elite of the Indonesian army that wanted to seize power from Sukarno.

The crushing of communism in Indonesia cannot be separated from the global context, namely the Cold War at that time. After the end of World War II, world political and economic power was divided into two completing blocs. On the one had there was the force of democracy-capitalism, driven by the United States and Western Europe, and on the other side was the force of socialism-communism promoted by the Soviet Union. Each side tried to extend its influence over the whole world, including Indonesia. Even though Sukarno, as Indonesia's president at that time, stood for non-alignment, still the two world forces had their own reasons to drag Indonesia into their bloc.

Both Moscow and Washington DC saw Indonesia as important. First, in geo-political terms, Indonesia's location was extremely strategic and would benefit whoever controlled it. Secondly, Indonesia was a large nation, the fifth most populous nation in the world at the time. Another reason was that Indonesia had a wealth of natural resources.[16] Each side tried to wield influence over Indonesia through foreign aid, both as direct funding as well as loans.

Diplomatic relations between the Soviet Union and Indonesia, which had commenced in 1954, opened the way for economic contacts. This was strengthened by exchange visits, Khruschev, the president of the Soviet Union, visited Indonesia in 1956, and Sukarno visited Moscow in 1960. Even though Indonesia was not a communist country, it was the largest recipient of Soviet aid in Asia. It even exceeded the Soviet aid to communist Vietnam. Unlike Western countries, the Soviet Union gave aid in the form of loans (not as grants), which were intended to create a mutually beneficial

---

16  See further John Roosa, *Pretext for Mass Murder: The September 30th Movement and Suharto's Coup d'Etat in Indonesia*. Madison: University of Wisconsin Press, 2006: 14–16.

relationship and to emphasise equality. The agreement made in January 1959 between Indonesia and the Soviet Union stated that the USSR would provide aid for heavy industry, agroindustry, energy, and infrastructure (roads and buildings), also for educational institutions for shipping and marine science. However, not all the agreed projects bore fruit. One that was successful was the Senayan sports stadium, which was built in just two years. The building was used for the 1962 Asian Games, and for the Games of the New Emerging Forces (Ganefo) in 1964.

The United States had had interests in Indonesia since the 1920s. American businesses in the fields of oil, gas and agriculture were in operation from this time. Even though Sukarno chose a political stance of non-alignment, at the same time he exploited the hatred between the two world economic-political forces, for Indonesia's interests. In 1959, Sukarno asked for American support to take Irian Jaya from Dutch hands. However, President Eisenhower chose to remain neutral in this matter. Sukarno therefore asked for the support of the Soviet Union. By 1961, Soviet aid to Indonesia had reached one billion dollars. A large part of this aid was used in the campaign for Irian Jaya. John F Kennedy, who replaced Eisenhower, saw that the Soviet Union could use this opportunity to entrench its influence in Indonesia. Therefore, after the transfer of Irian, America increased its loans to Indonesia and gave material aid.[17]

Meanwhile, the Indonesian Communist Party (PKI) was experiencing a resurgence after its setback in 1948 (as a result of the Madiun uprising). In the 1955 general elections, the Indonesian Communist Party came in at fourth place in the polls. By the beginning of the 1960s, its influence was strengthening not only in Indonesia, but over Southeast Asia.[18] Indonesia's communist party had the third largest membership in the world, with membership in the millions plus 20 million members in its mass organisations.[19] Communist Party leaders had influence in Malaysia, the Philippines, Singapore and Thailand. They campaigned for socialism and motivated opposition to imperialist-capitalist countries.

Domestically, Sukarno attempted to act as a balancing force between the Communist Party and the army. He needed the Communist Party for

---

17  Muhammad Farid, 'How the Cold War influences US-Indonesia relations', *The Jakarta Post*, 9 February 2007, http://www.thejakartapost.com/news/2007/09/02/how-cold-war-influenced-usindonesia-relations accessed on 10 April, 2012.
18  See Justus M. van der Kroef, 'Indonesian Communism's Expansionist Role in Southeast Asia', *International Journal* 20:2 (Spring 1965), 189.
19  Ragna Boden, 'Cold War Economics: Soviet Aid to Indonesia', *Journal of Cold War Studies* 2008 10:3 (Summer 2008), 117.

popularity. On the other hand, he needed the army as a safeguard against Communist Party threats to his own position. As things developed, the Communist Party became closer to Sukarno in order to secure its own position against the anti-communist army leadership. This made the anti-communist powers within the army realise that Sukarno and the Communist Party could limit the effectiveness of their political role.[20]

The Soviet Union saw the strides being made by the Communist Party as important to support, whereas America saw them as a dangerous threat. If Indonesia were to fall into Communist hands, this would be a serious blow to American interests over all Asia. Post World War II American politics saw things in terms of the domino effect. According to this theory, the collapse of one non-communist country to communism would cause the further collapse of neighbouring non-communist governments.[21] In the case of Indonesia, the United States was concerned to crush the Indonesian Communist Party, and knew of Sukarno's anti-imperialism. This seems to be why America exploited the split that occurred within the Indonesian army, namely between the Ahmad Yani group on one side, and the Nasution and Soeharto group on the other.[22]

As many researchers have shown, the 1965 tragedy was state violence. The slaughter was more planned bureaucratic violence than spontaneous mass violence. In the various outbreaks of violence in various areas over Indonesia, it is clear that the army's Special Forces (RPKAD) took an initiating role. If there were groups of youths involved, they were usually trained and facilitated by the military, and their impunity also guaranteed.[23] So the 1965 Incident was not 'horizontal conflict', namely civil conflict, or between the people and the Communist Party, as the version promulgated by the Indonesian authorities has explained it to date. What happened was a 'vertical conflict'. It was the State authorities who perpetrated the greatest human rights abuse against their people, and in particular against

---

20 Mohammad Farid, 'How the Cold War influenced US-Indonesia relations', *The Jakarta Post*, 2 September 2007.
21 John Simkin, 'Vietnam and the Domino Theory', on the Education Forum web page, accessed 10 April 2019. See http://educationforum.ipbhost.com/index.php See also the entry 'domino theory' in the Encyclopedia Britannica, http://www.britannica.com/EBchecked/topic/168794/domino-theory accessed 10 April 2012.
22 Peter Dale Scott, 'The United States and the Overthrow of Soekarno, 1965–1967', *Pacific Affairs* 58 (Summer 1985), 239–64.
23 Hilmar Farid, 'Indonesia's Original Sin: Mass Killings and Capitalist Expansion 1965–1966', *Penebar e-News*, No. 9 (January 2006), accessed 10 April 2012; also Robert Cribb, 'Unresolved Problems in the Killings of 1965–1966', *Asian Survey* 42:4 (July/August 2002), 550–63.

members and sympathisers of an official political party that was fully legal at the time.

The 1965 tragedy in Indonesia can thus be seen as the foundation of the New Order, as well as the foundation of the expansion of capitalism in Indonesia. The killings and mass arrests, the eviction of people from their homes and their lands, and the paralysing of the critical sector in Indonesia was an integral part of New Order politics. The military group led by Soeharto relied on foreign funds for the development of the national economy. In this way, they promoted the expansion of capital and tied themselves to the power of the Western economy, ending Sukarno's anti-imperialism program. When elephants fought – both global elephants (the United States versus the Soviet Union) and national elephants (Ahmad Yani versus Nasution and Soeharto), ants got trampled.

## Regional themes and structure of the book

In the following chapters, readers will find six reports from different regions containing description, analysis, and in some of the reports also a little theological reflection from the area's team, with separate themes. The themes in the writing emerged from conversations with the informants and between the research team members. The book is divided into two parts with the first part focused on the regions where the GMIT is dominant, and the second part concentrates on the GKS areas.

Part One of the book focuses on the regions of Sabu, Kupang, Timor and Alor where the Christian Evangelical Church in Timor (henceforth GMIT) is the dominant church. The report from Sabu in Chapter One takes as its theme the destruction by the state of the female teachers in Sabu-Raijua, where both Communist Party sympathisers and members of the Indonesian Women's Movement (Gerwani) were mainly teachers. Ideas of social justice championed by the Communist Party were well received by the educated on the island of Sabu. However, it was precisely because of this that they became targets of state destruction. This report depicts the suffering of these female victims and their strategies to remain strong and raise their children in the face of this destruction. It also pays attention to the effects of the 1965 events on the church, on Sabu-Raijua culture, as well as the world of education in these environs. The murder of a number of male teachers and the firing of a number of female teachers resulted in the decline of education on the island, and in the creation of a climate of fear that grips society to this day.

Chapter Two, the report from the city of Kupang, the capital city of NTT province, concentrates on stories by Gerwani activists. In general, Gerwani activists were educated women of the time. The 1965 tragedy led to these educated women not only losing their jobs that were a source of income for their families, but also to them being ostracised from the church and society. They were branded as 'sinful women'. Many of the female victims found spiritual strength to continue to live in the fellowship of prayer.

In Chapter Three the East Kupang team focused on the theme of the destruction of kinship relations that was a result of the 1965 tragedy in this area, together with an assessment of the church's response to this. In societies where the pattern of family relations is marked by communality, choices of differing political ideology by certain individuals within that community can easily be branded as rebellion. And when this political choice conflicts with the desires of those in authority, then pressure can be extremely strong. In this kind of context, the church tends to be fearful of speaking out. The church is unable to fully play the role it should, namely to assist with reconciliation between family members and the congregation, because the church is itself trapped in fear. The old saying that 'fear is a high fence' is true indeed. The church's healing today must involve it liberating itself from fear, breaking down that fence, and becoming a free community which is then able to free others; it must become healthy in order to heal.

In Chapter Four the team writing about South Central Timor selected the stories of a few women in order to depict the complexity of the situation at that time. When the 1965 tragedy happened in Indonesia, the area of South Central Timor (TTS), like many other areas in NTT, was suffering a famine after a severe drought that had caused failure of the planting season and harvest. The upheavals in national politics and the economy made things worse. In this situation, there arose what was called 'The Spiritual Renewal Movement'. The research team for South Central Timor attempts to analyse the relationship between these various events and their effect on the identity of women from that region. When local culture and religions were crushed because they were viewed as atheist and communist, and people were forced to convert to Christianity, how did the women survive, both physically and psychologically?

In Chapter Five the research team for Alor offers stories of female victims whose husbands were killed at that time. These widows also experienced violence: they had their heads shaven, they were made to stand in the hot sun in town squares, and they were turned into exhibits for the crowd.

Some experienced sexual abuse. They were considered to be 'infected' by the Communist Party virus transmitted by their husbands. Their punishment was intended to be a lesson to other members of society, to not oppose the state. To some women, their families were their essential support, but others were rejected or insulted by their own families because of their status. As best they could, these women developed any talents they possessed to survive and raise their children: by trading, traditional healing, weaving and so forth. In this way, they opposed the imposed stereotype, and created a new image of families bringing good.

Part Two of the book focuses on the Sumba region where the Christian Church of Sumba (GKS) is the largest Protestant mainline church. In Chapter Six the Sumba team focuses on the issue of sin that was raised by the female victims they interviewed. The Christian Church of Sumba (GKS) required victims to confess their sins before the gathered congregation. Even though not all the women arrested were members of the Communist Party, they were still considered to have disturbed the congregation, and therefore they had to confess their 'sin'. The question that arises from their stories is: What did the church mean by sin? This question encourages the church to rethink its teachings about sin. In Chapter Seven the Sumba team reveals the abuse of civil rights when victims were unilaterally fired from their positions as state civil servants. To this day, some of them are still battling for restoration of their rights in this matter. Chapter Eight examines the views of Dutch and German missionaries in Sumba during this period. This report is made based on direct interviews with former missionaries, as well as their writings.

Each of the regional teams presents its report in its own style. But there is one thing common to all the regional reports. They all call for the church and society today to act to restore the rights of the victims, which will also be a self-healing for the church and society from the collective trauma that continues to haunt the life of this nation.

## The path to healing is still a long one

Apart from listening to the stories of the victims through interviews, the research teams also gave space to those who wanted to have a voice, by organising a two-day meeting of victims and their families at the end of March 2011 in Kupang. We were moved to see that some women who had to date been marginalised by their communities because of the state-sponsored violence inflicted upon them, agreed to come and to share their strength among the invitees and with us, the researchers. A group of grandmothers and their children from Sumba, Sabu, Alor, South Central Timor, East Kupang and the city of Kupang shared with us the incredible suffering they had experienced their whole lives. But that was not all. They also talked about the strength and spiritual sources that allowed them to survive so that their own humanity was not crushed.

They made plans to reach out and invite other friends still living in fear to have the courage to state the truth that they were actually victims of a huge evil inflicted upon them, and not the instigators of that evil. They also took the initiative to make memorials at the places where their loved ones had been massacred.[24]

This meeting also encouraged us to think of broader projects of community reconciliation in the church and society. We hope this publication will foster public awareness, particularly in the church, of the need to listen to the victims and begin to create a safe atmosphere for them to talk; to acknowledge the violence inflicted on them, including by the church; and to work together to fight for restoration of their rights. Indeed, this is the duty of the church, both to proclaim the voice of prophecy and to bring about its fellowship as a healing community.

We are well aware that the publication of our research findings is not the end of a process. Precisely the opposite, it is the beginning of a long, ongoing path. For this particular stage, we took about one year from the time of preparation through to publication. This is an extremely short time to express the complexity of the problems of the period we were researching. When we completed the stage of story gathering in our research, there were still many questions that needed to be explored further about actors, methods and the chronology of the violence. Apart from that, many parties in Timor, Alor, Sumba and Sabu, encouraged us to go on gathering these stories. We are committed to creating a wider space in the future to listen to and promulgate the voices and perspectives of victims in more varied ways and with more varied methods (including popular writing, documentary film). This can be seen as pastoral action for the future that springs from the reflections we have developed together thus far.

In this, we stand together with the victims to unsettle those forbidden memories: to break open the grave of history that is so ridden with violence in Indonesia, for the sake of a just and civilised future for this nation. As a

---

24  The word 'massacre' is used in this book in the sense of deliberate cruel murder at one place of more than four defenceless people.

challenge, the stories of these female victims come from a self-image that was not expunged by the violence inflicted upon them, and from the longing to contribute to the healed life of the church and nation.

# PART I

Part I of this book examines the 1965 violence in Sabu, Kupang, Timor and Alor, regions in East Nusa Tenggara (NTT) served by one of the two dominant mainline Protestant churches in the Province, the Christian Evangelical Church in Timor (GMIT). Each of the chapters in Part I focuses on a particular geographic location and highlights various themes that emerged as the local teams carried out their research.

Chapter One examines the destruction by the state of the female teachers in Sabu-Raijua, where both Communist Party sympathisers and members of the Indonesian Women's Movement (Gerwani) were mainly teachers. This report depicts the suffering of these female victims and their strategies to remain strong and raise their children in the face of this destruction.

Chapter Two focusing on the city of Kupang, the capital city of NTT Province, concentrates on stories by Gerwani activists. The 1965 tragedy led to these educated women not only losing their jobs that were a source of income for their families, but also to them being ostracised from the church and society. They were branded as 'sinful women'. Many of the female victims found spiritual strength to continue to live in the fellowship of prayer.

Chapter Three examines the theme of the destruction of kinship relations that was a result of the 1965 tragedy in East Kupang, together with an assessment of the church's response to this. Chapter Four examines experiences of economic hardship and the 'The Spiritual Renewal Movement' in South Central Timor. It analyses how, when local culture and religions were crushed because they were viewed as atheist and communist, and people were forced to convert to Christianity, women were able to survive, both physically and psychologically.

Chapter Five presents the stories of female victims in Alor whose husbands were killed at that time. These widows also experienced violence: they had their heads shaven, they were made to stand in the hot sun in town squares, and they were turned into exhibits for the crowd. Some experienced sexual abuse. They were considered to be 'infected' by the Communist Party virus transmitted by their husbands. Their punishment was intended to be a lesson to other members of society, to not oppose the state.

## Background: The Christian Evangelical Church in Timor (Gereja Masehi Injili di Timor, GMIT)

The Christian Evangelical Church in Timor (henceforth GMIT)[1] is one of the largest Protestant churches in Indonesia. Like the Christian Church of Sumba (GKS), it is shaped by Calvinist teachings as they were taught by Dutch Protestant missionaries. However, the GMIT and the GKS continue different theological traditions as a result of the split within the Protestant church in the Netherlands in the early 19th century.

The development of the Protestant religion in the area that is now known as Nusa Tenggara Timur (NTT) was influenced by the power of the Dutch East India Company, the VOC. As the military and political position of the VOC was relatively weak, Protestant proselytising did not develop before the 19th century. The Netherlands Missionary Society (NZG) had been successful on the island of Rote in the mid-18th century with the opening of a school there. In 1854, proselytising by the NZG in Timor was given over to the state (Dutch) church called the Protestantse Kerk in Nederlands-Indië or more commonly, the Indische Kerk. By the end of the 19th century, Protestantism was limited to Kupang and its environs. In the interior of Timor, there was not much development before the arrival of Pieter Middelkoop in 1922. He translated the New Testament and many songs into the Timorese language, *uab Meto*.

Although the process of church autonomy in Timor began to take place with the establishment of some regional church councils in 1935, the GMIT was established only with the first synod assembly in 1947. The GMIT was funded by the Dutch government, and then by the Indonesian government until 1950. The church faced a financial crisis when its funding ran out at the same time as it was rapidly expanding.

---

1   This summary is based on information Frank L. Cooley's *Benih Yang Tumbuh XI* Jakarta: Lembaga Penelitian dan Studi Dewan Gereja-gereja di Indonesia, 1976), (English translation *The Growing Seed XI* pub 1982) and *A History of Christianity in Indonesia*, eds. Jan Sihar Aritonang & Karel Steenbrink (Leiden, the Netherlands: Koninklijke Brill NV, 2008) pp 300–310.

The GMIT made a great contribution in the field of education through its organisation, the Christian Education Foundation (Yupenkris), and training in theology that developed into what is now the Faculty of Theology at Artha Wacana Christian University (UKAW), a university that is jointly run by the GMIT and GKS. The GMIT also provides medical services, which included the establishment of a small hospital in Alor (which has since been handed over to the state) and a hospital for mothers and children in SoE, Southern Central Timor. The GMIT also runs orphanages in Kupang, provides agricultural training through its Alfa Omega Foundation (established in 1967), and has a micro-credit program that it runs through the Tanaoba Lais Manekat Foundation (TLM), established in 1995.

Both the GMIT and the GKS serve in the context of the province of NTT, which is noted for both its ethnic diversity and the poverty of its people.

## Sabu

Hanga Loko Pedae, Mab'ba (Seba): Massacre site.

*[They were taken] by foot from the Seba hospital… Towards the police barracks, and then… they turned… towards East Sabu to the square, and then to Hanga Loko Pedae [meaning The Dry Riverbed that is always talked about] to the edge of the Terdamu airstrip. I remember that name Hanga Loko Pedae to this day. It took about an hour to get there. There were people accompanying them and crowds of people following behind. When we got to the location, there were also crowds of people already waiting there.*

*After we got to the location, Wadu and I… put Mara down in the hole… holding him by the hands. When he was down there, we made him sit down while we climbed back up. While we were still climbing up, and our feet were… still dangling in the hole, there was a blinding flash followed by a booming sound.*

*I turned back, and saw that Mara's head was gone, blown right off. The others, after I got to the top, followed one by one, like the first one – the second, the third, and so on until it was finished. After the hole was half full with bodies, they sat the ones to be executed on the western edge of the hole, with their legs dangling down. They were ready to be shot or macheted. And as far as I know, only two people were macheted. The one who did it was a soldier [from Sabu] … by then I had been given a new job to hold the petromax light up beside the person that was going to be executed. So, after he was beheaded, the victim was almost lifted up and immediately fell. After he fell, he was kicked into the hole. I stood about one metre away from the victim, so I didn't just get blood stained, but I was sprayed with blood and brains.*

*Informant's testimony*

# Chapter 1

# State Destruction of Sabu-Raijua Women Teachers

### Paoina Bara Pa and Dorkas Nyake Wiwi

Gad'i, one of the women victims who is now 83 years old, was full of emotion as she told her story about the bitter history of 1965–66: 'What did I do wrong?' Sobbing, beating her breast, exhausted, on the sofa, she continued to speak of one violent experience after another that she experienced.

> One day the mob came and dragged me away when I was heavily pregnant with my third child. I kept passing out on the way, until they threw me into detention. There were lots of men and women detained in people's houses accused of being communists or Gerwani.[1]

The coup d'état in Jakarta in 1965 spread to every corner of every village in the country, Sabu-Raijua included. The violence and cruelty against humanity took the form of arrests, detention, abuse of women detainees, the killing of 34 people – both Communist Party activists and non-communists – forced labour, the imposition of a requirement to report to authorities, dismissal from positions as teachers and other government civil service positions at the district level, and restriction of political rights. The trauma and stigma perpetuated by the New Order continues in Sabu-Raijua society to this day. Whenever there is any disturbance or trouble it is always linked to the Communist Party, and out come the old insults, 'What do you expect of a communist/Gerwani?' As a

---

1   Gad'i, interview at Ledemanu, Sabu, 21 November 2010.

victim's child explained, if anyone is critical and clever, then he or she too is branded communist/Gerwani.[2]

We, the research team for Sabu, tried to map the impact of the 1965–66 Incident on education, and in particular on women teachers. Many teachers were executed without trial, both as Communist Party officials and as people merely branded as such. Women teachers, whether they were activists or not, suffered physical, economic and psychological violence, and ongoing trauma.

The destruction of teachers, both men and women, was a severe blow to the GMIT as a civil institution in Sabu-Raijua society, which had pioneered education long before the Indonesian state had done anything in this field. GMIT's human resources were wasted when its members became victims of the 1965 power politics in Jakarta. The customary societies (*masyarakat adat*) were also trapped in an experience of state evil through killing and terror. In the name of the destruction of the Communist Party, they were forced to change their beliefs (from indigenous religions to Christianity) as a sign that they were not atheist. Strangely, some people, without any knowledge whatsoever of the cause of the problems, still carried out violence against others. The 1965 Incident is like taboo history: *loe diam, loe aman; loe tanya, loe mati* (keep your mouth shut, and you're safe; ask questions, and you're dead). But now, the victims in Sabu-Raijua want to open up this silenced history, as this written report records. During their research, team members found that the victims were open because they trusted the team that had taken the time to visit them, listen to their suffering, and pray together with them. There was another reason why they were open, as one of the children explained, namely that they have been able to follow on TV developments in the history of 1965, particularly President Abdurrahman Wahid's decision to give political space to the victims as full citizens.[3]

This research was something new and startling to the victims, witnesses and perpetrators, but on the whole they were very open, and this in itself is extraordinary. Everyone said that what had happened in Sabu-Raijua was a humanitarian tragedy.

---

2   Alu, Wila's child, said this at the time of the interview with Wila on 24 November 2011 at Ledemanu, Seba.
3   Ibid.

# Profile of Sabu-Raijua

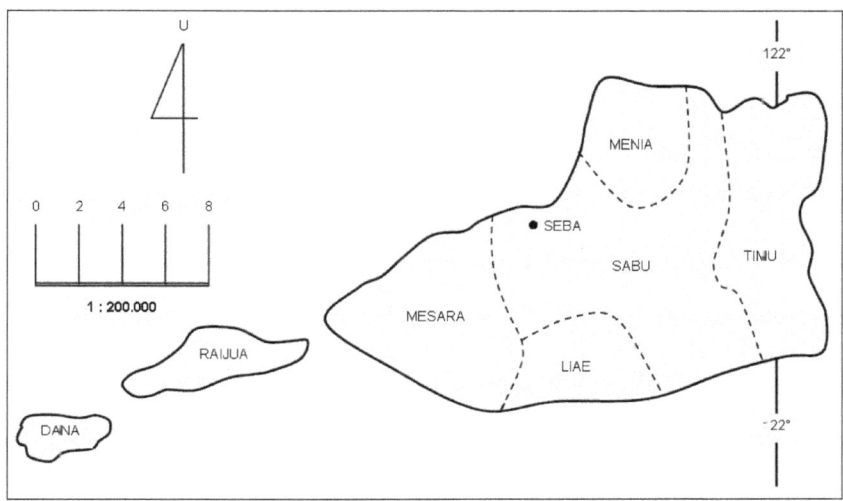

This map of Sabu-Raijua shows the division of the territory into five traditional areas. Today, the territory has become the district (kabupaten) of Sabu-Raijua with six sub-districts (kecamatan). The Sabu-Raijua district also includes Dana, an uninhabited island that is also known by the epithet '*Dana wila kole*' meaning 'the kole flower of Dana'. People believe that this island was the resting place for the Sabu ancestors on their way to and from Sabu, both physically and spiritually. Today, Dana Island is still the place where the people of Sabu-Raijua hold special ceremonies.

The District of Sabu-Raija is located in the province of East Nusa Tenggara (NTT) between the island of Sumba to the west and the island of Rote to the east. According to the 2010 census, the population of Sabu-Raijua is 74,136 of which 37,655 are male and 36,481 are female. The land area is 420 square kilometres. The sea that surrounds the islands of Timor, Sumba, Flores, Solor and Alor is called the Sabu Sea. The island of Sabu has five traditional areas, as seen in the map above. The islands of Sabu, Raijua, Dana and Cole (which is not shown on the map) were separated from the District of Kupang in 2010, and now form a district of their own.

This new district is made up of six sub-districts whose borders are almost contingent with those of the traditional (customary) territories, namely West Sabu, Liae Sabu, Central Sabu, East Sabu, Hawu Mehara, and Raijua. Sabu-Raijua can be reached by boat from Kupang, the capital of NTT, by boat in 15 hours, or by plane in around 45 minutes.

The people of Sabu-Raijua have a traditional form of government, divided according to territorial divisions that were carefully maintained until

2009, when they underwent change because of the formation of six subdistricts to fulfill the requirements of the establishment of the district of Sabu-Raijua.

## Education

Formal education was introduced to Sabu when the Dutch government established schools not long after the Dutch arrived around 1850–1860.[4] One of our informants, Kitu, a former teacher, now aged 70, talked about his family's introduction to education via the church:

> When my ancestor left his original village, Rae Loro, he had a son and the colonisers asked his father for permission for him to be sent to school and baptised as a Christian…[5]

Kitu talked about how that son's descendants were Christian, and to the present they all enjoy education. Then he spoke about himself:

> My father once strung me up because I skipped school.[6] My parents were very strict about their children going to school. Back then, the government appointed school prefects who had to take the children to school, and also to check whether there were children skipping school or who had forgotten. So, you can understand why many parents decided to keep their children at home to work.

From 1948 the GMIT had to support itself, independent of Dutch funds, and so the schools that were previously colonial were taken over by the School Board (PAP) of the GMIT. In 1964, there was government legislation that all private schools had to be managed by a foundation, and so

---

4   It is unclear when the Dutch first arrived in Sabu. One Sabu family holds a document dated 19 June 1868 signed by a Dutch official about a government complex owned by the Sabu king at the kampung of Rae Pana, Seba (a photo of this document is held in the JPIT archives). According to *A History of Christianity in Indonesia*, eds. Jan Aritonang and Karel Steenbrink, (Brill: Boston, MA: Brill, 2008, p.301), records of the Dutch Church in Batavia show that in 1756 there were 600 people in Sabu ready to be baptised, and in 1760 there were five congregations with a total membership of 626. This means that the Dutch introduced Christianity even before many Dutch people lived in Sabu. However, when Pastor W. Donselaar arrived in Saba in 1870, he began his proselytising from zero.
5   Kitu, interview 17 November 2010 at Eikepaka, Rae Loro.
6   This used to be a common punishment for children who had done wrong: their feet were tied together with rope made from palm fibre, then they were hung upside down from a mango tree that was covered with large ants. The informant cried as he spoke about this experience.

in 1967 the GMIT School Board changed its name to the Foundation for Christian Education (Yupenkris).[7] This Foundation established branches in every area, including Sabu. The Foundation's principles were set out in article 2 of its constitution, as follows:

1. The founding principle of Yupenkris is the Bible which witnesses that Jesus Christ is the Redeemer of the world, including in the field of education.

2. Yupenkris acknowledges the Pancasila (Indonesia's five principles) as the basis and moral content of national education.[8]

Two years later, on 22 February 1969, The Indonesian Union of Christian Women (PWKI) established the first kindergarten in Sabu-Raijua. The congregation in Seba provided the land, and the women looked for funding from the local office of the Department of Education and Culture to construct the building. The women founders included: Ibu Huma-Penu (the wife of Pastor Huma), Ibu Bilik-Miha, Nyora Agustina Nuban-Heke, Nyora Welhelmina Lado-Raja Riwu, Nyora Paulina Amalo-Manu, Ibu Sarlin Ragalai-Tung (nurse), Mariana Manu (nurse), and Nyora Paitiba-Kake. Nyora Agustina was head teacher and director of the kindergarten. She was assisted by Ibu Billik and Ibu Huma, while Ibu Mariana and Ibu Sarlin did occasional teaching with a focus on health.[9]

The teacher Kitu, who was a student at the primary school and the vocational school for primary school teachers (SGB), also described the role of the church and the condition of schools and education in Sabu:

Our [primary] school back then used to be called People's School (SR). The school building was not fit to be used. So we used the church and people's houses.

This information shows that the church was the founding pillar in the field of education before the government took over this important role. Until

---

7   Discussion with retired teachers on 15 October 2011 at an event at Lasiana beach, Kelapa Lima district, Kupang. See too the information in Frank Cooley, *Benih Yang Tumbuh XI: Gereja Masehi Injili di Timor* [*The Growing Seed XI: Christian Evangelical Church in Timor*] (Jakarta: Lembaga Penelitian dan Studi Dewan Gereja-gereja di Indonesia, 1976) p. 238.
8   Frank Cooley, *Benih Yang Tumbuh* XI, 244
9   Phone interview with Nyora Agustina Nuban-Heke on 20 January 2012. The wives of male teachers were called *nyora*, while women teachers themselves, whether or not they were married, were called *enci*. All the names of the founders here are their real names.

the 1960s, apart from primary schools, both the GMIT and the state had established secondary schools like the national junior high school (SMPN) and the vocational school for teachers (SGB). At the beginning, the teachers in the GMIT schools were both private teachers paid by the GMIT as well as state teachers. However later, after the government built its own schools in the 1970s, the GMIT schools suffered a shortage of teachers.

Since colonial times, teachers have had a dual role as teachers at both school and at church (Bible study). This dual role made them extremely respected in society. Teachers were a new social class and the bearers of new values to society. Teachers had to have a real desire to learn. Back then, books and radios were limited, so teachers who wanted to learn from the world of politics became members and organisers of political parties. At that time there was also no ruling that limited the participation of teachers in politics. The office bearers of the national political parties in Sabu like the Communist Party, Parkindo (Indonesian Christian [Protestant] Party), Partindo (Indonesia Party) and PNI (Indonesian National Party) were predominantly teachers.

Two teachers, Mone Dami and Kitu, gave their reasons for becoming active in politics and party officials. Pak Mone Dami said:

> I was attracted to the PNI back then because its ideas were in keeping with Pancasila. I thought this was the party that could forge the spirit of the people to know Indonesia as their nation... Many government civil servants did not work properly. The teachers here, for instance, did not work well. They worked more for political parties rather than fulfilling their duties as teachers.[10]

According to Kitu, who was a teacher and PNI official at the time

> People invited us to join, but it was also because we wanted this, we wanted to try it out, being participants in the political climate so that as educators we would also know the ins and outs of politics.[11]

Many teachers married other teachers: for instance, Manu and Tenga, Bara and Moili, Rihi and Lena, Kitu and Natada, and Doro and Moj'o. These young teachers were also active in providing informal classes in the afternoon and evenings to people who were still illiterate. Locals like Bire Here

---

10   Yermi Mone Dami, interview on 20 November 2010 at Tanalara, Mab'ba precinct, Seba city.
11   Kitu, interview 22 November, 2010.

Riwu (Sabu) and Gaja (Raijua) assisted them. Bapak Bire Here even fell in love with and married one of his former students in this literacy class.[12]

One can see, then, how over these years the movement for education, led by teachers in both the formal and informal sectors, both in the church and government, and the way the people responded to it, was passionate indeed. The demand for teachers in Sabu was high, so there were courses for training primary school teachers, as recounted by Rihi, one of the first students at the State junior high school (SLTP), who now lives in Kupang.[13] Teachers were the new intellectual group in society, schools, the church and political parties at that time.

## Socio-economic map

Over 1964–65 Sabu-Raijua experienced a very long dry season and an environmental crisis that meant food supplies for the people were in dire straits. Long dry seasons had become a regular disaster, which led the people to make their own predictions of odd-numbered years being dry years of hunger, and even numbered years as years of rain and plenty. In the midst of the food shortage, the political temperature heated up. Political promises about helping the people became increasingly aggressive, as two witnesses recounted:

> Back then people were experiencing a severe food shortage. There was not enough corn and rice, and when there was distribution of rice it was often a Communist Party initiative so we were upset about that. There was probably something going on between the different party officials, who were competing for advantage in attracting the people's sympathy.[14]

> The Communist Party was making promises that the farmers would be given hoes and other farming tools, and the Party would defend them in any land disputes. Government officials were promised promotions and a raise in salary, and that they would be heard and defended when they faced any problems. The Communist Party promised people they would get things for free, everything would be free. So that's why the Communist Party was well ahead here.[15]

---

12  Bapak Bire Here is his real name.
13  Ibid
14  Yermi Dami, interview.
15  Mahe, interview 26 November 2010 at Pedami, Seba

Kati, a woman from a customary community, described the situation in a similar way, depicting her family's situation in the customary kampung of Rae Loro, Seba.

> My aunt died around this time. When we had the funeral gathering, there was no food in the house. This was a miserable situation. So I went to a few families (near Seba) to ask them to help out with food, but no one had anything. Then a family member took me to East Sabu. We walked for a whole day, and at last I got one sack of sorghum. I had to go back home through the forest at night alone, terrified. With that sorghum we could hold the ceremony for my aunt. That was truly a disastrous year.[16]

During the dry season it was common for fires to break out in the fields, and also people's houses, as Dina and Kati recounted about the traditional kampung of Namata and Rae Loro in Seba:

> In the month of *koo ma* [meaning the month of clearing the fields, namely October 1965), we were all out doing the clearing. At the ceremonial house called the *pulodo* [according to the traditional hierarchical structure, this is the house of the sun grandmother] there was just my grandfather left alone. When we went back home, the house and my grandfather had gone up in flames. According to our customs, if there is a fire no one comes to help. This is taboo because those who help out will then have the same thing happen to them. And no one is allowed to rebuild on the site of a house that has burnt down.[17]

Dina's family home in the customary kampung of Rae Loro burnt down around July-August 1965. After that, the kampung was deserted. Other fires broke out in Kota Seba in July 1965, beginning with the house belonging to Pak Mone Dami, a PNI official, and spreading to the GMIT-run primary school at Lederaemawide in the Mehara area. In Sabu there are often fires around July-August because apart from the fact that it is the dry season, there are also strong winds. But in 1965, people from other political parties suspected that Communist Party members had lit the fires in Seba and

---

16   Kati, interview on 16 November 2010, Rae Loro.
17   Dina and Kati, interview on 18 November 2010 at Namata.

Lederaemawide, yet it was Pak Mone Dami himself who was accused and arrested in relation to the fires in Kota Seba.[18]

## Socio-cultural map

In Sabu culture, the men usually sing when they tap palm trees (lontar) for their sap, to 'encourage' them to produce lots of juice. Parents sing these same songs as lullabies to their children.[19] Even though people still grow sugar palms today, only a few old men still tap for the juice, and the tradition of singing is lost. In the past, both men and women used to sing when they weeded the beans and sorghum to encourage the bean plants to produce lots of beans, but this practice in now also forgotten.

The people of Sabu-Rajiua also have very strong family ties that are maintained by the practice of pressing noses when they meet. Pressing noses (called *hengad'o*) has various meanings: as a greeting, as a way of emphasising family connection, and as a sign of reconciliation.

Since the beginning of Sabu-Raijua history, weaving has been the main occupation of women. Through their weaving motifs, the women of Sabu-Raijua document genealogies, clan histories and so forth, so women have an important role in society, particularly in safeguarding the maternal line. In the customary societies of Sabu-Raijua, one also finds a rite of special teaching for girls. Every year in April, girls gather in the traditional house to learn from their mothers about the intricacies of weaving, about ancestry, and food traditions.

On the one hand, one cannot deny that the Christian schools had a positive effect on the women and girls of Sabu who received a good education. Through education, they were introduced to a wider world and received knowledge and skills so they could work in and become leaders of organisations.

On the other hand, the Christian schools, as tools of Christian proselytising, helped to wipe out traditions and customary practices. Through the world of education, the people of Sabu-Raijua were uprooted from their cultural roots with the demand that they had to be baptised, change their names, speak Indonesian, and they were not permitted to wear sarongs and

---

18  Interview with Pak Mone Dami. Pak Mone Dami and some other teachers named a teacher from Timor who was suspected of being a Communist Party member or sympathiser and the arsonist. Pak Mone Dami also said that the fires in Seba City happened in early June, whereas other informants insisted that the fires happened in late July.
19  Some brief information on the history of Christianity in Sabu can be found in, Aritonang and Steenbrink, 2008, op.cit. p. 301.

traditional cloth to school. Education also had an influence on the world of work, because if someone went to school, then it was not considered fitting for them to go back and work as a farmer, palm-tree tapper, or weaver. The loss of traditions could also be seen in the practice of cutting the hair of customary leaders when they were baptised, and the reticence to speak or sing in the Sabu language at church. Even though the customary practices still exist, their value has begun to fade.[20] Seeing the threat of destruction of their traditional ways, the people of Sabu-Raijua have produced two cultures. They have done this by forbidding from going to school those children who have been selected to inherit and pass on traditions and to safeguard original identity. Therefore, there are now two societies: those who follow traditional religion with customary leaders, and the 'modern' society that is Christian.

## Socio-political map

The developments in national politics in Jakarta in the 1950s and 1960s influenced even Sabu-Raijua, with the birth of big political parties like the Indonesian Communist Party (PKI), the Indonesian National Party (PNI), Parkindo (Indonesian Christian Party) and Partindo (Indonesia Party). According to one of the top PNI officials and a Gerwani activist, in 1963 the party that most appealed to the people was the Communist Party. This is understandable because their programs answered local needs. These programs – which were spread through their literacy classes, education about people's land rights, and food aid – produced political awareness and also emboldened the people to fight for land rights. Mudji, who lost her husband, explained why he became involved with the Communist Party's programs in Sabu:

> It was probably because of his own desire to defend the rights of the people.[21]

Some time around 1965, teachers, Communist Party members and others initiated a protest demanding the return of their lands. One of the victim's children said that his father had managed to get settlement of his land dispute because of the assistance of the head of the Communist Party.[22]

---

20   The loss of value placed in customary law (*adat*) can been seen in the common male Sabu practice of cock-fighting. This is no longer a rite that safeguards relations between people, and between people and nature, but now just a form of gambling.
21   Mudji, interview on 20 November 2010 in Seba City.
22   Ibu Rade, interview on 24 March 2012 at Oetete precinct, Kupang,

The various political parties' different interests created competition between them.

> It was clear that there was competition between the Communist Party and other political parties like Parkindo and PNI. You could see it in the parades and in the parties' anniversary celebrations; sometimes they would just photocopy names of members of other political parties to include in their own line up.
> This did not affect the church too much. There was some effect; like when church officials themselves were sometimes influenced and in their pastoral care they chose that system of care [meaning they ignored their congregations, especially Communist Party members]. They considered themselves to be party this or that. And the Communist Party they particularly ostracised, they thought those people were outside the fence; that's what they thought.[23]

As the war between political parties began to heat up, so too did the tension in society and the government. According to an informant:

> It was the government itself that was saying this, including the Sub District Head… They said that if the Communist Party wins, then that will be it for us. According to the news going around, the core members of the Communist Party leadership were in Surabaya getting eye gougers, weapons, and bombs. People suspected the Communist Party was behind the house and school fires and all the fighting going on.[24]

Towards September 1965, the situation in Sabu was marked by competition between the parties in which teachers were involved. Other parties were envious of the Communist Party's popularity.

## Modern women's organisations

### Gerwani *(Indonesian Women's Movement)*
Gerwani is always equated with the Communist Party. However, many people of Sabu did not even know the term Gerwani. This women's organisation appeared in Sabu at the same time as the Communist Party, and its path was similar. It was the Sabu head of the Communist Party who

---

23  Ibu Rade, interview.
24  Kitu interview, interview.

determined the membership of the executive board of Gerwani, as Wila in Sabu-Raijua explained:

> All the wives of Communist Party members had to join Gerwani, to fight for Indonesian women. So I went along, but I was never a member. I just knew the members. When the army interrogated me I said that I had never joined their activities or taken part in their membership drives.[25]

Gerwani was one of the national women's movements which existed right down to the village level with its programs for improving the lives of women, as is clear in its mission and vision, known as 'The Manipol Family'.[26] Gerwani's programs were supported in parliament by the Communist Party. When the Communist Party was extending its programs in Sabu-Raijua, it also formed the Executive Board of Gerwani and promoted its activities.[27]

Raising the quality of life for women spurred the teacher Wila and her friends Ibu Gad'i and Anne to join the Gerwani board. The process to select officials was extremely top-down, even though there was an informal channel of recommendation between teaching colleagues or family, as one victim said, 'Well, they just decided the placements.'[28]

The women of Sabu-Raijua, especially the educated, were very much attracted by the Gerwani enthusiasm, because traditionally in Sabu culture women were involved in social organisations. The island of Sabu used to have a matrilineal structure with social organisations run by women together with their oldest male relatives.[29] Women were familiar with organisation and leadership within their clan organisations through the special training given to girls in the customary houses.

Gerwani found easy acceptance in Sabu because people had this familiarity. Sabu families already had the *hubi* (the traditional organisation for women) and the *udu* (for men), so that the collaboration between the Communist Party and Gerwani was seen as a form of collaboration that already had cultural roots. Here it is interesting to note that in Sabu, the

---

25 Wila, interview on 24 November 2010 at Ledemanu, Seba.
26 Manipol refers to President Soekarno's 'Political Manifesto' of 1959. For a discussion on 'the true Manipol family' see Ita Fatia Nadia, *Suara Perempuan Korban Tragedi '65* (Yogyakarta: Galangpress, 2007), 9–11.
27 See Wila's account that follows, where she tells how the Communist Party head encouraged her to join Gerwani's executive board in Sabu-Raijua.
28 Wila, interview.
29 Dr. Genevieve Duggan, *Bunga Palem dari Sabu* [Palm flower from Sabu] (Jakarta: Himpunan Wastraprema, 2010), 2.

head of Gerwani was not the wife of the head of the Communist Party. It is possible that the local head of the Communist Party chose Wila (who was also his relative) as head of Gerwani based on her particular skills. Wila spoke several languages including Dutch, German and French.

### *Indonesian Union of Christian Women (PWKI)*

Information about the Indonesian Union of Christian Women (PWKI) as a national women's group in Sabu-Raijua is hard to find because of the loss of oral tradition. One former official, Tenga, does not want to talk openly because of the trauma she still feels. She spoke about her involvement with PWKI in her youth:

> Informant: Back then, the PWKI was already established and I wanted to join. So while I was still at school in Seba I joined so I could take part in the church as a Christian youth.
>
> Interviewer: So it was not like the PWKI today, all its members are old. Back then the PWKI members were young, is that right, Mama?
>
> Informant: Yes… the pastor's wife invited me to join.[30]

Women teachers, wives of male teachers (*nyora*), and civil servants became office bearers in the women's organisations. For instance, office bearers at Gerwani included the teachers and teachers' wives, Wila, Gad'i, Anne and Ota, and in PWKI there was Ibu Ester (a pastor's wife) and the teacher Tenga (also the wife of a pastor).

The Christian women's organisation, PWKI, probably appeared in Sabu-Raijua along with the Christian party, Parkindo. The synergy between them was strong because PWKI officials were women from the church, especially the wife of the church pastor (*nyonya*). One informant said that the church's political stance in Sabu (the GMIT in Seba City), through the influence of its pastors, was pro Parkindo.

# The 1965 Incident in Sabu-Raijua and its effect on society

The 1965 incident had a huge impact on Sabu-Raijua. The development of a civil society and the unity of the traditional society were extremely important in Sabu. This can be seen in the struggle for land rights, the development of women's organisations, and the nurturing of culture. All these suffered a

---

30   Tenga, interview on 21 November 2010 at Rae Liu, Seba.

serious setback. The high regard for education was also destroyed with the murder and firing of many teachers. Teachers who were not detained, were forced to accept an increase in students from the classes of teachers who had been detained or killed. Even though no schools were actually closed, the standard of education declined.

## Mass detention, the execution of 34 men, and firing of teachers

The coup d'état in Jakarta in September 1965 spread to Sabu-Raijua. Proof of the spread of political violence can be seen in the arrival in Sabu of the army from Kupang, the forced departure of Communist Party officials for a meeting in Kupang from which they never returned, the formation of a civilian militia by the army and sub-district government. Other proof is the war of blame. The accusation that the Communist Party was the source of the confusion and the fires that happened at that time led to the formation of a 'justice forum' or interrogation team. The hastily created 'justice forum' was made up of people from the army, the police, political party figures, religious figures, teachers, and government authorities at the sub-district level.

The army arrived in Sabu for the first time around October–December 1965 (before this, only the police were there). Their presence changed the situation in Sabu-Raijua to one of utter confusion. The security officials and the militia were free to carry out acts of abuse and violence through accusation, arrest, capture by force, detention, hiding the location of detention centres, terrorisation and torture, including the murder of 34 people who were Communist Party officials or branded as communist. Gad'i, who was an office bearer of Gerwani, described this situation of utter confusion:

> One day, the mob arrived and asked where my husband was… My heart was thumping. I said, 'He is away at Liae on duty.' They beat me and called me a liar. They ransacked the house and took away all the office equipment that was stored at the house. The one in charge of the attack was a PNI official. The next day, they took my husband to the police station and put him into the prison at Seba. Not long after this, I experienced the same thing. I was also dragged away by the mob although I was heavily pregnant. I kept passing out under the guard of this wild mob. [They] beat me, kicked me and hurled abuse at me on the way to the police station, then I was detained at the Jariwala centre,

in the Seba village complex. My children, who were still small, were just left behind at home.

On the night before he was to be executed, I met my husband at the gate of the prison. We knelt and prayed together, and sang the hymn of surrender, 'I surrender to Jesus my body, spirit and soul'. That night was the last night we met [before his planned execution].[31]

The Bible was my strength during detention. We were considered trash. People felt disgusted if they passed us on the street. We hid ourselves at home and could not communicate in any normal way with the neighbours. Even so, we ignored this suffering; as a family we formed a choir to sing at church, even though we were the targets of insult. In this way, we gave thanks to God for the life He had given us, especially my husband who, I have no idea how, escaped being killed.[32]

When she recounted her experience, Gad'i frequently sobbed and gasped for breath as she lay on the sofa in her oldest daughter's home. Now aged 84, Gad'i does not understand why these events happened, or what she had done wrong. The easy accusation of being a communist or member of Gerwani had been reason enough for them to bear the burden of state political evil.

From the eight people who were informants, as victims, witnesses and perpetrators, we compiled a list of some of the names of those who were imprisoned, both men and women, as far as people could remember them. This list can be found at the end this report.

The process of execution of 34 men who were Communist Party members or accused of being communist happened in two stages. The first stage involved 31 men and was carried out on the night of 29 March 1966, as Kitu recounts:

On the 29th, the 31 men were ready with their hands bound behind their backs. I don't remember who did the tying. I was merely asked to hold the hands of those who had been tied and lead them to the execution site. I had to lead the person at the very front, who was my own relative, Mara. I was together with someone from Raenyale. Each victim was led by two people. We led them, already bound, from the Seba hospital. The gathering place was in front of the Seba hospital, maybe because there was a wide open space there and maybe there were other considerations too, so everyone gathered there, and then

---

31  As Kitu explains below, Gad'i's husband was freed at the last moment before the execution of 30 March 1966.
32  Gad'i, interview 21 November 2010, Ledemanu, Seba.

they were led off to the execution site. A large crowd was there to watch.

Even though we only had a petromax lamp, my relative Wadu and I held Mara. After everyone was ready, the army gave the orders: 'If anyone tries to escape, we will not be responsible, so the first one we shoot will be the one holding the victim.' So, there was no talking at all, let alone any showing of mercy. That was the ultimatum – so, get moving! Tell me, who, under such pressure in in such a situation, would dare try to let them go?

[They were taken] by foot from the Seba hospital towards the police barracks, and then they turned into the road going towards East Sabu to the square, and then to Hanga Loko Pedae [meaning The Dry Riverbed that is Always Talked About] on the edge of the Terdamu airstrip. I remember that name Hanga Loko Pedae vividly to this day. It took about an hour to get there. There were the people accompanying them and crowds of people following behind. When we got to the location there were also crowds of people already there.

After we got to the location, Wadu and I, as the people at the front of the march of people to be executed, put Mara down in the hole, still holding him by the hands. The hole was about two metres deep. When we got down, we sat him down and started to climb back up. While we were still climbing, and our feet had not even got to the top, they were still dangling in the hole, there was a blinding flash followed by a booming sound.

I turned back, and saw that Mara's head was gone, blown right off. The others, after I got to the top, followed one by one, like the first one – the second, the third, and so on until it was finished. After the hole was half full with bodies, they sat the ones to be executed on the western edge of the hole, with their legs dangling down. They were ready to be shot or macheted. And as far as I know, only two people were macheted. The one who did it was a soldier [from Sabu]... that's what people said, anyway, I don't know if it was true or not. By then I had been given a new job; to hold the petromax light up beside the person that was going to be executed. So, after he was beheaded, the victim was almost lifted up and immediately fell. After he fell, he was kicked into the hole. I stood about one metre away from the victim so I wouldn't just get blood stained. I was sprayed with blood and brains.

From the start, the people had it drilled into them that they must not show any sympathy towards the victims, or disgust with the killing.

You could not show any mercy, and if required, you had to threaten and curse the victims. In the end, your feelings turned even though you did not like the killing and could not bear to see your own relatives killed. Nobody screamed, because screams could be taken as a sign of denial, so it was totally calm and quiet. The soldiers ordered them to pray before they were shot: 'Pray, if you still believe in God.'

Towards the end, there were still seven or eight people left, but the hole was full because the bodies were all over the place. When they fell, some went head first, some feet first, so we had to arrange the bodies, like stacking firewood. After that, there was probably only around 30 centimetres left. So we had to cover the bodies and pack the earth tightly because we were afraid that pigs or dogs would come and dig it up, because the earth was loose. We packed it with earth and turf, like stones, so it was a mound.[33]

The second stage of execution took place around nine in the morning on 30 March 1966, and happened at the same time there was an order that the Gerwani women were not to be killed. There were three unmarried men executed – two teachers, and one person who worked at the sub district office. Kitu recounted that the process of execution was almost the same as the earlier one, starting at the Seba hospital, but took another route to the site:

[The march to the execution site] went via Raepana, through the ricefields, towards Hanga Loko Pedae. I was there the whole time, and it was I who had to lead the victims and their guards, under police leadership. The policeman who was the commander that day was Maman. When we got to the location, the victims were made to sit as the victims before. Then they were told to pray before their execution. After they prayed, they were immediately shot. The ones who did the shooting were the commander, Maman, together with Tulu and Bole (heads of the District Police) because by now all the soldiers had returned to Kupang. They went back the morning after the first execution.

I remember something that made an impression on me, when Tulu shot Jungu [at the second execution]. Maybe because his conscience was troubling him, he did not have the concentration when he shot, so the victim was only grazed. When he saw this, Tulu went running off

---

33  Kitu interview, op.cit.

> towards the barracks. The Commander called him back and said, 'You, Tulu, finish your job!' Tulu answered, 'I did finish it, I have to go back to the barracks now.' Another policeman brought him back, but Tulu gave the same answer. [Jungu] was badly wounded but still not dead. In the end, the Commander shot him, but still he did not die. Probably the shot missed its target. So when we filled in the hole, he was still alive. It was the same with Bura, he was still alive too but very badly wounded.

All the male detainees in the prison were murdered except for two, who were unexpectedly released.

> The second lot of killing took place on the morning of 30 March 1966. They were taken from the old Dutch prison, near the hospital. I myself took part, from opening the doors, to asking them to face the prison wall, and I was given the job of tying their thumbs together using the twine you use to make balls. As I was handing one of them over to the ones on duty, the head of the team came and asked me, 'Who is this?' I replied, 'It's Aa'. Then the team leader ordered me to untie him and take him back inside the prison. And again, as I was handing another one over, the team leader asked me, 'Who is this?' I replied, 'Laga'. Then the team leader ordered me to untie him and take him back inside the prison. Then I opened the door and brought out someone called Hila, a teacher and unmarried man from Mesara. After that, my job was done, and I handed him over to the one on duty to guard him, but I forget who that was. And then I opened the door again and brought out someone called Dipa, an unmarried teacher from Menia. And last was Jungu, who worked at the Forestry Office. So there were only three people killed that morning.[34]

## Women teachers' accounts

After they were interrogated, the women who were members of Gerwani – or who were branded as such – were divided into groups and held in four locations around the town of Seba, namely at the police station, at the house of Ma'u, at the Seba district complex, and at the house of Kana, which was encircled with red cloth (red being the Communist Party colour). Before they all were taken to Seba, they were held temporarily in each area: at

---

34  Kitu interview, op.cit.

Raijua (at Talimiri kampung), Liae (at D'aba kampung), Mesara (Pedarro) and Dimu (the Sub-district Head's office). While held in detention, they experienced various forms of abuse, like being given no food (they had to find their own); being beaten, kicked, forced to work, forbidden to speak, terrorised, separated from their newborn babies, and having their hair cut roughly. After they were released, they had to regularly report in at various locations, like the local office of the Department of Education and Culture, and the Sub-district Head's office. Some were fired from their jobs.

The original plan was for all the Gerwani women to be executed in the second wave of executions on 30 March 1966. But on that day, the district head of police at Lima Sabu, at the meeting of the execution team, issued the order that the Gerwani women were not to be executed. They were to have their hair cut. The reason given, according to Rohi (a perpetrator and witness) was that 'they were women who were merely following their husbands'.[35]

The names of Gerwani women and those branded as Gerwani, as far as informants and witnesses can still recall them, are listed as an appendix to this chapter. However, there are still many other women whose names are not included because informants were afraid to mention them, or because they had forgotten as it was 45 years ago.[36] The accounts below detail the experiences of three informants who were willing to share their stories.

## *Teacher and Nyora Wila*

This is my sin, so I must endure…

Wila is the daughter of Bapak Lede and Ibu Lena. She was born at the kampung of Keka in Sabu on 20 December 1934. She was born to a well-educated family for those times. Her father had left Sabu to go to school. He decided that he did not want to be an office-worker, and chose to return to Sabu and be a farmer. Wila's aunt, her father's sister, graduated from school in Makassar and then came to Sabu and took Wila with her, first to Rote, then to Baun and Kupang. Wila grew up in this educated family, and was used to hearing different foreign languages such as Dutch, Japanese, English, and German. She began her own schooling at the Nahagadai primary school (SR) in Sabu, then moved to Rote with the Dena family

---

35  Rohi, interview, 20 November 2010, Air Nitas, Seba.
36  Kitu, interview and Rohi, interview.

This former home of a Communist Party leader in the village of Rae Loro was used as a detention centre for Gerwani women and women accused of being Gerwani. When they were detained there, the house was encircled with red cloth. – JPIT archives.

(Bapak Dena worked for the Dutch colonial government in Rote before he moved to Amarasi, South Central Timor, where he was a civil servant, then returned to Kupang-Fontein on his retirement). Wila continued her education in Kupang, qualifying as a teacher. This is the story of her studies.

> When the Japanese were here I was in the fourth class of Nahagadai primary school, and there was a bomb in Meda Harbour. From then on, I was not allowed to go to school, for a whole year. Then Mama Maria came to my father and asked permission for me to go with them to Kupang. Not directly to Kupang. I moved to Rote first. I went to a school there that was near the hospital, near the prison. The headmaster was Pak Josua; he lived at Oemau. It was really long walk to school.
>
> Everything was pretty normal; I can't remember any special experiences. Except that I loved school. Once, when I was going home from school, someone was smoking out a beehive. The queen bee came out of the hive and stung me on the head, but I kept going to school.

> Just imagine, in Kupang, I had to walk all the way from Fontein. But if I was told to stay home, I cried.
>
> In the 1930s, not many girls had ambition for higher education. This was because it cost a lot of money to leave Sabu, transport was still a rarity, and to get the opportunity to do higher education, you had to pass a national selection.[37]

Wila's family valued education. Her father and her relatives all furthered their education as much as family finances would allow. Wila wanted to change ideas about women, which were still backward, so she struggled and was prepared to make sacrifices for education and her future as a woman.

> When I was in Rote, the school was very far away. I had to climb hills to go to school, and climb hills when I went back home again. And on the roadside, there were often men who sat around drinking the local alcohol called *laru*.[38] They were usually drunk. They liked to tease me when I went past, but I would always go on home from school. What's more, I had to walk all by myself to school every day.
>
> Oh my, I was treated like a servant at home. In the morning I would cook, and go down to fetch water. All of them would bathe at home. Mama [her aunt] used to wash early in the morning, and as soon as I got home from school I would go to the river to wash. Mama never went to the water. I would water the flowers, and after that I'd go and bathe. I had no time to do any sweeping, because I would leave for school before it was light. I was beaten on the nose, and I still have the mark to this day. That's all. Food and clothing were alright. Actually, my uncle was good, it was just my aunt who was cruel like that.

After finishing primary school, Wila continued her junior high school and then senior high school (a vocational school for teachers) in Kupang until 1957.

> My junior high school was at Airnona [a neighbourhood of Kupang]. I graduated in 1952. Then I went on to the state high school (SMA) in Kupang, but did not stay through to graduation because they opened the vocational high school for teachers (SGA). So I changed schools when I was in second year, but because of the different curriculum, I was put back to year one. The head of SGA was Ibu Sia. She was also head of the state high school. I graduated from SGA in 1957.

---

37  Wila interview, op.cit.
38  Laru is mafrom the fermented juice of the lontar palm.

Wila was on the direct path towards working as a teacher. But there were always obstacles placed along that path. Her adoptive mother asked her to be a servant:

> I was told I had to go and help out Ibu Lina as she was a distant relative, so I went to help. But can you imagine… I had finished high school, and now was working as a household servant. I heard about Pak Hede, so I went to talk with him at Yode. He asked, 'What do you want?' I said, 'I have graduated from senior high school for teachers, but I have not found a placement yet, and I hear that they are going to open a state junior high school in Sabu. So, if it is possible, I want to go back to Sabu to teach even though I have not yet officially joined the civil service.' He said, 'Well, that sounds good.' Luckily, there were not enough teachers there, so he gave me a letter of introduction and eventually I was accepted. The headmaster at the time was Pak Liwe.
>
> So in 1957 I started teaching at the state junior high school (SMP) in Seba, and was formally accepted into the civil service in 1961, the letter of appointment came directly from Jakarta, along with a regular raise in salary. I taught algebra, history, and arithmetic.

An interesting point in Wila's account is that in the 1960s in Seba, the number of males and females was about equal. Both the boys and the girls were really enthusiastic about going to school.

> The number of girls and boys enrolled was about the same. In the first year of junior high school, there were 12 boys and 12 girls. In the 1960s, the children of Sabu were really enthusiastic about schooling. For instance [one of the students]… lived in Labba [on the Dimu border]… but went to school in Seba. This was because he was determined to go to school. And the children from the hills would also walk to and from school.
>
> I got married in 1960 to a primary school teacher in Ei Wou called Huki. He was a good man and always smiling. We met in Sabu as teaching colleagues, and fell in love. It was not an arranged marriage. We were blessed with three children.

Around 1960, the political parties (PKI, PNI, Parkindo and Partindo) and the women's organisations (Gerwani and PWKI) started to flourish in Sabu. Wila's husband sympathised with the Communist Party and Wila herself was chosen by the head of the Communist Party to lead Gerwani.

She wanted to refuse the offer of this position because she had no one to help with child care. But because Gerwani had a good vision and mission to fight for women's rights and for equality between men and women, she agreed even though she had no time to do any membership drives or to hold meetings.

> Uncle Radja... came to the house and asked me to be head of Gerwani because all wives of Communist Party members had to join Gerwani. So I was interested in joining at the time. Yes, because my husband favoured the Communist Party, I joined. Radja said that Gerwani's aim was to improve and fight for the fate of Indonesian women. Yes. So every wife of a Communist Party member had to join Gerwani to fight for Indonesian women. So I joined, but I never went looking for members. I did not even know the members.
>
> Gerwani was good because its articles of association stated that it wanted to fight for the rights of women; there was equality between men and women who should get the same education and work.

As an organisation, Gerwani was invited to attend the Indonesian Independence Day celebrations and the Communist Party anniversary celebrations in Sabu. Wila was asked to go to these celebrations to represent Gerwani.

> In the anniversary celebrations for the Communist Party before 1965 and also for Indonesian Independence Day, I was asked to give a speech. I said, 'The women of Indonesia should not be restricted to three things: giving birth to children, bringing up children, and the kitchen, but they should fight alongside their husbands for the progress of Indonesian women. If our duty in the past was to marry, look after the children and the kitchen, today it is no longer like that.'

Wila and her husband were both victims of the 1965 Incident. Her husband, who was only a Communist Party sympathiser, was one of those executed in the massacre of 29 March 1966 at Hanga Loko Pedae, Sabu.

> My beloved husband was 'secured' [meaning detained and murdered]. I don't know if he was persuaded or what... just because his name was on the list, he was taken away and killed. [Ibu Wila started to cry.] My youngest child was just one month old. My husband was executed, shot at Hanga Loko Pedae. Because he was no one important, just a sympathiser, he was not arrested... he handed himself in because he knew about the cruelty of the army and the mobs who came to pick

people up. When I came home, I met my husband on the road. He said he was going to turn himself in. And from that day on, he came home only once, when he was ill. He was home for about three days, then he went back, and that was forever.

Wila's husband was not given an opportunity to meet his wife before he was executed, or even to leave her a message. Wila heard the news that her husband had been executed from a pastor who was detained along with him. When she heard this, she could do nothing except restrain her tears and sadness. The person she loved who should have been alongside her to support the family and the children had gone forever. From that moment on, she had to be both mother and father to her three children who, at the time their father was killed, were aged five years and seven months, two, and two months.

There was no message because when they were going to be executed they were taken to the hospital. They were taken at night, and the next morning I went to sweep the road. I met Pastor Para. He was also detained along with my husband. I have no idea why he was being held. He told me that it was done. [Wila beings to sob, and continues to speak between the sobs.] I held back my tears. I had to remain strong for my children so that they would get a good education. There was no message at all. Bapa departed forever. God knows what they did to us.

When the arrests and detentions began in Sabu, which according to most informants was already underway in October 1965, Wila was in Kupang. Her family told her not to return to Sabu because the situation was bad. But she rejected their advice. Although heavily pregnant, because of her love for her family, she returned to Sabu by boat. When the boat arrived at Sabu wharf, there was a furious mob waiting.

When the 30th September Movement happened I was in Kupang visiting a relative. I heard about the 30th September Movement on the radio in Kupang. My family in Sabu told me, 'Don't come back. Things are crazy here.' I thought, what is this all about? When I got off the boat in Sabu, there was an old man called Tobe on the same boat with me. The minute he got off the boat, the mob attacked him.

The accusation that Wila was a Gerwani woman was going around Sabu.

> At the time, I was accused of carrying a bomb in my trouser pocket, even though I never wore trousers.[39]

After her return to Sabu in December 1965, Wila was taken in for interrogation. But because she was pregnant with her youngest child, she confronted the West Sabu Sub-district Head.

> I was heavily pregnant with my youngest child, my time was almost due. So I asked the Sub-district Head, 'how will it be if I have to give birth in detention?' And he said, 'You may return home for now, but after you give birth you have to come back.' While I was back home giving birth, I heard that friends of mine in detention were jealous of me. 'She's got it good', they said.

A few months after she had given birth, Wila was arrested.

> In the evening the army came and took me to the hospital to have my hair cut short. It was deliberately cut roughly. They just did what they wanted – as long as it looked terrible. There was no questioning at all. I was just picked up with no reason about why I was arrested and why I was being taken away. After we got there, they cut my hair. Another family came and brought my newborn baby, because I thought I was going to be killed, and if so, then that family would take my baby back to the house. Yes. I was resigned to whatever was going to happen. If I was going to be killed, then I wanted to make sure my newborn baby would be given to my husband's family. Thanks to God Almighty, this did not happen, because I knew I had done nothing at all to undermine the unity of the nation and state.

Wila was required to report regularly and to do forced labour like cleaning the police station, the Sub-district office of West Sabu, the roads, and the Seba church. She once felt embarrassed because one of her former students was a guard when she, together with other women, had to clean the church. What was most saddening of all was that she lost her future, for no reason that made any sense.

> I was fired [as a teacher] because I was pregnant outside marriage [after her husband had been executed] so my letters of appointment as teacher and my placement letter were held by Pak Uli [the head of Parkindo].

---

39  Wila wore a dress. At that time, teachers and students were forbidden from wearing traditional woven sarongs to school.

> Yes. He was also the headmaster of the State Junior High School 1 in Seba. I think those official letters had been issued earlier, but because of the political competition of the time, he held on to my letters.

Even though all paths appeared to be blocked to Wila, she continued to try to regain her rights as a teacher and civil servant. But in the end, she failed. Many other teachers experienced the same thing as she did, losing their rights to teach, for reasons that were never clear. There were also some teachers who were fired from teaching, but were later reappointed without any clear explanation, like Mudji and Tenga. But Wila never had any of her rights restored.

> I received no salary either after I had been dismissed. In 1972, my friend Ma'e, who had been my friend since we were at senior high school told me, 'I am very sorry, there is nothing more we can do. You know yourself the political problems now. You are already in your 40s, so you should give up.' So I had to leave and never teach again.

Tragic indeed. The saying 'already fallen, and still hit by the ladder' is probably a suitable description of the way that Mama Wila's life was destroyed as a result of the 1965 incident. She lost not only her husband, but also her work, and the future of her family and children was also in jeopardy. When her children later applied for entry to higher education or for work, they were scrutinised and obstructed.

> When my oldest child applied for work, there was a policeman who knew us. He said, 'Your mother was Gerwani, right? But she's no longer red.' And my younger brother too, who worked in the governor's office, got locked out of promotion. He got no further post, even though formerly he had been head of a department.

Alu, Wila's daughter said the same thing, talking about her older brother, Obed.

> When Obed wanted to do the test for joining the police force, Uncle Titus said, 'Your Dad was communist, right? Hang on a minute while I take a look at this...' So Obed just went back home. He cried. He said, 'why did we have to have a father who joined the communists? We all suffer because of it.' ... Back then... whenever anything happened at church or in society, people always said, 'It's because of those communists'.[40]

---

40   Alu interview, 24 November 2011 at Ledemanu, Seba.

Wila's family still bears the stigma of being trash, evil, and the cause of problems, from her own family members, society in general, as well as from the church. As Alu said:

> It wasn't only when I was young. Even when I was at senior high school it was still like that. Until the end of Soeharto's regime we were still stigmatised by society and the church as bad people. As I said, communists and Gerwani were considered to be trash, or people no longer needed. This was political wickedness.

Mama Wila, who had never before worked to the bone in the fields, now had to do this just to go on living and for her children's future. But from all this, she knew that God is just, as was proven in her children's success.

> As a person, of course there were things that made me deeply sad. [She cried.] Even though people thought we had done bad things, Almighty God is just, so my children were able to further their education and my oldest child graduated with a degree in social work, and my second child is now studying for a bachelor degree in agriculture. Even though there is nothing I could do about the loss of my husband and everything that happened, I accept it, because maybe this was God's way because I had too many sins. And according to the word of God that the payment for sin is death, I was forced to be determined. I had never before done any farming, worked in the fields, or rice fields, or looked after children. But because of what happened, I had to do all this.
>
> As for women, I say to them that when organisations are formed, don't be in a rush to join. Wait for a while and watch, because don't ever let happen to you what happened to me in the past. I do not know what I am supposed to have done, but the reality was the bitter experience I had.

### *The ship Tenggiri, 29 July 1966*
#### Paoina Bara Pa

The Sawu sea is seething,
after the humanitarian tragedy of 29 and 30 March 1966,
The ship has sailed into Seba for the umpteenth time
Its mouth is open wide, welcoming the passengers

The passengers crowding in as usual
Especially because it is education month, student enrolment month.
Among the passengers are some military cadets
Returning from the battlefield;
Not a battle because of threats to national sovereignty,
A battle they were made to fight against innocent people; Fighting
With self control, killing their own relatives; Fighting
using weapons purchased with money from the ones they kill;
Fighting in front of the mothers who gave them birth: Threatening,
terrorising, preaching, hitting, throwing, slapping, controlling,
killing, shaving the mothers' crowns,
tearing babies away from their breasts,
kicking wombs, and violently making them march.
Yes, the soldiers are surely full of pride as they go to Kupang
They carried out their noble duty,
They are sure to get medals and promotions
Maybe their leader is waiting for their report
To report to his leader above him
Yes, not long now
We will get in to Kupang Harbour in the morning
Wives, children and families are all sure to be there
Along with the official transport.
On the ship... the nation's cadets are being given good service
After all, just look at their uniforms, their threatening manner
And the aroma of order-giving... yes, on the ship Tenggiri they...

The ship's whistle blows once... a warning to the sea and to the people
Second whistle... not long now
Third whistle... the ship moves leaving Seba harbor
Passengers and those on shore wave to each other
Farewell, Goodbye, Sayonara!!!
Who knows how far out, sea, winds and storm
Rage against the Tenggiri, screams of fear,
The captain cannot control the sea
Nor can the prayers of the passengers

Nor the weapons that have done the killing
The waves of 29 July 1966 are the killers' judge.
'Is this the justice of Almighty God?' the victims ask,
Whatever you sow, so shall you reap.
Their deeds have come back to them…
Ahhhhhh, they try to make theology from this reality…

*Lasiana, 7 February 2011*

## *Teacher Mudji*

Teacher Mudji, usually called Mama Mudji, is the daughter of Bapak Soleman and Ibu Marta. Her father was a village (*fetor*) chief in East Sabu. Mama Mudji was born in Metei, East Sabu, on 13 October 1941.

> Our family could be said to be relatively well off. Although the school was far away in Bolou, I still attended school, taken there on horseback. After all, my father was a village chief. So anyone who stole chickens, committed adultery, or did other bad things, was held at our house. While there, they had to work like feeding the pigs, pounding rice and so on. They only did work for everyday needs. When it was planting or harvest season, they helped with that work but also shared the produce. While my parents were alive, God still blessed [us] with rain and harvest.
>
> I started school when I was about seven. From our home in Matei to school was about 4–5 kilometres. I was taken there on horseback. I would sit on the horse, which was led by children who lived at the house. There were people who were given the special job of taking me to school and waiting there to take me home. But there was food for them as well as for me. The horse was tethered to eat grass, and the children who had brought me would go and play until it was time to take me home.[41]

Mama Mudji also went to school in Kupang, and had plans to move to Java, but her father would not allow it, so she returned to Sabu and continued her education there.

---

41 Interview conducted on 20 November 2010 at Seba City

All of us children went to school. After being at the Bolou school for a year and a half, my relatives took me to Kupang to stay with Ibu Tius, Jami's mother. The school at Sabu only went as far as the second grade, so I was taken to Kupang and to the Bonipoi primary school. When I had reached the fourth grade, my father ordered me to return to Sabu because he did not want me to be taken to Java. I returned to Sabu and went to the Yeruel church school in Seba Kota. My teacher was Pak Adu. At that time, the first teacher from Sabu was called Yakob. In the sixth grade I moved to Nahagadai primary school.

As long as my father was alive, we had a comfortable life; all our needs were met. When we wanted to eat, we would all sit at the long table. Mama would sit to my father's right, and I would sit on his left. My father made his sons sit further away. Father once said, 'You boys, when I die, it is good if your future wives embrace your sisters. So if your wives are not of good character and do not feed you, then you still have relatives. So when you get married, do not follow your wives' wishes when it comes to inheritance, and make sure you look after your inheritance wisely, and divide it among your sisters.' That's what he said. And his older sister, Bu Heo made sure his wishes were followed.

Although Mama Mudji was a girl, she had the same rights as the boys, both in schooling and in attention and love in the family. This is why in 1956 after she completed primary school, she continued her education at the vocational high school for primary school teachers (SGB). She started SGB in 1956, as part of the second intake. She graduated in 1960, in 1961 became a teacher, and in 1962 married Bapak Gadja who was also a primary school teacher. They had two children, a girl Eda and a boy, Weka.

Pak Gadja became a member of the Communist Party, but Mama Mudji herself was not involved in any organisation. After she became a teacher and got a teaching position, she dedicated herself fully to school teaching. But then the arrests and detentions of 1965–1966 struck her.

At the time I was surprised: how come my name was listed as Gerwani? I have no idea who listed me as Gerwani. When I got to the police station, they asked, 'You are Gerwani, aren't you?' I said that I knew nothing about it. 'I don't even know who the head of Gerwani is', I said. He asked, 'Well why is your name listed here?' I said, 'I don't know'. I was surprised that my name could be there, as I didn't even know about their activities. I said, 'I never joined Gerwani. I never go outside the house except to go to school [to teach].' 'How many times have you held meetings?' he asked. I said, 'Never. I don't even know who the Gerwani members are.' I was surprised. Who was actually the head of Gerwani? Maybe because a husband was a member of the Communist Party, then his wife was considered to be Gerwani. And there had never been any meetings. This what surprised me. Because there was definitely no leader.

When the police came to pick up Mudji, accusing her of being Gerwani, she had just given birth to her youngest child, Eda. Her husband had gone to Kupang two months before the 30th September movement, giving no clear reason. When Mudji was arrested and detained the first time, he was still in Kupang, so she had to endure everything alone. When she was arrested, Weka was still small and Eda only a newborn. Weka was not taken to the detention centre, but Eda was, as she was still nursing.

> What could I say? Everything that happened was just as they designed. My mother brought Eda to the detention centre to be breastfed, and then she took her home again. My children were at home with their grandmother.
> In the evening I was taken from the house to the police station where I was held and interrogated. After returning home, about a week later, I was picked up again, held at the house of a neighbour, Bapa Ma'u, and then released.

When she was released, Mama Mudji still had to fulfill certain requirements. She had to live quietly, as though she had done something wrong or committed some terrible crime.

> I was told to go and be good and live quietly in society. I had no idea what was the crime I had committed. Maybe they thought this attitude was provocation, so they told me to live quietly.
> My husband was arrested in Kupang, I have no idea where exactly, because until today I have had no information. I got no news at all about him. About two months before the 30th September movement, he went to Kupang by ship, on the Lampu. Eda was not yet born when he left. He gave no date of when he would return and did not say why he was going to Kupang. I tried to find out news from his family, but they didn't know anything either. So that was how it was. All we could do was be resigned and place our trust in the Lord Jesus.

Mama Mudji was not reticent to talk about things with her two children, Weka and Eda, when they were still at school. So when they grew up, they were not shocked to know what really happened. As a result of the events, Mama Mudji was fired from her job as teacher.

> When I was fired from teaching, there was no official letter at all. You can imagine that as a mother who had to support her children I felt this deeply, but in everything, I place my trust only in Jesus. My relatives and family helped out. So we were able to get by.
>
> Then in 1969 I was reemployed. This was the initiative of Pak Uli in 1968. A member of parliament – I'm not sure from what political party. He was head of the state junior high school (SMP 1). He had returned from Kupang, and gave instructions for my case to be reviewed as I had received no salary all this time. So in 1968, I went to Kupang. The Foundation for Christian Education (Yupenkris) that was in charge of running the church's private education system was already formed then. Pak Wadu was the head of the foundation. I was told to collect my pay, because it had come through. They had calculated not from 1965, but from 1966 to 1968. Then Pak Wadu gave me a letter of appointment. So I taught for one year at Menia, and then I was moved to another GMIT school. The head of Yupenkris, Pak Rano, also chose me to help out with the distribution of salaries and rice to the GMIT teachers.
>
> My sense of loss was lightened because my children thought of my older brother, Heo, as their father. They even took his name. They took my family's clan name as their own. Well, what could I say? I kept my faith strong in the Lord Jesus. I never complained, because every day God gave some of his Blessing; that was all. We always had enough every day to get by.

Before 30 September 1965, Mudji's husband had taken his leave to attend a meeting in Kupang. Because of this, Mudji's children lost their father, to this day. Not only that, they lost the right to use their father's family name.

> Actually, my children's clan name is Leo, but based on an agreement of our parents, if bride price is not paid in full, then the children take the mother's family name. So my older brother made the decision that the children should not be part of their father's clan. He was the one who organised the papers so they were officially part of my father's clan, and have remained so until today.

After what happened in 1965, Mama Mudji had a message and hopes for the generation today, so they do not fall into the same traps.

> Well, I just talk to my grandchildren and tell them be careful of who you keep company with. If someone tells you to do something, don't just do it. Think about it, reflect on it, because I was once branded like that. So don't just make the decision yourself. Ask your mother. 'Mother, is it alright to do this? From this point of view, is it good or not?' School groups are okay, but nothing outside of that. We must be very careful. Remember, don't be too influenced by people who come with high-sounding this and that, but then later on it is not right. As for government sponsored programs, think about them first. Which one is good? And even if the government program is for the thousandth time, still we have to think, who is this, exactly?

## *Teacher Tenga*

> I have been a member of PWKI since I was a teenager, hoping to be active in the church.[42]

Tenga is the name of a woman well known in Seba society as courageous and with talent in leadership in the 1960s. She was born in Bolou on 13 October 1939, and comes from the sub district of East Sabu. She worked as a primary school teacher and married a GMIT pastor. She found that her profession as a teacher was satisfying only if she could supplement this with involvement in broader organisations. She needed an outlet for her aspirations and enthusiasm to develop the fate of Sabu women. This is why she became involved with the Union of Indonesian Christian Women (PWKI), encouraged by Ibu Ester, the wife of Pastor Rano who was a Parkindo official. Even so, Tenga had her own reasons for joining PWKI:

> PWKI was already established back then and I wanted to become a member. I was still at school at the time, so I could socialise with young Christian men and women. I wanted Sabu women to be involved in organisations, but organisations that recognised God.

---

42  Interview with Ibu Tenga, 21 November 2010, Rae Liu, Seba.

On Labour Day in early 1965, the PWKI was invited to participate in events, by sending a representative to give a speech. The head of PWKI asked Tenga to do this. The main message of her speech was this:

> PWKI is a Christian organisation that is progressive and revolutionary. Women should not be involved in the wrong organisations, or not recognise God. Long live the revolutionary life!!

Mama Tenga was a strong woman with great leadership skills. She dared to say something risky. And this daring brought her great trouble. There were some who did not agree with what Mama Tenga said in her speech. They were angry, and later, when there were all the arrests of women suspected of being Gerwani and Communist, she was also arrested for no good reason.

> Back then, I was, well, good at it… he he… So I was asked to give a speech on Labour Day… to encourage the women involved… and that was considered wrong. They were angry. Yes, because I gave a public speech, and I said that this organisation was good, progressive and revolutionary. So I had to report regularly and clean Pak Sani's house.[43]
>
> At that time there were a lot of women. One afternoon I said to sister Gad'i, 'Try to sing a song,' because I don't have a good voice. Try to sing *'Meski Akupun Dinista'* ['Although Even I am Reproached']. So, they sang. It was hot, whew, it was 10, 11 o'clock in the morning. Pak Sani was lying down in his room and he asked his wife to make sugar water for the women, you know. So for a while I ran away. I said, 'You go ahead and drink.' So sister Gad'i said, 'If you are here, we always get a little help, a blessing'. That's what she said. I would make jokes so they wouldn't feel stress.

Generally, the children of families suspected of being communist found things made difficult for them when they went to school, and especially when they went into higher education. But thankfully, Tenga's children did not experience this.[44]

> The children's schooling went on as before, none of them were kicked out of school… because there were some children who were not allowed to continue their schooling, weren't there? Like Madue's children.

---

43  Pak Sani was a government official at the time.
44  It is interesting to note that Tenga's husband did not experience difficulties because of his wife's status. Had their situations been reversed, this might not have been the case. In general, if a man was involved with the Communist Party or accused of being so then his wife was automatically also suspected, detained, and fired from her job.

When they started university, there was a check done on them, and they had to leave. I said to my children, 'Go to school. [Wait until] after they have done the checking, just go back in.' They said, 'But what is all this about? We don't know anything, Ma.' So all my children went to university. Just this one son here came back home because he dropped out. He failed.

It was determination, sheer determination, always looking for ways around things. Whenever we could find ways, we would for the sake of our children's education. For the sake of their futures according to their individual talents. Six people is no small feat... I had some earnings, but nothing much. I had to divide it out – this, this, and this... the oldest one would share what he earned with his younger brothers and sisters. When he got a job at Yupenkris, he immediately shared [his earnings]. Sometimes I would get Rp 16,000 for all of them, but whenever it was enrolment time I would have to sell something; goats, pigs, cupboards, anything I had, I would sell. Only one child failed. He was not strong enough to struggle.

As a mother who was a female leader herself, Mama Tenga has a message for women of the young generation:

If you experience anything like this, then I say to other women that the only thing is determination. You have to try hard and be able to choose which path to follow in order to move forward.

\* \* \*

# Women's suffering

There were women of Sabu-Raijua who experienced various levels of state violence. They also experienced violence from their own society.

### *Physical violence*

Sabu-Raijua women were dragged away, tortured, killed, had stones thrown at them, had their hair roughly cut, were detained without any reason, intimidated, forced to work, and required to report to authorities regularly. This treatment, together with the view that they were not even human, traumatised them, made them afraid and made them blame themselves.

On the night of the first massacre of 29 March 1966, the people were ordered to watch a film about development that was shown in the yard of this house beside the Seba police station.
– JPIT archives

## *Psychological violence*

It was not only the physical violence and social ostracising that traumatised the women, but also the loss and death of their husbands. They explained how they experienced deep depression when their husbands disappeared and they had no idea where or how they were, or when they were killed. Mama Mudji and Mama Wila (the head of Gerwani) talked movingly about when their husbands disappeared without trace. They themselves were also stigmatised as the cause of problems, and their families, society, the church, the world of work and politics, all blamed them for anything and everything bad that happened. This psychological violence also had a multi-layered traumatic effect, including the trauma that prevented them from being further involved in any kind of organisation.

## *Economic violence*

The women of Sabu-Raija who lost their salaried positions because they were fired and banned from working, had to be prepared to work as farmers and traders to make ends meet. Those who had lost their husbands became single parents, and had to bring up and educate their children alone. Economic violence extended to when their family members were failed in their application tests to join the government civil service, and when they were banned from promotion to any higher leadership position in an organisation because of their parents' or siblings' backgrounds.

### Social violence

The stigma of being ostracised from society applied not only to the victims of arrest and detention, but also to their children and to members of their families. This can be seen in the three women's stories presented above. Apart from losing their father or the support of their mother's salary after she was dismissed from work, there were also children who lost their father's family name, who were taunted at school and at church, and who, when they were adult, faced problems when they wanted to marry (impediments to paying bride price) or in their work places where they were never promoted. The social violence extended to education. The loss of female teachers seriously affected the supply of teachers and the provision of subjects in the curriculum, but no less important was the loss of women as teachers of children in school, society, and the church.

## Impact on the GMIT in Sabu-Raijua

The effect of the 1965–66 events on the church in Sabu, particularly on the GMIT, was both positive and negative. On the one hand, the communist issue benefitted the church in an increase in membership though baptisms, confirmations, and mass weddings at the time.[45] But on the other hand, it was not clear whether the increase in membership was the product of good proselytising, or because people were driven by fear. The issue of the Communist Party spread to Sabunese customary groups [who were not Christian] because the pretext was that they were atheist. The church was also used as a safe house where they were baptised so they could escape being branded as atheist. People changed their original Sabunese names to Christian names, to stress that they were now believers. This model of proselytising continued in Sabu, namely through attacking and accusing others rather than through good example.

---

45   People who spoke of baptisms, confirmations and mass weddings after 1965 included Kitu, Rohi and Mone Dami.

The negative aspect included the arrest of members of the Christian Women's movement, PWKI, because members were accused of being communist activists.

> I always wanted to join the PWKI, from when I was a teenager, so I could be active in the church, and then... look at what happened to me, accused of everything, arrested, made to report to authorities.[46]

Mudji is another example of the effect of 1965. Even though she was extremely active in the church, and a teacher at the GMIT school, she advised her children:

> Don't rush to believe in any organisation at all, either government or church. I will not allow my children to join any activities.[47]

There were also church leaders who were deeply conflicted when the government wanted to use the church to do bad things:

> My father... was a pastor at [one of the churches in Sabu] from 1963... Father rarely spoke about those sad events. As far as I remember, he only spoke about them once or twice when he agreed to what mother said about him running home as fast as his legs would carry him when his name was called to join those executing communists at Hanga Loko Pedae. He came home with his shirt covered in mud; because of his panic, as he was running home, he had collided with a buffalo wallowing in a mud hole.[48]

In many cases, the GMIT joined the government in taking action against members of the congregation or pastors who were members or officials of the Communist Party or Gerwani, or who were branded as such, by firing them from their church duties. To this day, when there are elections for GMIT office bearers in Sabu, the issue of communist or Gerwani membership can be raised, with sentences like, 'He/she was involved', or 'He/she is from a family that was involved.' The church perpetuates this stigmatisation as truth. According to Malado, who used to serve the GMIT congregation in Sabu:

> When nominations for the council [for one of the congregations in Sabu] for the period 1995–1999 were announced at Sunday worship,

---

46   Tenga, interview.
47   Mudji, interview.
48   Email correspondence with Laku, 25 March 2012.

after the service was over, a church figure – a military man – came to the church council [to complain about one of the people] nominated as an elder, because the person was thought to be a former communist political prisoner. This matter was then raised in the meeting of the Church Board. As head of the Church Board at that time, I reacted strongly against this objection. 'Give me a single solid theological-ecclesiastical reason why a former political prisoner should not be a member of the Church Board! I want a formal, written objection so that this can be used by the appointment committee!' In the end, as there never was any formal written objection from anyone, I ordained that person as an elder.[49]

It is important to note that not all pastors dared do such things. A former pastor who was also a teacher and an official for PNI noted this about the impact of the 1965–66 incident:

> Many GMIT congregations were destroyed because they lost their bearings. The sense of a dead end and confusion made many people seek safer protection in other churches that would accept people branded as communist and Gerwani. They had many personal reasons for eventually changing churches and changing religion.[50]

The competition and hatred between people of different parties was also brought into the church. Often, in Sunday worship, when a priest or an elder gave a sermon, an official from a different party would criticise, spit or even call out words like *keb'aro* (rubbish!).[51]

Apart from that, there were some people in Sabu who suspected the church of being deceitful by exploiting education and the massacres to increase its own membership. Those who followed local indigenous religions saw that the victims of 1965 were Christian, but the ones who arrested them were also Christian; they saw that both the dead and the living were supposed to be clever people, and Christian. This certainly weakened their belief in the church. To this day, there are still customary groups that suspect the church, even though there are pastors who have no intention of converting them.

---

49  Ibid.
50  Interview with Kitu. Many GMIT church members joined the Seventh Day Adventist Church.
51  Kitu, interview.

## The effect on Sabu-Raijua culture

People experienced arbitrary murder, in Sabu and beyond Sabu, even though both witnesses and perpetrators who were interviewed admitted that they themselves never saw the victims do anything bad. Some of the core Communist Party officials, supposedly summoned to Kupang, disappeared, as one of the women teachers said:

> Bapak went to Kupang around September 1965. He never said what he was going for. We looked for him; there was never any news, and we finally gave up.[52]

The killing and social confusion was something huge that had never before happened in the history of their culture. Murder was something taboo. In the eyes of people from the customary groups, the killing of 34 people was *'made harro'* (salt death), meaning wrongful death. This kind of death brings misfortune and disaster to the cosmic balance, and therefore requires a special burial rite. The customary groups were confused and asked: how can people who are government civil servants and church goers kill one another, and how can people who were not involved with politics become victims?

A well-known figure from a customary community called Mone was chased by the mob and took shelter under the roof of the house of a leader of the customary council in the kampung of Namata. The frenzied mob threatened to burn the house down if he would not give himself up. Eventually, the house owner persuaded him to come down, and he was then paraded home, beaten all the way.

The destruction of the customary communities as a result of the incidents of 1965 intensified with the increase in the number of church denominations that came to evangelise in Sabu, like the Indonesian Bible Institute in Batu Malang. Around 1969–1970, an evangelist who had graduated from this Institute was vigorous in his efforts to cleanse a location on Mesara of its of traditional religious altar, in the name of Jesus. The local leaders asked him not to enter this location, as it was not the correct time, but he took no notice of them. When he came back out, he said his body felt as though it was burning and when he arrived back where he was staying in Seba, he died.[53] This might be something extraordinary, but to people in the

---

52  Mudji, interview.
53  This story was told by a number of people in different interviews, including Mama Kati, Kitu, and Mahe.

customary communities, actions like his are considered to be infringements of their rights to their own rites, and also strengthen the impression that Christians are rude.

The customary communities were intimidated by being accused of being atheists and communists. Prominent church figures who debated with leaders of customary law tried to cleanse anything considered to be idolatrous and atheistic by belittling and stigmatising people; by burning traditional altars and items used for rituals, including works of art like woven cloth and jewellery; abandoning ceremonial houses, and felling trees at water springs. These were all difficult things for customary communities to accept and they asked: Why are we being attacked? The author herself (Paoina) experienced how her grandfather, her mother's father, almost died one night after drinking poison because he was so disturbed after being accused of being an atheist at a thanksgiving ceremony. Many people in these communities wept to see the treasured work of their ancestors burnt as a sign that they were now Christian.

Tegid'a, the women's house in a customary village. As a result of the events of 1965, the cutomary groups in Sabu suffered intimidation, accused of being atheist. – JPIT archives

## Effect on education at Sabu-Raijua

The destruction of the Communist Party and Gerwani reached its peak in Sabu with the murders of 34 men on 29 and 30 March 1966, and the arrests of family members from families of teachers. Those who were not murdered were fired from both their church and teaching positions. Even though at that time all the schools in Sabu were run by the GMIT, the church was unable to protect its teaching staff. The church was actually exploited to help in cleansing the teachers who were considered to have been poisoned by the evil spirit of communism, and were seen to be traitors, murderers, and destroying the moral fibre of the nation. Formerly, a pastor could lead a congregation and also advise on curriculum and teach at school. After the events of 1965, these duties were separated, and the GMIT schools began to be taken over by the government.

The education foundation Yupenkris experienced a shortage of teachers and a decline in the standard of education. For instance, GMIT schools that used to have one teacher for every grade, after the 1965–66 Incident might have only one or two teachers in total. This was also because, apart from teachers being killed or fired, there was not enough funding to pay teachers' salaries. As a result, the church's management of the schools worsened, and teachers lost their enthusiasm.[54] Families lost their enthusiasm to send their children to school, and the congregations' trust in Yupenkris declined. After the 1965 Incident, the congregations' interest in the GMIT schools also declined. This can be seen in the allocation of funds for education, which was small in relation to funds for places of worship. This most likely reflects the church's trauma after the terrible experience involving GMIT teachers in 1965–66. One can say that after that, there was a crisis in education in Sabu-Raijua, and it took a lot of time for things to improve, particularly with regard to the state education system.

GMIT might have been the property owner of the buildings, but it was the government that was in charge of the policy for teachers, curriculum, and funds. As time went by, the GMIT school buildings were also handed over to the government, and state schools were constructed as well. Teachers who had previously been allocated to teach at the GMIT schools were

---

54  It must be admitted that the decline in the GMIT schools in Sabu-Raijua was also caused by the GMIT's own management. For instance, the centralisation of the different congregations' budgets at the central office of Yupenkris created a rift between the congregations and the GMIT schools. Apart from this, Yupenkris's own weak administration and organisation were also to blame for the decline in GMIT schools in Sabu-Raijua.

'reclaimed' by the government. The system of teaching was designed by the state, no longer by the church. Not only politics, but education too, became something in which the church should no longer interfere.

Another after-effect of 1965–66 was the weakening of the image of women teachers as role models. The firing of teachers from their positions as elders and deacons also weakened their prestige in society. Rather than being models for the young generation, teachers were feared. People were afraid that if their daughters became teachers and were active outside the house, they might go wild, and become like those women with short hair, so a common saying among Sabu-Raijua families to discourage girls from furthering higher education was: 'Even if a girl goes to university, she will return to the kitchen.'[55] There are also congregations who consider themselves to have been 'clean' of any communist contamination who are cautious about accepting anyone with 'communist involvement' as a leader in the church because they think they will brainwash people. Once again, it will take time to change the views of the people of Sabu-Raijua about women teachers.

Another effect was the meaning of education itself. Whereas formerly education meant seeking and discovering something for oneself, sharing information, and encouraging students to discover the world through reading and writing skills, after the 1965–66 events, students had to be passive and accept anything the teacher taught. Students may not criticise or question because it is considered to be rude to question a teacher, and especially rude to have a different opinion to the teacher. So the method of teaching and learning strengthens a hierarchical culture, with knowledge always at the top, and coming from the top (Jakarta), to the bottom (Sabu, Kupang, and so on).

## Why were teachers crushed?

In the official New Order version of history, teachers were entirely forgotten. The teaching profession in society is tarnished, so people, even the children of teachers themselves, are not interested in studying to become teachers. Even today, Eastern Indonesia (NTT province) has a shortage of teachers, so that minimal qualifications are required – even junior high school graduates can become teachers. The current government is aware of this situation.[56]

---

55 This saying probably dates only from the time of slander against the communists and Gerwani, because traditionally, women in Sabu were active as leaders and teachers in traditional community organisations.
56 Most information here is taken from chapters 1 and 8 in Saskia Wieringa's *Sexual Politics in Indonesia* (2002).

Teachers as educators of values to their students and society are a potential force to teach other values. Teachers became office bearers in the Communist Party, a party banned by the government since 1966 because its ideology contradicts Pancasila. The New Order was worried that communist values could be taught to children, so the space for teachers to move was limited and diminished.

All the information we gathered from victims, witnesses and perpetrators shows that many teachers were crushed. Saskia Wieringa helps us better understand the national context as to why teachers and the world of education in Sabu-Raijua were destroyed. According to her, the Communist Party was considered to be a dangerous threat because it did not believe in God, was destructive, and betrayed Pancasila. Gerwani women were considered to be dangerous, wild, savage, and prostitutes who assisted the murder of the generals by dancing naked, cutting off their genitals, and slicing their bodies at Crocodile Hole. People's knowledge about all this came through indoctrination from the source (Jakarta), and this was accepted as truth. The vulgar accusations made of Gerwani were spread via newspapers and the radio, from 1 October 1965 through to early 1966.[57] The campaign spreading the news that the Communist Party, Gerwani and the mass organisations associated with them were all traitors became the rationale for acts of cleansing, like torching Gerwani offices and demanding that the Communist Party be banned. The campaign became increasingly virulent and there were demands that Gerwani be banned and its criminals be publicly hanged.

Saskia Wieringa shows us how teachers in particular became a group that had to be protected from communist influence. The methods used to 'safeguard' families, society and the nation was to 'crush them', as was fitting for traitors ('it's just as well they were killed', is something you still hear people say today). The murders can be seen as fortunate, a blessing, because they are regarded as having saved people from the influence of a group of atheists who rejected religion and Pancasila. The message was that those communist women teachers and Gerwani should go back home and keep quiet, to be taught a lesson so they stop their whoring, wickedness, treachery and atheism. Firing them from their teaching posts was an act of salvation for families, society, and the nation of Indonesia that adheres to Pancasila.[58]

---

57  In Sabu-Raijua, this propaganda was known via the radio because there were no newspapers at the time.
58  In her book, Saskia quotes the army newspaper *Angkatan Bersenjata* of 9 November, 1965, which published a resolution along these lines from a union of women's

The image of Gerwani manipulated at the top was passed down to the teachers who were Gerwani leaders and the *nyora* in Sabu-Raijua. They were condemned and considered to be the enemy. The role of the teacher as the one who fosters certain values made teachers a target for accusations of being a dangerous threat to the future of the nation. How could criminals and prostitutes educate people? This could not be allowed! People were provoked so that they would believe the stories and join in the duty of 'crushing the communists and Gerwani'. But those accused feel they did no wrong. To quote the head of Gerwani for Sabu-Raijua who was both a teacher and a wife of a teacher: 'What did we do wrong? We did nothing bad to the country.'[59]

## *HANGA LOKO PEDAE 1966*[60]
### Paoina Bara Pa

They were the ones who wrote this poem that had been stifled in their hearts and souls for 45 years. They poured it out and I was there with ink and paper, to share it with others. I offer my thanks to you women for the trust shown that allows this bitter water to flow.

> From the land of the lontar palms laments are heard
> Laments of blood without blood,
> Laments of bodies without bodies
> Laments of eyes without eyes
> Laments of heads without brains
> Laments of mouths that are gagged
> Laments of wives without husbands
> Laments of husbands without wives and children
> Laments of children who are orphans
> Laments of the earth: why were graves dug?
> Laments of the night made dark

---

    organisations sent to Major General Soeharto and Brigadier General Duhartono. Weiringa 2002.
59  Wila, interview.
60  Hanga Loko Pedae, situated at the edge of the Terdamu airfield in West Sabu, was the site where 34 men connected to the 1965 Incident were executed in March 1966. This location is known by this name until today. The name means 'The dry river bed that people always talk about.'

Laments of the morning made hot
Laments of the seekers not knowing what they seek.
The God-believers say,
'You are anti-God.
Go on, pray if God is still there.'
In their hands, those God-believers
Machetes are raised, bullets fired
Dooooooooooooooooooooooorrrrrrrrr!!!!!!!!!!!!
Aduuuuuuuuuuuuhhhhhhhh, heeeeeeeellllpp!!!!
We are being pulled from the womb of mother earth,
Hanga Loko Pedae, 29–30 March 1966.
Like worthless worms,
Thirty-four men die in the name of power
How worthless is life in the eyes of politics.

*Lasiana, 7 February 2011*

## Appendix to Sabu Report

List of detainees and people killed in Sabu-Raijua linked to the 1965 Incident*

| TEACHERS | | | | |
|---|---|---|---|---|
| **Grouping** | **Women detained**† | **Men detained (those executed in italics)** | **Men executed in first round (night of 29 March 1966)** | **Men executed in second round (9 a.m., 30 March 1966)**‡ |
| Teachers and wives of teachers (*nyora*) | Wila/Gerwani official Sabu (husband killed), Bitu/Gerwani official (husband killed), Moj'o (husband killed), Tenga, Moli (husband killed), Mudji, Kuji (8) | | | |
| Married teachers | Wenyi (1) | *Mara*/primary school headmaster, *Huki*/husband of Wila, *Hane*/husband of Bitu, *Doro*/husband of Moj'o, *Rihi*/husband of Lena, *Bara*/husband of Moli, Laku, Haja (8) | Mara/primary school headmaster/Huki/husband of Wila, Hane/husband of Bitu, Doro/husband of Moj'o, Rihi,/husband of Lena, Bara/husband of Moli (6) | |
| Teachers and unmarried | Anne/Gerwani treasurer, Sabu, Hab'a, Dil'a, Tati, Heti (5) | *Ke, D'ida, Tobo, Hekei, Dje, Hila, Dipa,* Mika, Nada (9) | Ke, D'ida, Tobo, Hekei, Dje (5) | Hila, Dipa (2) |
| Teachers (marital status unclear) | Wini (1) | *Laka, Kiko, Maja, Kanni, Geje, Jemi, Dju,* D'adi, Higa (9) | Laka, Kiko, Maja, Kanni, Geje, Jemi, Dju (7) | |
| nyora | Edo, B'ui. Yane, Pula, Neta, Piga (husband who was head of Sabu PKU disappeared in Kupang) (6) | | | |
| Married civil servants | | Laga, Aa (2) | | |
| Civil servants, marital status unknown | | *Jungu, Nope, Make* (3) | Nope, Make (2) | Jungu (1) |

\* This list of detainees and victims is compiled from nine informants: Kitu, Rohi, Dina, Gadja, Lodi, Kora, Mone Dami, Tada and Wila

† All the women detained were considered to be Gerwani, even though many rejected this 'stigma'. Many said that when their husbands or a member of their family were a member of the Communist Party or a communist sympathiser, then automatically, the wife would be branded as Gerwani. Of those interviewed, the only one who acknowledged her Gerwani position was Wila, as head of Gerwani for Sabu, and she mentioned some of her colleagues whose names she could remember.

‡ At the time the men were executed, there was an order that the Gerwani women should not be killed.

| NON-TEACHERS | | | | |
|---|---|---|---|---|
| Grouping | Women detained | Men detained (those executed in italics) | Men executed in first round (night of 29 March 1966) | Men executed in second round (9 a.m., 30 March 1966) |
| Wives of civil servants | Gad'i, deputy head of Gerwani for Sabu (1) | | | |
| Pastors | | Para (1) | | |
| Ordinary people | | *Bura, Jore*/bachelor and jingitiu, Djawa, Gela, Kiri, Gaja/ married (6) | Bura, Jore/ bachelor and jingjitu (2) | |
| Unknown category, possibly civil servants, possibly not | | *Lakki, D'ara, Pau, Adu, Pile, Jagga, Lede, Buke, Ludji,* Ngadi, Lado, Dani, Tuka, Ari, Nguru, Mapeki, Maroda, Dope, Madohe (19) | Lakki, D'ara, Pau, Adu, Pile, Jagga, Lede, Buke, Ludji (9) | |
| TOTAL | **22 women detained** | **57 men detained** | **34 men executed** | |
| % TEACHERS IN TOTAL NUMBER OF VICTIMS | Of the women detained, 74% were teachers (16/22) | Of the men detained, 46% were teachers (26/57) | Of the men executed, 59% were teachers (20/34) | |

## City of Kupang

Merdeka Stadium (Freedom Stadium), Kupang City. Female detention centre.

*Merdeka Stadium (Freedom Stadium), in the area of Oeba, Kupang, is a sports stadium. At the time of the 1965 Incident, it was used as a detention centre for female political prisoners. Some of the women we interviewed were detained there. According to informants, two to four people were housed per room, each with their own bed. The women were detained here for periods ranging from one week to a month.*

*The construction of this building and sports arena began in 1962, as a project led by an army man (also a sports coach) assisted by his personnel. The dormitories, constructed in 1964–65, were used by athletes from various districts from across NTT province.*

*Each dormitory consisted of 15 rooms measuring about 4 x 4 metres, a large meeting room, a shared kitchen, two bathrooms and toilets. At that time, soccer matches between Indonesian and foreign (Portuguese, Australian) teams were held at the Merdeka Stadium. It was also used as a place for motorcycle racing. From around the 1990s, the building was no longer used as an athletes' dormitory, as a new facility was built. Today, the Merdeka Stadium is still used as a venue for football matches.*

**Statement from a member of the research team for the City of Kupang**

*Chapter 2*

# The 1965 Incident and Female Activists in the City of Kupang

### Nela Loy Bhoga, Martha Bire, and Golda Sooai

In the 1950s and early 1960s, the living conditions of women in NTT did not differ significantly from those of women in other areas of Indonesia. Whilst there were new opportunities opening for them to pursue education equal to men, their lives remained obstructed by a strong patriarchal culture in society. Even so, some women managed to complete higher education. Because of this, they found work and could live independently from their own earnings.

Apart from working, they were also offered the opportunity to take active roles in all kinds of women's organisations including the Indonesian Union of Christian Women (PWKI) and Gerwani. Their social interaction was no longer limited to the domestic household, but extended to the public domain. At this time, this was something new.

No one ever dreamed that participation in these women's organisations would later prove to be dangerous, for at the time these women joined these organisations they were public, legal, and officially recognised by the government. Furthermore, the activities the organisations carried out were positive and well received. It is not surprising that a few clever women became extremely active and were given central positions in those organisations.

In our research for this book, we, a few women of a younger generation, had the opportunity to meet and chat with some of these extraordinary women. We met two of the top officials of Gerwani in the city of Kupang, and the wife of the local head of the Communist Party who was murdered in the operation for the 'restoration of security and order' at that time. These three women were willing to share and entrust their stories to us, but only two of them agreed to their stories being published. Apart from them, we also met a male victim, the child of a victim, and some witnesses who were then important figures in the Indonesian Christian Party (Parkindo), as well as church leaders and ordinary people. Their accounts support the evidence that this period witnessed violence against civil society, including violence against the activist women within it.

This violence has left a deep and lasting trauma in society, especially among women. Women who had only just begun to take up opportunities to enter a wider circle than the limited domestic world, had to accept the bitter reality that their involvement in certain organisations became the reason for their arrest and for the loss of many important things in their lives. Work, their rights as citizens and even their own loved ones were torn from them, and replaced with arrest, detention, and stigmatisation from the government and the society around them. In order to better understand the struggle that the women activists in Kupang have had to face from the 30$^{th}$ September 1965 until today, it is necessary to first map out the context of social life in Kupang from 1960 to 1970.

The city of Kupang is the capital of the province of Nusa Tenggara Timur (NTT) and its main harbour. It is 180.27 square kilometres in area and comprises six sub-districts: Alak, Kelapa Lima, Kota Raja, Kota Lama, Maulafa, and Oedobo.

## The role of women in politics

According to informants, at the time of the 30$^{th}$ September movement in Jakarta, the role of women in the formal world of politics in Kupang was not particularly prominent.[1] Among other things, this was because women there did not yet have a good political education. At that time, opportunities for further education were more open to men. As far as membership of the Communist Party was concerned, the number of official members was also not great when compared to the total population of Kupang at the time.[2]

---

1   On the involvement of the women of NTT in various organisations, see further *Buku Peringatan 30 Tahun Kesatuan Pergerakan Wanita Indonesia, 22 Desember 1928 – 22 Desember 1958* (Jakarta: Kementerian Penerangan RI, 1958), pp 384–85.
2   Nyongki Ndili, interview on 25 November 2010 at Oeba, Kupang. Pak Ndili was a civil servant at a provincial level office who was arrested, detained and tortured by the military. Because of this, he lost his job and the right to his pension. After it was determined that he was not involved with Communist Party activities, he was released, but he still lost his job. Along with 11 colleagues, he fought for restoration of his rights through legal channels, and requested the support of the Department of Internal Affairs. However, nothing changed, and until this day none of them have received the

Gerwani membership was also not high.³ In general, those who joined Gerwani's activities were housewives and some were also teachers.

## Economic situation

At this time, the majority of the population of Kupang were farmers, agriculturalists, civil servants and workers in the private sector. They managed to get by with what they earned from their work. Between 1958 and 1965, Indonesia experienced soaring inflation and with it increased economic difficulties. At the peak of this inflation, on 13 December 1965, the rupiah was revalued: Rp 1000 was revalued at Rp 1.⁴ As a result, the price of daily necessities skyrocketed and this had a huge impact on peoples' lives. The situation was made even worse by a famine that struck all of the province of NTT around 1965–1966, making it extremely difficult for people to find even basic foodstuffs. They were forced to eat cracked wheat – called bulgur – which was sent as aid from the United States. People who were earning barely enough to live were forced to eat cassava flour and drinking corn juice just to fill their stomachs.

Generally, during this time in Kupang city women were in charge of the household economy. They were the ones who had to balance the household finances in the midst of these extreme economic challenges. This was even more difficult for those women who were victims in 1965 and who lost their jobs and their husbands.

## Women's access to education

The number of schools was still very limited at this time. In the city of Kupang there were primary schools, junior and senior high schools, one vocational high school for primary school teachers (SGA), one vocational high school for

---

  right to their pensions. A more complete chronology of their legal case can be found in Appendix 2b.
3 Ibu Marsa, survivor, interviewed at Oeba, Kupang, on 4 December 2010. In the early 1960s, she was a primary school teacher and also a core office-bearer for the Kupang branch of Gerwani. Ibu Marsa was involved with various Gerwani activities. At the time of the operation for 'restoration of security and order', she was arrested and detained along with many other women. She was summarily dismissed from her job, and lost all rights as a teacher. In 1975, together with two other core Gerwani women, she was detained once again in Bali and held for three years as political prisoner.
4 For more on inflation, see 'Sejarah Bank Indonesia: Moneter, Periode 1959–1966' (Unit khusus Museum Bank Indonesia: Sejarah Bank Indonesia), 3, at http://www.bi.go.id/we/id/Tentang+BI/Museum/Sejarah+Bank+Indonesia/Sejarah+BI/sejarahbi_3a.htm accessed on 15 December 2011.

secondary school teachers (SGB), and Nusa Cendana University, which opened on 1 September 1962 in the district of Naikoten 1 (the old campus). Very few students from the vocational teachers' colleges were able to continue their education to tertiary level. Generally, they graduated from SGA or SGB and immediately found work as teachers, becoming civil servants. For the families who could afford it, their children could further their education in Java.

The women who were able to pursue an education were generally those from relatively affluent families, or those who had some special connection with officials including colonial officials at that time. For instance, Ibu Nona's parents had connections, which assisted her to attend school:

> [I had gone to school] at the Dutch School at Terminal Bakunase. [Before I was accepted] I had to do a test. Luckily, my father was a barber. He used to shave and cut the Dutchmen's hair; you know, the assistant resident and the resident. So I managed to get into school. After that, I moved to Bonepoi primary school, which was a model school. [Later I went on to] junior high school, which was also a Dutch school.[5]

## Channels of information and communication

There were few public channels of information for the people of Kupang at that time. The Kupang branch of the national radio station, Radio Republic Indonesia (RRI) opened on 19 November 1958. Prior to the 30th September Movement incident, the regional committee of the Communist Party (CDB) published a weekly in Kupang titled *Pelopor* (Pioneer). This magazine ceased publishing in 1965 after the communist elimination. In 1962, a well-known PNI figure and orator launched a weekly titled *Mingguan Pos Kupang*, as a rival to *Pelopor*. This magazine only lasted for a few months. The same person later published the weekly *Mingguan Kompas* having been granted permission to publish by the *Kompas* daily newspaper in Jakarta. Again, this weekly lasted just three months, as the publication did not have its own separate publishing license.[6]

---

5   Ibu Nona, survivor, interviewed on 15 December 2010 at Kelurahan Manulai, Kupang. In 1965, she was a civil servant, working in the administration of a state high school in Kupang. Her husband was a Communist Party leader in Kupang. According to Ibu Nona, she herself never joined or became an official member of Gerwani. Nonetheless, she was fired from her job and lost all her rights as a government civil servant.
6   See W. Therik 'Perkembangan Pers di Nusa Tenggara Timur', The World of Wilson Therik, http://wilson-therik.blogspot.com/2010/11/perkembangan-pers-di-nusa-tenggara.html accessed on 18 August 2011.

It was from these limited sources that the people of Kupang got their news about developments at the national and local level. According to one of the respondents, Pak Adi, people were told about the dangers of the Communist Party through broadcasts on national radio, RRI:

> (T)hat was the official information, and generally accepted truth, that the seven generals were murdered by the Communist Party. Of course that incited hatred. This shaped social opinion. Everyone hated them. [The news] deliberately incited people to oppose the Communist Party. Because of that, [Communist Party members] were considered to be atheists, and because of that people tended to be violent. Well, that's what the situation was like at the time, and the economic situation was also like that, and the communists had gained support because of the poverty everywhere, and [combatting poverty] is the communist image, after all.[7]

## The role of women in the GMIT

The role of women in the Timor Evangelical Church (GMIT) in Kupang at this period was not much different to what it is today. Women were included in all kinds of church ministry, as deacons, elders, and even as pastors. The GMIT already had female pastors at this time, although their number was limited.[8] There was also a group within the church named Christian Women (Wanita Masehi, now called GMIT women). When the GMIT was established in 1947, Kupang was the first congregation with a Christian Women group, led by Mrs LSY Arnoldus.[9] Christian Women then developed in other areas as its members moved elsewhere, for instance when Ibu Pastor Radja Haba-Nalley moved to SoE she formed Christian Women there.[10] In Kupang their activities included working alongside (foreign) doctors and

---

7   Pak Adi, son of a survivor, interview at Kelurahan Naikoten 1, Kupang, 8 November 2010. He is a pastor serving in the GMIT. His father was also a pastor and civil servant in a provincial government office at the time of the 1965 incident. Pak Adi was then 11 years old and in 5th grade of primary school. He and a few of his friends had just returned home from school and he witnessed the arrest and torture of a neighbour who was accused of being a communist.
8   A number of women had already been ordained as GMIT pastors in the 1950s, whereas in the GKS, the first woman to be ordained as pastor was in 1990.
9   Interview Ibu Maya, church staff, interview at Oetete, Kupang, 4 March 2011 and 19 February 2012. LSY Arnoldus is her real name.
10  Ibu Pastor Radja Haba-Nalley is her real name.

nurses to give cheap medical assistance to pregnant women and women in childbirth at the maternity clinic, Ora et Labora.[11]

According to Ibu Pastor Ruth Sabuna, before GMIT Women was recognised at a synod level, every congregation had a Christian Women's group or Church Women's group, the names being determined by the local congregation. It was only in 1968 that a formal structure for women was agreed upon at the synod level and named GMIT Women. It consisted of five sections, including the religious obligation section; spiritual section; and welfare section. Ibu Sabuna was the Secretary from 1968 to 1979, and her main activity was to lead the women in the congregation. Apart from that, together with the Synod Council, the GMIT Women visited congregations wherever the church was active, and created branches at the presbytery level in places including Flores, Sabu, Alor, Rote, Amarasi, and South Central Timor.[12]

## The GMIT position on the communist purges

The GMIT had stated its position towards the Communist Party long before the 1965 incident. Through its synod at SoE, which was held from 31 May – 3 June 1960, the GMIT issued a pastoral letter which was sent to all GMIT congregations. According to Pak Tony, an emeritus GMIT pastor, the letter stated: 'All GMIT officials who are ordained must adhere to Christian ideology.'[13] This stance was further strengthened at the extraordinary GMIT synod meeting held in Kupang from 30 October-1 November 1965. The synod council in its sixth meeting held on 8 December 1965 resolved to take cleansing action within the body of GMIT with reference to the decision made by the synod at SoE (1960) and the extraordinary GMIT synod meeting in Kupang (1965).[14] This cleansing was done by expelling anyone linked to the 1965 incident from the body of the church.

---

11 Ibu Maya, church staff, interview at Oetete, Kupang, 4 March 2011 and 19 February 2012.
12 Interview with Ibu Ruth Sabana (her real name) on 19 February 2012 at Kelurahan Oetete, Kupang. Also see Frank Cooley, *Benih Yang Tumbuh XI: Gereja Masehi Injili di Timor* (Jakarta: Lembaga Penelitian dan Studi Dewan Gereja-gereja di Indonesia, 1976) who discusses the activities of Wanita GMIT (1971–72) as these were reported in the reports of the Komisi Pekabaran Injil, Pendidikan, dan Perlengkapan Jemaat, pp 255–58
13 Pak Tony, emeritus pastor of GMIT, interview, Desa Baumata Barat, Kec Taebenu, on 3 November, 2010.
14 Anna Ch, Salukhfeto, 'Perhatian Gereja Terhadap Anggota Jemaat yang Terlibat PKI di Mollo Utara: Sebuah Tinjauan Kritis Theologis terhadap Cara Gereja di Mollo Utara Memberlakukan Disiplin Gerejawi bagi Anggota Jemaatnya yang Terlibat PKI' (S1 [BA] thesis, Fakultas Teologi UKAW Kupang, 1993), see her appendix 3, 'Pedoman Kebijaksanaan Umum dalam Tindakan Pembersihan Tubuh GMIT dari

The church rejected communism through a series of official statements, and it made no comment about the State when it carried out massacres. In fact, the church (church leaders) benefitted from the situation by accusing as communist those people or church officials who were at odds with them personally. This is the dark side of the church's stand at the time of the 1965 incident.

## The flow of arrests and detention

The Communist Party was one of the national political parties with large membership in all areas of Indonesia. It had become common practice for political parties to make promises for programs to answer people's specific needs. Like other parties at the time, the Communist Party leaders also made promises to potential members that they would receive various benefits if they joined. These promises included things like free handouts of basic food, land, agricultural tools, work, and promotions if the Communist Party won in the next elections. The Communist Party was determined and enthusiastic in its membership drive. They were skillful in discussion about issues linked to politics.[15]

All this strongly influenced people's decisions as they were facing various difficulties. Many people were attracted to become members because of these promises, not because they had any understanding of communist ideology. According to a former Parkindo member, many people in Kupang whose names were listed as recipients of rice, agricultural tools, and land from the Communist Party, later discovered the list had been changed to say they were members of the Communist Party. So people who in fact might be official members of other parties, found their names listed as Communist Party members.[16]

Many names were added to lists at the time of the arrests because of bad feeling and personal disputes. Personal conflicts could be exploited in this turbulent political situation.[17] Pak Adi's father was an example. Pak Adi recounts that his father was accused, arrested, and detained at Kupang prison for three months because his name was on a list of Communist Party members. This list had been drawn up by one of his work colleagues who

---

Unsur-unsur Gerakan Tiga Puluh September.' The research team has to date been unsuccessful in its efforts to obtain copies of original documents.
15   Pak Edi, former core official for the NTT branch of Parkindo, interview 1 November 2010 at the precinct of Nunbaun Delha, Kupang.
16   Ibid.
17   Pak Adi, interview.

was a pastor. His father was eventually released because that same pastor admitted that he had added Pak Adi's name to the list.[18]

Gerwani began to be active in Kupang around 1961.[19] It usually held its activities at the government-owned Gedung Wanita (Women's Building) located at Oebobo, near the current national radio station building. Activities included courses like sewing and cooking. Sometimes similar courses were given at the home of one of the core Gerwani officials, in Oeba. According to a survivor, when asked if Gerwani held activities related to politics, most informants denied this; the activities were about domestic skills.[20]

The 30th September Movement in Jakarta had a huge effect on the lives of Gerwani members in Kupang. They were dragged into it all because they were considered to be members of an organisation that was a branch of the Communist Party. The effect on them was wide-reaching. Those who were working (usually as teachers and civil servants) were summarily dismissed with no explanation. They were also arrested and interrogated by the military. They were separated from their families, and three members, including Ibu Marsa, were also separated for three years by distance when they were held as political prisoners at a prison in Bali. At that time, Ibu Marsa's youngest child was just 11 months old. She wanted to take her baby daughter with her, but the four soldiers who came to take her away would not allow it.

> When I was in prison, she was only 11 months old. I was detained for three years in Denpasar. So she was with her father.

In Kupang the arrests of Communist Party and Gerwani members and those suspected of being members, took place from around December 1965 until the end of 1966.[21] The military made the arrests. Some of them came with warrants issued from the Kupang district military command (Kodim), but others had no warrant at all. Some victims experienced intimidation, for instance people who lived nearby surrounded their houses.[22] They came bearing sharp weapons and blunt things. There was also 'sweeping' carried

---

18   Ibid.
19   The information about Gerwani in Kupang is from an interview with Ibu Marsa at the precinct of Oeba, Kupang on 4 December 2010, and with Ibu Nona, at the house of a pastor at the precinct of Manulai, Kupang, on 15 December 2010. Initially, Ibu Marsa was unwilling to grant permission for us to include her story, but after she was given more detailed information about the research, and also had the opportunity to join a meeting of victims, she agreed for her story to be documented and shared with others.
20   Ibu Marsa, interview.
21   Pak Adi, interview.
22   Ibu Marsa, interview.

out by the head of the neighbourhood.[23] Everyone would turn out to watch, and it served as a warning to others. The victims and their families also bore the brunt of suspicion and cynicism, as Ibu Marsa described,

> I did not understand. Suddenly there were people, just ordinary people, carrying knives and such, my own neighbours, can you imagine. I had done nothing wrong. I couldn't understand it. The mob, all those people, there they were with weapons, knives ... I was inside the house. I was alone. My husband was out at sea. I wanted to say to them, there's nothing here. I was surprised. What was going on? What had I done wrong? And you want to kill me? But I kept quiet. I said [to myself], 'God, I do not know what is happening. Help me, God, give me strength.' They did not stay long. Then they came – namely the Neighbourhood Head. They searched my house. They were looking for any books about politics. They came in and examined all my books. But there were no political books, just primary school text books.

When the 30th September movement broke out in Jakarta, followed by the arrests of Communist Party members in towns and regional cities, the situation in Kupang became edgy. The situation was extremely tense and unclear, making people tend to think only of themselves and not of other victims.

The situation was frightening because often the military (decked out in full uniform and weaponry) went around arresting and torturing people suspected of being Communist Party members. These arrests and torture were done in public so they would 'teach others a lesson'. In this way, civil society in general became fearful, and people were afraid to go out of their houses or to defend others when they witnessed violence inflicted on their neighbours or people close to them. They were afraid they too would be arrested, as happened to Pak Nyongki when his neighbour, who was in charge of Kupang prison, was arrested.

> [I] sort of went up to them [those who arrested my neighbour] and said, 'This person is the head of the prison, what do you want him for?' They tied him up, put him in the car and beat him. So I said, 'Don't beat him.' Well, that was it. That was a big deal. I was immediately branded, said to be a communist. It was the paramilitary civil defence guy (Hansip) who did it... Now he is retired and lives in Camplong.[24]

---

23  Neighbourhood Head, ketua Rukun Tetangga (RT). Pak Adi, interview.
24  Nyongki Ndili interview. Camplong is a village about 30 kilometres to the east of the city of Kupang.

Old prison, Kupang: Male detention centre. – JPIT archives

Anyone who defended communists was treated inhumanely and considered to be communist themselves, in other words, they were opposing the government.

## Experiences of detention

The people arrested were taken to various places. Some were taken to the District Military Command base in Oepoi for interrogation. The men were immediately taken to the old prison in Selam in front of the old office of the District Head in Kupang. The women were taken to a temporary detention centre at the Merdeka Stadium in Oeba. The victims were subjected to various forms of physical and verbal abuse. The physical abuse included being beaten with weapons, having their heads smashed against the wall, and being given no food for 24 hours while being held for interrogation. Ibu Marsa explained,

> I was not beaten. I was tortured, given no food for a whole day. I was ordered to confess that I had been a witness. I had no idea what any of it was about. Whenever I was asked, I would say I didn't know anything. And I did not know, how could I say I knew?

Some women had their breasts and crotches bared so the interrogators could check whether there were any communist marks on their bodies:

> I was taken to the hospital; I was examined. [I asked] 'What are you examining me for? I am not sick. I am not sick, so why are you examining me? What are you looking for?' [They answered], 'Ibu, you are going to be examined; there might be marks.' [I said] 'On my thighs, here, you see, there is nothing.' I kept my underpants and bra on. 'Go ahead', I said, 'do your examination.'[25]

In prison, the detainees were kept in separate rooms from ordinary criminals. This was because of a classification system determined by the 'extent' of their involvement. There was cell A where core Communist Party officials were held, the ones who were going to be executed. Cell B was for official members of the Communist Party, and cell C was for those suspected of being involved (and were currently being interrogated). From time to time, some prisoners in both cells B and C were moved to cell A if it was proven that they were active officials. The cells measured 3 x 5 metres. This clearly was not proportional to the number of detainees they housed. Nyongki Ndili describes his place of detention,

> I was held from around February until March [1966]. We were divided into rooms; room 1, room 2 and room 3. I was in room 3. There were about 83 people in that room. We had stacked bunks for sleeping. [The location] was at the Kupang prison in front of where the Kupang District Head's office used to be. There used to be a prison there.

The women were taken to the Merdeka Stadium and held in rooms measuring 4 x 6 metres. There were between two to four people per room and each detainee had her own bed. There were twelve detention rooms at the Merdeka Stadium, two bathrooms, one shared kitchen, and one meeting room. The length of detention differed. Some stayed for only about a week, and others for up to a month. There were soldiers watching every single move they made. This made the detainees keep to themselves and not talk to one another.

> We could not go outside. At the most, we could go out on the verandah. I asked my children to bring me clothes because we could not go out,

---

25   Ibu Marsa, interview.

just to the verandah, not to any other room. One room, four people. So we ate our own food [we could not share].[26]

The children of one of the detainees, whose house was near the Stadium, every day brought food to their mother in detention, but the other women had to eat whatever was provided at the centre.[27]

## Continuing intimidation and detention

According to one of the female former political prisoners, after being freed from temporary detention the victims went back to their daily lives. However there were exceptions. Ten years later, in 1975, three women were re-arrested with an official warrant from the District Military Command. The women, all former Gerwani officials, were taken on a commercial airline under police guard to Bali. They were held there as political prisoners for three years, with no clear legal process.[28] Their husbands, though, were not detained and were able to continue their lives as usual in Kupang and care for the children.

In Bali, the women were held in cells at the Pekambingan prison on Jalan Diponegoro in Denpasar together with political prisoners from other places. There were four women to a room. They were allowed to send and receive letters from outside, via the prison censors of course. They were also allowed to have visitors once a week on Wednesdays. In detention, they were given the opportunity to learn skills so they could earn some money. Ibu Marsa, for example, did weaving and sewing. She produced some items that she sold to the prison staff, and so was able to earn a little money.

Some of the women interviewed found that their lives became increasingly difficult after all these events. They had lost their jobs, just like that. At the time, Ibu Marsa, a teacher, questioned her head of school about her dismissal:

> When I was dismissed, I was shocked. I said, 'What have I done? Why can't I teach anymore?' The head of school said, 'Because you were a member of Gerwani.' 'But what did Gerwani do wrong?... When I was in Gerwani, I didn't think there was anything wrong with that. I never did anything wrong to another person, let alone to the government.' So when I went home I told my husband about it. He said… 'Just let it be.' I said, 'What do you mean, just let it be? I worked like a fiend, I taught

---

26  Ibid.
27  Ibid.
28  Ibid.

for 11 years, and then I am just shown the door? What are we going to eat? What, I ask you?'

Everything the women experienced left a deep and lasting trauma. Subsequently, they became afraid to join any organisation at all. They also became closed and sensitive, particularly in connection to the traumatic events that left such wounds in their own private lives, including their family life.

### *The effect of the 1965 incident on women activists in Kupang*

Women like Ibu Marsa, who formerly enjoyed taking part in organisations and all kinds of activities outside the house now had a kind of trauma about doing so.

> So from then on, I left Gerwani. People invited me to join this or that organisation, but I did not want to; I did not want to join. I was afraid, afraid. I did not want to. That was the first and last time.

They preferred to stay at home and manage the house than take part in any activity that might cause problems.

> I just go to church. I do not want [to join the Christian Women's organization]... truly, I just don't want to.[29]

Survivors of 1965, and women in particular, not only became more selective in choosing organisations, but they also no longer dared and no longer wanted to do anything at all outside the house. Apart from that, they became sensitive and easily angered, particularly if there were offensive words or phrases referring to Gerwani. Some of the women saw this as a past best forgotten. It was a thorn in their side, and they did not want that wound opened. As Ibu Nona remarked,

> That wound is almost dry now, if you open it, I will have to go through all that again.

Many of the women who had been members of Gerwani, or who had been accused of being so, often had a sense of having done wrong. They felt that their involvement in Gerwani had been a sin. Their involvement affected not only them personally, but spread to their families and people close to them. Some female victims felt that their families and loved ones would never have suffered, had they themselves never joined Gerwani.

---

29  Ibu Marsa was referring to the Indonesian Union of Christian Women, (PWKI) whose activities raise women's skills.

We are sinners… [when] people say that we are sinners, I say, 'Yes, thank you, you are right.' We women are all the same, and we are the ones who sin most. So there's no point in interviewing us and asking us for data.[30]

After the events of 1965, inevitably the women survivors were branded in their own societies. This included the church where they worshipped, which meant the church was no longer a safe place for them. According to one informant, Ibu Maya, in 1965 the number of prayer fellowships in GMIT congregations in Kupang was very small, because they were considered to be a different denomination: 'their spirit is not that of the GMIT.'[31] However, later many women decided to withdraw from their own churches and join these prayer groups because they found them more welcoming.

Some women decided to become more active in a prayer fellowship because after the incident, there was no care or special help from the church. In trying to overcome her trauma, she found that prayer fellowships strengthened her relationship with God and with other members.

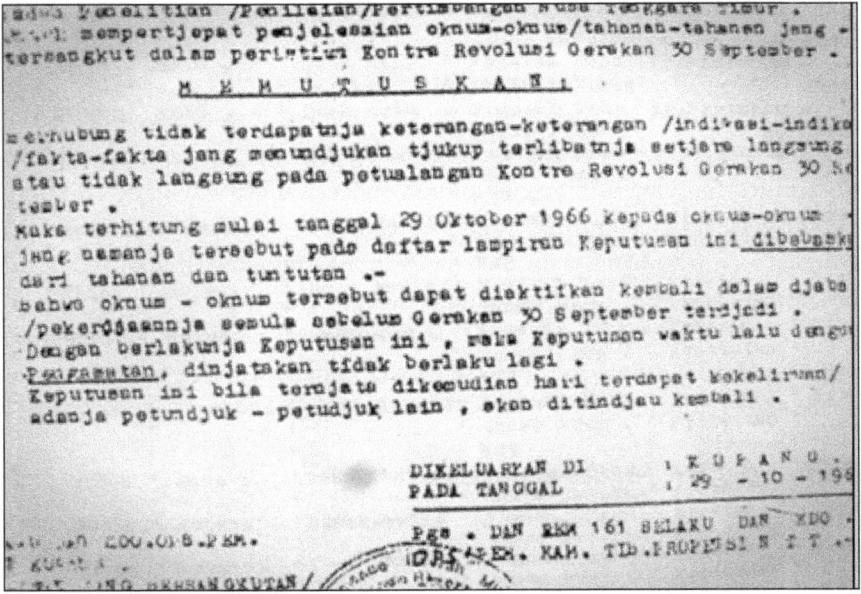

On 29 October, 1966, the Military Resort Command 161 decided that Pak Nyongki Ndili and other colleagues should be freed from detention and from suspicion. Even so, Pak Ndili never regained his rights. See further Appendix 2. – Archives JPIT

---

30   Ibu Marsa, interview.
31   Ibu Maya, interview at Oetete, Kupang, 2 March 2012.

## Analysis

### Power play

Although the research team for Kupang did not give particular research attention to the dynamics between political parties in Kupang at that time, it is important to note that, as today too, there was fierce competition between parties to attract the people. This is the reason why so much attention was given to social organisations in NTT with large memberships, like the churches.

The power contest within certain organisations encouraged people to do wicked things to opponents or work colleagues. Because of a lust for power, certain people exploited the situation to put the names of people they considered their enemies on the list of communists. Even organisations that civil servants were obliged to join, and which had been established by the government, were suddenly considered as '*onderbouw*' – namely organisations affiliated with the Communist Party. For instance, officials in the local Forestry office as employees, were automatically made members of the All Indonesia Union of Forestry Workers (Sarbuksi). When the 30th September Movement erupted, all members of this union were suspected of having connections with the Communist Party.[32]

This power play did not stop at one generation, it was passed on to the next. The State perpetuated ongoing violence in the special investigation of families considered to be communist or Gerwani, particularly children. People with skills who fulfilled all the requirements for a certain position, whether in government or in the church, could automatically fail selection because of the 'special investigation' report. This meant they would be banned from holding a position of authority over others; for instance, organisational positions in the church, a sub-departmental head, or a district head in government.[33]

### Difficulties faced by women victims

The biggest impact on the life of the women victims was their summary dismissal from their work and the loss of their rights to a pension. When they were first dismissed, the financial situation of their families was severely affected because they still had to support their families.[34] Those women

---

32 An informant from the Kupang research team.
33 Pak Adi, interview.
34 Interviews with Ibu Nona and Ibu Marsa.

whose husbands had died had to take on a double role in the family. They had to work extra hard just to survive with their children. This was made more difficult because of the stigma that was attached to them, as Ibu Nona explained:

> I was a teacher, and I had my teaching qualifications. But because I was 'involved' with the 30th September movement, I was fired... This was very difficult, because formerly I used to receive a regular salary every month and rice, and so on.

The difficulties these women activists faced in finding work after their arrest and detention affected their views about working. They were able to survive with different strategies, but with the same principle – they would have nothing to do with any government organisation. One of the survivors chose to work for a foreign firm. She was able to do this because she had good language skills in English and Dutch:

> [I worked] from [late] 1969 until [early] 1973, but on contract, a three year contract. I worked for... [a private foreign business in Kupang] in the field of water surveying. [My income] was not bad, enough to cover my children's needs.[35]

Ibu Marsa chose to earn money working at home, making the most of her sewing and weaving skills:

> I was used to managing money; luckily I had a skill. I could do embroidery. I made lace and sold it. In order to earn some money on top of my husband's salary, I could also sew. When my seventh child went to university in Salatiga, I had to find money for food, university fees, more food, and boarding costs. I asked God, 'God, what am I to do?' That was my struggle. One of my children has to serve God. The others all serve in the world, so one should serve God. And sure enough, suddenly someone I did not know came and ordered sewing from me. I didn't know her. She came and ordered clothes from me.

The path these women had to follow was not an easy one, yet they had no other choice. The trauma they felt at the state violence they experienced meant they no longer wanted to pursue any field of work linked to the government sector.

---

35   Salukhfeto, 'Perhatian Gereja', appendix 3.

## Finding spiritual comfort in prayer groups

After their release from prison, the victims returned to society bearing the label of 'ex-political prisoner'. The Indonesian word for this was *ex-tapol*, and often just the initials ET are used. This label had enormous repercussions on every aspect of their lives. No matter what they did or where they went, they were never free from negative comment. These negative opinions that flourished in society, also carried into the life of the church. The church was therefore not a place free from issues and negative opinion. Church leaders were not merely silent, but in fact contributed to this negative opinion, as reflected in the church guidelines on cleansing the body of the GMIT from elements of the 30$^{th}$ September movement.[36]

Even though not all members of the GMIT might have shared these feelings, the official GMIT position at the time was to consider the Communist Party as atheist and therefore as the enemy of the church. Therefore, the church saw that people's membership in political organisations the government considered dangerous, was indeed a sin. There was no pastoral care or special assistance given to the victims. They had to struggle on their own to heal the trauma they had experienced.

In their struggle to heal themselves from trauma, the women victims found prayer groups more welcoming. Their acceptance helped them to regain their strength and self-respect, and to heal their wounds. This in turn helped to strengthen their spirituality. Furthermore, their life stories as ex-political prisoners, with all their suffering, could be borne as witness, which strengthened other members of the prayer group. Their stories were no longer something shameful to be kept hidden, but valuable experience. Even today, prayer groups within the GMIT remain safe places for women to share their life experiences in a more open way.

This is just a small part of the story of experiences of some women survivors in Kupang; part of the long journey of their lives from the 1965 period until the present. The hardship and suffering they went through did not made them weak and despairing. They have proved that they are able to turn that suffering into valuable experience. Through those events, they found another strength within themselves. This strength enriched their spirituality in viewing God's almighty power. This is what helped them to endure, rise up, and move on to organise the rest of their lives.

---

36　The Indonesian title of the guidelines is *Pedoman Kebijaksanaan Umum dalam Tindakan Pembersihan Tubuh GMIT dari Unsur-unsur Gerakan Tiga Puluh September.'* See Salukhfeto, 'Perhatian Gereja', appendix 3

## East Kupang

Behind Oesao Market: Execution and mass burial site.

*An execution and mass burial site is to be found at Oesao, at the Public Cemetery behind the market. The mass execution of 18 men occurred there on 16 February 1966. Initially, the hole was dug for eleven Gerwani women who were to be executed. However, when they were interrogated, no marks of the sickle [the communist logo] were found on their bodies, and it was discovered that none of them had been formally appointed to the executive committee of the Kupang branch of Gerwani. They were therefore released. The hole was then used for the murder of these 18 men who were suspected of being members of the Communist Party, the majority of whom came from outside Oesao. This execution was the last in East Kupang.*

**Statement of a member of the research team for East Kupang**

*Chapter 3*

# There is a Gulf Between Us

The 1965 Events, the Destruction of Family Relationships and the Pastoral Role of the Church in East Kupang

**Welys Hawuhaba-TaEdini, Elfrantin de Haan, and Fransina Rissi**

The 1965 incident greatly affected the social fabric of East Kupang, in ways which are still felt today. In our research, we met a number of informants, including witnesses, victims, and even perpetrators of the violence of the 1965 incident. They spoke to us about how the events came about and their involvement with them. But not all informants we approached were willing to give information. Some who we had hoped to be informants chose not to talk, and some even avoided meeting us. This in itself shows how they are still traumatised, afraid, or embarrassed to open up old, painful stories. However, we cannot presume their reasons.

The most dominant theme in our research was the destruction of family relationships and the weakness of the pastoral role of the church. This was apparent in the sense that the church was weak in caring for, listening to, and understanding the struggles of its own members.

## The importance of family

This report focuses on the importance of the family because in the area of this research (selected places in the subdistrict of East Kupang), the communal aspect of family relationships is extremely important. The joy of one person within one family group or local community becomes the joy of all; so too does difficulty. For instance, when one family wants to marry off one of their children, the cost is borne by the larger family group. These relations create a communal pattern of life, which is not merely a way of life, but an entire system that supports every individual's sense of security within that system. The positive side is that when people who are part of a certain community have problems, then the community protects them, and every individual is also expected to take responsibility for his or her community. This also means that a person can also be banished, branded as a traitor or not supported by his or her community, if that community is convinced that he or she has not chosen the same path as the majority. The risk is that he or she will be banished by their community and family relationships will be destroyed.

## Profile of East Kupang

East Kupang is a subdistrict of the district of Kupang, with its government centre in Babau. The area is geographically defined as follows:

- To the east it borders Fatuleu subdistrict
- To the west it borders central Kupang subdistrict
- To the north it borders East Amarasi subdistrict
- To the south it borders Kupang Bay

Before this area was divided administratively into districts and subdistricts in 1959, the area to the east of Kupang comprised three *kefetoran* or villages (*fetor* being the Portuguese word for village chief), namely Oninama, Amabi, and Amabi Oefeto. Oninama became the subdistrict of East Kupang, and the other two *kefetoran*, Amabi and Amabi Oefeto amalgamated to become the subdistrict of Amabi. In 2008, Amabi was subdivided to become the subdistrict of Amabi and Amabi Oefeto.[1]

The majority of the population of East Kupang are from the Timor and Rote ethnic groups. The Rotenese who live in East Kupang moved there in the early 20$^{th}$ century.[2] Almost the entire population works as farmers, both those who work their own fields, and those who are employed by others.[3] Most of the area of East Kupang is wet ricefields, as can be seen along the main road from Tarus (in Central Kupang) to Oesao (in East Kupang) to Camplong (in Fatuleu), all of which is considered to be the area of East

---

1   Pak Gaspar, interview, 27 January 2011 at Tanah Putih.
2   According to a story told by Pak Charles in an interview on 7 February 2011 at Oli'o, in colonial times, in 1900, an agreement was made between a hero from Rote island and the Dutch colonial power.
3   Interview with Pak Charles

## Execution sites in NTT

| PLACE | DATE | NUMBER OF VICTIMS |
|---|---|---|
| **Sumba** | | |
| Mamboro beach, Mananga | April 1966 | 7 |
| Rua beach | September 1966 | 13 |
| Padadita beach | 1 March 1966 | 7 |
| Old Wharf, Waingapu | August 1966 | 13 |
| **Sabu** | | |
| Hanga Loko Ped'ae, Seba | 29 March 1966 commencing 19:00 | 31 |
| Hanga Loko Ped'ae, Seba | 30 March 1966, 09:00 | 3 |
| **Oesao** | | |
| Kujawas forest, Oben | Early 1966 | unknown |
| Tanah Putih, Oebelo | 27 December 1965 | grave number 2: 16 Total 100+ in more than 7 graves |
| Public cemetery, Oesao (behind the market) | 6 December 1966; 16 February 1966? | 18 |
| **TTS** | | |
| Cendana forest, SoE | January/February 1966 | |
| Nonohonis bridge, SoE | January/February 1966 | |
| Nasi Metan, North Mollo | January/February 1966 | |
| Fafinisin, SoE | January/February 1966 | |
| Kolbebe, south Amanuban | January/February 1966 | |
| **Alor** | | |
| Air Kenari, Kalabahi | February 1966 | 70 |
| Alor Kecil | February 1966, midnight | 200 |
| Dulolong | February 1966, midnight | 70 |
| Tanjung 9, Kalabahi | March 1966 | 9 |
| Tombang, Kalabahi | Unknown | 60 |

Kupang. This area is known as the best rice-producing area for the Timor plains. The largest wet rice field area is in the village of Oesao.[4]

Apart from working in farming the women in East Kupang, also sell cakes. In the past they would go around the ricefields when the farmers were out working, but these days they sell their wares at small roadside stalls.

Prior to the 1965 events, the people of Oesao participated in politics. In the lead up to the 1955 elections, the political parties active in this area were the Communist Party (PKI), the Indonesian National Party (PNI) and the Indonesian Christian Party (Parkindo). The parties competed fiercely for membership. One way to attract support was to establish programs that responded to the people's needs, for instance the Communist Party established the Indonesian Farmers' Front (BTI), and Parkindo the Christian Peasants' Alliance (Pertakin).[5]

In 1955, when Indonesia held its first general election, the PNI party won the most votes nationally. However, in many regions in Eastern Indonesia including East Kupang, the Indonesian Christian Party, Parkindo, won. After the elections, the parties continued their efforts to increase their membership.

## The 1965 Incident in the subdistrict of East Kupang

In 1964–65, the East Kupang region suffered a severe drought. The wet ricefields did not produce a good harvest so the people became poorer and there was famine. The people were forced to eat a sago gruel made from tree bark called *putak*, usually only fed to animals, until they received some government aid in the form of cracked wheat (bulgur).[6] At the same time, politics was heating up with increased competition between the parties. In the midst of this, the news arrived about the murder of the generals in Jakarta and the 30th September movement. In East Kupang, beginning around December 1965, anyone who was a member of the Communist Party, the Farmers' Front or Gerwani, or was merely suspected of such, was arrested, interrogated and murdered.

---

4 "Pengertian Kawasan Agropolitan," Kementerian Pertanian RI, Badan Penyu- luhan dan Pengembangan Sumber Daya Manusia Pertanian" See Maximus Sikone, 'Tingkat Partisipasi Masyarakat Dalam Pembangunan Sarana dan Prasarana Wilayah di Kawasan Angropolitan Oesao Kabupaten Kupang, Nusa Tenggara Timur' (Master's thesis, M.Si., Salatiga: Program Studi Magister Studi Pembangunan, Program Pascasarjana Universitas Kristen Satya Wacana, 2006
5 Interview with Pak Sam, 8 November 2010, Oesao.
6 Interview with Pak Jack, 4 November 2010, Oesao.

## Who were the communists and Gerwani?

The slaughter at Oesao, the trading centre of East Kupang, began around December 1965, with the arrests of people suspected of being members of the Communist Party, the Farmers' Front and Gerwani.[7] Their names were taken from a list of recipients of land aid from the government. The government program, called *mekatani*, was meant to provide people with aid in the form of land to manage. Anyone who wanted to receive aid had to first enrol.[8]

The term *mekatani* was mentioned in a serveral interviews. The research team has not succeeded in finding out the common name, but they think this must be a local term for the implementation of the Agrarian Land Reform laws, because the informants spoke about the distribution of land and wet ricefields to workers who did not have land of their own. According to Gerry van Klinken, a senior researcher at KITLV:

> Mekatani seems to have been a government office for giving aid to farmers. These offices were all over Indonesia, However, they were politicised in Kupang by the Mekatani Workers Union which was affiliated with the Communist Party. Probably this union distributed aid as though it was from the Communist Party even though in fact it was a regular government program. Political parties taking over government organisations was common practice at the time – Parkindo in NTT also took over the Education and Culture office, PNI got the Department of Internal Affairs etc.[9]

The Agrarian Land Reform Law was ratified during the Soekarno period. The Communist Party, as a party supporting the government at the time, helped with its implementation. Members of the Communist Party went out to the rice fields to distribute land to farmers who owned no land. When the 1965 incident erupted, those who had received this land were arrested and accused of being communists.[10]

There were also lists of names that the mobs handed to the village head, and these lists were used to arrest people. According to Pak Sam, apart from the people arrested at Oesao, there were two Communist Party members who disappeared and never returned home after attending a training workshop in Jakarta. He also mentioned some members of Gerwani who were arrested at Oesao, but the majority of them have since died. Two of the

---

7   Pak Kobus, interview, 23 November 2010, Oesao.
8   Ibid.
9   Email correspondence, 22 March 2012.
10  Interview with Pak Ben, 18 November 2010 at Oesao.

Gerwani women he mentioned are still living, but they declined to speak to the research team.[11]

## Arrest and detention

The process of detention began when the civilian militia and police would arrest someone accused of being a member or sympathiser of the Communist Party and take them to the house of the *barnemeng* (village head).[12] They were then made to do a 'board run', meaning to run around the yard in front of the Imanuel church in Oesao with a placard hanging from their necks on which was written their name or 'PKI' (Communist Party), and they had to sing the Nasakom song.[13] They were then taken and detained at the house of the Oesao village head, which also functioned as the Oesao village hall. They were detained at night, and during the day they were permitted to return to their homes. However, some people chose not to return home because they were afraid of being attacked and tortured by the mob.[14] At the village hall they were examined by a Team for the Annihilation of the Indonesian Communist Party, formed by the army. In Oesao this team was made up of three people, namely Pak Sam (representing Parkindo), Pak Tinus (representing PNI) and Sergeant-Major Leksi (representing the police). According to Pak Sam, the team's duty was to ascertain whether the detainees were really members of the Communist Party and Gerwani or not, based on some criteria that had been pre-determined. The criteria included: the detainee was a member of the executive board or an active member; had at some time served on the executive board; and especially for the Gerwani women, whether there was a stamp or tattoo of a sickle on their thigh.[15]

There were also witnesses, namely people in local positions of authority (including members of the PKI Annihilation team, the village head, and leaders of other political parties) who came to the Oesao village hall. According to an interview with Pak Sam, the presence of the PKI

---

11  Interview, Pak Sam, 8 November 2010, Oesao.
12  *Baarnemeng* is a local term for a government position that at the time was the level of a village head. The term probably comes from the Dutch term *waarneming*, meaning representative.
13  The story about the 'board run' was told by many informants, including Pak Kobus and Pak Sam. [Nasakom is the acronym from **Nas**ionalisme-**A**gama-**Kom**unisme, or nationalism-religion-communism, which was Soekarno's ideological formulation that called for a united front of nationalist, religious and communist elements in Indonesian political life. Trs.]
14  Pak Kobus, interview.
15  Pak Sam, interview.

Annihilation team was extremely important. After ascertaining whether or not those detained were Communist Party members or not, they would then sort them into different categories: active members, executive members, or just sympathisers. At the village hall, the names of detainees would be checked against the list held by the Annihilation Team. If their names were on that list, then they would be processed; if not, they would be released. It important to note that at this stage, if a detainee who was initially saved by the Annihilation Team or by someone else, later turned out to be 'guilty of involvement', then the team or the witness had to add five new people as detainees. This was a kind of deterrent or threat by the army to the Annihilation Team against too easily releasing suspects. Even so, the Annihilation Team did manage to release a few people (because they were neighbours, or members of their family) even though the person released had been proven 'guilty'. Meanwhile, the Annihilation Team also exploited its power to topple people they did not like. It did this even when there was no proof of involvement with the Communist Party at all, merely because of political rivalry or some other reason.[16]

From late December 1965 through to February 1966, those detainees whom the Annihilation Team had accused of being active Communist Party members, were transferred from the Oesao village hall at eight at night and taken to the East Kupang subdistrict office in Babau, on a truck owned by an Indonesian-Chinese businessman, to be processed further.[17] The subdistrict office was a house owned by an Indonesian businessman of Chinese descent. The government rented this house as a subdistrict office initially for a period of six months. After the 30$^{th}$ September movement, it was used as a detention centre. The government used the house for six years without paying any rent.[18]

## Execution of communists

After being processed at Babau (which took several days), at nine in the evening the military took the detainees to the execution site. People knew that if someone was taken to Babau, they would never come back, although there were exceptions, as Nona Asmi's story below shows. Before being taken to the execution site, the prisoners had their thumbs tied together behind

---

16  Ibid.
17  Ibid.
18  Pak Fanus (son of the owner), interview on 28 January 2010 at Babau. The research team calculates this was from 1959 to 1960 (when the first sub-district office opened in Babau) until 1966.

their backs with palm twine and were blindfolded. If they took too long getting on or off the truck, they were pushed with a gun at their buttocks.[19]

Apart from the men who were arrested as Communist Party members, there were also eleven women in East Kupang suspected of being Gerwani members because they were wives of members of the Farmers' Front (BTI) and prepared food for the BTI members working in the fields. These women were taken to the village centre in Pesao and interrogated, but the Communist Annihilation Team released them because none of them had been made committee members. Only Nona Asmi and Ibu Nina were held under suspicion of having been on the Gerwani executive for East Kupang. Nona Asmi was taken and processed at the subdistrict office at Babau, where she was often hassled by young men, because she was pretty. When the village chief heard about her harassment he helped her escape one night through the window.[20]

## Execution and mass burial sites

In East Kupang the locations prepared as sites for executions and mass burials were centred in the village of Tanah Putih, but there were also sites at the villages of Pulu Thie, Tanah Merah, and Oesao. There was another site prepared at Oesao for the execution of Gerwani women, but because there was no proof that they were members of Gerwani, the women were freed. The grave prepared was then used for 18 male members of the Communist Party killed on 6 February 1966. As far as is known, this was the last massacre that happened in East Kupang.

Based on the information uncovered, the first massacre in East Kupang took place after Christmas in the area of Tanah Putih in December 1965. Subsequently there were a few other massacres between December 1965 and the beginning of February 1966. Among the execution sites, the one with the largest number of graves is the village of Tanah Putih, which is an area under a traditional village chief (*fetor*), and the centre of his power. Seven graves were found there. The first is estimated to have 24 victims buried in it, the second 16, and there are no estimates for the other graves. However, the total number of victims in the seven graves is thought to be more than 100. The local people dug the graves at the order of the village head (*fetor*) who said it was for planting bananas. However the holes were then used as places to kill and bury the victims. The victims were taken to the holes and ordered

---

19   Pak Ben, interview.
20   Pak Sam, interview.

This is one of at least seven known graves for 1965 massacre victims in Tanah Putih, East Kupang. – JPIT archives

to stand facing it, then they were shot by soldiers, police, or civil personnel who had been designated this task. If someone was shot and did not die, their throats would be cut with a machete, or they would be buried alive.[21]

The people remember this as an incredibly tense time when they did not dare leave their houses or do any activity. They describe this time with the saying, 'the lizards made no sound and even the cocks did not crow.'[22]

## Destruction of family relations

The findings of the research team for East Kupang show that the greatest impact of the 1965 incident was the destruction of relations between the former political prisoners and members of their own families (for instance,

---

21  Interview with Pak Gaspar, 27 January 2011 at Tanah Putih. Pak Gaspar is a high ranking figure for customary law in the area of Tanah Putih. The information he gave us came from his grandfather and father. It is not exactly clear when the 'holes for planting bananas' were dug, but it could be that from the outset when the *fetor* ordered them to be dug, they were intended as execution sites and mass graves.
22  Pak Kobus, interview.

between parents and children, or between siblings), and also relations between former political prisoners and their children with society.

## *Putri's story*

The people of Oesao follow a system of communal life, as do the majority of people in Timor. They live communally not only because they are within a community, but there are also strong blood ties between them. They take care to maintain good family relations, and even though there may be occasional differences of opinion, these are never serious enough to threaten their relations as family members. Their close kinship is threatened when someone chooses a path that is different to that of the community.

An example of this is Mama Nina.[23] After her husband Pak Yusuf died because of illness, she decided to take a new partner, Pak Doni, a Communist Party leader in Oesao. Her decision to live with Pak Doni as husband and wife without any formal marriage was problematic, because in Mama Nina's community the communists were seen as a threat to the pattern of ownership of rice fields (because they wanted to change the system of land ownership). They were also seen as agents of destruction of the social-cultural order, and considered to have no religion. Because of this, people did not want to have relations with them, including Mama Nina.

Indeed, there were some people who were sympathetic to the Communist Party because they thought they were the ones who helped them get land and fields to work.[24] But the landowners saw the presence of the Communist Party as a threat to their status. They did not like the Communist Party, which they thought acted arrogantly by taking land that belonged to them.[25] With such views, anyone who was linked to or had any relationship with the Communist Party was automatically branded as bad. They were seen to have taken the wrong path and made the wrong choice. Therefore, when the 1965 incident occurred, anyone involved with the Communist Party was accused, arrested, and killed.

---

23  Mama Nina herself was not willing to give information to the research team. The information presented here with Mama Nina's permission, is from her daughter, Putri, who was interviewed on 9 November 2010 at the pastorate of the GMIT Emanuel church in Oesao.
24  Pastor Emeritus Markus, interview on 4 November 2010 at Pukdale.
25  Pak Ben, interview.

The 1965 incident worsened relations within families where relationships were already fragile, which was the case for Mama Nina's relationship with her children. After her first husband died, Mama Nina chose to live together with Pak Doni. She did not take the children from her first marriage with her. Because of this, they felt abandoned. When the 1965 events occurred, Mama Nina was involved with Gerwani. She was arrested and detained for about a month in the old prison in Kupang. After her release she was ostracised by society. Her children too, even though they had lived apart from their mother, were also ostracised. They were angry at their mother for this discrimination that continued for years afterwards. They felt it was their mother's fault. The gulf between Mama Nina and her children widened.

In 1967, Pastor To'o from Oeba in Kupang, arranged for around six children of former Communist Party and Gerwani members to be taken to the GMIT orphanage in Oeba so they could go to school. They continued to live at the orphanage until they finished high school. Mama Nina's children were among those taken to the orphanage with the exception of her youngest daughter, Putri, aged only three years old at the time, who was brought up by Mama Nina's younger sister, Ibu Dorkas. In her new family, Putri helped sell cakes, beginning when she started primary school at age six. She recalls that she was constantly taunted as being a 'communist child'.

> It was because I was her daughter. It really hurt. Wherever I went people would taunt me. Call me names. I felt it the most when I was living at Oesao. My three older brothers and sisters were at the orphanage, I was all alone in Oesao. I could get by; mama [her adoptive mother, Trs] could cook cakes. I used to sell them at the market, the one over there. I never went anywhere. Never went very far; just stayed home. So in the morning I would sell the cakes, and people would talk about me – there goes that communist kid.

Apart from the accusations against her, relations between Putri and her biological mother, Mama Nina (who she called 'older mother') were not good, because of their separation. After Putri's father (Mama Nina's first husband) died and Mama Nina left to live with Pak Doni, Putri and her mother never lived together again, so their relationship as mother and daughter weakened.

> I never lived with Mama. I only ever lived with her for a few months; three months when she was sick, because my brothers and sisters were not around. So my [adoptive] mother told me to go and stay over there

and help my older mother eat and drink. I was there for only three months, then I went home. I said that one of my older brothers or sisters should come, because I wanted to go home. I wasn't used to it. Even now I am not very close to my older mother.

The fact of Ibu Nina's detention embarrassed Putri and left her bitter towards her:

> Interviewer: Do you think your mother did not take you with her because she did not care about you, or was it because she thought it better that you did not go along [so as to protect you]?
>
> Putri: It was like that – she just didn't care. And my mother was trying to get free. That's what I think. You and I are both women, and, you know, there is a woman's instinct. Like me, for instance, I could never just leave my child. If I really think about it, it makes me mad. Aduh! How could my own mother have just left her children? I don't know how my three older brothers and sisters feel, but I look at the way they live with their children, and I think it's the same for them.

People's accusations and bad feeling towards those who were ostracised as communists continued until the 1980s. This was proven when Putri wanted to get married, but her fiancé's family refused to accept her:

> Everywhere I went, there were brick walls. When I wanted to get married, my prospective mother-in-law objected because I had that black line, communist. I didn't try to force it. I knew that was how things were. My [adoptive] mother said, look, if [your fiancé's family] don't want it, there's no point in pushing it. There was no point in me going to live with them if I was just going to be a burden. So I just let it be. There was nothing I could do about my mother. Best just to be safe. Well, what happened to our parents should not happen to us children. I was aware of my position. So I just said, well, I am not going to force it. If the family does not agree, then that's it. I didn't want to go over there and be a nuisance. That'd be no good. I went to the house and my prospective father-in-law invited me to sit down, and talked to me about the communists. He advised me, he told me what they were like. But I said those people who were involved didn't pass on their communist nature to their kids. The one who was involved was not me, it was my mother.

The old East Kupang Sub District Head's office, where Nona Asmi was interrogated.
– JPIT archives

## *Pak Kobus' story*

Another example of the 1965 events worsening already problematic relations between family members is the case of Pak Kobus and his sister Ibu Fina. The siblings fell out over a land dispute and because of a misunderstanding between family members. Their relationship worsened when Pak Kobus was arrested because he was suspected of being a communist. He was later released because there was no proof of his involvement with the Communist Party. However, his freedom meant little, because the people around him including his own family, ostracised him, his wife and children. They were considered to be 'communist dregs' and 'rubbish'.[26] They were treated in this way because of the ambiguous government statement accompanying their release: 'these people are being returned to society to be socialised'.[27]

---

26   Pak Kobus, interview.
27   Pak Ben, interview. The Indonesian term is '*dimasyarakatkan*' [Trs].

Following his release sometime in 1966 until the 1980s, Pak Kobus was required to report regularly to the village office. The stated purpose was to ensure that he and a few other former detainees were still alive and not acting in ways harmful to the government. Even today, he is still haunted by this stigmatisation. His status as an ex political prisoner legitimised any kind of treatment and apart from the effect on him personally, there is also the effect on his children. When they were still at school their own friends, teachers, and parents of other students would often taunt them as 'communist kids'. Apart from the teasing and abuse at school, their neighbours would also taunt them. They would feel the stigma particularly painfully when they took part in Independence Day celebrations (17 August), and their father, as an ex political prisoner, had to report to the authorities.[28]

Pak Kobus explained that another thing that would happen was that whenever he had a difference of opinion with his sister, Ibu Fina, she would always bring up the accusation that Pak Kobus was showing 'traces of communism'. This accusation of communism still comes up today. Ibu Fina once reported Pak Kobus, her own brother, to the police because she said he wanted to take her land. As his son, Pak Sef, explained,

> In 2006, there was a problem. There was a plot of land on the main road, which [Pak Kobus] wanted to measure for the land title. He went to clear the land on Friday and Saturday. On Sunday the police came and arrested him: they had pistols and surrounded the house. Even though all he had done was clear the elephant grass. But in the police report, he was accused of carrying out sabotage, and latent communist activity. When the police came, he was asleep. He went out just wearing his underpants, with no shirt on. It was Ibu Fina [his sister] who had reported him. He was taken to the police station, but released because there was no clear proof. Because of that, Ibu Fina was very angry. There is also a story about when one of their relatives died and Ibu Fina did not go to the funeral because Pak Kobus was there together with his children.

Communities can be a space to give a sense of security and protection to the individuals within, in economic, political and social terms. But at the same time communities make demands on individuals to take responsibility for communally accepted values.

When an individual acts in a different way to those values, he or she will be branded as a traitor. Family members cannot greet one another, and families

---

28  Pak Sef, (son of Pak Kobus) interview 12 March 2011, Oesao.

are ostracised from their communities. They are no longer regarded as part of the community where they lived and grew up together. They have to stand alone, stigmatised and badly treated by their fellows. It is extremely regrettable that until today even though their intensity may have lessened, and even though there are attempts to repair those rifts through pastoral action – 50 years since the 1965 incident – there still remain unhealed family rifts.

## The Church's pastoral role

*Impact of the 1965 incident on the church and its pastoral role*
In the aftermath of the 1965 incident attendances at Sunday church services in East Kupang increased. The churches were packed for worship. The rise in attendance can probably be attributed to fears in the community of being branded an atheist communist. Sadly, after the political crisis died down, church attendance declined and many never attended church again.

The 1965 incident involved families in the congregation of one of the central churches in the subdistrict. It not only destroyed family relations, but also damaged relations within the fellowship of the congregation as a whole. The family is the smallest fellowship within the body of the congregation and when the solidarity of the family is disturbed, so too is the body of the congregation. When family relations were destroyed, this had an indirect effect on the church as a fellowship and as a place of shelter for Christian families, including the church's pastoral role.

The pressures within and outside the church at this time provided contrasting and deeply conflicting responses.

Sometime in December 1965, a GMIT pastor, Markus, was asked to pray for victims beside the grave at the execution site before they were shot. He then had to visit the victims' families, accompanied by the congregation council. Pastor Markus explained that this initiative came from one of the elders, but was carried out only once. Pastor Markus said that he himself did not take the initiative to do this, because he was traumatised and terrified after his experience at the execution site.[29] Pastor Markus also talked about what happened at a church service the night before the massacre, when the congregation and the pastor felt terrified and under severe stress as they faced the threat of the arrests and killings. Because they could not express this in words or actions, in their communal prayer they shared some time

---

29  Pastor Emeritus Markus, interview on 4 November, 2010 at Pukdale.

of silence, and could only weep at their fate and that of their relatives and friends who were under the threat of death.[30]

At the same time, the church disciplined members of the congregation named as communists or sympathisers, labelling them sinners because they had been involved with the Communist Party, which was atheist. They were not permitted to attend services in the church. They were also not permitted to take part in the sacraments; for example, their children could not be baptised and adults could not join communion and were prohibited from holding positions in the church. They were subject to this discipline for a number of years.[31]

Why did the church carry out this disciplining, and yet find it difficult to carry out its pastoral role? According to Pastor Lexy, the church at the time was itself afraid of being accused of being communist, or maybe it was just afraid. The situation at the time forced the church to keep silent or it would be attacked. Another probable reason was that the church was not yet free of the influence of its role as the state church in colonial times, so it obeyed and agreed to whatever the state did, even though this could destroy the values and meaning of the church's presence. As a result, the church was silenced, and took the safest stand, namely to silence itself.

### *The church's pastoral role in the healing of family relations*

In 1979, there was a change in leadership in one of the large churches in East Kupang. The new pastor, Pastor Lexy, introduced new initiatives through pastoral action. He visited every member of the congregation, including those who had been disciplined by the church. This included those disciplined for adultery to those involved with the Communist Party (or accused of this), although at that time he did not know of the disciplinary action against those accused of being Communist Party members and so his pastoral visits were more of a general nature. As a consequence of his visits, most of the congregation returned and joined church services, and also took on positions in the church; all the disciplinary action was erased. Pastor Lexy considered this the right thing to do because the correct pastoral role of the church is not merely to look at things in terms of black and white.

> People viewed those who were 'involved' with the Communist Party as though they were lepers in the Old Testament, as something filthy to be isolated and reviled. But I personally did not agree with that

---

30 Ibu Kobus, interview 23 November 2010, Oesao.
31 Pastor Lexy, interview 7 January 2011 at Oebufu.

common view because I had studied at the Tarus Theology College. I had studied there about Marxism, and read its criticism of religion that did not carry out its function and was just an opiate of the people. I also studied Soekarno's ideology, and there were no leaders who matched him, from his Nasakom ideology that could combine three ideologies – nationalism, religion, and communism. I also studied the theologies of various religions, and together all of that informed my approach to the congregation.

Pastor Lexy saw that getting to know his congregation was important so that they would also know their pastor, especially when they are recent arrivals from another area. Through pastoral visits, a pastor can get to know many people and understand new things. Pastor Lexy explained:

> During the Suharto era, there was a letter that went around to all institutions instructing them not to include former communists; this included social organisations and the church. And it was not just the church doing the disciplining, they themselves [those accused of being communist] consciously, and maybe because of fear, disciplined themselves [withdrew themselves from fellowship]. All of Indonesia had been possessed by an evil spirit, and consciously or not, the church went along with it, so it was not entirely the church's fault.

One can say that now there are congregations in East Kupang that have begun to adopt pastoral care of victims of the 1965 events and their families. Even so, there is still much to be done, and the church itself is wounded. It is time for renewal of the pastoral role of the church.

## *Renewal of the church's pastoral role*

One hopes that the church can act as a community made up of families within. However, to date the church has tended to be more fearful of worldly power, meaning the military and the government, rather than taking seriously its role as protector and bearer of peace. The church is not fully carrying out its role of protecting those who become victims of state violence. The church's silence obstructs the healing of destroyed relations, and this is still the case today. Because of this, the presence of the church has lost its meaning. The destruction of the smallest fellowships results in wounds in the larger fellowship of the church.

There is need for pastoral action towards the victims and their families, namely to receive them back into the fellowship of the church and to eliminate all church discipline of them. This is an important first step towards reconciliation, but it must be acknowledged that beyond that there are still cracks in family relations. A further step must be taken to encourage other church members to introspectively examine their own attitudes in judging victims. The church's role now is to heal itself and renew its pastoral role.

The research we carried out helped us to understand the weaknesses in the church's pastoral care to date. Renewing pastoral care means that the church, as an institution, needs to ask itself: whose voices and whose struggle has the church been ignoring? Creating the space and time to listen to the voices of victims who have not been heard can help us understand the problems and hatred so long buried in our midst. Our research provided such a bridge for us.

It is time for the church to acknowledge and apologise to the victims for its weakness and neglect of them and also its tendency to join in the ostracising and accusation of them. This is a church process to heal itself so that its pastoral role will be renewed and the church can then listen to its voice of prophecy, namely to expose violence and speak up for justice for the victimised. In this way, the gulf between us will begin to be bridged.

## South Central Timor

Naismetan Forest, sub-district of Mollo Tengah: Massacre site.

*According to some informants, victims from various places in South Central Timor were brought to this forest to be executed, about 20 kilometres to the north of SoE. There are about 16 graves in the forest, and each grave has more than one body buried there. The victims dug the holes themselves, and they are so shallow that when the research team went there for documentation, one could clearly see skulls and other bones. The forest is still covered with thick undergrowth. The people living nearby are afraid to plant anything in the forest, or even enter it or the immediate surroundings.*

**Statement from a member of the research team**

*Chapter 4*

# The 1965 Incident and the Women of South Central Timor's Fight for Identity

Dina Penpada, Ivonne Peka, and Anna Salukhfeto

This report gives an account of the survival strategies of the women of South Central Timor during the terrible famine that struck the area in 1965, the inhumane events that were later labelled 'G30S', and the Christian Revival Movement, all of which happened virtually simultaneously. The stories of victims also show the impact of these three things on their identity as female civil servants, members of customary societies, farmers, Christians, wives and mothers.

## Research area

Three areas in the district of South Central Timor were chosen as targets of our research, namely South Amanuban (the subdistricts of South Amanuban and Kualin), the area around the town of SoE (the subdistricts of SoE Town and Central Mollo), and the village of Boti in the Kie subdistrict. We chose the area of South Amanuban because it had the largest number of people considered to be involved with the Communist Party, namely 1213 people.[1] The area around the town of SoE revealed many holes that are suspected of being execution sites. Furthermore, as the centre of the district of South Central Timor, SoE is the judicial centre for the people around West Amanuban and Mollo as well as other sub-districts. Lastly, even today Boti is known as the area where the majority of the population are followers of traditional religion, and we therefore considered it important

---

1   Hans Itta ed., *Timor Tengah Selatan dalam Jangkauan Zaman* (SoE: Pemerintah Daerah Kabupaten TTS, 2006), pp 162–71.

for our research to find out how people there survived the turbulence of 1965, which required many people to adopt other religions to avoid being considered communist.

## Profile of the subdistricts of South Central Timor before 1965

The district of South Central Timor was created on 20 December according to the 1958 law on the formation of districts at the second level of government within the first provincial level of Bali, West Nusa Tenggara and East Nusa Tenggara. South Central Timor district covered the area that was previously *Onder afdeeling Zuid Midden Timor* (South Central Timor sub division), which comprised three administrative districts called *swapraja*, namely Mollo, Amanuban, and Amanatun.

In 1955, when Indonesia held its first general elections, four political parties participated in South Central Timor, and their results were as follows: Indonesian Christian Party (Parkindo), 6 seats; People's Front (Front Rakyat) 5 seats; National People's Party (Partai Rakyat Nasional), 4 seats.[2] However, these results did not last for long, because of a Presidential Decree issued on 5 July 1959 together with a Presidential Instruction. The elected Regional Head was declared to be Kusa Nope. However, according to a subsequent Presidential Instruction announced on 27 March, 1960, the name of the regional parliament, hitherto known as DPRD or Regional House of Representatives, was now changed to DPRD-Gotong Royong (DPRD-GR) or Mutual Cooperation DPRD [in accordance with the changes at national level, Trs.]. The various political groups were brought together into two large groupings; namely Golongan Politik (Political Groups) and Golongan Karya (Work Groups).[3] As a result, the sub districts of South Central Timor had to be brought in line with the new mapping for the period 1961–66. The new groupings were as follows:

---

2  Rufus Ony Yunliu, *Kilas Balik DPRD TTS*, unpublished manuscript still in compilation. Those elected to the DRPD seats for South Central Timor were formally appointed in the Governor's decision SK Gubernur/Koordinator Pemerintahan Nusa Tenggara TImur, no, Des. 2/1/133 dated 26 May 1959.
3  Ibid.

| Political Grouping (Golongan Politik) | Work Grouping (Golongan Karya) |
|---|---|
| Christian Sub-group<br>• Parkindo (Indonesian Christian Party)<br>• Partai Katolik (Catholic Party)<br>Nationalist Sub-Group<br>• PNI (Partai Nasional Indonesia, Indonesian National Party)<br>Communist Sub-group<br>• PKI (Partai Komunis Indonesia, Indonesian Communist Party) | Armed Forces<br>• Army<br>• OPR [Organisasi Pemuda Rakyat]<br>National Police<br>Religious leaders<br>• Christian religious<br>• Catholic religious<br>• Muslim ulama<br>Spiritual development<br>• Youth<br>• Women<br>Material development<br>• Farmers and cooperatives<br>• National business persons |

Based on these changes and new groupings, the regional parliament for South Central Timor gained three seats, making a total of 20 seats in 1960. The parties that received extra seats, one each, were the Indonesian Christian Party, the Indonesian Communist Party and the Work Group's sub group Material Development, which was held by the Indonesian Farmers' Front (BTI).

All of our informants stated that the Indonesian Communist Party was a legal political party in Indonesia, which worked via political channels for the wellbeing of the Indonesian people. The legality of the Communist Party is also seen in the fact that in the 1955 general elections, it won 16% of the vote nationally, making it the fourth largest political party in Indonesia.[4]

In order to bring the party close to the people, the Indonesian Communist Party, like the other political parties, broadened its structure at all levels of government across the country, including South Central Timor. In order to reach out to all levels of society, it formed support organisations that are today known as 'party wings'. On 9 July 1960, the Communist Party established a branch of the Indonesian Farmers' Front (BTI) in South Central Timor, and on 14 August 1960 it established a branch of Peoples Youth.[5] In their membership drive to fill this structure, the branches recruited people who later became victims when the Communist Party was systematically attacked. In general, informants explained that the victims of

---

4 'Pemilu 1955' in the Election Commission's online series about the history of Indonesian elections, *Pemilu dalam Sejarah*, at http://www.kpu.go.id/index.php?option=com_content&task=view&id=43&Itemid=66 accessed 22 November 2011

5 Rufus Ony Yunliu, *Kilas Balik DPRD TTS*.

the 1965 incident in South Central Timor did not really know about either the Communist Party or the Farmers' Front.

In order to get the votes of the people, the Communist Party along with its 'wing organisations' developed programs for basic necessities, agricultural tools, and weaving materials for women. These programs were greatly appreciated as they answered people's needs at a time when there was a severe food shortage. Many people signed up with the Communist Party or the Farmers' Front in order to receive this aid. All those who received aid, or just promises of it, were considered to be members of the Farmers' Front, and so after the 1965 incident they were dragged into the problems concerning the Communist Party and became targets of the annihilation of the 'Communist threat'. One can conclude that the 1965 incident, which caused thousands of deaths is therefore inseparable from the competition between political parties leading up to the first General Elections of 1955.

## Famine in South Central Timor: The example of Boti

The Boti people are one of the indigenous Timorese groups living in the area of East Amanuban in the sub-district of Kie. They practice their traditional beliefs, and do not follow any of Indonesia's official religions. According to their belief, apart from Uis Neno, Almighty God the Creator and Organiser, there is also Uis Pah, or God who is around them and protects them. Uis Neno takes the form of the *usif* (the king). The people therefore greatly respect and obey their king.

### *Mama Bifemnasi's story*[6]

Mama Bifemnasi recounted that in 1964 there was a serious food shortage in Boti as a result of a drought that caused the harvest to fail. There was no food in storage. As a wife whose duty it was to guard the rice storage house (*pana*) and prepare food for her children and husband, this was a very serious situation. To help out, her husband went to Tune (Kolbano), a village one full day's walk away to buy sugar palm trees, dried cassava and coconut, by bartering pigs or goats (one pig or goat was bartered for one sugar palm). He extracted the inside of the palm and took it home for Mama Bifemnasi to prepare. The preparation was laborious – the palm was pounded, strained, left to settle, and then roasted. The whole process, from her husband's search for

---

6   Interview with Mama Bifemnasi on 12 March 2011, Boti, Kie.

sugar palms until the product was ready to eat, took 4–5 days. During this time, Mama Bifemnasi would look for alternative food like wild taro to feed her six children who were still young, but cooking wild taro was also difficult, because if not treated properly, it can be poisonous and even cause death.

### *Mama Anita Besi's story*[7]

Mama Anita Besi also spoke about the foot shortage and hunger. While her husband went searching for food outside the kampung, Mama Nita did other work like weaving cloth, plaiting mats and trays, and taking them to the markets in Bele and Oinlasi to sell. She worked hard, treating dry cassava and mixing it with corn. She also mixed *putak* (the inside of the *gebang* palm) with cow's milk she milked herself, as food for her family. She said that people ended up owning no animals, because they had bartered them for staple foods. She and her husband had the principle that no matter how hungry they were, they must not steal. They had to work to get food. She even taught her children to help clean other people's gardens so they could get some food. In the 1970s there was another food shortage, but not as severe as that of 1965.

### *Mama Sance Nelo's story*[8]

Mama Sance Nelo's story is very similar to those of Mama Bifemnasi and Mama Anita. She said that during the food shortage, she and her husband bartered pigs for *putak*, but her husband had for walk for days to the village of Oetuka in Kolbano to get it. While he was away finding *putak*, Mama Sanci would look for wild cassava, and treat it so she and her children could eat it.[9] She would cut it up, dry it, pound it, and then mix it with coconut and cook it. The drought lasted a long time, and her husband had to go out looking for food in other places eight times before the drought ended.

---

7  Interview with Mama Anita Besi, 12 March 2011 in Boti, Kie.
8  Interview with Mama Sance Nelo on 12 March 2011 at Boti, Kie.
9  Wild cassava is actually poisonous, so it has to be boiled a number of times to make it edible.

## *Mama Ernasani Nulu's Story*[10]

Mama Ernasani Nulu (known as Mama Sani) was born in Boti and is now aged about 70 (she is not sure of the actual year she was born). Her husband is Fanus Tasuit. They were blessed with one daughter and four sons. Before converting to Christianity, Mama Sani's name was Nope Nulu, and her husband's name was Nuba Tasuit.

In 1964, Mama Sani and her husband already had two children. It was extremely difficult to find enough staple foods like corn and rice, because there was none for sale at the markets. They had to travel to distant places to get corn, and it was very limited. So all they could eat every day was *putak* and wild cassava. That was all they had for their children, too, and as a result their children's growth was stunted. The first child could not walk until two years old, but was paralysed and went back to crawling. As a mother, Mama Sani suffered deeply to see her two children suffering from hunger and malnutrition. The famine and difficult situation of the time drove her to help her husband look for work just to meet basic needs.

Her husband, Fanus Tasuit, tried to earn some money by making weaving equipment used by Mano women, called *bnini* and *ike suti*. The *bnini* is a tool that prepares the cotton for making thread, and the *ike suti* is a spindle. Mama Sani herself did weaving and spun thread, and what she earned from selling, she used to buy food. As she told the story, she explained that she used all her ten fingers to weave and earn money, as well as going to the forest morning and evening to dig for wild cassava.

There were times of extreme suffering. All the plants died because of the long drought. In the midst of this difficult economic situation, in 1965 the 30th September Movement occurred, which, Mama Sani recalled, made the people afraid. They were hungry, but too afraid to go out of the house to look for food because they might be accused of being communists. At that time, none of the people of Boti were communist, because their head, the *Temukung* called Bapak Benu, had not permitted it.[11] Mama Sani and her family remained calm and continued to struggle to face their economic difficulties. At the time of the famine, Mama Sani and her husband had not yet converted to Christianity, but neither did her husband wear his hair in the traditional style [as non-converts did, Trs.], long and tied up in a bun.

---

10   Interview with Mama Sani Nulu on 12 March 2011 at Boti, Kie.
11   *Temukung* is a government administrative position of pre New Order times, equivalent to a sub-district head *(camat)*. Pak Benu is his real name.

Before converting to Christianity, Mama Sani joined in performing the traditional Neno rites of the people of Boti. Every ninth day, all the people of Boti would gather in the place of worship on the top of a hill, and work together at that place. The women would bring palm (*lontar*) leaves or *gewang* leaves and plait them to make mats, trays, baskets and boxes for carrying food. They would also spin thread and weave. The men would pray in a certain place where the women were forbidden to enter. This would go on from 7 o'clock in the morning until 5 o'clock in the evening, then they would all return home. Through the Neno rites, the Meto men and women learned to work. The women learned to weave and do plaiting and wickerwork, and became extremely proficient at weaving. This is how Mama Sani helped support her family during the famine. According to her, if a Meto woman does not know how to weave, it means she is not yet adult and therefore not yet fit to take a husband. She will also be an embarrassment to her family, and her own marriage will not succeed.

\* \* \*

## Christianity and the Holy Spirit in South Central Timor

### *Before 30th September 1965*

According to Frank Cooley's book, *The Growing Seed*, in the Portuguese time (1556–1613) missionaries visited all of Timor. Efforts at conversion began at this time and continued into the Dutch period (1614–1942).[12] However, until 1850 Dutch evangelizing had not touched the interior of Timor. It was only in the period 1916–1925 that the interior of Timor attracted attention. By 1920, the number of Christians in South Central Timor totalled 500 people. However, those who had undergone mass baptism returned to their own local religions, probably because there was no follow up after this mass conversion. In 1922, Ds. P. Middelkoop arrived in Kapan and began his mission by paying attention to local language and customs.[13] He translated both the

---

12 Frank L. Cooley, Staf Proyek Survey Menyeluruh DGI, *Benih Yang Tumbuh XI* (Jakarta: Lembaga Penelitian dan Studi Dewan Gereja-gereja di Indonesia, 1976), 24, 48–49. The English version of this book titled *The Growing Seed* was published in 1982 (Jakarta: Christian Publishing House BPK, Gunung Mulia).
13 It should be noted that P. Middelkoop replaced Krayer van Aalst who served in Kapan, South Central Timor, before him. Van Aalst's presence there was part of what was called a 'pacification campaign' by the Dutch Indies government. However it was Middelkoop who was more intensive in his conversion efforts in the interior. Middelkoop translated the New Testament in 1947.

Old and New Testaments into Timorese. By the end of World War II, the number of Christians had risen dramatically, reaching 80,000. This may have been the result of Middelkoop's efforts to contextualise Christianity.

In his book *Curse-Retribution-Enmity*, Middelkoop writes about the indigenous beliefs of the Timorese, which remained even after they had been baptised as Christians:

> The development of schools and education since the last war has been enormous. There is an increased open-mindedness to listen to the Gospel and to surrender to the Lord in many places. On the other hand, the Independent Timor Church has to grapple with many problems, especially of finance, discipline and faith.[14]

By the mid-1960s, many people in South Central Timor had converted to Christianity, but at the same time they retained their pre-Christian beliefs and practices, like magic charms and mantras.

### *Birth of the Revival Movement* [15]

September 26th 1965, is recorded as the birth of the Revival Movement in South Central Timor, however, its origins were earlier. In 1960 an evangelist called Mr Cheng from the school of Stephen Tong came to bear witness and evangelise to the Chinese living in SoE, successfully converting almost all of them to Christianity.[16] After Mr. Cheng's departure, in 1962 the prayer group in SoE enjoyed the presence of a teacher who was also a GMIT evangelist from Amfoang, called Ratuwalu.[17] He came to SoE to expand the Evangelisation Service (KPI; now called Spiritual Awakening Service, KKR) and performed various miracles for spiritual healing, which influenced many people to repent. When Ratuwalu's period was over, in

---

14   Pieter Middelkoop, *Curse-Retribution-Enmity: As Data in Natural Religion, Especially in Timor, Confronted with the Scripture* (Amsterdam: Drukkeerij en Uitgeverij Jacob van Campen, 1960): 41.
15   All names in this section are real names except for Pastor Topan. The information in this section is from various informants including: interviews with Mama Kaci Beti at Supul on 31 August 2011; with Pak Dian Asnat at SoE on 12 October 2011; and with Pastor Yefta Topan in Loli on 13 November 2010. This oral information can be compared with *Atoni Pah Meto: Pertemuan Injil dan Kebudayaan di Kalangan Suku Timor Asli* by Ds. P. Middelkoop (Jakarta: BPK Gunung Mulia, 1982) especially the chapter 'Gerakan kebangunan baru di Timor (1967)': 218–33.
16   Stephen Wong taught at the Southeast Asian Bible Institute (SAAT) in Malang, East Java, for 25 years.
17   After Middelkoop returned to Holland in 1957, he received letters from friends in Timor about the Revival Movement in South Central Timor that began around mid-1965 and continued through 1966–67.

June 1965, an Evangelisation Service was held at the Maranatha church by a group from the Indonesian Evangelical Institute (III) in Batu Malang, under the leadership of the then rector Pastor Oktavianus (who was from Rote). The rector prophesised that after their return from the gathering the young men and women of SoE would flourish like mushrooms in the rainy season. After the three-day gathering, they returned home.

The movement flourished, with many people forming small groups giving witness about what they called 'miracles of the Holy Spirit'. When the KPI team returned to Batu-Malang, all kinds of unusual or miraculous spiritual events took place, beginning with the presence of Mama Heny Tunliu, a teacher who received the gift of sight and hearing to pray over people and destroy their magic charms. Among the miracles recorded at this time, apart from healing of the sick, was the miracle of a deceased person who came back to life and water turned into wine.

Then there was Nahor Leo, a junior high school student who lived with Pastor Daniel and worked as a 'runner' at the markets around SoE. He was known to have various magic charms that made him win running competitions at the time. Then in September 1965, as he tells it, God 'caught him in an extraordinary way', which he claims was a direct sign from the Holy Spirit. He began to burn his magic charms, then went from school to school bearing witness and encouraging as many people as possible to believe and join in gathering things including magic charms to burn.

Pastor Manuain and Pastor Daniel asked him to bear witness before the congregation at Maranatha, SoE. Following on from his witness, on 26 September, he asked people to collect all things that were 'worldly', like cassettes of pop songs and books of fiction. That night, all these things were gathered, then the people prayed until 11 o'clock at night while confessing their sins, crying, and some were even 'gripped by the holy spirit'. This continued until the night of 28 September. They made a fire to burn the cassettes and books that had been collected. Nahor Leo said that in accordance with the direction of the Holy Spirit that had descended upon him, he would name the people who were to enter his team as assistants or followers. They would form a prayer group of twelve people and be sent on a mission to Kapan. The twelve included Pak Nico Fallo, Pak Christian, Pak Mariman Adisuparto, Mama Ros Kase, and Mama Ester Sapa, who had been prayed over on 29 September and left that same day to evangelise in Kapan.

The movement continued to grow, and new prayer groups were formed and sent to new areas. There were so many teams that they had to be given numbers so they could be identified. Mama Kaci was in team number ten. In the beginning, the teams were active only in SoE and surrounding areas, but later they spread further, beyond South Central Timor, namely to Sabu, Rote, Flores, Alor, and even beyond the province of NTT and overseas.

The teams' chief activity was to pray over the sick, and to bring people to repent their sins. It was often discovered that the cause of someone's illness was their belief in evil powers and charms. The first thing done to the sick person was to determine that he or she had magic charms, then to locate them, and after praying over them to release their power over the sick person and his or her family, finally to burn them. The teams also prayed over people who still followed traditional religions. When they met them, they encouraged them to destroy their traditional places of worship, their sacred places, and the equipment they used for their rites (sacred stones, healing sticks, and things like necklaces, antique jars, Chinese porcelain etc).[18]

Many groups were formed. Seventy-two teams, with between six and seven members per team, are recorded at the Maranatha church in SoE. According to Pastor Topan, when Nahor Leo and Mel Tari bore witness and convinced people that miracles had occurred, without their realising it and without any direction, many people joined in and uncontrolled groups began to appear. Apart from the rapid spread of activities, there was also confusion when cases of adultery occurred among some members of the prayer groups, and one unmarried girl became pregnant.[19] Further, understanding about the Holy Spirit had begun to diverge from Scripture. A public meeting was held at Maranatha church and Pastor Topan was asked by Pastor Daniel and Pastor Manuain to give theological explanation about the Holy Spirit and his work. Pastor Topan spoke to 72 groups. After this meeting, many groups disbanded. Only a few then combined and became the Yayasan Utus SoE (SoE Messengers Foundation). In 1968, Pastor Topan became seriously ill, and many people said this was because he had opposed the Holy Spirit when he explained its working in theological terms. The other reason the prayer groups disbanded was probably because after the 1965 incident, the government prohibited gatherings because the country was in a precarious situation.

---

18   On antique jars and Chinese porcelain there are often pictures of dragons which are considered to be the sign of the devil, so this is probably one reason why these items were destroyed.
19   Information from a peer reviewer, email, 23 February 2012.

The SoE Messengers Foundation formed by some witnesses and participants of the foundation prayer groups of the Revival Movement, determined that 26 September would be commemorated as Spiritual Awakening Day in South Central Timor. Prayer groups in South Central Timor still commemorate this day by gathering every year at the Maranatha congregation, SoE.

## Women victims of 1965

### Ibu Neltji's story[20]

In 1968, accused of being a member of the South Central Timor branch of Gerwani, Mama Neiltji was fired from her position as a government civil servant, summarily dismissed until pension age. This was the punishment she received from the state.

Mama Neiltji's full name is Neltji Kumar. She was born in Nunukniti-Pisanin in the sub district of East Amanuban in 1942, and now lives with her husband (Bapak Nabin) and children in the precinct of Sentosa at Desa Noemoeto, in the sub district of the town of SoE. Mama Neltji began her education when she was seven years old in 1949 at primary school at Pisan. Upon completing primary school, she continued her education at the Aermata Christian junior high school in Kupang.

In her last year of school she did not pass the examinations. Rather than repeat a year, Mama Neltji decided to return to SoE and see what work she could find with the schooling that she had. In October 1960 she applied for a position as a civil servant in the South Central Timor district administrative offices and was immediately accepted (there was no entrance examination as they were in need of staff). She worked in the finance section and earned Rp. 177 a month. By chance, the head of her office was a man called Bapak Paulus who later became known as the head of the Communist Party for South Central Timor. This was the start of the disaster that struck Mama Neltji and became a bitter experience affecting her life to this day.

As the only woman in the Finance Section at the time, Mama Neltji was often asked to represent Bapak Paulus's wife at various Communist

---

20  Interview with Mama Neltji and her husband, Pak Nabin, on 19 November, 2010 in SoE.

Party and Gerwani meetings.[21] Mama Neltji attended these meetings at the instruction of her boss, and his instruction to do so was given with a somewhat threatening tone, as she recounts:

> Bapak Paulus told me to go so that I could listen and then report to his wife as the head of Gerwani. If I did not want to go, he would threaten me. He would get angry and say, 'Your fate is in my hands, if you remain stubborn, I will fire you.' So I had to follow his orders, as his subordinate. He told me to go, and then report to Mama Paulus.

Because of this, Mama Netji was later accused of being a member of Gerwani. Even so, she remained determined, and would not admit to this accusation:

> So they suspected I had probably joined Gerwani… But I never joined. I was summoned to the police headquarters… Questioned there… But I never joined that organisation… that organisation, what was it… the Communist Party one… Gerwani. I never joined, I have never joined any organisation.

So how did Mama Neltji view the South Central Timor branch of Gerwani? She and her husband, Bapak Nabin, said that Gerwani was not very active as a dangerous organisation. All she knew was that Mama Paulus was the head, and this was only because Mama Paulus's husband was the local head of the Communist Party. Mama Neltji talked about Mama Paulus:

> She was also Timorese… didn't work, just a housewife.

Bapak Nabin expanded on this:

> Well, if you look at her, at the most she had finished primary school, so she could not take part in meetings… We were involved with political parties, and we knew everyone… Mama Paulus was just a name there. Her husband was the head of the Communist Party so therefore automatically his wife had to be head of Gerwani, but it was just her name, she wasn't active. It is Ibu here [his wife, Mama Neltji] who was active together with Mama Paulus's daughter.

But power is in the hands of the state, and it was Mama Neltji, a helpless ordinary civil servant, who had to face the state violence. One day, around 5 October 1965, when she returned home after participating as one of the

---

21  One of the reasons Mama Neltji was asked to go and not the wife of her immediate boss was because Mama Neltji's education was a little higher, and thus she was considered more fitting for this kind of role.

regional dancers at the opening of the Asian Games in Jakarta, she was summoned and interrogated at the SoE police station, where she was accused of being a member of Gerwani. She had no sign or intimation of what was going to befall her, except that on her return journey from Jakarta, she lost six traditional Timorese necklaces, which made her extremely sad. It was only a few days later that she was called in for questioning. There were no reasons given for her interrogation other than suspicion because she was a member of Bapak Paulus's staff.

> They asked, did you join… did you join that organisation or not? I had never joined, but they just suspected me because I was a member of Bapak Paulus's staff. Head of finance.

Even so, Mama Neltji had to undergo regular questioning, and was even detained for two or three weeks without any warrant at the sub-district military command in SoE. She was then moved to a house where Bapak Liufeto now lives.[22]

Mama Neltji described her detention as being the most terrifying time because every morning there were always detainees who were called and taken out, but never returned. Then the news went around that they had been executed at a few places around the town of SoE (for instance at Fafinisin, Nonohonis and Nunumeu).

> Every night at midnight a vehicle would come. Usually a soldier would stand at the door and say a name. The person called would have to get into the car and would be taken to the 'Crocodile Hole'. We would only hear the name being called out. The name called… into the car… at midnight… so when we heard the sound of the car coming, we would all pray.

Although she was not called and did not experience physical torture in detention, Mama Neltji still had to fight hunger as the political prisoners were given no food. Luckily, at the time she was not yet married and had no children, although she and Bapak Napin (now her husband) were already sweethearts, and he was the one who brought her food when she was in detention.

> My parents were living in the kampung… At the time… I was going out with Bapak, so he used to bring me food.

---

22 The military sub-district command was called Bintara Urusan Teritorial dan Perlawanan Rakyat (Buterpra) and is now known as Koramil.

Strangely, after two weeks of detention, and with the constant support of Bapak Nabin, she was released, but she still had to regularly report to the District Military Command for one or two months.

After a period of enjoying free air, and marrying Bapak Nabin, disaster struck Mama Neltji again, as the accusation of being a Gerwani member was not yet settled. She had to face a state sentence of guilt, and as punishment, she was stripped of her status as civil servant.

> Just like that... I was fired. I had to wait until pension age before I could organise my right to a pension.

This situation caused Mama Neltji deep grief, as she recounts:

> Back then I was deeply sad. When would I ever work again?... I was miserable, my future was destroyed, I was like a broken plate, I was sad...

Bapak Nubin said the same thing:

> We just prayed to confess, I don't know how, but Mama cursed saying she did not want to have anything more to do with the government. And the same for our children. We were asked to work then later arrested like this. They [the government] created a lot of political parties but then they arrested us for it.

Even though this was the situation with work, socially not many people ostracised her after she was accused of being a member of Gerwani. According to Bapak Nabin, this was because most people were ignorant of politics. To this day, Mama Neltji and her family give thanks to God for her freedom from that accusation, even though she had to pay for it by losing her job.

> Yes, it is still a deep hurt, but what can we do about it? It is in the past, but God protects us. Consider it God's love towards us that we were saved.

Today Mama Neltji spends her old age (she is 69) with her husband and seven children, supported by her pension and that of her husband.

Apart from talking about her own life problems, Mama Neltji and Bapak Nabin also talked about other events that happened around the same time in 1965, including water turning into wine near SoE, famine and food shortage, and the local political contest between the Indonesian Communist Party, the Indonesian National Party and the Indonesian Christian Party.

Some informants said that the miracle of the water turning into wine (which happened near Pak Nabin's house) and the Revival Movement that happened right around the time of the 30th September movement were religiously linked to God's way of teaching the faithful. This is what Bapak Nabin said:

> Yes, because they were afraid, afraid of the 30th September Movement, because at that time there was information going around that anyone who did not want to embrace religion must be communist. So, we should immediately join a religion. It could be Islam, Catholicism, Protestantism, the main thing was to convert... everyone rushed to convert. That was when the church started to flourish. And at the same time, there were the Gifts of the Spirit at Pak Daniel's house. And it was with that Gift that in 1966 there was that water changing into wine.

Meanwhile there was the food shortage, which in 1965–66 became famine. There was no food anywhere because of the long drought and also because of the terrible economic conditions, as Bapak Nabin recounted. 'There was drought, no rain fell until late November. So because of the drought, we ran out of food.' And it was not just the drought. As a result of the tense political situation, basic foodstuffs disappeared from the market. 'Yes, because suddenly there was no more corn or rice in the shops, and meanwhile in the kampungs there was none at all.' To support their families, they had to go from kampung to kampung in search of food.

> People went looking in the kampungs, they would go to find one or two people who sold corn. You might be able to buy some, but it was expensive... there were only five or seven cassava trees. Five trees would buy a cow. Everything was expensive.

As far as the political constellation in the region went, Bapak Nabin thought that the Communist Party was just a normal party, whereas in South Central Timor the main competition was between PNI and Parkindo. This is why Bapak Nabin questions why the government, if it legitimised the existence of all these parties including the Communist Party in the first place, later allowed its legitimation to be used as the weapon for arresting people.

> They established many parties, and then we were arrested.

It must be acknowledged, though, that the Communist Party's strategy, through its associated mass organisation (the Indonesian Farmers' Front), and particularly though its distribution of aid to the people, made itself a new party popular with the people. Even so, the Communist Party did not get a significant vote in South Central Timor.

> I think if there was competition, it was between the two major parties. As for the Indonesian Farmers' Front (BTI), it also existed, but it was not really competing. It is just that at that time it was influential because it set up co-operatives. So they brought clothing and rice and distributed it to the people with sugar, all kinds of things, and they would write down your name. Then we would go. But whoever had received aid, they had their names written down, and then they had joined the BTI.

The PNI and Partindo, however, did not do the same thing. The competition continued until the 30th September Movement when, to safeguard all the members of their own parties (especially the PNI and Parkindo), party officials from various levels were summoned to the local military command to certify that their members were not members of the Communist Party. Because Bapak Nabin had an official position in the Parkindo party, he was able to save many people by stating that they were members of Parkindo. As he recounts:

> I was called in, the judge was Jaksa Lerek... he was from Ambon, a big, tall man. He called me in.
>
> 'You know this guy?'
>
> 'Yes, I know him.'
>
> 'Is he a member of Parkindo?'
>
> 'Yes, he's a member of Parkindo.'
>
> 'OK, that's all. Go.'

This also was part of the story about what happened around the time of the annihilation of the Communist Party in the sub-district of South Central Timor, as told by Bapak Nabin and Mama Neltji Kumar.

## *Mama Yulianti's story*[23]

Mama Yulianto Meno was born on 30 September 1950, and now lives in Oenasi, Nonohonis, SoE, with her children. She is one of countless women in Indonesia who had to suffer as wives of husbands who were accused of being Communist Party members with the classification B2. Mama Yulianti talked about her life with her husband, and how she bore the burden of supporting her family of ten children after the death of her husband Bapak Meno on 6 December 2007.

Before marrying Bapak Meno on 30 January 1975, Mama Yulianti already knew that he had been sentenced as a member of the Communist Party. 'Pak Daek and a few other people had already been released. They were taken to Fafainisin. Back then, Bapak Meno and I were not yet sweethearts. I was still afraid.' Then, without any clear reason, Bapak Meno had charges against him dropped and he was merely required to report daily over a three month period to the local military command. He was also told to return to his teaching at the Sinar Pancasila junior high school in SoE. Mama Yulianti's doubts were dispelled and they eventually married on 30 January 1975.

However, it turned out that Mama Yulianti's married bliss did not last long. Shortly after, another round of accusations attacked their domestic life. Bapak Meno was dismissed from his work as teacher after just three months, and then in 1980 had to undergo a process of investigation. Even though after six months he was ordered to teach once more, not long afterwards he was again dismissed while he was still being investigated. Then one day in 1983, around ten in the morning, he was summoned by the District Head.

> The District Head gave my husband a dishonorable dismissal. He said 'Stop. If you want, you can work outside of the government, you can still earn money.'

And his government salary ceased from that moment.

This was a severe blow to Mama Yulianti and her late husband as he had to support the family of now ten children. Bapak Meno could not bear to face work that had any connection to government, nor do anything about trying to get money put into his pension fund. Not long after he had been fired from his work as a teacher, a colleague and female official who worked at the local office of the Department of Education and Culture came to see him and told him he should collect his pension contributions in Kupang,

---

23   Interview with Mama Yulianti on 2 November 2010 at SoE.

and also argue his case to the Minister. But Bapak Meno refused, despite her encouragement:

> He said, 'I don't want to take it'. I said, 'why not? Take the money because we can use it to pay for the children's schooling. But he said. 'I'm not going to take that money. Later when I'm dead you can organise it.'

In the end, nothing was done, and Mama Yulianti never tried to get those savings.

The troubles of Mama Yulianti's family in relation to the Communist Party did not stop with Bapak Meno losing his position as teacher, but included the insults they had to endure as a 'communist family'.

> The children, their family name was no longer Meno, or whatever else it could be, they were just 'communist'... Well, so be it. I myself don't even understand what the Communist Party is. I am speaking with tears pouring from my eyes... we were so abused! These children, 'communist kids', 'kids of communist trash'... No matter where they applied for work, they were refused.

Even at school, the teachers would often insult the children with these names.

So it was that the victims who should have received support and encouragement from others, on the contrary felt alone and undefended by anyone at all, even by their pastors.

> No one defended us. If a pastor defended us, then he would be branded as communist.

All they could do was pray to God and keep faith that God is just and that God's kingdom will come. Apart from that, to support everyday costs, Mama Yulianti often cleaned other people's gardens, took in the neighbours' laundry, babysat the neighbours' children, and even bought fish in the market, dried it, and sold dried fish. Mama Yulianti worked like this until the death of her husband, just to find money to pay for the children's schooling, and to raise them. The worst suffering was when her husband, Bapak Kristofel Meno, died in 2007 leaving her with ten children. With moist eyes and a quivering voice, Mama Yulianti recounted:

> When my husband died, he left me with all these children, it truly made me suffer. Even when he was still alive, I worked as hard as I could with every one of my ten fingers... When I think back on it, it makes me very sad.

Victims from various places were brought to these barracks, detained here and tortured. – Archives JPIT

Now, after about twenty years of suffering as the wife of a man accused of being a member of the Communist Party, Mama Yulianti has a smile on her face to see three of her children now in settled jobs, and able to send her money periodically to pay for electricity, water, and to help her in her old age. Sometimes Mama Yulianti gets the urge to sort out the pension savings her husband left. But when she imagines the injustice of the way he was treated, and the intricacies of the bureaucracy, she decides it is better just to get by with what she has.

### *Mama Melda's story*[24]

Mama Melda's name came to the attention of the research team when there was a focused discussion session held at the Pniel church at Noekmuke, at Amanuban, to identity possible informants. Mama Melda was known as the

---

24  Mama Melda, interview on 17 November 2010 at the village of Linamnutu, Amanuban Selatan.

wife of one of the Communist Party figures from the village of Naip, namely the late Teofilus Kiubani.[25] According to the Naip village head:

> Teofilus Kiubani had a wife who now lives in Linamnutu, called Melda Sarkin. She is married to Efraim Tuflaka, who is also from Naip.

This information was the start of our search to find where she lived. We found her at Linamnutu, in the precinct of Oenoah, hamlet C, the village of Linamnutu, in the subdistrict of South Amanuban.

Mama Melda lives with her three grandchildren in a simple house with a palm-leaf roof, about two metres high. Her three grandchildren are the children of the son she had with Efraim Tuflaka.

Mama Melda's smiling face makes her look younger than her years. She still has a good physique and sometimes helps her son with the garden of hundreds of chilli plants. Mama Melda cannot remember the date of her birth: she just remembers that she was born during the Japanese occupation in Timor [1942–1945, Trs.].

> I was still very small when the Japanese were here. When we saw them, we would run away.

These days, she celebrates her birthday on 31 December as that is the date entered on her official government identity card.

Melda was born as one of four children, three girls and one boy. She is illiterate. When she was small, she did once go to a school in Oepliki but did not pass. This was after the Japanese had gone. One thing she remembers vividly is that when children did not study, they were made to eat chicken manure. That is why she and some of her friends stopped school. Something she remembers about the Japanese time is that the Japanese stole their pigs. With her limited education, Mama Melda lived her life in the village of Naip until the communist-related mass arrests and massacres occurred.

When she talked about the start of the arrests and mass killings, Mama Melda recalled that before this, there was large-scale famine in their area.

> There was hunger everywhere. It was incredible. Even the police were just eating *putak*.

She remembers there was very little rain.

---

25  Mama Melda lived with Teofilus Kiubani although they were never officially married. She later married Efraim Tuflaka after Teofilus disappeared, but according to Mama Melda herself, and to others, both men were regarded as Mama Melda's husbands.

Melda's parents, to support the family, went out with the children and relatives to look for *putak* and wild cassava, to treat it and make it edible. Once her mother wove some cloth and traded it for some corn. The famine continued until the 1965 incident happened.

Mama Melda had been with Teofilus Kiubani before the arrests and mass murders, but as she said:

> Teofilus lived the wrong kind of life, so I was not serious with him.

In the end, even though they were not officially married, the 30th September Movement separated them. According to Mama Melda, her parents compared their union to 'the brief meeting when you are out getting water at the well, and looking for firewood'. That is how she describes her union, even though they were blessed with a son, Frits Nomleni.

As if suffering was not enough because of her husband's involvement at the time as local head of the Indonesian Farmers' Front (BTI) for South Amanuban, Mama Melda herself had to go to court to answer the accusation that she was a member of Gerwani.

> I was taken all the way to SoE because I was accused of being a member of Gerwani. We had to go to court, but I didn't know what was going on.

She did acknowledge that indeed her partner, Teofilus Kiubani was head of the BTI.

> Yes… he did that kind of work… I think he was head of BTI.

Mama Melda did not know exactly what Pak Teofilus's activities were outside the house as far as BTI was concerned because she never went with him on BTI activities. But she did know that they travelled very far – as far as the village of Kusi, to list Communist Party people.[26] Pak Teofilus would not talk much about his activities. According to Mama Melda:

> He never talked to me about it, he just said he wanted to write down names [wanted to find] members for Gerwani and other BTI leaders in other villages.

It is interesting that Mama Melda notes the kind of person her husband was recruiting. According to her, most of the names listed as members were people with good education, so they became BTI and Gerwani leaders:

---

26  Many people in South Central Timor equate the Farmers' Front, BTI, with the Communist Party, PKI, even when they clearly mean BTI.

They would write down the names of men who had gone to school and women who had gone to school, to be leaders.

That was her everyday life with Teofilus Kiubani, and everything in her life was going smoothly until he was arrested.

Changing her tone, now Mama Melda recollected Teofilus's arrest, and how it all began with her own arrest, as his partner, by an official from the People's Youth Organisation from Naip.[27] Mama Melda was made to join the group of people going to Oe'usapi (in the sub-district of Takari) to arrest Teofilus. The official who went to capture him was fully armed, and from a distance she witnessed how the sound of gunfire was part of the arrest of her husband:

> We were told to sit like this, then the official went and arrested them in the kampung. It was about that far away [she indicates about 500 metres away]. All we could hear was gunfire.

At the time of this arrest, she was together with Mama Sipora, the wife of another person from South Amanuban who had been accused of being a Communist Party figure.[28] After their husbands were arrested, Mama Melda was taken back to Noemuke, then to Basmuti where her husband and Mama Sipora's husband had been taken. When they arrived at Basmuti, Mama Sipora complained to the officer because she was exhausted, having been taken from Oe'usapi to Oe'mofa to Bena, to Noemuke and then Basmuti. She said:

> Who has done something so bad that you have to force us to go so far without any rest? I want to go home. I will see you later in SoE.

When she spoke about the time her husband was arrested, initially Mama Melda seemed evasive, and even acted as though she was not sad about it at the time. But as she talked, it turned out that she was afraid that if she cried she would be accused of defending communists and would be tortured,

> Eh, I am not crying; I don't want to cry. I will be tortured.

---

27 The research team believes that this group, which she calls Organisasi Pemuda Rakyat (OPR) is not the same as the Communist Party's youth group, called Pemuda Rakyat.

28 The research team tried to find the whereabouts of Mama Sipora, and did manage to meet her. However, she refused to give any information. She answered all questions by saying she did not know, including her own name and date of birth. This is probably because of deep trauma, because until today there are many people or families of people who were accused of being communist and who were arrested, even murdered, who still blame Mama Sipora's husband, namely the late Yan Fandu.

Back to her story. Mama Melda then went with her friend to SoE. But when they arrived there they could not meet their husbands. They had to wait a whole week in SoE, and only then did their husbands come out with guards in attendance, their bodies full of torture marks, which Mema Melda found difficult to describe. All she could say was:

> They had been tortured. They had been tortured beyond belief. Their arms and bodies were crushed, and their bodies were black and blue.

Mama Melda talked about this while showing the way they had been tortured inhumanely and had their hair cut off. They were still being beaten right in front of her eyes:

> We saw it with our own eyes. It wasn't that we heard it from someone else.

Even faced with this, they dared not cry for fear of being accused of defending communists, and then punished. Their husbands were held for about two months at the barracks, and Mama Melda and her friend were also called for interrogation, until on the last day, the officer ordered them not to come back to see their husbands again.

> He said, go back home and don't come back, just forget them because we are going to deal with them here.

And from that very day, their husbands did not return home. They have no idea of their whereabouts.

When we asked about involvement in various Communist Party organisations, Mama Melda was familiar with BTI and Gerwani, but she said she had never been a member of any organisation. She only knew about the Communist Party after the 30th September Movement that led to the arrest of people, including her husband, and the information circulated that they were Communist Party members. When she remembers her husband being accused as though they were all a band of thieves, she cannot believe her husband was like this. And proof was that her husband never brought home any farm produce for the family to eat.

> I just don't believe it… how could you go and steal from someone and not be afraid?… And anyway, he ever brought home any food. Well, who knows, maybe they ate it all on the way.

After her de facto husband died, not many people treated her discriminatively; but there were a few who would sneer at her as the wife of a communist figure, because they accused her husband of being the cause of all the problems. About this, Mama said:

> Well, that's their problem; I don't know anything about it.

But that did not last for long. A few years later, Mama Melda married and left the village of Naib to live where she is now, in the village of Linamnutu.

## *Mama Yane's story*[29]

Mama Yane Netomela was born on 14 April 1942 in the village of Babuin, in the sub-district of Kolbano in Amanuban, South Central Timor. She was born into a family that could only just make ends meet, as her father was a farmer. Back in those times she had not yet converted to Christianity, and she had never attended school, so was illiterate. There was one GMIT primary school in her village, but many people did not go to school. In 1961, she married the late Bapak Yosua Netomela.

Between 1960 and 1970, there were harvest failures, which caused economic difficulty, especially the period 1964–66 when there was famine. As she explained:

> Back then no one was selling rice or corn. We only had *putak* and mangoes to eat. It was a very hard time.

Mama Yane's husband, Yosua Netomela, was a primary school teacher, teaching at the GMIT primary school in Babuin. Because he was a teacher, and therefore could of course read and write, the *usif* (local king) in Babuin asked him to write down the names of people who were members of the Farmers' Front (BTI).[30] According to Mama Yane, a communist figure in Babuin called Yusak Bei encouraged the people to join the BTI with the promise that whoever joined would be free from paying tax. Apart from that, they would get free rice, corn and cooking oil. As a consequence many people in Babuin village were attracted to become members of the Communist Party.

Because Mama Yane's husband, Bapak Netomela, had been given the job of listing the names, he himself was said to be involved with the Communist Party. So in 1965, soldiers arrested him, with no warrant. He was taken to

---

29  Interview with Mama Yane Netomela, on 22 November 2010 at SoE.
30  The *usif* was murdered in 1965 because he was considered to be 'involved' with the Communist Party.

the police station in Niki-Niki, and then brought to the police station in SoE for interrogation. While he and some other people from Babuin were being interrogated, they were beaten and had their teeth and fingernails pulled out. They were ordered to do hard labour at the police station, like digging and turning the soil in the courtyard, cleaning the toilets (using only their hands) and laying stones on the road entering the police station, which was then still unpaved. For some unclear reason, Mama Yane's husband was released after three months in detention at the SoE police station. She said that the others were not released. A prominent communist figure from Baduin, Pak Yusak Bei, was taken away and it is believed then murdered.

In 1966, after his release from prison, Bapak Netomela was fired from his position as teacher because it was said he had communist involvement. He was required to report regularly to the police station in Niki-Niki for six months. In order to report, he had to walk from his village of Babuin to Niki-Niki, a distance of 32 kilometers, every day. But then in 1973, the SoE branch office of the Department of Education and Culture called him to work again. He was not permitted to teach but instead he could work as staff in the office. However, in the 1980s he was fired once again, along with six other colleagues, because of a regulation direct from the main office.

According to Mama Yane, when her husband was fired, their life was extremely difficult. She said, with tears in her eyes:

> When Bapak stopped work we were sad. We made a garden and planted betel nut, betel leaves and coconut to sell. We opened a roadside stall. Our only child, Jemi, had to leave university in Kupang because we could not afford the fees.

The people around them did not make much fuss about Bapak Netomela's communist involvement. For instance, they still addressed him with the respectful term 'Teacher', even though he had been fired. The church, however, stood him down from his position as elder, without any prior discussion. Mama Yane still feels the impact to this day, namely she feels deeply hurt by the attitude of the government and the church. She feels she was unfairly treated. The effect was on her family, for her husband's loss of his job caused such financial difficulty that their child had to leave university.

Mama Yane hopes that no such event will ever happen again, and she has some points to make. The government must be fair and honest with the people; when there are problems, they should be studied properly. The church should not just go along with the government, because the church should be an institution that protects and stands by its members who are in trouble. It should not ostracise and hate its members. No matter what the situation, the church must be able to give its voice of prophecy.

### *Mama Bendalina Puai's story*[31]

Mama Bendalina Puai was born in Boti and is now around 70 years old. She lives in Latan in the village of Babuin, an isolated place that borders the village of Boti. Her husband is called Obed Nakamnanu. Before he converted to Christianity, his name was Noe Sae.[32] Mama Bendalina Puai's parents were already Christian. Mama Puai had eleven children, of whom seven survived. She and her husband suffered terribly during the drought and famine of 1964. They survived on *putak*, wild cassava and wild peanuts (*arbila*). Two children born during this period, Pitronela Sae, born in 1963 and Matheos Sae born in 1965, were malnourished.

In the middle of this food shortage, the 30th September Movement happened, and Bapak Obed Nakamnanu, Mama Puai's husband, was declared to be a communist. His name had been listed, without his knowledge, and so he was taken away and detained in Niki-Niki for two years, and released in 1968.

While her husband was in detention, Mama Bandalina tried to earn money to support her children. She spun thread to sell, and wove blankets and sarongs, then took them to the Oinlasi market. She used whatever she earned to buy food for the children and for her husband in detention. She also kept animals, and sold them to buy food.

Mama Bendalina suffered greatly along with her children, not only because her husband was in prison for two years, but because of hunger. However, she remained resolute and kept her faith that God would help her. At that time, both the government and the church ignored her, because as her husband had been declared communist, she was considered to have wronged.

\* \* \*

---

31   Mama Bendalina Puai, interview on 21 February 2011 at Boti village, sub-district of Kie.
32   Noe Sae is his real original name.

## Connections between the Revival Movement and the 1965 events

In the middle of the food shortage, famine, and the Revival Movement, the 1965 incident occurred, which had a huge impact on life in South Central Timor, including on Christianity and customary communities. Studying this helps us to understand the stories presented above from some women who were victims of the 1965 incident.

During the 1965 incident, the church found it difficult to protect its members and others. One example in South Central Timor is the Imanuel Congregation worship hall in the village of Kombaki, subdsitrict of Polen, which was used as one of the places of torture. – Archives JPIT

According to Pastor Topan, the prayer teams that began forming in SoE around this time were the result of the spiritual revival and had no connection to the trauma of the killings related to 1965.

> Those who bore witness were not the children of parents who had been killed in 1965–66... there was no connection to the Communist Party.[33]

---

33  Interview with Pastor Topan.

But some informants considered the 30th September Movement a test of faith from God.

Some Revival Movement activists thought the 1965 incident was God's punishment on those who had not worshipped him. They used the Bible as their justification for the violence going on. For instance, Pak Dian Asnat connected the 1965 incident to God's curse against the Egyptians that the Pharaoh would let the people of Israel go (Exodus 11). According to Pak Asnat, the first people to be arrested in South Central Timor were the communist leaders, as though they were like the firstborn of the Egyptians who were considered to be so evil that their firstborn had to be killed.[34] The killing of the firstborn was God's way of making the pharaoh (the Communist Party) 'repent' and free the Israelites from their captivity in Egypt (captivity of communist ideology). Those who were tempted by communist teaching also had to 'repent', using the threat of death. This was basically the logic behind Pak Dian's biblical interpretation.

Another view, similar in the sense that the killing seemed to be vindicated by the rise in church membership, is found in a document by a GMIT pastor about the history of one of the congregations in South Central Timor. The pastor connects the 30th September movement to the conversion of customary communities to Christianity in this way:

> Before 1965, the biggest thing the congregation councils had to wrestle with was how to win souls. How could the people who still followed traditional religions repent and become believers? God answered the prayers of the believers in His own way. When the 30th September Movement happened, here and there the authorities did carry out some killings of those involved. By witnessing these killings, the followers of the traditional religions, without having to think long and hard, immediately escaped into the church. A common understanding arose among them: those who followed traditional beliefs were the same as those who followed communism. This is why they wanted to become Christian, so they would find protection and escape the danger of being killed. The year 1965 can be described as the year when, without exception, the people from the surroundings all wanted to repent and embrace Christianity. The subsequent development and growth of

---

34  Pak Dian Asnat, interview. Pak Asnat had been very active in the prayer groups from the beginning in September 1965.

One of the execution sites in Kolbebe, village of Bena, subdistrict of South Amanuban.
– JPIT archives

congregations after 1965 happened in a natural way, namely through birth and marriage.[35]

Because of their fear of being killed, many of the indigenous peoples of Central South Timor gradually began to embrace Protestant Christianity. This can be seen in a letter from Pastor Daniel that Middelkoop quotes in his book *Atoni Pah Meto*:

> God is strengthening those bearing witness with miraculous healing, as happened at the time of the apostles: they are also receiving power to cast out devils. This is a huge miracle that one cannot rationally understand, but this is the reality we are experiencing here now; the communists are repenting and seeking God.[36]

---

35  *Sejarah Gereja Jemaat Wilayah Netpala* (1997, unpublished)
36  Middelkoop, *Atoni Pah Meto*: 225

In his book, Middelkoop comments as follows:

> ...in Timor many people who had joined the Communist Party are now turning away from it, and in their fear they are open to receiving the Gospel.[37]

He also writes:

> The spreading of the Bible by church members and the people is a kind of channeling, and this is happening more and more. Whether this is happening because it is driven by the Holy Spirit, or by our suffering, basically, it is happening. Many people are repenting, even though undoubtedly many are confused and uncertain.[38]

Frank Cooley, the author of *Benih Yang Tumbuh* (The Growing Seed) also thinks that the Revival Movement is inseparable from the atmosphere of terror at the time:

> Those who know about the events that followed the failure of the 30th September Movement do not deny that... in the end, the equation of those people who had no connection to or membership of one of the recognised religions (Islam, Christianity or Hinduism, Buddhism) with atheists (people with no belief in God), meaning communist – that all this was a very strong motivation for thousands and even tens of thousands of people to enter the church or to renew their membership with the church... It is this situation, much more than the Revival Movement, that caused the enormous growth in the Timorese church, if indeed this occurred, between 1965 and 1969.[39]

Cooley wants to stress that these three events are interconnected. The way we see it, anyone who understands these facts cannot deny that these three major events, namely famine, the 1965 incident, and the spiritual revival are connected. The famine and 1965 incident made many people, especially women who most experienced the pressure, need God, who they thought could fulfill their spiritual needs. When facing a prolonged crisis,

---

37  Ibid.
38  Ibid p. 228.
39  Frank L. Cooley, *Benih Yang Tumbuh XI*, p.203. Also see further part II of this book, on the circles and atmosphere of the Revival Movement in Timor, p.200–205. [The quote here is the translator's translation of the Indonesian text as the published English translation (*The Growing Seed*) was unavailable. Trs]

the women of South Central Timor longed for a direct experience of God, which they found through their involvement in the Revival Movement.

## Forced conversions

In the 1965 incident in South Central Timor, we find two different aspects. On the one hand, there were those people who were attracted by the enthusiasm of the Revival Movement. But on the other hand, there were some who felt forced to convert to certain religions in order to escape punishment. After the September 30th Movement, people commonly thought that customary communities that had not converted to one of the official religions were communist and therefore atheist. So both families and individuals chose to convert to Christianity, as one of the officially recognised religions.[40]

According to Pastor B. Topan, in Mollo at this time many people had already converted to Christianity because of Ds. P. Middelkoop's presence there since 1922. Bible teachers had baptised their students, and only old people remained unconverted. Christianity was already well established, so that many people chose to convert without coercion. They were willing to leave behind their sacred stones (*fatu kanaf*) and trees (*hau kanaf*) to become Christian.[41]

In the mid-1960s, the Spiritual Revival teams continued their drive to convert the people of Central South Timor, but there was an element of coercion, namely all the sacred items considered linked to paganism were destroyed. For instance, the teams destroyed woven cloth because it had the

---

40 In the field, people do associate the requirement to have one of the 'official religions' with the 1965 incident. However, actually the government regulation about official religions was issued only in 1978 as the Circular from the Minister of Internal Affairs, in relation to completing the information on identity cards: 'There was no official government decision about the implementation of official religions other than the Circular from the Minister of Internal Affairs No. 477/74054/1978 about guidelines for completing the column stating religion on identity cards, which, among other things, stipulated that the religions recognised by the government are: Islam, Protestant Christianity; Catholicism, Hinduism, and Buddhism...' quoted [and translated, Trs.] from Moh, Mahfud MD, 'Kebebasan Beragama dalam Perspektif Konstitusi'. 2, footnote 3, http://law.uii.ac.id/dokumentasi/task,doc_download/gid,62/ accessed 22 October 2011.
41 In Timorese custom, the *fatu kanaf* and *hau kanaf* explain the origins of a clan and also its relationship with its ancestors. The ancestors are considered to live in the world of the ancestors, *pah nitu*, which is also called *hau bian* and *fatu bian* (behind wood and behind stone). Christian evangelists considered worship at the *fatu kanaf* and *hau kanaf* as idolatrous, and something to be wiped out.

dragon motif, which they considered sinful.⁴² So too with their 'medicines', meaning magic charms.

The people of Boti practice their tribal religion and believe that the *Uis Neno* is in the form of the *usif* (king), so they pay great respect to and obey their *usif*. In October 1967, during a funeral ceremony, a soldier called Pello (wearing his green uniform) came to Boti, gathered all the adult males in the square (in front of the village head's office) including the king, Nune Benu, and demanded that they agree to convert to Christianity.⁴³ Because they would not agree, they were whipped, had their hair cut, and were left out all day in the hot sun until sunset.⁴⁴

Mama Sance Nelo recounted that when this soldier called Pello came to Boti, he whipped her husband with a rattan whip edged with brass. The soldier was wearing a pistol and was in full uniform. Her husband was beaten and tortured for a full day. Eventually, she and her husband decided to convert to Christianity. The same thing happened to Mama Anita Besi who said that when the soldier called Pello came, she and her husband, and all men in the kampung who had not officially converted to 'official' religions were treated as just described. She and her children had to watch her husband being beaten and having his long hair cut off. She also saw how the king was repeatedly kicked and had his hair cut. The king made an oath:

> Let the God above and the God on earth witness all this, because I have done no wrong.

In the end, Mama Anita and her husband decided to convert to Christianity because they were afraid the king would be killed. She said,

> It was better that we became Christian so the soldiers would leave the king alone.⁴⁵

For a few years after this happened, whenever someone from outside came to Boti, all the adult men who had not converted to Christianity ran into

---

42  There is a legend that the island of Timor was formed from the body of a crocodile, and this is why its shaped is like a crocodile. The indigenous people of Timor, particularly the Meto people in Central South Timor, believe that the crocodile (*besimnasi*) is the chief of the water (*Uis Oe*) while the python snake is the chief of the land. They both are considered to be transformations of the master of the world (*Uis Pah*).
43  Nune Benu is the king's real name.
44  Traditionally, Boti men wore their long hair in a bun on top of their heads. They believed that their strength was in their hair, so cutting their hair was a severe blow and insult to their culture.
45  Mama Sance Nelo, interview and Mama Anita, interview.

the forest to hide. In 1969 another soldier arrived and looked for the king, but he had escaped. Some people were captured and threatened with death, including Miu Besi, Mama Anita's husband. According to Mama Anita, he was prepared to become Christian.

> [Because he agreed] he was told to go back home, while the others were all whipped, beaten, and tortured.[46]

They were beaten in an open square in the middle of the kampung.

The violence connected to the 1965 incident encouraged the people of South Central Timor to discard their customary identity and accept a new identity as Christians. This change of their essential identity happened at a time full of tension, so it is not clear whether their decisions were made of their own free will. Even so, one cannot deny that the women in customary societies saw their baptism as something extremely positive. At the outset, they converted to protect their king, but gradually they found there were benefits for their children because they had the opportunity to go to school and get good jobs. The women who converted to Christianity felt there was something new in Christianity. As Mama Anita said:

> My life became clearer.[47]

But on the other hand, they had to pay dearly for their conversion, because their relations with the customary communities weakened. Those who had converted chose to move their houses far from their former location in the Boti kampung. They were no longer involved in customary ceremonies and activities, particularly in rites. Families who had converted to Christianity were considered to have severed relations with customary communities. There were some cases of the king sending emissaries with silver and *muti* or bead necklaces to entice people to return to the customary circle they had left, but these enticements were rejected.[48]

The gulf between Christianity and customary beliefs and practices can be seen in Mama Anita's story. After converting to Christianity, Mama Anita had a dream that a man with white skin wearing a white robe came and changed her sarong for a white cloth. She saw this as a sign that she had been called by Christ to leave her customary circle behind, and become Christian. This is why she had to distance herself from customary practices so she could cast aside her identity as a member of that community.

---

46   Mama Anita, interview.
47   Ibid.
48   Mama Sance Nelo, interview.

In the midst of the violence inflicted on the Boti people who refused to convert, the church exhibited a kind of arrogance because suddenly it had power over so many people who had not previously been attracted to Christianity. The Church sidled up to the New Order regime, because it benefited from the regime's policies. One can see the increase in church membership as something positive if one sees religion only from the point of view of membership numbers. However, it can also be seen as something negative, because people used religion as an escape or merely as a temporary place of protection. People became religious not because of faith and conviction, but only to be free of the overpowering disaster. Once things were safe again, a number of them returned to their former lives, including their tribal religion.

All these things occurring simultaneously; the violence surrounding the 1965 incident, the famine, and Christian conversions in South Central Timor together combined to impact on women. There were many psychological, economic and social burdens that some women felt keenly. They faced interrogation by the police and the army even though they knew nothing at all about the activities of the Communist Party. The stories of some of the women victims help us to understand what happened and how they were able to survive while facing that wave of savagery.

## The women of South Central Timor face their challenges

The stories presented above demonstrate the reality of the women's struggle in the face of these events, as they fought for their families' survival. Their ability to survive gives us an opportunity to better understand the women of South Central Timor, but to do so we need analytical study that shows the causes and effects of each separate event, the relationship between them, and the effect of that.

### *From guardian of the family food storehouse to supplier*

There are two versions of the causes of the famine in South Central Timor around mid-1965. The first version attributes the famine to natural causes because of the long drought that resulted in a failed harvest. The second version attributes the famine to the bad political and economic situation that led to limited food distribution. Most likely it was both, with the result that there was severe shortage of all food supplies, affecting the entire population of South Central Timor, regardless of socio-economic status.

While the famine caused severe suffering in general, it was the women who bore the brunt of it, because in South Central Timor society, it is the women who are entrusted with the role of guardians of the family food storehouse. Women are the ones most responsible for the preparation of food for the family. When the family food storehouse was empty, it was the women who most suffered the psychological pressure of this. They had to find food alternatives, like wild cassava and *putak* to replace corn and rice, but the preparation was laborious. There could also be nutritional problems with the children. But the women were creative in finding ways to keep their children healthy.

When women also had to cope with the deaths of their husbands (as, for instance, Mama Yulianti and Mama Melda), or when their husbands ran to the forest to hide (as happened to the women in Boti), then the severe food shortage was even harder to cope with. The women now had a double work load – at home doing the domestic duties of cooking, cleaning and looking after the children, and travelling far from their own kampungs looking for food to bring home. Going far from one's home was very risky; the women were already traumatised, and the situation was full of terror. One can only say that their determination in going out at night wandering from one kampung to another showed extraordinary courage. Women also helped to find other sources of income by spinning, weaving, and doing wickerwork, to make things that could be traded for food.

Some informants said that one of the reasons they had to go so far searching for food was because when their neighbours had food, they would not share it. On the one hand, the women's wandering to more distant places meant they made new connections and relationships, but on the other, the situation led to the destruction of socio-economic relations. In South Central Timor at this time, people preferred to barter than to use money. But when one person wanted to barter while the other refused, then both social relations and the economic system began to crumble.

The famine also had an effect on the way the women saw themselves as mothers. The women of South Central Timor consider neglect of one's children equivalent to murder. But the extreme challenges the women faced in finding alternative food, and taking on a double role, were severe burdens. They had no time to rest and were forced to risk many things. The situation created by the 1965 incident made the traditional role of women as guardians of the food storehouse now change to become that of the suppliers of the food storehouse. This was done for the sake of their children, so they would not 'kill' them with hunger through neglect. As Mama Sance Nelo put it:

> I watched over our children carefully so I would not kill a single one.

## The women of South Central Timor and the impacts of the 1965 Incident

The long period of violence worsened the economy, already fragile due to the famine. The 1965 victims who lost their jobs, incomes, and faced severe shortages of basic necessities ended up in poverty. This happened all over the sub-district of South Central Timor, and struck people in the towns as well as the villages. They either could not send their children to school, or their children quit school. Job losses had a severe impact on the family economy. Mama Yulianto Meno was used to her husband receiving a salary and quota of rice, then suddenly she was forced to completely change her life to support the family. Mama Yulianto took in laundry and sold fish just 'to keep the kitchen fire burning.'

Mutual suspicion also affected social life, particularly during the New Order regime. The village head of Naib said that in every village office the list of names of 'communists' was still on file. Indirectly, this led to discrimination of those people as being of lower social standing, and shaped the public opinion that these people were the cause of a huge problem and were dangers to society.

The 1965 incident, which happened right at the time the women of South Central Timor had to cope with famine, also brought a new layer of threat. Although the women never directly discussed the psychological effects when they were interviewed, it was clear that that they tended to be closed to people from outside their kampung, and to be suspicious of others. This was evident at a meeting organised for this research project in March 2011, attended by two former victims from each of the research areas. Some of the women, including those from South Central Timor, preferred not to speak about their experiences.

Psychologically, the 1965 incident has left its own particular impression. For instance, Mama Neltjis's traumatic experience of losing her job as a civil servant of which she was so proud, led her to reject the government and to discourage her children from working for the government. This was her own way of declaring her innocence.

On the other hand, when wives like Mama Melda, were forced to go along with their husbands, or when they visited their husbands in prison, they went out of a domestic world that traditionally was relatively closed and began to see a wider world, albeit full of pain and terror. This experience gave them courage as single parents, to go beyond their kampung in search of food.

## Women of South Central Timor and the Revival Movement

The problems the women of South Central Timor faced at this time were extremely complex. The period 1963–64, was a time of economic pressure, followed by the political pressures of 1965. In this climate, the Revival Movement reached a climax on 26 September 1965, just four days before the 30<sup>th</sup> September movement erupted in Jakarta. It was as though the Revival Movement gave many people in South Central Sulawesi a language and new way of dealing with huge, complex problems.

The Revival Movement was seen as a form of help. Some people thought that it helped to save many customary communities, because prior to the 1965 incident, evangelists were already entering these areas and establishing prayer groups, so when the army began moving in, many people could not be branded as atheist.[49] The movement also strengthened their faith and helped them endure both the trauma of violence and terror and the huge problems as a result of famine.

As the theologian Eka Darma Putera puts it:

> God is not only for people to believe in, but also for people to experience. God is not the symbol of power and controlling man's power, but rather the power within man, namely man himself, created by God and often called a conscience that influences all human thought, feeling and action, including influencing people, guiding them to the need for 'The Other', namely God.[50]

The Revival Movement which emerged in SoE answered that need. Through the prayer groups, the women of South Central Timor experienced meeting God. Through this, they hoped that the problems they were facing would soon be solved. They also hoped that things would get better.

The involvement of women in South Central Timor in politics at that time was non-existent, however, in the spiritual arena they were extremely dominant. Their involvement in the spiritual revival took them outside their homes and into a wider social world. But why were they not more active in politics? According to Pak Dian this was because:

---

49  Ibid, and interview with Mama Riat at Desa Supul, Amanuban Tengah on 12 October 2011.
50  Eka Darmaputera, 'Religiositas Meningkat, Tapi ke Mana?' *Penuntun: Jurnal Teologi dan Gereja* 2:5 (October-December 1995; Sinode GKI Jawa Barat), p. 23.

> (w)hen the women participated in prayer groups, they did not need any formal education. However, for politics and other work, formal education was required.[51]

Aside from that, the women were also looking for something that could help them overcome the crisis they were facing. When they prayed, gave sermons, or carried out miracles, even travelling overseas, they experienced a meeting with God. Opportunity fostered their talents, and receiving praise increased their self-esteem in the midst of a patriarchal culture that placed them as second-class citizens. Pak Middelkoop used the term 'awareness of women's emancipation':

> In Kupang where this new movement began, there is the daughter of one of the theologically trained congregational lay teachers called Johanna Taruwalu, and in SoE there is also the daughter of a church minister called Hennie Tunliu. This reveals the trend towards awareness of women's emancipation, which is made manifest by the Spirit.[52]

## *Imago Dei* – the Image of God

Through our experiences with women victims of 1965 in South Central Timor, we discovered that in the midst of the bloody tragedy when human lives were not valued, the women fought to maintain life and give new hope. This struggle is depicted in the change from their roles as keepers to suppliers of the food store houses. It is seen in the change from their roles as managers of domestic problems to leaders of the Revival Movement in the public domain, and also when they were willing to give up their cultural identity to convert to Christianity to safeguard the lives and futures of their children. Their courage can inspire and motivate all women, especially those struggling in the midst of many crises, to know that women have the power and courage to overcome many odds.

---

51  Pak Dian Asnat, interview.
52  Middelkoop, [Atoni] p.231. These are the women's real names.

## *Alor*

Tanjung Sembilan, sub-district of Teluk Mutiara (in 1965 the sub district name was Alor Barat Laut, or North West Alor): Execution site.

*Tanjung Sembilan is located around one kilometre to the west of the centre of the town of Kalabahi. Its name reflects the shape of the Cape – tanjung is cape, and sembilan is nine – for the Cape is shaped like the number nine. Here, nine men were killed in the jungle late one night in March 1966. A hole was dug and after the men were executed, the bodies were thrown into the hole, and the hole covered up. All signs of the execution at Tanjung Sembilan disappeared. Today, people are living at this location, but the forest is still there.*

**Statement from one of the Alor research team members**

*Chapter 5*

# Widows Fight Against Injustice in Alor

**Dorkas Sir, Erna Hinadang, and Ina Tiluata**

Throughout history the fight of widows against injustice is an important issue. While activists add their voices to the struggle for human rights, reality shows that at the same time all kinds of injustice and violence that consume so many people and material things are flourishing. Almost every day one hears, sees and perhaps even experiences various kinds of injustice. Injustice happens in every corner of the world, both individually and integrated into social, cultural, economic and political affairs, large scale and small. Many of the victims of injustice and violence are women and children.

In this report, we, the research team for Alor, take as our theme the fight of widows against injustice following the 1965 Affair.

Our primary informants are five widows who, with their children, were victims of the injustice and violence of 1965. They include Neto, the wife of Pak Mel Kelatanu; Fero, the wife of Temukung[1] Tera Sekalau; Karo, the wife of Temukung Kiel Talitai; Ribka, a literacy teacher and also the wife of the teacher Titus Manitapa; and Koba, the wife of the evangelist Nani Pelotata. Some other respondents we approached include: Apeles Tankalau, as a figure of customary law; Pastor Fredrik Pulinggomang as a religious figure; Pak Harun Dokana as a community figure; and Aris Tungga as a member of the police force. These people are historical witnesses and perpetrators.

In our field research, we chose locations in a few sub-districts. The sub-district of East Alor was selected because there were many victims of the 1965 Affair in this area, while the sub-district of Southwest Alor was chosen because this was known as the area where the head of the Indonesian

---

1   *Tamukung* is a local title in the local government system, with a ranking roughly equivalent to a sub-district head (*camat*).

Communist Party in Alor came from. The sub-districts of Teluk Mutiara and Kabola were at the time both part of the sub-district of South West Alor. Teluk Mutiara was the centre for political prisoners where many people turned themselves in and where there was also an execution site. Kabola was the location of some key informants.

## Alor today

The district of Alor is an autonomous district with its capital the town of Kalabahi. This island region borders the marine border of Timor-Leste. The land area of Alor is 286,464 square kilometres, covering two large islands, namely the island of Alor and the island of Pantar, along with many other small islands including Tereweng, Pura, Ternate, Buaya, Batan, Lapang, Marisa, Kumbang and Sika. The land is mountainous and hilly, with valleys, ravines, rivers, sea and fertile fields. Administratively, the district is subdivided into 17 sub-districts with 158 villages and 17 *kelurahan* (larger village cluster).

Today, the people of Alor embrace the officially sanctioned religions. According to the 2008 data from the Alor district office of the Department of Religion, religious adherence in Alor is as follows[2]:

Protestant – 134,039 (74.27%)
Moslem – 40,437 (22.4 %)
Catholic – 5,882 (3.26%)
Hindu/Buddhist – 129 (0.07%)
Total – 180,487

Florens Maxi Un Bria in his *Introduction to the Wonders of the Canary Island* summarises as follows:

The district of Alor is made up of dozens of ethnicities and languages. Hidayah Zulyani, in Ensiklopedi Suku Bangsa Indonesia (*The Encyclopedia of the Ethnics in Indonesia*) writes that there lives a number of sub-ethnics in Alor such as Abui, Alor, Belagar, Deing Kabola, Kawel, Kemang, Kui, Lemma, Maneta, Mauta, Seboda, Wersin, and Wuwuli. ... Stokhof and Woisika (1975), *Preliminary Notes on the Alor and Pantar Languages,* mention that there are 17 local languages used by the people of Alor Regency. Those languages are: Alor, Abui,

---

2   Table 5.3.1.2. The figures for religious adherence are from *Alor dalam Angka 2009*, Badan Pusat Statistik Kabupaten Alor, Katalog BPS: 1403.5307,160

Blagar, Hamap, Kabola, Kafoa, Kamang, Kelon. Kui, Kula, Lamma, Nedebeng, Retta, Sawila, Terewang, Tewa, and Wersing.[3]

The kinship system is marked by a pattern of family relations as expressed in these words from a traditional poem in the Baranusa language of Pantar:

*Onang tou danga alang, ateng tou wurang tou, takka tou tenung tou, pekke tou hanga tou.*[4]

One heart listening to one another, one heart one breath, eating from one plate, drinking from one vessel, one embrace, one domain.

Kinship is based on connections of blood, marriage, and *bela* (customary vows). The *bela* connections are made with a ritual that is called *bela sakang*, meaning to swear on the earth and the afterlife. The two parties swear they will never harm each other, and this vow has no time limit and cannot be revoked by anyone from any generation.

## Political developments in Alor prior to the 30th September Movement Affair

In the 1960s, power in Alor was still predominantly held by elite groups in various traditional kingdoms. The central figures were the kings, and their high status was acknowledged by everyone they governed. Political developments in Alor followed the steps taken by their leaders. Apart from royalty, there were also religious and customary leaders. In this structure, the society around the leaders automatically accepted any information the leaders considered to be good.

When political parties in Alor were beginning to form, the people as a whole failed to understand their purpose. The topographical conditions of Alor, mountainous and hilly with communities separated by ravines, made the process of distributing information difficult, including political information. Political parties that came to Alor used the local leaders as their bridges to spread political information to distant villages, and this is

---

3   Florens Maxi Un Bria, *Introduction to the Wonders of the Canary Island* 2001:39–40. The same 17 language groups are listed on the map of Pantar-Alor found in *A guide to the people and languages of Nusa Tenggara* by Charles E. Grimes, Tom Therik, Barbara Dix Grimes and Max Jacob (Kupang: Artha Wacana Press, 1997), with spelling differences. According to Bria, the two Alor languages are Tereweng and Nedeang, whereas Grimes et al spell them as Terewang and Nedebang.

4   Bria 2001: 33

why the power held by traditional leaders became the focus of attention of all political parties at that time.

Indonesia's first elections held in 1955, marked the first time that some political parties entered Alor, including the Indonesian Communist Party. At that time, there were basically two large political parties that flourished in Alor, namely the Indonesian (Protestant) Christian Party (Parkindo), and the Catholic Party (Partai Katolik). Alor was predominantly Christian, so people accepted religious parties more easily. The party that was slightly more dominant was the Christian Party (Parkindo), which won the election in Alor in 1955, and the head of this party, Arka Molaka, became leader of the regional House of Representatives (DPRD).[5]

Under the leadership of Sem Talmaka the Indonesian Communist Party (PKI), developed slowly, particularly making use of the party's strategy of forming the Farmers' Front (BTI) and the Indonesian Women's Movement, Gerwani through existing social groups. Even though people considered the Communist Party to be atheist, its attention to social needs saw it grow in many places, particularly in Alor. The economic condition of the country at the time was precarious, with inflation and a harvest failure leading to a shortage of food supplies and daily necessities. In this context, with its attention to social needs through its cooperatives, the Communist Party flourished in Alor. As some of the victims of the 1965 Affair point out, food supplies were available only through the BTI cooperatives, which were well managed. Anyone listed as a member of the cooperative had the right to shop at the cooperative and to receive free aid.

According to one customary figure, the Communist Party's recruitment drive in Alor extended to far-flung kampungs, and was not carried out through the BTI cooperatives, but primarily through kinship or family relations. If someone became a member of the Communist Party the names of people related to that person were also listed as members of the Party.[6] Because of the lack of information from the mass media, the recruitment

---

5   See Pemilu Legislatif DPR 1955, Kepulauan Tenggara, Sunda Ketjil (bagian timur) http://www.pemilu.asia/?opt=1&s=44&id=15 accessed on 15 January 2013. In the 1955 elections, Nusantara Tenggara was part of Sunda Kecil (Lesser Sunda) that won eight seats in the national parliament (DPR). For the whole of Sunda Kecil (the east, which then included both Nusa Tenggara Barat and Nusa Tenggara Timur), the Catholic Party won 40% of the votes, while the Christian Party (Parkindo) won 18% and Masjumi 16%. Parkindo and Masjumi were close. We have not found data specifically for Alor/Pantar.
6   Pak Apeles, interview 19 November 2010 at Felakanai, the village of Fanating, in the subdistrict of Teluk Mutiara.

drive in Alor was still going on even after the 30 September movement and the order to arrest all members of the Communist Party.

Even though the Communist Party did not win any seats in the Regional House of Representatives (DPRD) in the 1955 elections, the Party's position was strong across the region of Nusa Tenggara Timor (NTT) as a whole. The head of the Communist Party for Nusa Tenggara was a member of the national People's Consultative Assembly (MPR). In the provincial capital, Kupang, the heads of the Department of Information, the national radio station (RRI) and the regional military command were all members of the Communist Party.[7]

The lists of names of the members of the cooperatives later became death lists. At the time they joined, these people had no idea at all that doing so would have such dreadful consequences. It can be said that the Communist Party's efforts to respond to the terrible economic conditions in Alor, meant that many people who had no understanding at all of the Communist Party, later became victims of violence and massacre.

## The arrests

In Alor Communist Party leaders and members, along with people suspected of being involved in the Communist Party movement, were arrested, tortured and some were murdered. The operation took place under the command of the central government via the district heads and the army leaders at the district level, assisted by staff in the field under the operational control of a few corporals, together with the support of the community through civil militia.[8] There were a few methods used at the time to trace those involved with the communist movement. Rumor was spread that some members of the Communist Party had the party symbol (hammer and sickle) tattooed on parts of their body like their stomach, chest, thighs and so forth. However, on inspection people suspected of being communists turned out not to have these markings. Apart from this, there was the structure of the Communist Party leadership for the Alor district, the lists of members of cooperatives and lists

---

7   See Stephen Farram, 'From "Timor Koepang" to "Timor NTT": A Political History of West Timor, 1901–1967', doctoral dissertation Charles Darwin University, 2004, http://espace.cdu.edu.au/eserv/edu:6450/Thesis_CDU_6450_Farram_S.pdf

8   The army command at kabupaten level at this time was called PUTERPRA, (Perwira Teritorial dan Perlawanan Rakyat, Officers for Territorial Affairs and People's Opposition). At the sub-district level, the army command was called Buterpra. In everyday speech, the people of Alor were more familiar with the term Buterpra, even though in fact in Kalabahi, as the district capital, the military command there was Puterpra.

of people who had received free aid. This was the data used to drag people off to the military for examination and torture, often ending in killings without any summons or arrest warrants. Bapak Apeles testified to this:

> There were no warrants for the arrests, all they did was read the names of the members of the Communist Party on a list that the military [Buterpra] had. The detainees were divided into three categories, A, B, and C. Category A were the heads or people in senior bureaucratic positions; B were ordinary bureaucrats; and C were ordinary people. Many in group A were executed, whereas those in group C had to report regularly and had to work as prisoners for periods from six months to two years.[9]

The widow Fero, whose husband Tera Sekalau was arrested, tortured, made to do forced labour and to regularly report, also testified that:

> The Buterpra [sic] called him in.[10]

The widow Koba (wife of victim Nani Pelotaka) was another witness:

> They summoned, just like that, everyone to report to Kalabahi. [The summons] was with a letter.[11]

They had to undergo serious interrogation, and were then housed in special places for further questioning.

> The political prisoners were gathered in front of the Buterpra office, in the police station yard, and in the small field where they had to line up, and then they were put into the long house.[12]

Those considered to be directly involved received the most inhumane treatment. They were left out in open fields in the hot sun, some were tied up and tortured like animals, their heads were shaved (using pieces of broken bottles), and other rough treatment. The head of the Communist Party in Alor, Pak Semi, together with his members and people suspected of being involved in the Communist Party movement, were given electric shock torture before they were killed. Pak Arka, a retired member of the police force, witnessed the process leading up to the killing of the prisoners:

---

9   Interview with Pak Apeles.
10  Interview with Mama Fero on 21 November 2010 at Felakanai, Fanating, Teluk Mutiara.
11  Mama Koba, interview on 15 November 2010, Adagai, Kamot, Northeast Alor.
12  Aris Tungga, interview 6 November 2010, Jembatan Hitam, Kalabahi.

> Their thumbs were tied together behind their backs, then they were tied together in a line with the others and the army and police took them at midnight to a pre-determined location for execution.[13]

Eventually, the authorities determined that a number of people had been directly involved with the Communist Party movement and they were disappeared or murdered. The massacre of Communist Party members was carried out in a few locations around the town of Kalabahi, and in the sub-district of Northeast Alor. Harun Dokana listed these in detail:

> The execution sites of the Communist Party members are: in Alor Kecil or Kumba Wutung 200 people; in Dulolong or Lubang up to 70 people; in Tanjung Kenarilang or Tanjung Sembilan nine people; in Air Kenari up to 45 people; and in Tombang or Bunta up to 60 people. The civil militia dug the graves, assisted by the local people. The distance of these graves from residential areas was about 300–500 metres.[14]

One Communist Party member, Pak Simon, escaped the massacre in Alor Kecil because of a mis-fired shot. He managed to run away and hide for three or four years in the jungle in the sub-district of Southwest Alor.[15] He surrendered after the situation had calmed down, then was released and required to regularly report to the authorities.

The situation was extremely painful for all family members who had no idea of the where their husbands, fathers or relatives had been killed and buried, and were even forbidden to shed any tears.

> …he came home, said nothing to the kids, told us nothing… then went out at night, we did not know where. After Bapak… never came back, I was deeply sad. I sobbed, but someone scolded me saying, 'stop crying so loud, or they'll come and get you too.' So we cried, but with closed mouths, into the pillow.[16]

In Alor the 'crushing the Communist Party' period was a dark time for the victims' families. They had no idea where their husbands, relatives and families were. The authorities took into detention by force prominent figures in the community like teachers, civil servants, and evangelists. Mama Karo

---

13  Ibid.
14  Harun Dokana, interview 3 November 2010 at Adang Buom, Teluk Mutiara.
15  Daka Lomang, interview 16 December 2010, Jembatan Hitam, Kalabahi.
16  Mama Ribka, interview 12 September 2010, Kadelang, East Kalabahi, Teluk Mutiara.

told the story of how her husband was killed at the order of his own older brother who was in the army at the time:

> Back then people were summoned, and everyone went. It was early in the morning, I think. People went to the office of the tamukung… There were crowds of people, thousands, hundreds in Kalabahi, Pura, Pantar, Kolana, all those places. Here there were four people. We did not know they had killed Bapak. Someone came to tell us. My son's uncle… Moses, an army guy, my husband Kiel's older brother – he came… he said, 'you, come here. Now you don't have your helper. Last night I ordered someone to kill Kiel. You watch it. No tears, now.' That's what he said. I said, 'It's this child in my belly, and I have been out weeding and I'm half dead.' That's what I said. But my oldest child understood what he had said, and started crying, rolling on the ground saying, 'Adu, niming koi, e niming koi' (No, my Dad, my Dad). Screaming. And the women came running to hear a child screaming. There were lots of people, but his uncle [the soldier Moses] said, 'You watch it now. There's to be no crying, do you hear me?'[17]

The execution of those people considered to have been involved in the Communist Party movement was not the end of the suffering for the families left behind. They too had to undergo intense interrogation. Some victims' family members were forced to regularly report to authorities and carry out forced labour, their heads were shaved, and they were kicked, beaten, and even raped.

## Widows experience violence

The suffering that the victims' family members had to undergo began when they were summoned with force for questioning. From then on, the widows who had to report regularly to authorities were made to leave their homes and their small children who needed their attention, and cover long distances of between 7 to 24 kilometres, to report.

> We didn't know anything. Back then I had to carry my baby Ayub who was just 20 days old. We walked all the way to the military (Buterpra) office and then six soldiers surrounded me. Bapak Ahmad asked… 'Are you involved with the Communist Party? Do you know about Gerwani?' I answered in the Kabola language, 'Aai' [I don't know].

---

17   Mama Karo, interview 17 November 2010 at Palibo'o, Kabola.

> They kicked me out... They said, 'you goat, you mad goat, get out of here!'... [I told] my other friends... when they ask you anything... make sure you answer in your local language... We were all kicked out [of the interrogation room].[18]

Mama Ribka also had to travel a long distance to report to the authorities after her husband had been killed. She even had to sail to another island.

> We were called into Kabir [on the island of Pantar], Baranusa [Pantar]. And also Kalabahi [the island of Alor]. Someone would say, on such and such a date you had to be at such and such a place... We would get there before that date, we could not be late... We would be gathered together in one place. If one person from the group was not there, the family would be called in.[19]

When she had to go and report, Mama Ribka left her children with her family, but when the authorities started asking about her children, she denied she had any, in an effort to save her children and safeguard their future.[20]

Mama Fero also talked about her experience when she had to report:

> They kept on asking me questions. I was so afraid when they took Bapak away. All I could do was cry in secret. But after that the army called me in as well. They slapped me and said, 'You know about the PKI, don't you?' I was terrified. Paralysed, the police kept on slapping and hitting me. I was absolutely terrified.[21]

When the head of the Christian Party, Arka Molaka, produced his Parkindo membership card, it helped free other members who were being interrogated:

> Back then I was the first to be questioned... I was holding my baby Ayub, like this. He asked me, 'Are you a Communist Party member? Gerwani?' And I said, 'I'm a member of the Christian party (Parkindo). Back in the elections, I pierced the symbol of the candle [Parkindo's symbol]'... Bapak Molaka, he was in the national parliament, he was head of the party. He's got the documents.' I said the name of the old man, Molaka, so they called him in. They asked him if it was true I was a member of party. The old man said yes, it was true, so they ordered him to come back at eight the next day and bring the documents. They

---

18  Ibid.
19  Mama Ribka, interview.
20  Ibid.
21  Mama Fero, interview.

In February 1966, the army killed around 200 people in Alor Kecil in this isolated forest, so that people did not know about the killings. People dug the graves in the middle of the night. – JPIT archives

told me to go home. The next day the old man went to the office, he looked for the names and showed my name there. Then the old man gave me a yellow membership card. Bapak Molaka said, 'this is your soul; watch you don't lose it.'[22]

Those who did not have this card were considered to be members of the Communist Party.

We were members of Parkindo, [but were considered to be PKI] because we didn't have a [Parkindo] membership card. Back then, you just went along. All the office workers were told to join the Communist Party, and the whole family was listed. Someone listed my name. I only knew that someone had put my name there so I was a member. So the army came and arrested me, and said they had my name and all the men who had their heads shaved were taken.[23]

---

22  Mama Karo, interview.
23  Mama Neto, interview on 21 November 2010 at Felakanai, village of Fanating, Teluk Mutiara.

During the period of interrogations, the victims were treated extremely inhumanely. They were tortured and forced to work at various places like open public squares, in ditches alongside the main roads, government offices, places of worship, and even in the houses of the officials, including church officials – working with tools like crow bars, machetes and shovels, but also working with makeshift tools.

> They ordered us to work, they ordered us to go and get sand at Buono and put it at the mosque or at their houses. If we did not put it at the mosque, we would get the sand, go together and take it to a construction site where they would collect it for building the local government office. The workers there, they would give us some of their food.

Mama Koba continued her story:

> We would do laundry, go to feed the pigs, go and gather grass… we would do all kinds of things. All of us had our hair cut short; the old, the young, everyone, shaved off. Men, women, everyone. And when we did this forced labour we had nothing to cover our heads. In the morning we would work until 12, or until 1, then go home. The next day, the same. As for food and drink, it was terrible. We would eat these seeds from the kapok tree, kapok that you use to stuff mattresses, you can fry the seeds, that's what we would eat before we worked. Afterwards we would go home. We would knock fruit off the papaya trees, then grate it and mix with a handful of rice – mix it in a pot with some sliced cassava leaves, then cook it. We would divide this between us all, 20–40 people; we never had enough to eat, you never felt full. That's what we did, for food and drink. There were so many of us. There were 30 or 40 people in one house.[24]

If any of the tools used for the forced labour went missing, the one who had lost them was yelled at, slapped or kicked. Some people got sick, but were never given enough medicine and some even died because they were sick when they were interrogated.[25] Shaving all the political prisoner's heads (men and women) was a way to give them a stamp of humiliation and also to shame them.

Some among them who had very small children took their children with them when they went to the office to report. The children were left lying

---

24  Mama Koba, interview.
25  Pak Daka, interview.

on the shop verandahs without any food and drink. They were forbidden to communicate with anyone around them or with any family member that happened to pass by. These conditions continued for around three to six months. It did not stop there. Those whose husbands had been killed were required to report in three times a week, and this continued for two to three years.

> Yes, I would take the little one with me... I would carry some cooked banana. When he was hungry, I would chew a bit and feed it to him. We had to carry sand to the government [DPR] building. We would lie the kids down outside the shop, on the shop verandah. That's where we would lie them down. We would carry the sand. The Chinese there were good, so we could leave the kids there and not worry about them; but I would worry that my child would fall over, would wander off and fall. So I would put my child there first and then go to carry the sand for the DPR office.[26]

Mama Ribka spoke of a similar experience:

> I would take my kids with me. Someone gave us space for them; if one was sick, I'd leave it with the family. No one cared whether there was food or not, whether we were sick or not. No one cared, I felt like... 'oh mother, I am so sad'. We would tell our children, 'people are calling me, I don't know when I will be back. But you be good and stay right here.'[27]

The women also had to put up with sexual harassment from the army when they went to report. Some women were raped and became pregnant like Mama Dora:

> Mmmmm, many women got that, including Mama Dora. Her husband was killed. She was raped and gave birth to a baby, but it died. She's also dead now. Many of the women were raped, but what could be done about it? We were living there, and there was one good policeman who tried to keep our spirits up... he said, 'you women, don't be afraid'. But what could we do about it? All of us were raped when we got in there, we just wanted to save ourselves. There we were, we had lost our husbands, and that's what they did to us.[28]

---

26  Mama Koba, interview.
27  Mama Ribka, interview.
28  Mama Ribka, interview.

The widows and children were struck a second time – 'after falling over, the ladder hits you', as the saying goes – because apart from losing their loved ones, they also lost their respect and self-esteem. Their families and society saw the widows and children as rubbish to be thrown away. Mama Karo spoke about a bitter experience when she returned from one of her regular reports to the authorities and found that all her household effects had been thrown on the rubbish heap:

> It was when I came home from reporting to the authorities – all my things – plates, spoons, glasses, bowls, mats, pillows – they had all been thrown in the rubbish; it was [my in-laws] the Talitai family. I knew Aston Talitai, I knew his wife. They threw all my things on the rubbish heap. Our local word for rubbish is 'labata'. They said, (in our local language) *'Ni witiang labata'* meaning, 'We chucked it all in the rubbish'.[29]

The women were susceptible to violence from all quarters, including their own families. As Mama Ribka said when we asked her about her family's reaction to her having to report to the authorities, she answered:

> The family preferred to keep a distance.[30]

Some family members distanced themselves, like Mama Ribka's family, and others perpetrated violence themselves. Mama Karo told of her husband's older brother, Moses Talitai, a soldier who was involved in the murder of her husband when her two sons, Maski and Bastion were still small. After her husband was killed, Moses treated them harshly:

> The last time you were here my son Maksi told you, right? I was just abandoned. We were half dead. The boys didn't have any clothes. They were both at school. The little one was running around, and his uncle [the soldier, Pak Moses] came and called the kids: 'Hey, tell your kids to go and carry some wood, they'll like to get some clothes.' He gave the boys some old ripped trousers. He brought them over. I patched them. They wore them to school for two or three days, and in two or three days they were all ripped again. The kids were big now. Their uncle came and said, 'Hey, tell the kids to go and fetch water from the well, because my kids want to take a bath.' It was like that. Like that. The older one, Bastion, was sitting down eating some cassava after

---

29  Mama Karo, interview.
30  Mama Ribka, interview.

school. His uncle said: 'Hey you, throw away that cassava and go and fetch water!' But my son was stubborn, he did not want to do it. He was not afraid of soldiers, he did not want to do it. This made his uncle mad and he got a belt to hit him. But Bastion grabbed the belt and threw it in the forest, and ran away.[31]

The women were detained, forced to work and were sexually abused in the army (Puterpra) office in Kalabahi, Alor. – JPIT archives

To Mama Ribka, the violence she experienced as a result of the 1965 Affair was just one link in a chain of violence that she has experienced throughout her life. When she was small, she was both witness to and victim of the domestic violence in her home, followed by arguments in her own marriage that involved physical, psychological and economic violence on the part of her husband, and then her 'non-acceptance' as a widow because she was considered to be from a 'communist family'.

> I remember my father and mother did not live well together. They always quarreled because my father had three wives. When I got married I thought my husband was a good man. He led a choir, but he

---

31  Mama Karo, interview.

turned out to be wicked. 'Bapak, why are you so cruel to me?' When I asked him that once, he did not answer. He would often leave the children and me, for ages at a time. We were married, but he never handed over his wages. So I got some corn from Rote and pounded it to feed the kids. And when I fed the baby milk, he would often kick me. I would go around begging for food, looking for wild cassava and mix it with dried coconut for the kids to eat.[32]

At the time of the 1965 violence, Mama Ribka became a victim herself. She heard about the Communist Party from a civilian militia man who asked whether her husband was involved. Mama Ribka answered, 'I don't know'. As a result of her husband's 'involvement' she herself had to suffer endlessly.

My family took everything I owned; I had to cope on my own. In what was left of the garden I planted bananas and coconut palms; I took good care of the garden. I worked to find just 500 rupiah. I tried to get money any way I could so we could eat, and once a soldier [from Pantar]…said to some other people, 'leave this woman to work at whatever she can so she can live'. He was sort of defending me. What can I say? My family chose to distance themselves, and we could not fight with others.[33] I would plant corn and rice; if there wasn't any, then I couldn't ask people, I just had to quietly get on with it. As for my children, people called them 'communist kids'; they couldn't find work. My oldest boy, Filius Manitapa, became a soldier. I let another family adopt my other child so I could find work. Eventually my children did well in life.[34]

## Widows against injustice

When the killers murdered the women's husbands, they expected the widows and children to also be destroyed. That was a kind of wish for injustice. It is undeniable that the widows and their children, were gripped by fear, anxiety, stress, shock, trauma and low self-esteem. Even so, they demonstrated their ability to oppose this injustice. They did not sink, on

---

32  Mama Ribka, interview.
33  What she means here is that the families of victims had to take extra care not to enter into any conflict with anyone, because they would be branded as communists who like making trouble.
34  Mama Ribka, interview.

the contrary they tried to rise up and they fought as hard as they could to oppose injustice in various ways.

One example is the way the women took on a double role as both mother and father; as head of the family, fulfilling the traditional male role of guaranteeing food for the family. With this double role, they fought against hunger for their children even while they were traumatised from violence. Mama Karo, Mama Koba and Mama Ribka were the backbone of their family's economy, searching for rice, corn, cassava, bananas, coconut and other food for their children. In this way they were even able to survive a time of famine and food shortage in 1965. Mama Karo looked for seeds from the kapok trees.

> I would eat the seeds to make my own milk flow to nurse the baby.[35]

Mama Ribka also talked about how she staved off hunger:

> I would go out looking for wild cassava and horse chestnuts. Almost every day I would look for cassava. Bapak had been murdered in 1965. You can't feed horse chestnut to children, but it is okay for adults. I would never go out with friends, only with my younger sister. She didn't know how to look for wild cassava. The children were old enough to be left alone at home.[36]

Taking on the double role of mother and father did not mean that the widows gave up in their difficult situation or that they suffered any less stress, but they all had a special skill they could draw upon to earn money, like weaving and farming, which they did tirelessly. They continued to be the main breadwinner for the family because they were solely responsible for the household. Women who had to work outside the home had a special burden of work, and they also contravened traditional cultural views that considered it wrong for women to work outside the home. They survived through being scrupulous at organising their time —working from dawn until late at night, whilst still having to report regularly to the authorities and prepare food for their children.[37] It is surprising, then, to hear men, or even women themselves, say that women are weak, because when you consider the duties these widows shouldered, it shows how tough and resilient they really were.

Faced with a whole swathe of problems, and with such a heavy burden, the widows continued to place their trust in God for protection and as

---

35  Ibid.
36  Mama Ribka, interview.
37  Mama Karo, interview.

their constant defender. They also took on the role of teaching the faith to their children, educating and leading them to also put their faith in God. According to Maksi Talitai, one of Mama Karo's sons:

> We never forgot to say our prayers, morning and evening. We would pray together after Mama finished her work at night, and before she started work in the morning. When we had to memorise excerpts from the Bible at Christmas time, we would have to recite in a loud voice, and Mama would stand about 25 to 50 metres away to check.[38]

Mama Karo even taught her son Bastion how to give sermons in the local language, and then translate them into Indonesian for the children's Christmas celebration. Apart from this, she ensured her children had formal education so they would have a good future. Maksi Talitai managed to become a pastor, Filius Manitapa, Mama Ribka's son, a soldier, and the others also did well. As Mama Ribka said:

> I told them if I die, so be it, just as long as my children can go to school.[39]

The widows' fight was not only for themselves and their children. Even though their communities had rejected them, they also strived for the good of their communities. For instance, although Mama Karo and Mama Koba were in such dire straits, they used their training as midwives to offer their time, energy and experience to help women in childbirth.[40] This shows their concern for saving lives and for ongoing human life.

They showed this concern not only after the 1965 Affair, but also in the midst of the time of violence. The widows fought against the army's efforts to shame them by supporting their fellow victims when they had their hair shaved. Mama Karo tells this story:

> We had to go and report to the authorities for up to five or six months and we had our heads shaved at that time. Some were afraid. I said, 'We don't need to be afraid. What have we done wrong to be afraid of?' I told my other friends, 'After all, we know ourselves. We did not know anything [about PKI]. If we have hair, we will die. Somebody cuts it, we will also die. Or did you others know [about PKI]? I really didn't know.' I stood up and said, 'God knows [the

---

38  Maksi Talitai, interview on 15 November 2010 at Palibo'o, Kabola.
39  Mama Ribka, interview.
40  Interview with Mama Karo and Mama Koba.

truth], so just let it be. If someone wants to cut your hair really short, just let them.⁴¹

Because of the 1965 Affair, the victims' widows were branded as dirty and wicked. Although they had to confront this stigmatisation, they themselves kept their self-respect, and educated their children in the same way. On top of this, they also showed concern for each other. In this way, they stressed their humanity and at the same time fought against the injustice of the state, family, society and even the church.

## The attitude of the Church

In 1965 the GMIT church was in a bind, partly because of its limited understanding of the Communist Party and what was really going on. In the midst of the climate of terror, the church's stand was varied. Some GMIT church leaders in Alor tried to protect their members, but there were also GMIT members who were suspicious of others. Further, the GMIT church leaders together with some leaders of other religions in Alor issued a statement in support of the government and at the same time referred to a 'revolution', the meaning of which was not clear.

> In the church, my name was listed to be on the council but the village headman said, 'Why is someone who is a communist going to be on the council? So the congregation said, 'We are the council', so they stopped us from being church council members.'⁴²

The victims were considered dangerous, and therefore the church had to be wary of them. The widows had to suffer behind their smiles, but so too did their children. One example is that of Pastor Maksi during his ministerial internship with a congregation in Alor. Mama Karo tells the story:

> … Someone scribbled on the church walls, 'how can a communist kid become a pastor? How can a communist kid lead a church?' I heard about this and I cried. Maksi was living… with his uncle Bapak Abas Talitai. On Saturday I took vegetables over there and Maksi told me about it. The congregation council… came and said that the walls of the church were covered with writing. I asked, 'what have people written? A communist kid can lead a church?'⁴³

---

41  Interview with Mama Karo.
42  Mama Ribka, interview.
43  Mama Karo, interview.

It seems that the church's understanding about the communist victims was minimal, and probably even today church leaders still have negative ideas about 1965 victims. Because many church members were considered to be communist, the church had to tread very carefully in giving assistance to victims. For example, a minister assisted the congregational lay teacher Pelotata, who was going to be arrested and detained because he once led the prayers at the opening of a Communist Party meeting at Taramana. According to Pastor Pulinggomang, the night before Pak Pelotata was handed over to the army, Pastor Pulinggomang gave him some words of advice – if he was interrogated, he should say that he went to the Communist Party meeting to get them to renounce Marxism and communism. In the end, Pelotata was released from detention.[44]

The army also summoned a church leader to order the church to hand over Sem Talmaka, the head of the Communist Party in Alor, who was hiding out in the church leader's kampung. A presbytery leader was sent into the hills to search for him. When he found Sem Talmaka, he convinced him to turn himself in to the army:

> 'If you don't turn yourself in, then there will be trouble, they'll send in a whole battalion' And Sem said, 'Who will take me down?' And the presbytery leader said, 'I will'.[45]

Some of the pastors in Alor like J.A. Adang, T. Pulinggomang and Chr. Dakamoly protested about the killing of people who were not members of the Communist Party.[46] They put on their church robes and walked in procession around the town of Kalabahi for six nights in a row, praying. On the seventh day (Saturday) they went to see the army command leader, Ahmad. Before speaking, they knelt and prayed at the door of his office. Then they made their statement, 'If blood is shed, then let it be shed in a respected place', meaning that the victims can be executed but they should be given decent burials. According to Pastor Pulinggomang, the next day the Pola Tribuana church (the largest GMIT church in Kalabahi) was heavily surrounded by soldiers. On that Sunday, Pastor Adang ordered all the pastors to attend wearing their church robes, and to kneel beneath the pulpit. Then three pastors got up on the pulpit to give a sermon. The first was Pastor Lahal. The second was Pastor Adang, who took off his church robe, held it

---

44  Pastor Fredrik Pulinggomang, interview on 13 November 2010 at the village of Motombang, Teluk Mutiara.
45  Ibid.
46  These are the pastors' real names.

in his left hand and his necktie in is right, and said, 'Wash bloody hands. We are all held in the balance of man, but also in the balance of God. Repent!'[47] The third was Pastor Pulinggomang who said, 'Be careful when you pull out weeds because they grow together with the wheat.' This metaphor shows that the GMIT church leaders in Alor wanted to protect their members (the wheat) from the state violence towards Communist Party members (weeds).

There are also signs that the church tried to protect not only its members, but also itself as an institution by maintaining good relations with the government. The church was facing false rumours going around about religions (Protestantism, Islam and Roman Catholicism), namely that they supported the Communist Party. So on 5 May 1966, religious leaders in Alor launched a set of 'Devotional Verses' that included eight basic points, of which these four are most relevant here:

> IV. Rehabilitation of morals and the life of service and obedience to God and loving one's fellow men is the basic duty and primary work of we religious leaders together with the rehabilitation of physical life working together with all State authorities in their various fields, hand in hand and with mutual respect;

> V. This current point of history represents to us a new 'starting point' in the history of our lives and work since God saved the Nation-State and the Government from the 'Gestok' [1st October Movement] disaster which repudiated and also obstructed spiritual peace and worship of Almighty God;

> VI. As long as all Indonesians are of pure heart towards God according to their various ways of worship and remain true to the revolution, then it is absolutely certain that there will never be, in shape or form, those strains of anti-God and anti-revolution;

> VII. We believe that God is with us in the sacred struggle of the Indonesian nation:

> VIII. Amen and again Amen.[48]

---

47 Fredrik Pulinggomang, interview.
48 Dorkas Sir, 'Pengorganisasian Pelayanan', (BA [S1] thesis, Faculty of Theology, UKAW Kupang, 1990), appendix 1.

This extract reveals the stand taken by religions in Alor, including the church, namely that the Communist Party was seen as an 'obstruction to spiritual peace and to worship of Almighty God.' We see here how the Communist Party was seen as an obstruction on two levels – the individual level (spiritual peace) and the social level (religious worship). With the religions in Alor taking this attitude, it was difficult for the church to oppose the violence carried out by the state towards those accused of being involved with the Communist Party.

And yet, from another angle it is evident that at certain times the church also acted well in supporting victims. For instance, the church carried out deaconal ministry, secretly providing corn and cassava to members of the church who were suspected of being communist. According to Apeles, a figure of customary law, during the 1965 affair the church protected many of the elders and deacons who were listed as Communist Party members. Church members hid them in the forest and gave them food by pretending to feed the animals. They would throw food along the path while calling out, so those in hiding would know there was food there to be collected. At night, they would hide in the forest and get the food to eat.[49]

Another example is found in Pastor Maksi's experience during his ministerial internship. Even though there were members of the congregation who rejected him, he was encouraged by the words of Pastor J. A. Adang: 'a spring that spouts and flows is not all dirty water, there is also a flow of clear water.'[50] Pastor Maksi interpreted this to refer to the life of his own family – his parents and relatives who did bad, but there were also some who did good. Pastor Maksi took strength from these words, and was able to renew his service in the church.

According to one pastor, much of what the church did in the situation of terror was not pointless, but had a positive influence on local leaders to stop the killings and instead continue with the requirement for suspects to regularly report to the authorities.[51] Even with their limited understanding about the Communist Party and the violence raging at the time, the pastors did not remain silent. When they did fight to prevent the carnage, they upheld human dignity and values that we receive from our Creator along with life.

---

49 Apeles, interview.
50 Maksi Talitai, interview.
51 Fredrik Pulinggomang, interview. Most people in Alor share the view that the killings in Alor stopped because church leaders dared to protest about them.

## Discovering the meaning of everyday resistance: Analysis

The widows' experiences provide us with some interesting points for analysis; namely gender-based violence, the widows' concept of justice, the church's ambiguous stand, and the widows' resilience.

The effects of the 1965 Affair were different for men and women. For instance, both men and women had their heads shaved, but the meaning of this was different. If a man's head is shaved, this is nothing unusual, but in the Alor culture and the cultures of Nusa Tenggara Timur, a woman's hair is a symbol of honour. When her hair is forcibly shorn, this is a very specific form of humiliation.

There was also gender-based violence seen through the cases of sexual violence. Although information about the sexual violence carried out by state authorities on the women of Alor is minimal, clearly, rape was carried out against the women, not the men, and the women had to suffer rape at a time and place when they were the most vulnerable. The women also experienced rape at a time when their traditional protectors, their husbands, had been murdered. And they were raped at a place where they were under the total control of the military. As Mama Koba said, these women had no choice other than to give in so they could live.

The widows did not speak directly about justice, but their understanding of it can be inferred. For instance, Mama Koba once spoke about Pak Ahmad, the head of the military (puterpra) who raped many women: 'they might think what they did was good, but the blood of the dead will take revenge'. The widows believed that if someone did good, then good would return to them and their families. On the other hand, wickedness will slowly but surely be punished. Pak Ahmad's acts of violence would return to strike him. When the widows were raped, they remained silent. But this did not mean they gave in, rather that they clung tightly to their ideas about justice. They also believed that the blood of their murdered husbands would demand justice and thus at a certain time the perpetrators or their children would face disaster. In this way, injustice was not something that happened at a certain time during the life of the perpetrator, but was something to be felt for generations to come.

It was not only the struggle for justice that was to be felt by generations to come, but Christians of Alor and Nusa Tenggara Timor as a whole saw that sin too could be passed down. The children of the victims, even though they knew nothing at all about their parents' political choices, were seen as inheriting the wrongs of their parents who were considered to be Communist Party members or sympathisers. This was evident in the graffiti scrawled on the church walls when Maksi was doing his ministerial internship. However, Pastor Adang rejected that understanding about inherited sin when he made his parable about the water in the spring.

The efforts of the three pastors in Alor to stop the killing can be seen as based on religious values, namely the commandment, 'Thou shalt not kill', but also on humanitarian values, namely the right to life. But their courage was intended as defense of the right to life, and not as defense of the people's political rights for freedom of thought, freedom to gather, and freedom to organise. It is evident that the church in Alor at the time was unable to see the struggle for upholding political rights as a church duty. Therefore, the church did not make any serious analysis of the various political parties and their ideologies.

Apart from all this, the existence of political parties was something relatively new to Alor at that time. One must remember that traditional leaders were still dominant, and so Alor societies, both within and outside the church, were not prepared to interact critically with the presence of these parties. The violence of 1965 took place before the people of Alor were ready to participate in politics in a mature way, and this in turn influenced relations between the church and the state, and continues to do so today.

The widows, faced with all kinds of violence intended to crush them, and faced with no protection forthcoming from the church, refused to be crushed. Their conviction that they had done no wrong made them not only able to persevere but also to help other women friends keep their spirits up. Even though they appeared to be submissive when their heads were shaved, this could be interpreted as an expression of defiance, that they themselves were stronger than their hair. As we quoted Mama Karo earlier:

> 'I said, 'Hey, what is there to be afraid of? We've done nothing wrong…
> I stood and said 'God is our witness, so let them do what they want; if people want to cut off [our hair], let them go ahead.'

## Conclusion

The conditions in Indonesia over 1965–1966 were extremely tense and rocked every part of national life. Many of the people of Alor who were suspected of being members of the Communist Party and Gerwani were tortured, and many innocent people died. These actions produced unease and trauma.

Looking back and contemplating the phenomenon of the widow victims in Alor is a heavy step to take. The determination of these widows saw them through their long suffering full of trials. The widows and their children had to experience acts of injustice inflicted by the state, their families, society and even the church.

To the widows, the 1965 Affair is a bitter experience that should never be repeated.

> I pray that this will never happen again. There was such suffering in 1965. We were afraid, we did not want to talk again, we prayed that God would take it all far away from us. We want to find our lives and wait until God calls us.[52]

---

52  Mama Tibka, interview.

# PART II

Part II examines themes the researchers discovered when researching the 1965 violence in the region of Sumba where the Christian Church of Sumba (GKS) is the dominant Protestant church. Focusing on West Sumba, Chapter Six critically examines the conceptualisation of victims of the violence as sinners. Chapter Seven reveals how victims in East Sumba narrate their versions of facts and history concerning this period. Chapter Eight presents a GKS missionary's account of his story of the 1965 events.

Firstly we would like to provide the reader with an introduction to some contextual history on the Christian Church of Sumba (GKS).[1]

## Background: The Christian Church of Sumba, GKS

The Christian Church of Sumba, or Gereja Kristen Sumba (GKS) emerged through the proselytising of three institutions of the Dutch church that came to Sumba over the 19th century. Their background was the pietist movement that arose in Western Europe in the 17th and 18th centuries. Another influence was the influx of immigrants from Sabu, both those who arrived spontaneously as well as those who were moved there by the Dutch colonial government. The Christianisation of Sumba also flourished as a result of the social mixing and intermarriage between the already-converted people from Sabu with the local people of Sumba.

After World War II, pastors from Sumba took over pastoral care of the congregations there, rather than foreign missionaries, as before. Some

---

1   This summary is based on information from F.D. Wellem, *Injil & Marapu* (Jakarta: BPK Gunung Mulia 2004) and 'Old and New Christianity in the Southeastern Islands' in *A History of Christianity in Indonesia*, eds. Jan Sihar Aritonang and Karel Steenbrink (Leiden, The Netherlands: Koninklijke Brill NV, 2008, 229–344)

congregations began to make their own presbyteries. In 1947, the GKS was established, becoming one synod. The missionaries who returned to Sumba after WWII now functioned more as advisors.

The transfer of leadership from the missionaries to the people of Sumba was also evident in the field of education. Missionaries continued to run the schools they had established until 1950, when the people of Sumba established the Foundation for Evangelical Education in Sumba (Yapmas). Apart from managing the existing schools, this foundation opened primary schools all over Sumba. Until 1974, these schools outnumbered government schools, but from that date onwards, Yapmas began to relinquish its schools to the government. Other schools the foundation took over from the missionaries included vocational and junior high schools.

In 1924, a special school had been established to prepare the people of Sumba to assist the missionaries. More recently, in response to the need for pastoral care in Sumba, a theology college (STT GKS) was established on 25 November 2005.

From 1947 to 2004, the GKS's activities included evangelisation, education, and Christian service. Members of GKS evangelised through sermons, singing, plays with Christian themes, visits to followers of the local religion called Merapu, dances, and forms of Sumba collective poetry called *tau li'i*. In 1950, the church established a foundation to operate Christian hospitals. By 1978, this foundation managed two hospitals, four clinics and ten medicine outlets.

In 1955, the Indonesian Communist Party opened a branch in Sumba and attracted a large number of Christians, including members of the GKS. After the 1965 tragedy, the number of converts to GKS increased dramatically. By 1971, the GKS had more than 43,000 members.

## West Sumba

Rua Beach, West Sumba: Massacre site.

*About 100m to the right of the jetty at Rua Beach is the site of a massacre that took place in the second wave of killings in West Sumba in September 1966. The victims (13 males) were blindfolded with black cloth, and their hands were tied behind them. They were made to stand facing the sea, and shot in the back. After a check to make sure they were dead, their bodies were put into sacks with large rocks, then taken by boat and thrown into the sea. Rua Beach is the beach closest to the city of Waikabubak, around 20 kilometres to the south. It takes about 30 minutes to get there by car.*

*About six kilometers from Waikabubak, the road is steep with sharp bends for about a kilometre. On either side there is a precipice about 100 metres deep. This place, called Lapaie, is well known to the people of West Sumba.*

*Rua Beach faces directly to the Indian Ocean. The coast here is known as particularly dangerous because of the huge waves, but it is good for surfing. Because of this, in 1990 an international hotel called Nihi Watu, was built there. A jetty was also constructed there for tourist ships and pleasure craft to moor. The locals of West Sumba, especially from Waikabubak, also come to this beach for recreation.*

**Statement of a member of the Sumba research team**

*Chapter 6*

# Victims of the 1965 Tragedy: Sinners?

Yetty Leyloh

## Introduction

I myself knew about the 1965 tragedy from history books at school. In history lessons we were told about the sadism of the Communist Party and all organisations associated with it. All schoolchildren had to watch the film *The Treason of the September 30th Movement/PKI* that depicted a story of the savagery of the Communist Party and Gerwani. It was only when the New Order collapsed that people began to be a bit freer to study and seek the truth of what happened.

I have a sliver of memory of the situation when victims were imprisoned and murdered. I was only five years old at the time. Our house happened to be beside the Waikabubak prison, so we knew what was going on. I can still remember hearing a religious service before victims were executed; it was probably the second wave in Rua (on the south coast) in September, 1966. The hymn that sticks in my mind is 'KuasaMu Ya Pengasihan' ('Your power, O Merciful One). Then, even though I did not really know who they were, I saw the blindfolded victims come out of the prison and get loaded on to a truck. This vision stays with me to this day.

In Waikabubak, the capital of the regency of West Sumba, I interviewed two women as key informants. It turns out that in West Sumba there were very few female victims. The research team found that only one person was accused of being a member of Gerwani, Mama Nel, a Sumba woman of

Laura ethnicity who married a man from Sabu. Their daughter, Ibu[1] Bunga, who was considered to be Sabunese like her father, was also arrested and held in prison for two nights. She was the wife of Bapak[2] Ama who was also arrested because he had been involved with a government run labour union. Ibu Bunga was fearless in her efforts to obtain justice for her husband while he was in prison. The second key informant was Ibu Ana, the wife of Bapak Angga, a government civil servant who was accused of being a member of the Communist Party, held for four months, and then executed even though he was not a member of the Communist Party or any organisation associated with it.

These two informants described two groups of victims of the 1965 tragedy. Ibu Bunga's family were victims as a result of family members' involvement in the Communist Party, Gerwani, or other organisations considered to be related to them; whereas Ibu Ina's husband was a victim of unproven accusations. Statistically, we must admit that just two informants cannot possibly be representative of all victims of the 1965 tragedy in West Sumba. Nonetheless, their experiences deserve our respect, including as an entry point to give meaning to the 1965 tragedy from the victims' viewpoint. While still seeking further female victims in West Sumba willing to speak out, we can listen and learn from these two key informants.

## Profile of the Area

When the 1965 tragedy occurred, the island of Sumba was divided into two regencies or administrative districts (*kabupaten*), East Sumba and West Sumba. It was only in 2006 that a third district was created, and then a fourth in 2007. Today the districts are East Sumba, West Sumba, Central Sumba and Southwest Sumba.

In 1965, Waikabubak already had a prison, a police station, a court and other government offices. The town was also the place of residence for government officials, and this is why, along with the town of Waingapu (the capital of East Sumba), these places were the centres of mass attacks against 'communists' who were thrown into prison.[3]

---

1   Translator's note: The word *Ibu* is the Indonesian honorific for 'Madame' to refer to an older or married woman. I have retained it throughout the book.
2   Translator's note. The word Bapak, which literally means 'Father', is the Indonesian honorific for a man, equivalent to Mr. and is also written as Pak or Bp.
3   Around 1985–86 a new prison was constructed on the western edge of the town, and the old one was no longer used as a prison. The law courts are also no longer in their original location.

In 1965, the prison was situated in the heart of the town right beside the law courts, and about 300 metres from the police station. The town of Waikabubak was still extremely quiet, and the climate was cold because it is situated in a valley. It is often said that the town is 'set in a wok'. Back then, there was still no public transport, only a few trucks owned by Chinese or Arabs, and a few government vehicles. The townspeople walked everywhere – to school, to the office – and walking two to six kilometres was perfectly normal. Electricity was also sparse. Electricity came on only from six in the evening until midnight.

The population of Waikabubak was made up not only of indigenous Sumbanese. The economy was dominated by Chinese and Arabs. So too with local officials, like the local head of Justice (Pak Herman, who was replaced by Pak Ahmad in 1965, both of whom were from Sulawesi); the chief prison warden (Pak Nali, from Rote), the chief of police (Pak Sonopati, who was Javanese), and the court, which did not yet have a judge (there was a judge only in East Sumba) but the court registrar was Umbu Ronggo (from Sumba). The District Head (Bupati) was from Sumba (Umbu Tinus), the District Secretary was Pak Taka (from Sumba). There was no district military command (Koramil), but there was a military command made up of non-commissioned officers called Puterpra which later became the Koramil. The teachers and civil servants were predominantly from Sabu, Rote and Ambon, so one can say that the 'intellectuals' and government officials in Sumba were predominantly outsiders.

In terms of religion, the population of Waikabubak was mainly made up of Protestant members of the Christian Church of Sumba (GKS), Catholics, Muslims and a large number of people who were still followers of the local indigenous belief, Marapu. At the time, the GKS was still hosting many Dutch missionaries who served as pastors, social workers, doctors and nurses.

## Arrest and torture[4]

The quiet, cool town of Waikabubak was suddenly rocked by the 1965 tragedy. After it broke out in Jakarta on 1 October, the waves reached Waikabubak just one week later. Anyone involved with the organisation of the Communist Party became the target of mob attack. A teacher had his house destroyed and set alight. All signs and symbols of the Communist

---

4   Information here is from interviews with Ibu Bunga on 9, 11, and 15 November 2010 and with Ibu Ina on 6 November at their homes in Waikabubak, West Sumba.

Party, like flags, banners and billboards, were destroyed.[5] Houses owned by communists or those suspected of being so, were attacked and ransacked.

The arrests and torture began around January 1966, after a rumour went around that the Communist Party was going to kill non-communists. As Bapak Jacob told it, this rumour began with a voluntary work program planned for the area of Lapale, around five kilometres to the south of Waikabubak. The voluntary work was intended as a government program for forestation by planting seedlings. At the time, the news spread that the Communist Party was going to take this opportunity to plant a bomb at Lapale to kill everyone taking part in the work program, including the local government officials. The rumour spread like wildfire over Waikabubak and instigated anger against the communists. Because of this, anyone suspected of being a communist or a member of any organisation associated with the Communist Party was arrested and summarily imprisoned.

Ibu Bunga's husband, Bapak Angga Derosario, was a civil servant in a government office in Waikabubak, and also head of the union at that office.[6] Because of this, he was fired from his position as civil servant.[7] He was then imprisoned around February 1966, and Ibu Bunga herself was arrested around May 1966 and held for two nights. Prior to her arrest, her house was ransacked. Everything in the cupboards was pulled out and thrown on the floor. The ransackers were looking for proof to back up their accusations, but could not find a single thing to prove that Ibu Bunga's family was communist.

> 'I was terrified when they came. I was not allowed even to change my clothes. The ones who came were not policemen. They had no papers of any kind, nothing… So when they came and started ransacking the house I didn't know what they were looking for. They were pulling things out of the cupboards, throwing them on the floor. Can you imagine! Was that right? Then there was one army guy. He saw a ring fall on the floor. He came over and said, 'Mama, perhaps this belongs

---

[5] Those leading the youths to arrest Communist Party people or those suspected of being so were government civil servants like Pak Dodi (who arrested Bapak Angga) and Pak Rocky (who arrested Bapak Ama).

[6] The union was the All Indonesia Trade Union Federation (SOBSI) which the people of Sumba knew as being the labour union closely affiliated with the Indonesian Communist Party. It was also crushed at this time.

[7] The three orders (SK) issued to fire Bapak Angga were: SK No: Kp.2.3/10/65, Kupang 3 December 1965, for 'temporary suspension' (*dinon-aktifkan sementara*'): SK Direktur Daerah Pemasjarkatan Nusa Tenggara Timur, No: Kp.2.3/II/66, Kupang 26 February 1966 for 'temporary dismissal' ('*diberhentikan sementara waktu*'); and SK No: TCP/II/09/70, Djakarta, 15 November 1966 for 'dishonorable dismissal from government service.' ('*memberhentikan tidak dengan hormat dari djabatan Negeri'.*)

to you?' I took it and said, 'Thank you, sir. That was my mother-in-law's ring that belongs to my husband.' He shook his head looking at the piles of things on the floor. Luckily, I had some premonition and had already hidden any official papers belonging to my husband. Maybe this is why they came and did the search, don't you think?'

When Ibu Bunga was arrested, her second child was sick, with breathing difficulties. She had to leave him with her younger sister. She was not allowed to change her clothes. She left immediately with those arresting her and walked to the prison, about a kilometre away. Neither her arrest nor that of her husband was done with any warrant. Ibu Bunga herself did not experience any physical torture, but she was traumatised by her experience of arrest. She had no idea why she had been arrested:

> [The people who came] said nothing at all except, 'Hurry up! Get your things together.' That's it. They had arrested my husband first. So he was walking in front, and I was behind carrying Welem who was still small, just a baby, still nursing, just four months' old. So when they came and said to me 'hurry up! Get your things to go!' I asked, 'go where?' 'Just go! You don't need to know.'
> 
> ... But my child was sick, having trouble breathing, I needed to get him to the hospital. So I said to them, 'what about my child who's sick?' 'Just leave him over there! Kids are none of our business', he said. In my heart I was saying, 'Oh God, Listen to what they are saying to me.' Luckily I have a younger sister, so I gave my son to her. I said to her, 'if anyone comes bringing medicine, don't accept it, don't take it. If God loves me, I will be coming back. When I do, I'll get him to the hospital.'
> 
> ... So we walked. What else could we do? We walked through the rice fields, where I had never walked before, straight to the prison. And they kept saying 'Get a move on! Hurry up!' [At the prison] there was no questioning, just straight into the cell. I was waiting to see what they wanted to ask me, but there was nothing. The next morning they said, 'You can go!' maybe because I had told them about my sick child. Maybe God drove them to some compassion, maybe they thought of my baby at home, still nursing. [In prison] the ones doing the torturing were from somewhere else, oh mama... there were no police or army there.

Ibu Bunga's mother, Mama Nel, was also imprisoned.

Mama had been active in the Indonesian Union of Christian Women (PWKI), but people accused her of being a communist. People who thought themselves 'clean' said that the initials PWKI actually stood for Partai Wanita Komunis Indonesia (The Indonesian Women's Communist Party). Mama Nel was actually also a member of Parkindo (Indonesian Christian [Protestant] Party) but people said that was rubbish. She was one of the founders of the orphanage [run by the GKS in Waikabubak], but people did not believe that either. They said, 'Where did she get her money from? It must be the Communist Party.' Even though my mother was always really angry if my brothers and sisters and I missed church. She used to say. 'What will people think? Here I am, head of PWKI, and my children don't go to church.' Mother was so kind, I can't tell you how kind she was, also to anyone who came to her asking for help. If she saw anyone sad, or children crying, she would always ask them what the matter was. All I can say is, 'Ooo... she was a hero.'

Ibu Rina, another informant, talked about Mama Nel in the same way as Ibu Bunga.

Aunty Nel was really clever. She was clever at talking, and pretty bold in the way she talked to anyone. She was an intelligent mother, and a regular churchgoer. So when people said Aunty Nel was a communist and an atheist, I found this hard to believe.

Mama Nel was imprisoned along with Bapak Angga and Bapak Angga's brother-in-law around February 1966. She was cruelly tortured. Ibu Bunga witnessed this torture when she was held in prison for two nights. She saw her mother, Mama Nel tied upside down, raised up, then suddenly dropped down. Whenever she was raised up, she was beaten with rattan. She was also burnt with cigarettes. Ibu Bunga said:

What had they done wrong that they had to be tortured like that? I couldn't stop crying watching that torture.

Mama Nel was freed along with Bapak Angga in December 1966. But what she had experienced ruined her life, both as a woman active in organisations, and as a housewife. Ibu Bunga also witnessed the torture of her husband, Bapak Angga, which took the same form as the torture of her mother, Mama Nel.

According to Ibu Bunga, when she and her husband were in prison, the family was not allowed to bring them food or to visit them. Ibu Bunga was held for only two nights and then ordered to go home. But the experience of Ibu Ina and her husband, Bapak Ama was different. Ibu Ina was able to take her husband food every day.

Bapak Ama, who worked in a government office in Waikabubak, was arrested on 18 January 1966. According to Ibu Ina, he was accused of being an organiser of BTI[8] which was the 'Communist Party's right hand'. But before their arrest at the home of one of Bapak Ama's relatives (Ibu Dani), the house was ransacked. Everything was taken out of the cupboards and thrown on the ground. Ibu Dani said they were looking for documents and lists of Communist Party members. They found a list of names that Ibu Dani said was a list of people who had given them some financial contributions when their mother had died a few months earlier.[9]

According to Ibu Ina, the people who arrested the 'communists' were not police or army, but local civil servants together with youths (church youth) or anyone who wanted to join and who was 'not communist'. Many of the perpetrators and victims knew each other, even had lived together side by side, as neighbours. After their arrest, the victims were taken straight to prison (or, as in the case of Bapak Ama, were first taken to the judge), then interrogated and beaten by the judge and the people who had arrested them, and thrown into prison cells.

There was no warrant for Bapak Ama's arrest, but the reason given when he was taken was that he had to answer to the judge. Ibu Bunga told how the people who arrested him took him to the judge's house:

> [The judge was encouraging] people to confess, but Bapak refused. At the beginning, people kept trying to get him to confess... come on, who made you join... you're part of BTI[10] aren't you? Bapak said, 'I don't know what you're talking about. I did not join.' But they said, 'If you confess, we'll let you go.' But Bapak kept firm. [The judge] said, 'ah, you're just like your brother.'

---

8   The transcript has 'Buruh Tani' which seems to be a mistake for 'Barisan Tani Indonesia' or BTI, the Indonesian Farmer's Front [Trans].
9   Interview with Ibu Dani, November 2010, Waikabubak. In Sumba, when someone dies, it is a custom for visiting mourners to donate money, food, and woven cloth. Usually the names of the donors are noted down so when a death occurs in their family, a suitable return donation can be made.
10  As previously, the transcript has 'Buruh Tani'.

According to Ibu Bunga, who was being held at the prison, Bapak Ama was put in the same cell as her that night. When they put him in it was dark and she could not see the jailors' faces clearly.[11]

> My own husband was in another cell – there were many rooms. He was in the room next to mine. At night he handed me a lamp. 'Why are you giving this to me?', I asked. 'So you won't be afraid', he said. It was really dark: and the lamps were dim. Suddenly a group of people came. They threw someone into the cell. I got the lamp and saw it was Uncle Ama. I said, 'Hey, what's going on? Why are you putting a man in this cell? I am a woman.' It was Ama, and he was unconscious. That evening someone came and brought him some food, so I took it and kept it for him. I held the lamp up to him, and I saw, wah!... I had been put in the cell OK. But what on earth had happened to him? There was blood flowing here [Ibu Bunga points to her face]. He had been beaten half to death... I said to him, 'Uncle, uncle, can you drink some water?' 'No', he said. 'You have food here, from home', I said. 'I can't eat', he said. I pitied him terribly. I said, 'Uncle, the food has been here since morning, come on, eat a little.' But he did not want to. Oh my, he was really suffering.

Torture went on from the time of interrogation to the time in prison. Bapak Ama was beaten before he was put in the prison cell, and many others were tortured almost daily in the prison cells, which were used as special interrogation chambers. According to Pak Jakob, who was a junior high school student at the time, there was another place of torture at the office of Soba Wawi village in the district of Loli, which is about three kilometres from the prison to the west of Waikabubak.[12] Yakob once saw people being beaten and strung up at this village office, and because the torturers noticed him, they were going to force him to join in beating the victims. But he managed to run and escape, because he did not want to do this. Anyone who witnessed torture was forced to take part.

The torture at this place was also a warning to other criminals. West Sumba at the time was rife with theft and murder, so another term was in vogue, namely 'night communist', which meant those who were most probably not

---

11  It is surprising that men and women were put together in the same cell, but according to this informant, this happened because the prison was full of communists, people accused of being communist, and criminals.
12  Waikabubak Christian Primary School and Kindergarten, both run by GKS, now stand at this location.

communist but were thieves and robbers. This term in effect equated the Communist Party, which was one political party, with criminal activity. Apart from the prison guards, people outside also witnessed the torture in the prisons of those arrested as communists, because the prison was directly below a kampung. Anyone who wanted to watch the torture could just walk up behind the kampung and look down on what was happening in the prison.[13]

Almost all the detainees accused of being communist were tied upside down to posts, then pulled up and beaten from behind, including their feet, with rattan and also barbed sticks. Then they were suddenly let go. This torture was repeated, over and over. When Ibu Bunga was still in the cell, she was right across from the cell used for torture. She saw her own husband and brother-in-law tortured like this. She asked herself:

> What crime could possibly be so bad to warrant torture like this?

She could not stop crying when she saw it.

The torturers were not police, army or the prison wardens, but the people who had arrested them (the mob, youths, civil servants) led by Bapak Dodi, an official from the regional government office of West Sumba. According to Ibu Melati who worked at the prison at the time, the prison officers knew that every day between 10 and 11 in the morning, the torturers were sure to arrive. They forced the prison officers to beat the victims, because if they did not, then they would be beaten. Once, when the head of the prison did not want to join in the beating, the torturers beat him.

Ibu Melati herself, as a prison warden, always used every excuse she could to avoid that 'duty'. She would say her child was sick at home so she had to leave, or she had a stomach ache, and so forth; the important thing was not to join in the violence. But when she could no longer avoid it, she herself was forced to join in. The prison officials were not allowed to show any signs of compassion whatsoever because if they did, they would be accused of being communists themselves. It was the same with anyone who came to the prison to watch the beatings (usually youths); they had to join in beating the victims. If they refused, they would be beaten themselves.

---

13   The town of Waikabubak is surrounded by kampung or hamlets of traditional Sumba houses built on the hills and surrounded with stone fences or cactus. Behind the prison was the kampung of Bodo Ede. This is where people would come and watch what was going on in the prison, in the middle of which was an open courtyard where most of the torturing took place.

## Murdering communists[14]

In West Sumba there were two waves of executions. In the first wave, seven people were killed at Mamboro on 5 May 1966.[15] Those executed were:

1. Rito: one of the Communist Party leaders in West Sumba
2. Malak: a rattan weaver (an outsider, not from Sumba or Sabu)
3. Ibu Bunga's brother-in-law: a Communist Party leader
4. A teacher who was a very charismatic speaker
5. A teacher from Lauli
6. A teacher
7. A teacher[16]

Of these seven, one was Muslim, four were members of GKS, and the religious status of the other two is unknown. When this first wave of executions took place, Bapak Angga, Ibu Bunga's husband, had already been loaded onto the truck that was to take them to the execution site, but for some unknown reason, according to Ibu Bunga, he was ordered off the truck and did not go with them to Mamboro.

Ibu Ina remembers the mood as the victims were being taken to Rua:

> As they were being rounded up [to be executed] they were singing. I remember the hymn 'Iring Dikau Saja Tuhan' (At Your Side, Oh Lord), but Pak Rocky [prison warden] stayed with me at his house [beside the prison]... [On the day they were taken to the execution site]... I was at Pak Rocky's place. His family was guarding me at their house behind the prison. Why were they afraid of me? I can't remember exactly, but there were two execution sites, the first at Mamboro, then at Rua. [The victims included] Rito; that man from

---

14  Information about the execution in West Sumba of people considered to be communists is from interviews with Umbu Dangu on 10 November 2010 at Mamboro (now in Central Sumba District), and with Pak Yakob, 5–12 November 2010, at Waikabubak.
15  Information on the date of the executions at Mamboro is from the collection of a former GKS missionary '*Salinan dari sebahagian surat kepada Deputat Sumba Zending*', 4 October 1966.
16  The list of victims was obtained from interviews with various informants in Sumba. The source mentioned above ('Salinan dari...') says: 'On May 5 last [1966] the death sentence was carried out on six Communist Party leaders in West Sumba. The death sentence was also carried out on 15 Communist Party members on 9 June, [1966].'

Bima, Malak; and I don't remember; [and]... [Ibu Bunga's brother-in-law was executed] at Mamboro; Erwin too; Ido, a civil servant; Kanis.[17]

They were taken by truck from the Waikabubak prison in the late afternoon to Mananga Beach at Mamboro, about 60 kilometres to the north. The killing was done at dawn and witnessed by many of the locals at Mamboro as well as village officials, from village to district level. According to Umbu Dangu, there was a government instruction ordering everyone to be present at the execution, which was carried out by the police and the army. The prisoners were blindfolded from the time the left the prison in Waikabubak, with black bands, and their arms were tied behind them. They were accompanied by their executioners led by the East Sumba regional military command (Dandim) from Waingapu (at that time, West Sumba had only the lower level military garrison called Puterpra).

Seven people are known to have been killed on Mananga Beach, Mamboro, on 5 May 1966. – JPIT archives.

---

17  Ibu Ina, interview.

The victims stood facing the sea, with their executioners behind them – the firing squad made up of three people, one policemen and two soldiers, or the other way around – who shot the victims at close range of about ten metres.[18]

Five of the victims shot fell at once and made no movement. But two of them, after being shot once, twice, still did not fall. So the executioners showered them with bullets until they fell on the sand and they kept on shooting until their bodies were shot through. People said that these two people possessed 'special magic potions'. After all seven were proclaimed dead, the bodies were put into sacks weighed down with big stones, and then taken by boat out beyond Managa Beach to the ocean to be tipped overboard.

Then in September 1966, the second wave of executions took place at Rua Beach, about 20 kilometres from Waikabubak to the south, about 100 meters to the right of the jetty. Thirteen victims were shot there. Their names should be easy enough to find because according to informants, there are records held at the police station in Waikabubak. However, when we approached a retired policeman who used to be in charge of police archives there, he said that the files had been destroyed because of the 'cleansing' [rehabilitation, Trs] of the former 1965 political prisoners at the time Abdurrahman Wahid was president.[19] Of the 13 people executed in this second wave, six are known, namely:

1. A market trader

2. One of the organisers of the Indonesian Farmers Front (BTI) from East Wewewa district

3. The relative of one of the traditional rulers of West Sumba

---

18  Interview with Umbu Dangu. Each victim was shot by a squad of three executioners. There were several squads at the time.
19  Interview with a retired policeman, 14 November 2010, Waikabubak. During Abdurrahman Wahid's presidency, he 'proposed policies intended to bring about national reconciliation', including: "First, based on the presidential decree [Keppres B 15/PRES/11/1999] to permit Indonesian political exiles to return, and have their citizenship restored if this is their wish… ; Second, to disband the state Body for Coordination of Assistance for Consolidation of National Stability (Bakorstanas) and cease the practice of 'special scrutiny'; Thirdly, the president personally offered a statement of apology to the families of victims of the massacres of 1965–66 and to those who were imprisoned without trial; Fourthly, the president had various reasons for his proposal to rescind the regulation [Tap MPRS No. 25/1966] banning the Communist Party and outlawing teachings of Communism-Marxism-Leninism. (Budiawan, *Mematahkan Pewarisan Ingatan: Wacana Anti-Komunis dan Politik Rekonsiliasi Pasca-Soeharto*, Jakarta: ELSAM, 2004, pp47–49. Based on the data gathered by the research team, the ending of the requirement for 1965 victims to report [to local security offices] varied from one area to another (see Appendix 1: Chronology of Events in Selected Areas of NTT).

4. Erwin, from Sabu

5. Kanis, from Sabu

Of these six, one was Muslim, two were members of GKS, and the religions of the other three are unknown. I did not get any information that members of the public witnessed this execution. But I did get detailed accounts about the time leading up to it, before they were taken to Rua.

One morning in September there were preparations made, including spiritual preparation for the victims. A Dutch missionary called Pastor van Oostrum gave the last rites to the victims, inside the prison. Their families and other people outside the prison could hear them singing hymns like hymn no. 147 'KuasaMu, Ya Pengasihan' (Your power, O Merciful One). Pastor van Oostrum who led the group out (because they were wearing black blindfolds), got on to the truck and helped them up, one by one.[20] They walked out of the prison towards the truck singing 'Kuserahkan pada Tuhan' (I surrender to God).

Around late afternoon, they left for Rua, and all the way they sang hymns. The beach was quite a distance from any houses, not like at Mamboro where people had built houses right on the beach. Based on the information from Pak Yakob, the method of execution was the same as at Mamboro.[21] The victims were blindfolded, their hands bound behind them. They stood facing the sea and were shot from behind. When they were all declared dead, the bodies were put into sacks with big stones, then taken out to sea by boat and tipped overboard.

## A wife's struggle: Ibu Ina's story[22]

Ibu Ina, Bapak Ama's wife, was deeply shocked when her husband was taken by force into custody, particularly as there was no clear accusation. Bapak Ama was accused of being a member of BTI, but according to Ibu Ana, he had no idea what they meant by 'BTI': he merely worked as a civil servant in a government office at Waikabubak. Ibu Ina described what happened, beginning with when Bapak Ama was arrested at their house on 18 January, 1966.

---

20  According to Pak Yakob, Pastor van Oostrum probably went with them to Rua.
21  Interview with Pak Yakob. A few months after the execution at Rua, one of the executioners, a policeman, fell ill and lost his memory (he was considered to have gone mad).
22  All quotes are taken from an interview with Ibu Ina on 6 November 2010 at Waikabubak.

It's a long story… Pak Dodi, who was the leader of the group that went around arresting people at the time, took Bapak to the judge's house…. they sent back home whatever he had in his pockets, saying that we should hold on to it meanwhile until there were further instructions; just that. 'Alright.' I said, 'You have to do your job.'

But when he did not return home that evening, I went over to the judge's house… I introduced myself as Pak Ama's wife. They said that Bapak had been arrested because there had once been a Communist Party meeting at our house. I said, 'As his wife, I can tell you that there has never been any kind of meeting at our house.' Then the judge said, 'Oh yes, that's right, my mistake; it was the house next door.' They meant the big house, my parents' house. Because Mama had passed away, my older brother from Waingapu came and stayed there for a while. The judge went on. 'Anyway, the basic accusation is about the meeting.' So I said, 'There never was a meeting.' And the judge said. 'Alright. We'll see how things go. If indeed Bapak Ama did not go to the meeting, he can return home.'

But he did not come home. So I went back, and asked the judge again. 'Sir, you promised my husband could come back home, but why has he not returned?' And the judge said, 'There is a new accusation.' 'What is that, Sir?' I asked. 'Well' he said, 'Pak Ama is accused of being a Communist Party spy.' I was shocked. 'How could that be?', I said. 'How was he a Communist Party spy?' Because I can tell you for sure that my husband never went out anywhere. He just went to the office, stayed at home, worked at home…' 'Well, he was opposing the government.' I said, 'how, Sir?' Bapak Ama was someone who did not agree with any funny business fiddling with people's pay, like when the pay was held back and so on; he did not agree with that. He wanted everything above board. So… that was what he was accused of.

I thought long and hard. If this was how things were, at least now I knew. But in my heart I did not agree, how could I? … From the judge's house I went to see the District Head (Bupati). I told him everything that I had heard from the judge. The District Head asked. 'What are they holding Pak Ama for?' So I told him. I don't know if the District Head was being honest when he replied. He said to me, 'Actually, he should be coming to me. Anything to do with civil servants should come the District Head. And I know him well. So calm down. I will look into it.' 'Thank you, Sir', I said.

After Bapak Ama was arrested and put into prison, Ibu Ina continued her efforts to see anyone at all with any kind of authority, so she could explain that her husband had done no wrong because he was not a communist. Indeed, one of Bapak Ama's relatives called Bapak Lius (see further the report from East Sumba) was one of the heads of the Communist Party in East Sumba, and had been executed along with other victims there. Probably this was the reason that Bapak Ama was arrested.

Ibu Ina continued to reject the accusations made against her husband; she said that her husband had never gone to any meeting of any kind, let alone a Communist Party meeting. She came to the conclusion that all the accusations were totally fabricated anyway; what was important to the accusers was just to put her husband in prison. About two weeks later, Ibu Ina went back to the District Head's house:

> The last time I went there [to the District Head's house] because I had been waiting and waiting. Oh yes, the first time I saw the District Head he had said to me, 'When Pak Ama was arrested I was not here. I was in Java, so I knew nothing about it.' 'Never mind', I said… The last time I went to the District Head's place he said… 'wah, sorry, sorry… it's their affair, there's nothing I can do. There are regulations…' 'In my heart, I saw he was washing his hands of it. And true enough God gave me inner strength. So I said. 'Yes, Sir. I know that you are not directly involved, so if I have made a mistake, then I ask you to forgive me. But all decisions made in this region are decisions made by the Assembly of local leaders (Muspida), and this body includes you, Sir.' The District Head was silent. When I took my leave, he said, 'Let's see what happens.'
>
> I said 'yes.' But I waited, and waited, and waited some more, and still nothing happened. The District Head did ask me, 'how are things with his salary?' and I told him, 'it is going smoothly. There has just been a cut.' 'Well, if anything happens, come to me,' he said. 'Yes, Sir, thank you,' I said. Then I just waited and waited for some settlement because Bapak was already in prison. When I knew he was in prison, I wondered how people were treating him. It was as though he had committed some terrible sin against the state.

Every day, Ibu Ina would walk about two kilometres from her house to the prison taking food, and checking on developments with her husband.

> I was absolutely determined, and kept on going to the prison, just by myself taking the food, I did not want the children coming along. I wanted to see how things were going with him. Pak Rocky (one of the prison wardens at the time) said to me, 'Usi, you don't have to keep on coming.' I said 'Yes. I have a responsibility, as a wife I have a responsibility.'

Even though there was no announcement, detainees' families got information from the prison wardens that there was going to be a second round of executions at Rua Beach after the installation of the new judge. This news made Ibu Ina even more anxious.

> The first lot were killed at Mamboro, so this was wave... two; yes, the second wave. The time drew closer. I could not tell the family, I did not want to, I just kept murmuring, 'God, if his time has come, I am ready.' I got things ready. Sack, rope, Bapak's clothes. I was told there were 17 things that had to be taken.... the new judge was installed... I thought, 'Oh, no... ' I got all them all together [Bapak Ama's relatives to ask them what should be done], I said, please help me think. What is all this about?
>
> I wrote a letter, and wrote down everything from the very beginning when Bapak was arrested. I wrote it myself. At the end of the letter, I wrote, 'I implore you sirs, having read this letter, if the things I have said above might be considered as something that condemns my husband, then I accept everything [Ibu Ina's voice gets louder now], but if, sirs, you are not satisfied with what I have set out, then I myself am prepared to be summoned.' I took the letter to the new judge myself. I went to his house. When I got there he was eating. He invited me in, and said, 'please, sit for a moment.' I took my daughter with me; she has died now. Wherever I went, I would take her with me. The judge asked, 'Who is the letter from?'. 'Myself, Sir', I said. He took it and read it. Then he said, 'Who wrote this letter?' and I said, 'I wrote it myself.' I kept looking straight at him, and I could see the expression on this face change as he took in the letter. I kept on watching him. When he finished reading, he said. 'Very well', just like that. 'Come back in a few days' time. I will take this letter to the office.'
>
> I went back home, praying all the way, 'Thank you, God'. All I could do was wait. I went back to preparing what had to be taken to Rua. Pak Rocky [prison warden] said that there were now 15 people getting prepared. When I heard that, I had some hope. But I did not

dare to be sure. I said, 'God determines all. Whatever happens, I will accept it.'

Ibu Ina prayed to God, full of hope, but still there was no positive response.

> On the last day before they were to be taken, I knew it was the last day because I took food to the prison… Pak Rocky came to meet me from inside the prison, at his house [next door to the prison]; he was afraid I would be traumatised. He said, 'come now, Usi.' But I said, 'No, I want to bring this, and if I'm allowed I want to go along to Rua.' He held me by the arm and said, 'Come along here first'. I said, 'No, I want to go to Rua.' He could not hold me back.
>
> Before they were taken away there was still interrogation. I could hear the judge asking. He said, 'you were… a member of which organisation?' Bapak answered as before, 'I was Parkindo [Indonesian Christian (Protestant) Party]'. But the judge went on with his accusation; he started out accusing from the beginning, I heard it. He said, 'Oh yes, just the same as your older brother.' He kept on saying he was Parkindo right until he died. I did not hear the judge do anything to Bapak, but he was hitting the others with anything around.
>
> [After Bapak Ama was released from prison] he had to go regularly to report to the authorities, this only stopped a few years ago. [When he got out] he had release papers [but when he was arrested] there were no papers at all. How could they have acted like this? People said that they had found a Communist Party flag at our house… the ones who came were not people we knew. The ones who came… [two males], one of them said to me, 'Aunty, we apologise,' but he was being forced to carry out this duty. I said, 'Don't waver in your suspicions of me. If this [action] is right, it is right; if wrong, wrong.'

It is not clear exactly why, but at the last minute Bapak Ama was not taken to Rua Beach to be executed. He was given release papers. Even so, this story is a bitter memory for Ibu Ina, who chose to keep it to herself and not share it with anyone, even her own children.

## The stigma of being a 'communist family': Ibu Bunga's story[23]

There was a stigma attached to being 'involved' with the Communist Party, and also to their families. 'Involvement' here meant involvement according to the government which did not necessarily mean they were ever members of the Communist Party. I also often heard that the stigma was attached to some families in Waikabubak, including Ibu Bunga's family. The members of Ibu Bunga's family who were stigmatised included her mother who was a member of Gerwani, her brother-in-law who was murdered, her husband (Bapak Angga) and Ibu Bunga herself. All of them were imprisoned. But the stigma did not stop with those who had been imprisoned, it extended to the Yapmas teachers who were strongly rebuked by the Yapmas leadership. One of Ibu Bunga's relatives was fired from her position as a Yapmas teacher.[24] Around mid-1980, Ibu Bunga's nephew-in-law was also fired from his position as a member of the police force in Waikabubak.

What Ibu Bunga found most painful of all was what happened to her husband. Bapak Angga was released from prison with a statement saying he could be reinstated in his former position. However, all he received was a final payout that amounted to about three months' salary.[25] This was particularly stressful because no one cared about the situation of Bapak Angga and his family.

> When [Pak Angga] had been working before, people were always borrowing money from him. [Now that he had no salary], he said people would remember this and give it back ... I kept hoping they would take another look at his salary because he was a civil servant. What else could we say? Because all this time no one paid us any attention. No one asked how we were coping, how we were. No one.

Without telling her husband, Ibu Bunga used the payout to buy some carpentry tools. She had a 'feeling' that this would be the only way to support

---

23  All the quotes in this section are from interviews with Ibu Bunga conducted on 9, 11 and 15 November 2010 in Waikabubak. During the interviews, Ibu Bunga's daughter was present and would sometimes comment.
24  According to the notes of the meeting of the GKS Synod at Kananggar, East Sumba on 20–28 July 1966 (p.55), seven Yapmas teachers in East Sumba and twelve in West Sumba were fired because they were accused of being members of the Communist Party or Gerwani.
25  The statement was SK No: EP/70/12/December/1966 issued by the Sumba District Military Command 1601, under Commander of the Operational Command for the Restoration of Security, signed by Moh. Moesa S.B. Letkol Inf. NRP 10850.

the family. Her son had inherited a skill for carpentry after being refused a position as teacher in Waikabubak.

All attempts to restore Bapak Angga's rights were futile. According to Ibu Bunga's daughter, her father was told that in order to work again, permission would have to be 'arranged in Denpasar'. Ibu Bunga's reaction to this was cynicism:

> That was the head of the prison [in Sumba]. Couldn't he just send the information [about Bapak Angga's release] up the line, to Jakarta?... So I thought to myself... 'What can we do?'

Until his death in 2009, no official statement about Bapak Angga's eligibility to work was forthcoming, so he died with an unhealed wound.

Until the early 2000s, Ibu Bunga was still required to report to the local authorities once a month. This also made it difficult to be freed of the stigma of being a 'communist family'.

> We still had to go and report... at the local government office as well as the city district level; we went wherever they told us to go. We never reported at the police station or army command. We would arrive, write our names, talk a bit, chew some betel nut, and then go back home.

According to one of Ibu Bunga's children:

> [Those offices received] designated funds for those obligatory reporting sessions, so to make sure the funds kept coming, they would just sit around, tell stories, chew betel nut and go home. It was all a waste of time.

The communist stigma was applied not only to Bapak Angga and Ibu Bunga, but also to their children, which meant the family was in desperate straits. Around the early 1980s, Ibu Bunga and Bapak Angga's eldest child got work as a teacher outside of Sumba. But he could not take the way he was ostracised by his colleagues because he came from a 'communist family'. Eventually he returned to Waikabubak. He and his mother tried negotiating with the local Education and Culture office for an official transfer to Waikabubak, but without success. Ibu Bunga said, with a note of cynicism:

> They always thought up reasons, but I knew that because we were the guilty ones, we were the sinners and they were the holy ones, that my son would never be accepted as a teacher in Waikabubak.

And so it was again when Ibu Bunga's daughter applied for work in 1983 and was given a paid job in an office at Waikabubak. When she was employed, they used her junior high school qualification rather than her high school qualification [so she could be paid less. Trs.]

> Then they said that she could not work in the office any more. Children of people who still had to go and report could not work in offices.

Ibu Bunga knew that everything that happened to her children was because of the accusation that she and her husband were communists. Even so, she continued to hope.

> I had eight children to bring up... not easy. But they were all good, none of them caused trouble, none of them fought with the neighbours' kids. My children never spoke harshly to each other. Of the eight, seven are boys, just one daughter. Normally boys get into fights, but not them. Once I bought some fish. I gave each of them some, from the oldest to the youngest. I gave some a bit more. I was testing them. The oldest one started taking some off his plate, giving it to the youngest, and none of them protested. My children are the best. The two youngest now earn salaries at the clinic and their names are listed on the database.[26]

## The GKS attitude towards Marxism/Communism

The GKS had been wrestling with Marxism and communism long before the 1965 tragedy. It issued its first official statement at the GKS Synod X meeting in Petawang (27 July-3 August 1956). This meeting established the Delegation for Inquiry into Marxism (DPM). Based on their report, the GKS position was affirmed at the next Synod meeting the following year (Synod XI at Tanggaba 15–24 July 1957). This 1957 position was reaffirmed in the decisions at extraordinary meeting of the GKS Synod held at Pameti Karata on 3–4 December 1965.

The first statement about Marxism issued at the Synod meeting at Petawang 1956 was as follows:

---

26  Ibu Bunga's daughter was forbidden from working in an office in West Sumba in 1983, but at the time of the current research, as Ibu Bunga says, her two youngest children were working at the clinic. This shows how a change in the political climate can change views in society.

G.K.S. regulations, clause 49.

We as Christians cannot possibly follow communism because:

1. This teaching denies the existence of God by stating that everything is just dust (material).
2. It denies the redemption of Jesus Christ the Saviour and bearer of wellbeing to man, because Marxism promotes conflict (enmity between one group and another), conflict that will be settled by the proletariat and from which will arise an earthly paradise (a classless society) where people will live in prosperity: as equals.
3. It despises all forms of religion (including Christianity) because it considers religion the opiate of the people.
4. Based on the three items above, we reject statements that Communism in Indonesia is different to Communism in Russia. Such statements are just lies because both Communism in Russia and Communism in Indonesia have their basis in Marxism.
5. This hateful lie has clouded the eyes of my Christians who are following Communist teachings either knowingly or unknowingly.
6. Because Communist/Marxism denies the existence of God and Jesus the Saviour, the Church should investigate all Christians who follow these teachings. However, this investigation should be carried out only after counsel has been given, and frequent warnings have been given.

This report, having been presented, is accepted by the Synod as its declaration. This committee is prepared to continue its investigation into these matters, and if anyone has any queries about any of these matters, they may contact the committee by letter.

(Syn. X article 50).[27]

At the Synod meeting in Tanggaba in 1957, the danger of communism/Marxism was formulated as an 'Encyclical':

---

27 *Susunan keputusan-keputusan synode geredja keristen sumba*, [Collection of GKS Synod Decisions] Synode ke-I (1947) ss/d. Synode keXX (1966), Kantor Geredja Keristen Sumba, Panjeti VII/93, Pos; Waingapu, Sumba, pp 74–75. This document provides summaries of the development of GKS's attitudes to Marxism from time to time.

Based on the report of the Delegation for the Investigation of Marxism, the Synod decided as follows:

The Synod should issue an encyclical to all Christians in Sumba to be read at the same time at worship on 1 September 1957. The sermons preached on that Sunday are to use the same Bible passage that will be prepared and distributed to all congregations before 1 September 1957, together with the mandate as found in article 49. (Synod XI, article 48).

The full text of the encyclical referred to in this article 48 was as follows:

ENCYCLICAL

The Synod XI of the Sumba Christian Church at its meeting in Tenggaba on 15–24 July 1957:...

Resolved the following:

1. Communism denies the existence of God by stating that everything is dust (material).
2. Communism denies the redemption by Jesus Christ as Saviour and the bearer of wellbeing to man, because it promotes conflict (enmity between one group and another), conflict that will be settled by the proletariat and from which will arise an earthly paradise (a classless society) where people will live in prosperity: as equals.
3. Communism despises all forms of religion (including Christianity) because it considers religion the opiate of the people.
4. Based on the three items above, we reject statements that Communism in Indonesia is different to Communism in Russia. Such statements are just lies, because both Communism in Russia and Communism in Indonesia have their basis in Marxism.
5. This hateful lie has clouded the eyes of my Christians who are following Communist teachings either knowingly or unknowingly.
6. Because Communism denies the existence of God and Jesus the Saviour, all Christians who follow these teachings should be investigated by the Church, but only after the aforementioned

refuse to change after counsel has been given, and they have been given frequent warnings.

(Synod XI, article 49).

The Synod resolution about Communism made in clause 6 of the Encyclical also applies to members of the congregation who have joined parties or organisations whose ideology is the same as Communism. Therefore, the Congregational Council must investigate the basis of all such parties and organisations. (Synod XI, article 50). [28]

A few months after the 1965 tragedy occurred in Jakarta, the GKS held a special meeting in December, 1965. At this meeting, the GKS decided that members of the Communist Party were communists who were atheist and therefore should be investigated.

---

28   Ibid, 74–75.

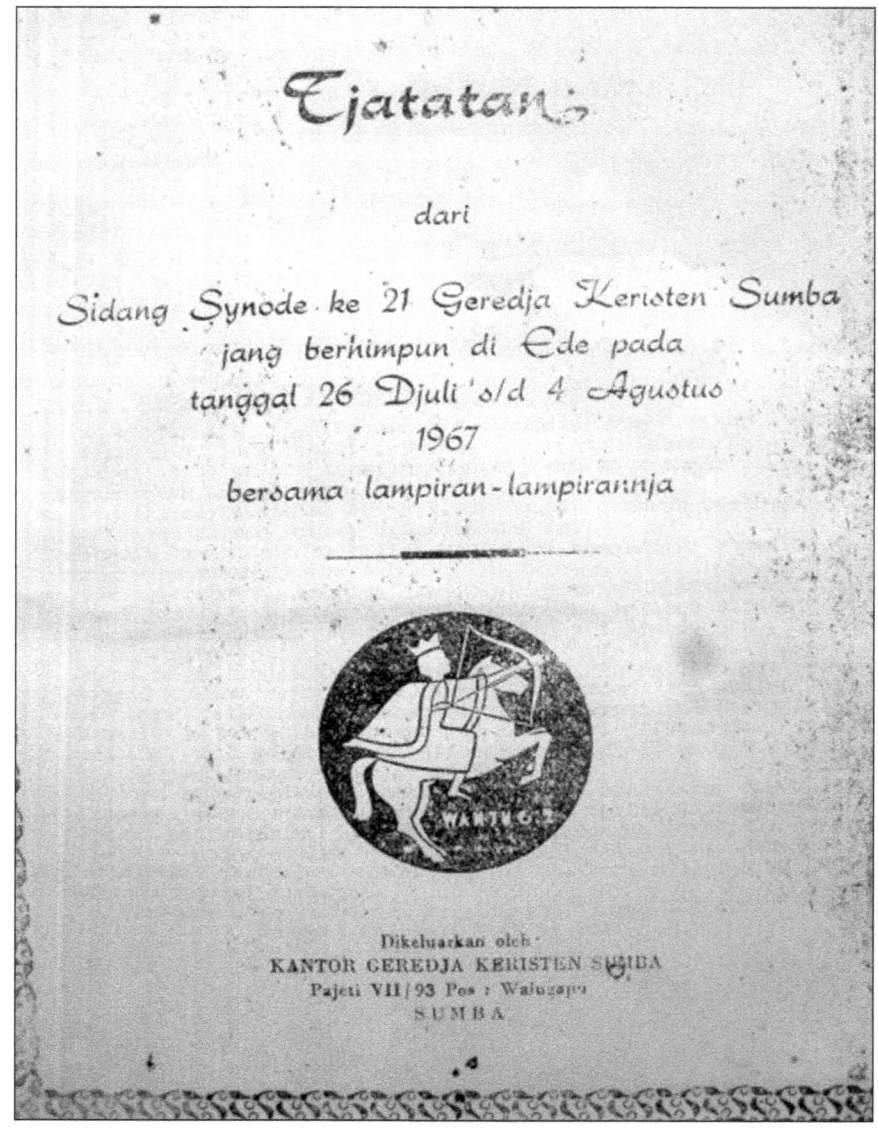

'What should the church's stance be particularly in the social-economic field so that Communism does not obtain an advantage? The Communist Party coup d'état has proven a bitter experience ... It is not impossible that it was our own fault that a social sickness like communism was able to influence Christians.' Report of the Delegation for Traditions and Beliefs in Society, in *Laporan Kedeputatan Adat-Istiadat dan Aliran dalam Masjarakat.* (Notes from the Synod XXI meeting in Ede, 1967) p. 161.
– JPIT Archives.

## Article 8
## The Thirtieth of September Movement

The 30th September Movement, which is a black page in the history of our nation, instigated by the Communist Party and its mass organisations, has carried out brutal murders on some of our Generals, murders that surpassed all humanitarian limits. This incident has caused a crisis in the Republic of Indonesia. In this national state of crisis, the GKS must take a stand, particularly when many GKS members were involved either directly or indirectly in that 30 September movement. The Synod Evangelism Commission (depis) representing the GKS in this sudden and urgent matter has wrestled with the events in an extraordinary meeting held at Pameti Karata from 3 to 4 December 1965. In our deliberations, we referred to the decision of the Tabundung Presbytery as follows:

1. Towards those directly involved or those in detention:

    a. The church does not hesitate from applying church investigation.

    b. Any officials of the Church are summarily dismissed

2. Any members of the meeting who follow communist teaching and who, following repeated advice refuse to repudiate those teachings, are to be investigated by the Church. 'Followers' means those who are directly members of a Communist party and those who in their attitude and propaganda take part in promulgating this ideology.

3. Any member who has deliberately become a member of any other organisation that is communist in spirit, who, after being given repeated advice, still refuses to repudiate, is to be investigated by the Church.

    Having given these matters deep deliberation, this meeting has formulated the following:

    <u>Special message from the Extraordinary Meeting of the GKS Synod Evangelism Commission to all Congregations of the Sumba</u> Christian Church upon reacting to the current situation in the Republic of Indonesia…

4. Parties involved, knowingly or unknowingly, with the 30th September Movement, include members of the church.

Resolution: To exhort all presbyteries and congregation councils of the GKS:

1. To repeat, in an orderly way, the reading at worship of the resolution of the Synod XI KGS at Tanggaba in 1957 about Communism

2. To give a reminder that the elements of Communism underscored by the encyclical of the Synod XI GKS at Tanggaba in 1957 are:

    a. Denial of existence of God

    b. Enmity between groups

    c. Hatred towards all forms of religion, which has now been publicly proven, therefore the Synod Evangelism Commission urges severity [by the congregation councils] in the investigation of members of the church who are proven to be followers of communist ideology.

3. To exhort all members of the congregation to be willing to assist the government and State apparatus in taking action against the 30 September movement, without transgressing existing Government regulations, or sanctions of the Divine law we adhere to.

4. To exhort members to pray for the State and its apparatus, and to pray also for those who have lost their way and have also led others down the wrong path so that God will protect the nation and the State and bring back those who have gone astray and led others astray.

5. To exhort all members of the congregation both through sermons and catechism and daily pastoral care to deepen their belief, meaning: 'Whosoever wants to follow Christ, follow Him and Him alone and adhere to His laws and His alone in every aspect of life.

*Pameri Karata, 4 December 1965*

Further to the above, the question that arises from the Synod Evangelism Commission to the Synod meeting is this: What further steps should the Synod be taking towards social justice in the Church after the above orders have been carried out? It seems necessary for this question to be discussed thoroughly so that the GKS can determine its further steps towards social justice.[29]

## Victims as sinners?[30]

Ibu Ina was waiting for my arrival at her house, because I had sent ahead notification about my intended visit. The meeting was also attended by her husband, Bapak Ama, their son and a female relative of Bapak Ama. Bapak Ama had suffered a stroke and was unable to speak, but could hear. After exchanging greetings and I had explained the purpose of my visit, Ibu Ina greeted me warmly.

Before I had pulled out my recording equipment or even asked any questions based on the interview guidelines, Ibu Ina started talking about her regrets and disappointment in the GKS because of the demand the congregation in Waikabubak made according to church regulations, for Bapak Ama to make a public confession of his sin after he came out of prison.[31] The Church had the opinion that all released 1965 tragedy detainees had to make public confessions at Sunday worship.[32] It was this position taken by the GKS that Ibu Ina found unacceptable, for she felt on the contrary the church should defend her husband and not side with those who arrested him. According to Ibu Ina, her husband had done nothing wrong, yet he was accused of being a Communist Party spy and imprisoned. When the members of the GKS Waikabubak congregation council came to visit the house, they asked for Bapak Ama to confess his sins.

> They were following rules, and they said, 'We don't know anything about that [that Pak Ama had done no wrong]. What we see is that he has come out of prison... what we see is that he was imprisoned.' So I

---

29  *Tjatatan dari Sidang Synodeke 20 Geredja Keristen Sumba jang berhimpun di Kananggaru pada tanggal 20 s/d 28 Djuli 1966 bersama lampiran-lampirannya.* (Kantor Geredja Keristen Sumba, Pajeti VII/93 Pos: Waingapu, Sumba) pp 16–17

30  All the following quotations are taken from an interview with Ibu Ina on 6 November, 2010 in Waikabubak except for a few quotations at the end of the section from an interview with Ibu Bunga on 15 November, 2010.

31  Ibu Ina knew me as a GKS pastor who works at the Faculty of Theology at UKAW in Kupang.

32  From the establishment of GKS until the present day, there has been a special liturgy for 'Confession'. Traditionally, there were specific sins that had to be confessed in this service. See further Maria Regina A. Pada, 'Praktek Pengakuan Dosa Pribadi di Hadapan Jemaat dalam Gereja Kristen Sumba (GKS): Suatu Tinjauan Dogmatis,' (The practice of confession for personal sins before GKS congregations: a dogmatic critique)(BA thesis, Faculty of Theology UKAW, Kupang, p.43).

> said, 'If you gentlemen cling to the fact that he was in prison, then I do not accept this, because there are also people who are imprisoned in the name of God. I am not saying that my husband was there in the name of God, not at all. I know for certain that he did nothing wrong, as his release says. He did nothing wrong, and yet now the church demands that he has to do this, has to confess his sin. Well, first say what the sin was. What was it he did?' But then the congregation council members said, 'Everyone knows that he has been in prison, so that means he did wrong.' He was being forced. But I said, 'Just so you gentlemen know', yes that's how I said it, 'don't worry about my husband. I myself', yes I said that, 'I myself want to stand up and confess my sins, but just so you gentlemen know, it is not your accusation that I will answer to. No. I know that I am a sinner, that everyone at every moment sins. It is those sins that I will confess before God, not the sins that you gentlemen are accusing me of.' Yes, I said that, and I took part in the Confession.'

After the visit by the members of the congregational council, Ibu Ina went to see the pastor of Waikabubak and spoke about the visit. But the pastor said that what they were asking of Bapak Ama, the confession, was a religious requirement. So in the end, Bapak Ama went along with what the church council had said and confessed his sin before the congregation.

> So... I went to see the pastor... so that he would not just hear things from the council, because they might put things differently, you know... So, I went to the pastor... I told him everything I was feeling. I know that my husband was in prison for one year and four months. But not a single member of the church council ever came to pray there, even though they knew that members of the flock were in that state, no one came, that's how it was. I had to get it out... And the pastor... said that people who confess their sins are not people with great sins, but they are showing maturity of their faith. That's what he said. So I said. 'I know that. That's exactly the point. So why my husband, then? If I am told to stand up and confess my sins, I will agree, because I know I have sinned'. So... I said that the church was not sincere in accepting the 1965 Incident.

Ina's anger at what her husband was experiencing increased. She had to fight to get justice for him, even be prepared to go to prison herself, because she was convinced her husband had done no wrong. Ibu Ina's refusal of the demand for confession was linked to the fact that no one from the church council had ever visited her husband while he was in prison.

> I was really mad, and I said to the church congregation members when they came to visit, 'When my husband was in prison, I didn't ever see you there. Don't you have a duty? When you see one of the flock fallen in a ravine, do you just stand there, saying, 'hey, you lamb down there, get back up here?'... [one of the congregational council] came and said [to my husband[. 'What's going on, uncle? I hear that uncle does not want to confess. I couldn't sleep last night, I was so upset.' That's what he said. And I said to myself, 'what an idiot'. What I said to him was, 'Maybe you couldn't sleep because uncle is released now. All the time he was in prison, you slept soundly enough... Let me tell you something, he was in prison not because of any accusation. Actually, I could have been in prison with him.'

Ibu Bunga told of a similar experience. No congregational council members ever visited them while in prison, and they too were disciplined by the church. When Bapak Angga was released around December 1966, he and Ibu Bunga made a public confession. Ibu Bunga said:

> Ibu Bunga: As for our congregation, did any of them ever come to visit? They ordered us to confess our sins, and I said, 'what sin, exactly, did we commit? It was the accusers, not us who did it.'... I asked the pastor, 'what is our sin? Probably you have sinned even more. Did you ever come and visit us? Did you ever ask questions, did you ever come? Not once', I said.

> Pastor Yetty: After you were released from prison, didn't you get visits from the church? So, we also went along with it and confessed our sins because of the church regulation. And what about Uncle Ama?

> Ibu Bunga: No, not a single one of them. We were the only ones who went to church and confessed, after others had done it already because those were the church rules.

The only one who came almost daily to lead worship and prayer was a Dutch missionary. Ibu Bunga said this about him:

> As for him... he was different. His faith was true, and he had fear of God.

## Lessons from the victims' history

Even though some of the victims did make public confessions, the stories above show that to this day they still do not understand why they or their husbands were considered to be sinners. There are at least two things the GKS can learn from the victims' stories, namely a lesson about the meaning of sin, and the need for reconciliation that involves church pastoral care.

### *Learning about sin*

Confession at GKS is grounded in the GKS's understanding of sin. As a church that is strongly tied to Calvinist tradition, so too is it tied to Calvin's teachings about sin. Calvin writes about secret and open sins, and each has different levels of church discipline.

Calvin's emphasis on individual sin is also the GKS's understanding of sin. In the 1965 tragedy, the GKS saw that because Bapak Ama, Bapak Angga and Ibu Bunga had been in prison because they were accused of being communist or Gerwani, this meant that they had sinned. Therefore, after their release from prison they had to receive church sanctions, as had been outlined in the resolutions of the GKS extraordinary meeting of December 1965. They were not permitted to take part in communion, and had to confess their sins before God and the congregation.[33] It is interesting to note that prior to 1966, and following 1956–57 when the GKS outlined its stand towards communism and Marxism, there had been no decisions about church sanctions for Communist Party members. The basis, both of traditional understanding about sin and for confession as carried out by the GKS, is that it is the individual who is considered to have sinned. But sin is not always individual sin.

The objections of some victims to confessing sin before the congregation helps us to learn about structural sin, or what Paul Tillich calls 'collective estrangement'. Tillich sees that sin is not limited to individual estrangement in relations with God and fellow beings, but it also includes collective estrangement, for example state evil carried out by leaders, and people encouraged by them to participate.[34] It is structural sin – 'collective estrangement' – that places the female victims of 1965 as sinners, by the

---

33   There are no notes about the number of 1965 victims who received church sanctions, but those known are Bapak Ama, Bapak Angga and Ibu Bunga. It is most likely that all the 1965 detainees were similarly sanctioned.
34   In *Systematic Theology II*, which he wrote after World War II, Paul Tillich emphasises the importance of the confession of wrong: 'And lately whole nations have been morally condemned for... atrocities...'. Chicago: The University of Chicago Press, 1957, p. 58.

state, the church, and by society as a whole. What we can see from Ibu Bunga and Ibu Ina's stories is that people in prison and people who have sinned are not the same thing. As Ibu Bunga said, she had done nothing wrong, and yet was branded as a sinner and was made to confess her sin.

Structural sin is connected to a system of injustice, intimidation, and violence that is difficult to avoid. In this structure, the church was cornered, because it had already rejected communism/Marxism, so it could not oppose the state when it wiped out the Communist Party with torture and massacre.

In West Sumba, we can see how the church accepted the state position. The moderator of the GKS Synod in July 1966 recommended that the speech made by the District Head of West Sumba 'be included in the GKS news'. Here are some words from that speech:

a. We should not judge the sad events and/or any bitter experience of the past from a narrow point of view because they led to suffering, but rather we should take advantage of them and exploit them.

b. As a concrete example, the escapades of the G30S/PKI [30th September Movement/Indonesian Communist Party] are a national tragedy, but they bring great opportunity to national life, particularly to those who profess religion, in the crystallisation of the situation in Indonesia, in various issues:

1. The truth of Pancasila and the Indonesian Revolution, particularly the truth of the first of the five principles of Pancasila, namely Faith in Almighty God.

2. Indonesians are made more aware of believing in God

3. There is a dividing line between the religious and those who are anti-God

4. We must not divert from the track of Indonesian revolution and particularly from religious teachings.

5. Man might make plans, but it is God who decides.

6. We must not idolise a theory or a leader as was done by former members of the Communist Party

7. Above all power in this world, we must acknowledge there is the highest eternal power, namely the Power of God The Creator of this universe. [35]

---

35 *Tjatatan dari Sidang Synod ke 20 GKS di Kananggaru pada tanggal 20 s/d 28 Djuli 1966* [Notes from GKS Synod Assembly 20 at Kananggaru, 20–28 July 1966] pp 35–56.

By accepting the state position as its own position, it was increasingly difficult for the church to defend victims. The victims' stories help us to remember what Paul Tillich said about sin as collective estrangement, so the meaning of sin also must be broadened from not merely individual sin, but also the destruction of solidarity as a result of a structure that is unjust and violent.[36]

A broader understanding of sin means that the confession of individual sin should accompany the confession of structural sin. The confession of individual sin before the congregation does not necessarily heal the condition of estrangement, but on the contrary can lead to other possibilities. Apart from the possibility that those not proven guilty according to law can be forced to confess sin, there is also the possibility that people who have done wrong can commit further sin as long as they feel the confession is just a formality. Further, there is the possibility that this will perpetuate the unjust system itself. Lessons learned from the victims' stories encourage the GKS to be aware that the GKS itself was cornered within a sinful state structure, and therefore it should reconsider confession so that there can be balance between individual sin and structural sin in the understanding of and dealings with sin.[37]

## *Learning about the need for reconciliation*

> I'm sorry… but whether it was right or wrong, I was angry with the congregation council back then because they ordered Bapak to confess his sin.[38]

---

36   See further Paul Tillich, 'The Marks of Man's Estrangement and the Concept of Sin', *Systematic Theology*, II, 44–59.
37   There are various other models of institutional apology to victims based on the institutions' awareness of involvement in transgression in a structural way. For instance, Gus Dur's apology when he was head of Nahdlatul Ulama, to the victims of the 1965 massacres, and to all those imprisoned without trial (see Budiawan, *Mematahkan Pewarisan Ingatan*, p. 49). Another example is the apology made by the United Church of Christ in America to the people of Hawai'i, not because their missionaries proselytised in Hawai'i, but because in their proselytising, the local culture was destroyed, and also many missionary families of the time were enriching themselves through involvement with the economy and politics in Hawai'i (see Charles McCollough, 'Why our church apologised to Hawai'i, on http://www.uss.orf/50/pdfs/mccollough.pdf accessed on 30 March, 2012. Apart from that, there is Pope Benedict XVI's apology on behalf of Catholic priests for child abuse in the Catholic Church in Ireland. In a pastoral letter to Irish Catholics he admitted victims and their families had experienced 'betrayal by the Church '. The Pope said that those who had done wrong had take responsibility before God for their sins and be tried according to the law. See 'Paus Minta Maaf', *Republika Online*, 21 March 2010, http://www.republika.co.is/berita/breaking news/internasional/10/03/21/107374-paus-minta-maaf, accessed 18 April 2012.
38   Ibu Ina, interview.

It turns out that Ibu Ina had never told her story about the 1965 tragedy, including her feelings towards the church, to anyone before the time of this research, including to her children. The 1965 tragedy happened decades ago, but it left bitterness and division among the GKS congregation, both among those who were arrested and killed, as well as their families, down to their children and grandchildren. The need for reconciliation means not only the healing of victims, but also the healing of unjust structures. Learning from victims' stories could help the GKS in this era of reformation to ensure that individual healing and structural healing go hand in hand. Structural healing is not merely church structure, including understanding about sin, but also state structure, including its duty to restore the rights of 1965 victims.

Learning from victims means that the church needs to take another look at the government's version of the 1965 tragedy, which has thus far been considered true, because both victims and Indonesian citizens have a right to the truth. Reconciliation includes the awareness that the state committed human rights abuse when victims were arbitrarily imprisoned, tortured and killed. This awareness will help to straighten the history of our country. Advocacy for the rights of victims to the truth and healing are steps towards reconciliation. As an integral part of the nation of Indonesia, the GKS can support victims who were government civil servants, in their efforts to obtain pensions and so forth. Other acts of reconciliation, which the church should also advocate, include official state apology for the terror and slaughter.

Although it is important for the church to demand a process of justice and protection of human rights by the state, this does not mean that the church itself can relegate its ethical and pastoral responsibility to secular justice, for among other things, state justice is not exactly the same as being wrong before God. The church, in becoming an agent of reconciliation for the 1965 tragedy, also must be prepared to listen to calls for the GKS to revise its position towards communism and Marxism. There is nothing wrong with the church revising its views of half a century ago, based on the victims' bitter experiences and the new research about the 1965 tragedy.[39] A review of those decisions would also be a step towards structural healing.

---

39 Some examples of this 'new' research that contribute to correcting the history of the 1965 Tragedy, particularly from women's perspectives, include: *Kejahatan terhadap Kemanusiaan Berbasis Jender: Mendengarkan Suara Perempuan Korban Peristiwa 1965* [Gender-based crimes against humanity: listening to the voices of women victims of the 1965 incident] (Jakarta: Komnas Perempuan, 2007): Ita F. Nadia, *Suara Perempuan Korban Tragedi '65* [voices of women victims of the '65 tragedy] (Yogyakarta: Galangpress, 2009); and Saskia Eleonora Wieringa, *Sexual Politics in Indonesia* (New York: Palgrave Macmillan, 2002).

Apart from this, the GKS can find a new basis for developing pastoral care that is more sensitive to the victims and to the healing of relations within the GKS congregations, for instance though a process of reconciliation, including religious services of reconciliation. Church discipline can be given new interpretation as pastoral action that involves justice and truth. Those serving the church are in a key position to create the situation and atmosphere of safety for victims to be able to describe their experiences, and for church members and other members of society to listen to them without judgment. It is important for pastoral care to include restoration of the victims' rights, and healing of the collective estrangement/ structural sin, so that reconciliation can take place within the church fellowship.

Chapter 7

# The 1965 Tragedy in East Sumba

## History from Victims' Perspectives

**Irene Umbu Lolo**

As in West Sumba, the incident that was called G30S caused havoc and unrest in East Sumba. From towards the end of 1965 until mid-1966, the upheaval of violence became increasingly obvious. Many people were accused of being involved with the Communist Party and Gerwani. They were quickly branded as communists, arrested and detained. Some were tortured, held in prison for months, even years on end, with no idea of any end in sight, and some were raped. Some were shot.

The situation in East Sumba became increasingly unsafe. The mood was threatening and tense. The military made people afraid, and suspicious of one another. The army and police encouraged the mobs to ransack and destroy houses of those accused to be communist or Gerwani. Hatred towards the communists and Gerwani reached fever pitch. For instance, the mob set fire to the house of Ibu Ria's parents in Melolo.[1] Angry youths dragged anyone they captured to the nearest police office. Coarse, brutal and inhumane action was commonplace. Everything happened very fast and smoothly, as though this activity was perfectly proper. No one dared restrain the mob.

This reality caused profound fear and trauma, particularly to those who became victims of mass violence. Communists or Gerwani (this was the usual label given to them, including those suspected of being so), who had previously lived normal, proper lives in the midst of society, now became despised or ostracised. Even their own families excluded them. They were discriminated against.

---

1   Ibu Ria, interview on December 2010, Payeti, Waingapu.

The accused were treated as second-class citizens, not only in society (having to report regularly to the police station, prohibited from joining the civil service, having no right to vote or stand for office), but also in church circles. At the Christian Church of Sumba (GKS) they could not be nominated or chosen as members of the congregational council. Those who had been in prison had to confess their sins with a personal confession in front of the congregation at Sunday worship, before they could be received back into the fellowship of the church and before they could join the sacrament of communion.[2] They were seen as the worst sinners of all, criminals, savages, atheists, trash, and bearers of disease in society. Here are two accounts:

> I was accused of all kinds of things, they said I was a seductress, a bad woman [cries]. Even though none of that was true [pauses]... Yes, I was taunted back then when I was still a young girl. They thought I was dirty. (Ibu Ria)[3]

> The children gave up. They almost did not want to go to school. They were afraid to go out of the house. They were teased, taunted and insulted. (Janda Mbulu-Dima)[4]

The stigma remains to this day. The victims and their families are still fearful and traumatised. Society is still reluctant to discuss the 1965 Incident because the subject remains extremely sensitive. Written information about the victims from East Sumba is difficult to find because it is lost or destroyed, or deliberately lost or destroyed.

So what actually happened? How could the events have occurred? Why were people detained and executed without any trial? Who were the executioners? And who were the people executed? How did the wives and children survive after their husbands and fathers were executed? What was the situation in East Sumba at the time? What was the effect of the incident on victims and society, including on the GKS in East Sumba? All these questions and many more demand answers.

This is why we, the research team for East Sumba, tried to investigate and study the events, to find answers. We visited victims, listened to their stories of their experiences, and paid close attention to the tragic stories that

---

2   See *Studi Kasus Pastoral II Nusa Tenggara Timur* (Jakarta: BPK Gunung Mulia, 1990), 105–107.
3   Ibu Ria, interview.
4   Interview with Janda Mbulu-Dima, 18 December 2010 at Kampung Wangga, Waingapu. See 'Gereja dan Pemerintah' in *Studi Kasus Pastoral II: Nusa Tenggara Timur* (Jakarta: BPK Gunung Mulia, 1990), 108.

they had kept to themselves for years. These stories cause them suffering. Their telling and bearing witness is what we want to retell and convey in this writing.

## Profile of East Sumba

In 1965, East Sumba, with its capital Waingapu, was one of two districts (*kabupaten*) on the island of Sumba.[5] Compared to Waikabubak, the capital of West Sumba, Waingapu was busier because the town had a harbour and an airport. The small town has been an important and strategic place since colonial times because of its location on the coast, which facilitates sea transportation and trade to and from Sumba. The police station and courts are located there. In 1965–66 these places were used as detention centres for communists. There is also a wharf, now called the 'old wharf', which was one of the execution sites. The Waingapu prison is located about 100 metres from the old wharf. Waingapu also has the Mau Hau airport located about five kilometers from the town centre, which used to be a landing place for visiting VIPs, including President Sukarno in 1955, and General A Yani who officiated at the opening of the Kambaniru Bridge on 26 September, 1965.[6]

Back in 1965, cars and transportation facilities in Waingapu were extremely limited. The only cars going around the streets were government vehicles, cars for foreign missionaries, and the vehicles owned by Chinese, Arab and local traders. Ordinary people went around by foot. Some people in Waingapu and the environs also rode bicycles.[7] If people wanted to travel outside the town (for instance to Lewa or to Waikabubak, about 60 kilometres away) they had to go by horse or take public transport, which meant trucks

---

5   The two districts were West Sumba and East Sumba. Since 2006, Sumba has been divided into four districts: East Sumba, Central Sumba, West Sumba, and Southwest Sumba.
6   According to Pastor Lian, when President Sukarno visited Sumba, he landed at Mau Hau and then toured the town of Waingapu by car that was driven by a young woman from Sumba called Rambu. The president visited the regional government offices, and after eating lunch in Waingapu, he continued his journey home via Mau Hau airport. General A Yani was shot in Jakarta in the 30th September incident only four days after his visit to East Sumba. See Umbu Pura Woha, *Sejarah Pemerintahan di Pulau Sumba* (Kupang: Undana Press, 2008), 298.
7   Interview with Bpk Muri Mada, 23 March, 2012 at Kambaniru. He started work as assistant Scripture teacher in Kambaniru in 1964. He often walked to visit his family in Melolo, When he wanted to do further schooling at the School of Evangelists (SGI) in Lewa on 14 August 1966, he and his friends chose to walk rather than ride on the back of a truck to Waingapu and back to save money. He often saw pastors cycling to their place of ministry in Kambaniru.

owned by Chinese. The journey from Waingapu to Waikabubak by truck took more than ten hours. As Bapak Loka Ndara said:

> You went from Waingapu to Waikabubak by truck, a truck called Radjawali that always broke down or got a flat tyre because the road was so bad. Back then the condition of the roads was terrible – just stones, mud, and many big holes. On top of that, the bridges were broken. Trucks could not go fast because the roads were so narrow. That's why it could take us a whole day. Once we had to sleep on the road because the truck had broken down. The government and the military had their own jeeps and trucks.[8]

The electricity was on only at night, and even then only in certain places like the hospital, the missionaries' houses, and houses of government officials. Most of the people who lived in Waingapu and the environs still used oil lamps and petromax lamps, and some wealthier people had generators.

The population, apart from Sumbanese, comprised people from Sabu, Flores, Timor, Rote, Ambon, and Java plus those of Chinese and Arab ethnicity. The majority of the population, namely the Sumbanese, worked as farmers and tenders of livestock. Some had government jobs, or they worked in the private sector, and there were teachers and traders. The trading sector of the economy was dominated by the ethnically Chinese and Arabs.

In terms of religion, the majority of the population of East Sumba was Protestant. There were also Catholics, Muslims and followers of the indigenous religion (Marapu). Between 1962–1967 various political parties had representatives in the regional parliament (DPRD) namely: Parkindo (Indonesian Christian [Protestant] Party) (8), Partai Katolik (Catholic Party) (1), PNI (Indonesian National Party) (3), PKI (Indonesian Communist Party)(1) and Masyumi (Consultative Council of Indonesian Muslims (1). The head of the local parliament for East Sumba was Mori Domu Tipa from Parkindo. The District Head of East Sumba for the period 1962–1967 was L.D. Dapawole who was replaced by Umbu Haramburu Kapita, appointed for the period 1967–1878.[9] The District Military Command (Kodim) 1601 for Sumba with its Military Commander was based in Waingapu, and the office was held by Letkol. Inf (Lieutenant Colonel Infantry) Moch. Musa for the period 1965–1967, while the office of Regional Police Chief was held

---

8 Interview with Bapak Lako Ndara, 18 October 2010 at the precinct (kelurahan) of Lewa Paku.
9 These are their real names.

Torture site. The old prison in Melolo, District of Rindi Umalulu, East Sumba. – JPIT archives.

by Drs. R.I. Suwondo.[10] The head of the court of justice in Waingapu at the time was Djahum Purba, S.H.

Apart from Waingapu, the other important place mentioned in relation to the 1965 Incident is Melolo, the capital of Rini Umalulu district, which is located on the coast about 60 kilometres to the east of Waingapu. This is where there were arrests and torture of communists and Gerwani, and also attacks and burning of houses. Victims were held at the Melolo police station and then taken by the police to Waingapu. The police chief at Melolo at the time was Bapak Nyoman. In Waingapu, the government office of the courts of justice and the office for agriculture were also used as temporary detention centres, because both these places were close to Padadita beach, which was an execution site.[11]

## Who suffered?

When the 1965 incident occurred, Bapak Loka Ndara was in the second year of Andaluri senior high school in Waingapu. According to him, when

---

10  See *Sejarah Pemerintahan*:246–8, 295–300
11  Interview with Ibu Ria.

the disturbance broke out in Waingapu, the Chinese school that was located directly across from the prison, closed immediately. One morning in January 1966, some students from his school demonstrated.

> The demonstration was organised by the teachers. The students walked to the Chinese school. We marched in line, singing national songs like 'Maju Tak Gentar, Membela Yang Benar' [Marching forward resolutely, defending the truth] and 'Padamu Negeri' [For you, my country]. When we got there we tore down the school sign [written in Chinese characters] and we wrote *'milik Negara'* [State property] on the walls. The staff of the Chinese school did not react, and it seemed that they had been given leave. The school was surrounded by a wall and had iron gates. It was taken over by the state and became a junior high school. The Chinese school was closed. The situation at the time was under military control. The people were asked to assist the military in their activities. It was a state of military emergency at the time.[12]

Chinese-owned shops were also closed. Many of the shopkeepers tried to escape to safer places.[13]

The people arrested were communists or Gerwani, but these labels meant many different things. Some people were indeed members or officials of the Communist Party (like Bapak Mbulu-Dima and Bapak Domi who were leaders of the Communist Party in East Sumba), or members and officials of Gerwani (like the Head of Gerwani for East Sumba, Ibu Liana).[14] Apart from that, the wives, female relatives or daughters of Communist Party officials were branded as Gerwani. For instance, Bapak Mbulu-Dima's wife was interrogated at the police station, accused of being a member of Gerwani, but because there was no proof she was finally sent home. However, later she was still penalised, even without any proof of any Gerwani affiliation. She had to report to authorities every month from 1966–1978 and was interrogated about the activities of her husband, her children, and herself.

> I was under 'town arrest' until 1978. I had to report to the police station. And then, around the 1980s, there was talk of a government plan to give some money to 'Gestapu' people. I did not want to take

---

12  Interview with Loka Ndara, 18 October 2010 at Lewa Paku
13  Ibid.
14  Both Mpk Mbulu-Dima and his wife were listed as members of the Payeti congregation of GKS.

any money. The way I see it: my husband was murdered, so why would I accept money from the government?[15]

According to some informants, some of those arrested were neither Communist Party members nor officials, but they were accused of being so merely because they had accepted help from the BTI (Barisan Tani Indonesia, Indonesian Farmers' Front) like tools, rice seedlings, thread, looms, money and basic food necessities.[16]

People who were involved with organisations with Communist Party affiliations, like the BTI were also arrested. For instance, Ibu Ria's father was the head of BTI in Melolo. He was immediately arrested and tortured at the Melolo police station. Her mother was also arrested and accused of being a member of Gerwani. A mob of youths torched their house in Melolo.

> My parents were finally arrested by the powers-that-be and taken to the police station. A mob of youth set fire to my parents' house at Melolo (60 kilometres from Waingapu). When my father was at the police station, they stuffed a stone rice pestle in his mouth, breaking his teeth, and he had to be treated at the Melolo clinic. My younger brothers and sisters went away to stay with our grandmother at Kampung Baru in Waingapu.[17]

Apart from this, the children of Communist Party, BTI or Gerwani officials were also arrested, whether they were siblings, in-laws, or nephews and nieces. Without any investigation or proof, they were accused of being 'involved' and therefore arrested. For instance, Bapak Luis ended up being arrested because his older brother, Bapak Ama, who lived in Waikabubak, was a Communist Party official (see the previous report on West Sumba).[18]

---

15  Interview with Janda Mbulu-Dima. 'Gestapu' is the acryonym of 'Gerakan September Tiga Puluh (Thirtieth September Movement). However, it sounds like 'Gestapo', the Nazi secret police established by the German Nazis whose duties included muzzling Hitler's opponents and seeding terror in society because of their terrible interrogation methods. See further John Roosa 'Dictionary of a Disaster' in *Inside Indonesia* 99 (January-March 2010); and Harsutejo (a former 1965 political prisoner), 'Gestapu, Gestok' on the Bingkai Merah web page, http://bingkaimerah-indonesia.blogspot.com/2011/09/gestapu-gestok.html accessed on 26 May 2012.
16  Informants who mentioned this include: Pak Bram (interview 4 December 2010 at Padadita; Janda Mblul-Dima; Pak Fredi Alelei, interview 26 February 2011 at Waingapu; and Ibu Ria. Informants did not always distinguish between the Communist Party (PKI) and the Indonesian Farmers' Front (BTI), using the term 'PKI' even when it was clear they meant BTI.
17  Interview with Janda Mbulu-Dima.
18  Ibid.

And Ibu Ria herself, whose father was head of the BTI, was also arrested and taken to the Melolo police station. 'I was accused of being a Gerwani official, even though I know nothing at all about politics.'

Although these victims were just the children and family members of Communist Party and BTI officials, they themselves kept trying to find reasons to understand why they had been arrested. For instance, Ibu Ria told the story about a hat emblazoned with the logo of Pemuda Rakyat (People's Youth). On 21 May 1965, there had been an all-Sumba Youth Assembly in Waingapu that included not only political parties, but also youth organisations like People's Youth, Christian Youth and Muslim Youth. This Assembly shows how, just a few months before the 30$^{th}$ September incident, relations between the various parties, including the Communist Party, were still good. According to Ibu Ria, representatives of the parties and organisations spoke at this assembly, including Bapak Mbulu-Dima as the leader of the Communist Party. People from the Assembly of Local Leaders (Muspida) also attended. Ibu Ria was delegated to attend the youth assembly, and when there, she was given a Pemuda Rakyat hat, but she did not wear it.

> In May 1965, the Education and Culture (P & K) office delegated me, via the head of school, to go and listen to the lectures at the youth conference in Waingapu, at the national building (Gedung Nasional). I went, because I had been ordered to do so. When I got there I was given a Pemuda Rakyat hat. I didn't wear it, because I had been sent as a P & K representative… It was really crowded. All the political parties and mass organisations were present.[19]

There were also people arrested even though they had no knowledge of, or links of any kind to the Communist Party, BTI or Gerwani.[20] They were the victims of slander, suspicion, bad feeling, and personal grudges. They were unable to defend themselves, given no opportunity to explain, and were helpless in confronting the frenzy of the mob. They were just arrested and taken off to the police station.[21]

---

19  Ibu Ria from interviews conducted at Payeti, Waingapu on 20 December 2013, and at Liliba, Kupang on 29 March 2011.
20  Janda Mbulu-Dima told the story of one of her neighbours, and a friend, who had no links to the Communist Party whatsoever, but was accused as such because of a personal grudge, and was arrested.
21  This is a summary of information from interviews with Pak Bram, Janda Mbulu-Dima, and Pak Fredi Alelei.

# Arrest, detention, torture, sexual violence, murder

## Women's experiences

Arrests of victims happened at night. Here is Janda Mblulu-Dima's account of when her husband was taken:[22]

> My former husband, Mbulu-Dima, was one of the officials of the Communist Party in East Sumba. He was also a member of the local parliament (DPRD)... back then there was a Communist Party sign in front of our house. In December 1965, my husband was arrested by a large group of people, the army – Kodim (District Military Command). [she lowers her voice, and her face shows anxiety]. They came to the house very late at night, arrested my husband and ransacked the house. They checked the cupboards and took away any documents they found. They took other things as well. I was told to keep quiet, not to ask questions. They took Bapak to the police station that night. He was detained there, then put into prison and he never returned.

When the arrests happened, wives and children were given no explanation at all, but were told to keep quiet. Often the people arrested were also forced to remain silent and follow orders. This happened to Ibu Ria:

> I was living in a 'teachers' mess' in [a certain village]. Late at night, a group of youths were told to kidnap and kill me. Fortunately, the local Melolo police chief came with some of his men. There were five of them. God had arranged it. Before the youths arrived, the police came first to get me... I was taken away on horseback. They covered me with a tarpaulin. When I asked where I was being taken, they told me to keep quiet – there would be time to talk when we got to the police barracks. When we got to the police barracks they kept heavy guard over me. I slept there night and day under the guard's table. I was not allowed to go out whenever I wished. I saw there were lots of people at the police station. Many of them were Christians – members of GKS, but we were not permitted to talk to each other. I was interrogated there for a month, asked all kinds of things, including what my activities were... What I saw, was that this was all because of envy, bad feeling, and revenge.

---

22  In Sumba, widows always refer to themselves as 'Widow' (Janda) with the name of their late husband. We have preserved that practice with our pseudonym, Janda Mbulu-Dima' – Widow Mbulu-Dima, but still protecting her real name.

At the detention centres (the Waingapu judicial offices and the agricultural office at that time) people were branded as communist and Gerwani and interrogated by the police. Following her husband's arrest in December 1965, Janda Mbulu-Dima was arrested herself:

> I was taken to the police station for questioning. They asked all kinds of things about my husband, about my own activities. I answered everything honestly; so the soldiers never beat me. While I was detained, I was forbidden to meet my husband. So from the time of his arrest until the end of his life (December 1965 – March 1966) I never met him again. The children were also not permitted to see him. [Janda Mbulu-Sima looks angry]. The children gave up hope.[23]

Some people were beaten and tortured. According to witnesses, the torture included pulling out fingernails and toenails, and being kicked by police wearing hob-nailed boots that broke legs or arms and cracked heads open.[24] All the prisoners had to do forced labour, as Ibu Ria described:

> Everyone who was being held at the police station was ordered to work every single day – cleaning floors, doing laundry, cutting grass, we were just like servants. Anyone who did not work was made to kiss the dirt or run around the barracks. One of the police chiefs ordered me to work. But I said I was sick, so I got out of it.

Some detainees were turned into objects of mockery, being made to dance, jumping up and down to entertain the others. All detainees were held under close guard, were not allowed to go out as they wished, and were not allowed to talk to each other.[25]

Those who did not carry out instructions were threatened, for instance Ibu Ria was threatened that her parents would be murdered if she resisted the interrogator raping her. Here is her account:

> Afterwards, they left me alone with the head of the [interrogation] team. There was just one oil lamp in the room. The team leader came up to me and stroked my hand. He asked me whether I had a boyfriend. I remained silent. Then he said. 'Do you know why you have been called in here? You want it, right? You're a woman now.' Then he tried to rape

---

23  In Sumba, widows always refer to themselves as 'Widow' (Janda) with the name of their late husband. We have preserved that practice with our pseudonym.
24  Ako, interview at Melolo village, Rindi Umalulu sub-district, 26 February, 2011.
25  Ibu Ria interview.

me [she stands up here, extremely emotional and angry]. I said... 'I'd rather die than lose my virtue.' So he said he would kill my parents. 'I am not afraid. Let us all die. I'd rather die than have to do this, I have self respect.' I kept on resisting and yelling. In the end, he did not rape me. About an hour later, his colleagues came in and asked him, 'So, all done?' The team leader answered 'She refuses!' I kept on crying, then they called in some of the male detainees who were going to be executed the next day. They made them dance to cheer me up. But I kept on crying. I felt one with them. At around two in the morning I was taken back to the place where I was being held.

Some of the women were sexually abused, and some were raped:

> I had a friend called Sarce. She was raped. She ended up hanging herself because she could not stand it. She was so traumatised, she killed herself [after her release].

According to Janda Mbulu-Dima, while they were in prison the detainees were visited and received pastoral care from a Dutch missionary with the GKS. This pastor would pray with those who were going to be executed, before they were taken away. He also went to visit the victims' families. Janda Mbulu-Dima talked about the visit of this pastor to her house:

> When he came, he was with a police guard. He told me to remain strong and to pray regularly. I kept silent because the policeman had already warned me not to ask lots of questions. I had to just sit there and listen quietly.

After their release, the female ex-detainees faced all kinds of problems. At church, 'Gestapu' families could not be nominated or chosen for the church council. They could only vote.

> Finally, I was released. I was considered to be a communist sympathiser. In 1967, I married my husband – a widower with three children. He was a policeman, a member of the team that had interrogated me, and who guarded me in prison. After I married, I wanted to teach again in Waingapu, but I couldn't because my certificates had been burnt when my parents' house in Melolo was burnt down. I also had to suffer church sanctions at the Payeti church. The pastor at the time was Pastor Mulipatty. I was ostracized from society, from the church, and also from my own family. My family rejected me. My children were not accepted as civil servants. Through the help of someone on the inside, a family

close to us that took pity on us, one of my children did finally become a civil servant. I have been a widow since 1979.

## Executions

All the people executed were men. No women were executed. Our research determined two execution sites in East Sumba; the old wharf, and the mangrove swamp at Padadita beach (about three kilometres to the east of the centre of Waingapu town). Even today, the people of Padadita still call that place the 'PKI forest' and it is deeply feared. Seven victims were executed on Padadita beach on 1 March 1966. Only five names have been obtained, namely:

1. Domi (a member of the local parliament, and Communist Party official)
2. Mbulu-Dima (head of the local branch of the Communist Party)
3. Hamid (a man from Sumba who had converted to Islam and had once been Village Head)
4. Ruben
5. Lalo[26]

The atmosphere in Waingapu was extremely tense when the executions were carried out. Beginning around 1 March 1966, there was a night curfew for more than a week, from 8 at night until 4 in the morning.[27] People were forbidden to leave their houses at night because there was going to be a police raid. People who lived close to Padadita Beach could hear the shots, as Bapak Bram recounted:

> Around midnight, I heard a volley of shots. I did not dare to leave the house. The atmosphere that night was terrifying.[28]

Janda Mbulu-Dima remembers her husband's execution.

> He was shot on the night of 1 March 1966. [She is silent for a while]. Before he was shot, he asked a policeman to come to the house. He

---

26   The information about those executed at Padadita beach is from interviews with various informants: Ibu Ria; Bapak Elo Ratapatt (25 February 2011 at Wainghapu), and Fredi Alelei.
27   Interviews with Janda Mbulu Dia and Bapak Bram.
28   Bapak Bram was a village official at Padadita at the time.

wanted to wear a Sumba cloth called *hinggi*.[29] I gave the cloth to the policeman. The mood that night was tense and terrifying. I trusted my fate to God although I was sad and desperate. That night there was an order from the government for everyone to stay indoors because there was going to be a raid.

The second wave of killings happened in August 1966. The victims were taken from the prison in military transport in the middle of the night to the execution site, the old wharf. Their hands were bound behind them, and they were blindfolded with black cloth. When they got to the beach they were loaded on to a barge and taken out to sea. There, while they were standing, they had stones ties to their feet, were ordered to pray, and then shot by an army firing squad, falling directly into the sea. According to an informant who heard from an eye witness, one of the victims did not die when he was shot, so that when he fell in the sea he was still floating and had to be shot repeatedly by the firing squad.[30] There were 13 people executed at the old wharf, including:

1. Henokh
2. Marten (from Tabundung, East Sumba, who worked in a government office)
3. Ony
4. Golu (from Walakaka sub-district, West Sumba)
5. Anton (Javanese, an official in one of the government offices)
6. Tius.[31]

After the execution, the people of Waingapu did not eat fish for months because they considered the fish to be poisoned from eating the bodies of the people executed. Fishermen were reluctant to go fishing because they knew they could not sell their fish.[32]

---

29  This woven cloth is still commonly worn by men in Sumba.
30  Bapak Dimu, interview 26 November 2010. He heard the story from an eye witness who was the driver of the army transport.
31  Elo Ratapatty, interview.
32  Interview with Pak Bram and his wife.

The old wharf. One of the execution sites in East Sumba. – JPIT archives

## The Christian Church of Sumba (GKS) in East Sumba wrestles with the situation

As part of this nation, the GKS has a duty to heal the wounds of the victims of the oppression, cruelty and violence of 1965. We can report that the GKS in East Sumba did carry out pastoral care to the victims and their families. As Pastor Matolang recounted:

> Other pastor colleagues and I in Waingapu took turns in serving at the prison. I went there to serve those who had been arrested and imprisoned, to give them encouragement. The atmosphere was exceedingly tense inside. I gave advice based on the word of God.[33]

Accompanied by military guards, pastors from Waingapu went to visit and pray with those in prison, even praying for them before they were executed. One pastor gave communion to victims before they were executed.[34] Pastors

---

33  Pastor Matolang, interview on 16 April 2012 at Kambaniru.
34  See 'Gereja dan Pemerintah' [church and government] in *Studi Kasus Pastoral II: Nusa Tenggara Timur*, 115.

also visited families, as in Janda Mbulu-Dima's account of when a pastor came to visit her and her children.

One can say that the pastoral care GKS gave at that time did not solve the problems or the suffering of victims in any significant way, because their husbands and fathers were executed, nonetheless. The church's role was limited to charitable diaconal ministry and did not extend to transformative diaconal ministry. The church was unable to prevent the executions from being carried out, even though the church acknowledges that according to the Christian faith, murder cannot be justified.

One can also say that the military supervision of the pastors while they were giving spiritual care to the victims and their families shows how helpless the church was in confronting military power. As has been said earlier, it was the military that the people, including the church, feared most of all. The military guard sent to accompany the pastors was not to give them a sense of security, but was a form of intimidation that increased the sense of fear. The military at the time also intervened in church matters, and the church was powerless and afraid to refuse this intervention that seriously interfered with the church's pastoral care.

Even so, one has to admit that the church's care at the time was somewhat beneficial to the victims, inasmuch as its intention was to give them strength.

## We, the living

One cannot ignore the fact that the 1965 incident left extraordinary suffering, bitter memories, and deep inner wounds on the victims' families. Ibu Ria experienced this when she had to witness the cruel treatment of her husband, She herself experienced sexual abuse. She could not continue to work as a teacher because her certificates were burnt when her parents' house in Melolo was torched. Janda Mbulu-Dima also underwent extreme suffering when she had to accept her husband's detention at the police station, imprisonment, and then execution. After her husband was killed, she still had to face life as a single mother, alone, raising her children and getting them through school.

It is absolutely clear that the 1965 Incident left the victims' wives and children stranded. Their lives, which had previously been normal, respected, enjoyable and secure, like the lives of others, were suddenly turned upside down, in total disarray, and uncertain. They lived for years in fear and uncertainty about the future. They experienced ostracism and discrimination in society, the church, and even their own families. Their children were often teased as 'communist kids' in daily life and at school. After they finished school, they could not get the same job opportunities as other children.

Ibu Ria and Janda Mbulu-Dima did not understand what they had done wrong. Although their 'crimes' were never proven in a court of law, they continued to experience injustice in many areas. Even so, they were able to survive these difficult times each in their own way. Janda Mbulu-Dima tried keeping chickens and pigs, sewing, making cakes and coconut oil to make ends meet. And from her hard work, she was able to send her children to school.

Ibu Ria's story was different. After being stood down as teacher, she tried to keep herself busy by filling the day with positive activities that would be useful.

> I am 68 now. I live simply, I try just to run the house and live off my husband's pension. I do some sewing, do some cooking at people's places, help sell things from Chinese traders, do some flower arranging and sell them, all to make ends meet. I try to keep myself busy to control this deep feeling of hurt and bitterness.

Their determination and hard work has borne fruit. They were able to put their children through school, even to a tertiary level. And with the passing of time, their children have become independent and have good jobs, some have even become teachers and officials, and they have married and got homes of their own. Increasingly, opportunities have opened up for the children of victims to pursue education and to find work.

According to Janda Mbulu-Dima's account, in the 1980s, the commander of the local army resort gave a talk in Waingapu. In the talk, among other things, he asked people not to insult and ostracise families of communists or Gerwani.

> Some time in the 1980s – I don't remember the date exactly – the military gave a talk asking people to stop using language that ostracised 'Gestapu' people.

As time went on, the families of victims were able to reintegrate with society and become accepted. They were able to organise their lives even though the stigma of being communist or Gerwani families is still not completely gone.

## Justice is only from God

One important thing to note in this report is their reflection that no matter what their experience of human injustice was, God remains just. This was a deep conviction. God's justice is seen in many things. For instance, God is just because He has blessed their effort and hard work so that their children have obtained a good education and good jobs. Even though initially they were ineligible for employment in the government civil service, they did finally find employment there. God is also just because he blessed them with good health.

> But God is good, and I have not been sick for 31 years. (Ibu Ria)

God is just because He helped them get through difficult times. God is just because he granted them strength and mental resilience so they could arise from their abyss and grasp the future.

Ibu Ria and Janda Mbulu-Dima are thankful for God's mercy and justice which they experienced in their own lives. It is this appreciation of God's mercy and justice that encourages them to forgive and to forget the bitter experiences of the past and to focus on building the future. They advised their children not to bear revenge and resentment.

> I told my children to be resolved and not to repay evil with evil. (Janda Mbulu-Dima)

> Even though people did wicked things [to us], I tell my children to be kind to others. (Ibu Ria)

## Our hopes

Apart from their spiritual reflection and appreciation of God's justice, they also have hopes, namely that that the bitterness they experienced will not be repeated. They hope that their children and grandchildren will never experience violence that brings enduring trauma. They hope that the government will pay attention to their children and grandchildren.

> I hope the government will do something to wipe the trauma that the Gestapu children and families went through. (Janda Mbulu-Dima)

Their hope is that their children and grandchildren will not be insulted, blocked, limited and marginalised either in the fellowship of the church or in social life, especially at school and at work. They hope that their children and grandchildren can live calmly and peacefully.

> What I hope for is that my children and grandchildren can live in love, live calmly, and not experience trauma like I did. (Ibu Ria)

Their hopes are entirely proper and it is not only the government that should pay attention to them, but also the church. The government and the church are fully responsible for bringing about reconciliation and healing. The government and the church must care about their fate and their future. They are part of the Indonesian nation and have the right to feel secure and have full rights as citizens. They are not second class citizens in society. They are not free riders in this republic. They are fully legal citizens.[35]

---

35 See A.A. Yewangoe, *Tidak Ada Penumpang Gelap, Warga Gereja Warga Bangsa* (Jakarta: BPK Gunung Mulia 2009), viii.

Chapter 8

# The 1965 Incidents through the Eyes of GKS Missionaries[1]

## Liliya Wetangterah

The 1965 incident changed the life of the Indonesian nation. It produced various stories from different points of view. So too with the foreign missionaries who were then assisting the GKS. They have their own stories about 1965. This report recounts the 1965 incident from the viewpoint of three foreign GKS missionaries. Pastor Hendrik Olde, a Dutchman, and Pastor Heinrich Baarlink, a German, did service in East Sumba, while Pastor Hendericus Jacob van Oostrum, also Dutch, served in West Sumba. The accounts from Pastor Olde and Pastor Baarlink who were both still living at the time of the research, are from interviews and also from their writings, while the account from Pastor van Oostrum, who died in 2010, is based on his writings and an interview with his daughter, Jeanette van Oostrum.[2]

Pastor Hendruk Olde, who is usually called Pak Olde, wanted to be a missionary from when he was still a child. It was this longing that brought him and his wife to serve in East Sumba. The Olde family arrived in East Sumba at the end of August 1965. Pastor Olde served in two places during his time in East Sumba – at Melolo from 1965 to 1967 and at Payeti from 1967 to 1972. This account is from a conversation between myself and Pastor Olde at his home in Zwolle, Holland, on 11 November 2011.

After listening to his story about his mission service in East Sumba, I asked Pastor Olde to talk about the events of 1965. Pastor Olde said that

---

1   The word used for foreign missionary in the Indonesian text of this book is the Dutch term, *zendeling*. The names of the missionaries in this report are their real names.
2   Pastor Olde was born in 1925, and Pastor Baarlink in 1927.

as he had only just arrived in East Sumba at the end of August 1965 and at that time did not have much understanding of either the Sumba or Sabu languages, he thought it better to discuss these things together with Pastor Heinrich Baarlink who, in 1965, had already served in East Sumba for many years. Pastor Olde and his wife then accompanied me to visit Pastor Heinrich Baarlink in Germany.

Pastor Heinrich Baarlink, who is usually called Pak Baarlink, served in East Sumba from 1960–1967. He greeted us warmly when we arrived at his house. After he understood the reason for our visit, he began to talk about the events of 1965.

## A list of names and the 'Crocodile Hole'

Pastor Baarlink opened his account with a story about a list of names of people the Communist Party were going to kill in East Sumba when their 'coup d'état' in Jakarta succeeded. He said:

> Immediately after 1 October, people did not know what exactly was going on. There were rumours, but no clear picture. Then a few days later the Executive Committee of the Foundation for Evangelical Education in Sumba (Yapmas) where I was working as an advisor, held a meeting.³ The secretary said to me, 'ah, Pak Baarlink, you name is also there on the list.' 'What list?' I asked. 'You mean you don't know about it? The list of all the people who were going to be killed after the revolution happened in Sumba.' And I was shocked... There was a detailed list of everyone that was to be killed [by the Communist Party] at the outset, namely the District Head, head of police, head of the army, the judge and so on. And... there were already [graves] that had been dug and called 'crocodile holes' in Sumba, at Wangga near Melolo where everyone was going to be buried. Anyone not killed at their own home was to be taken to Wangga and killed there, including me and my family and the Olde family who had just arrived.

Pastor Baarlink got the same story from the head of the army at the time. He went on with his story:

> About the list, well of course we wondered whether it really existed or not, or whether this was just rumour. Later, at the end of 1967 before we had to return home [to Germany] for good, I had to go to Kupang

---

3   Yapmas was run by GKS.

to organise my exit permit. And I said, 'Sir, may I ask about that list – was it real or not? He said 'I can give you proof, namely that list complete with all the names, except for the name of Pak Olde which was added with a different pen.'

To Pastor Baarlink, the fact that Pastor Olde and his family's name had been added with different ink showed that the list existed before the Olde family arrived in East Sumba in August 1965.

Pastor Olde also heard about the list of people that were going to be murdered by the communists and about the 'crocodile hole'. According to him, there was a Communist Party official who, when he was arrested, had concealed on him a list of names of people to be killed. He was not from Sumba. This information made a deep impression on him. He thought that the existence of the list of names showed that the Communist Party in East Sumba had made detailed plans for murder.

> Specifically, the Sumbanese communists were carrying out a detailed coup in Sumba. This was probably different to other islands.

But Pastor Baarlink and Pastor Olde pointed out that they never saw any such list of names with their own eyes. They only got this information from other people.

## Arrests and killings

According to Pastor Olde, the news about the list of people the communists were going to kill, and the existence of the 'crocodile hole' in Wangga was one of the sparks of the outbreak of violence against members of the Communist Party and Gerwani in East Sumba, and people who were accused of being involved with them.

A letter that Pastor Olde wrote on 29 November 1965 was later published in the *Bulletin Zendingcentrum, Bulletin situatie Indonesia No. 12*, a bulletin of the Dutch Reformed Church. Pastor Olde described the situation in Melolo:

> When the Communist Party plans became known, the police carried out raids, moving from house to house. The situation heated up. On 6 November, 1965 when there was an attack on the house of the leader of the Communist Party. Fortunately he and his family had been taken to the police station. This calmed the situation in Melolo. But this changed when a member of the congregation gave witness that one of the youths had seen an old man with suspicious movements. It turned

out that the old man was the father of the Communist Party leader. So he was arrested and beaten. In his hat, a new list was found. This news circulated widely. Youths then began to arrest anyone who had any connection with the Communist Party and took them to the police station. In the letter they found, it said there were 18 grenades, but [the police] had found only three of them. This made people afraid to go into the forest. Security was tightened even more. We even locked our bedroom for ten days, and every night we were woken by police shots, which signaled they were on guard.[4]

Pastor Olde expanded on the story he told in the letter, describing the situation in Melolo at the time of the arrests:

> On a Saturday morning [he did not recall the exact date] the communists were [chased and] beaten, taken to the police station, the polyclinic or the hospital, and beaten, but not to death. Very early on the Saturday, Willemien [Pastor Olde's wife] went to the market, and suddenly youths started chasing these people to the police station and hospital, from about seven in the morning until around eleven. The noise was incredible. About twenty people were beaten and taken to the police station. Some of the communists escaped. There was one man from Ternate, who had a grenade at his house. On that Saturday night we locked our house, boarded up our windows, and had patrols circling our house… Churches and mosques were all patrolled. And at four in the morning suddenly there was a bomb, and we thought our house was going to collapse. We went outside and whispered to the youths – asking what was going on. Then new police arrived by car from Waingapu. They sounded an alert so people would know the police were there. The next day was Sunday. After worship, all the young men and women from the whole district of Rindi-Umalulu left, walking even into the hills, searching for the person who had the grenade. One of the GKS pastors led this search.

Some church figures were actively involved in the arrests. Pastor Baarlink explained that there were three groups of people considered to be communists who were arrested in East Sumba:

> Then we also experienced how from then on people were just said to be involved in the 30th September Movement… the first and second

---

4   Pastor Olde was speaking in Dutch.

groups were to be sentenced to death, but not the third group, they were detained for various periods, more than one year.

As for the killing of Communist Party members, or those considered to be, Pastor Olde added:

> In West Sumba around 45 people [were killed], and in Waingapu, if I am not wrong, about 25.

Responding to Pastor Olde's numbers of people killed, Pastor Baarlink added:

> Yes, I think the first group was executed on a barge that was taken out to sea and they were killed there and thrown into the sea. And the others, I don't recall. If I am not wrong, there were two groups executed.

The stories about the arrests and executions of communists and those suspected of being so, made us all go quiet. I myself needed a few moments to imagine and to understand the events they were talking about. After a few moments silence, I went on with the conversation, asking about the involvement of GKS church members in the Communist Party. Pastor Baarlink replied:

> There were not many, but there were some. I did not know them by face, but it was not a large group. From the members of my church, I do not know whether they were people from Payeti, Waingapu, or Kambaniru; I do not know.

According to Pastor Baarlink, not many church members joined the Communist Party, but Pastor Olde answered differently. According to him, about 80% of the Communist Party members around Melolo were members of the church.

Even though their answers to questions about the involvement of members of the church in the Communist Party were different, they both remembered clearly that a former GKS pastor was an active Communist Party member. He was not killed, but was detained in the third group, to be a living witness. Pastor Baarlink went on with his account:

> One of the GKS pastors who was also a Communist Party official was in the third group and was not killed at the time because these people were to be used as living witnesses.

These two missionaries considered that the procedure of arrests and interrogation were carried out well. According to an informant, the church established relations with other policing bodies to guarantee this process and to ensure that the arrests were not based on personal interests. Pastor Baarlink emphasised:

> In Sumba, it is important [to note] that there was no revenge. The families of the detainees were protected, no one harmed them. This was not the case on other islands, also in [the province of] Nusa Tenggara, and especially in Java and Bali, as we heard about it at the time. We did not know, but we heard from other people. [In Sumba], this was smoothed by government institutions and there was excellent collaboration between the government, the church, and the judiciary.

## The GKS Resolutions on the Communist Party[5]

Leading on from the explanation about the active involvement of church members in Communist Party leadership, I then asked about the church's response to this. Pastor Olde explained that actually, at the Synod meeting at Tenggaba in 1963 the church had already taken a stand towards the Communist Party. At that meeting, the GKS had resolved that the Communist Party was in conflict with church belief.

After the 1965 incident, this resolution was distributed to congregations to be read out from the pulpit. Pastor Baarlink explained:

> The Synod resolution was read out again from the pulpit after 1 October 1965, and also became the guideline for giving pastoral service to them and for talking to them. They already knew for a long time that the GKS's belief that communism was in conflict with the tenets of the faith.

Even though there was the GKS circular about the Communist Party, the missionaries continued to give pastoral care to the victims. Pastor Baarlink continued:

> I went to see one of the Sumbanese pastors, and told him that the church had a duty towards those in detention. Even though they were communist, there were still church members, and therefore we had a

---

5   See the earlier chapter on West Sumba, and the report 'Victims of the 1965 Tragedy as Sinners?' for quotes from the Christian Church of Sumba's resolutions on communism.

duty. He and I went to the head of the prison and asked for permission to visit them. He replied, 'ah, they are just kids from hell; they've got no need for visits.' We said that we had a different opinion, because it was our duty. Then he gave us permission to visit them. So we went back home and discussed it together, and I said, 'Pak, as a foreigner, it is better that I don't go along. It is better that you and your Indonesian colleagues go.' So they visited them, and this was what could be done.

Another story Pastor Baarlink told about GKS pastoral care involved himself, and was noted in his letter to the Department for the Sumba Mission.

> I was included in a group that visited political prisoners. There were about sixty people who attended our witness of the resurrected Saviour. We gave this sermon to the political detainees. We also spoke with them to find out how they were feeling. What they said was deeply moving. One by one, all sixty of them gave witness, including some who were not yet baptised. They gave witness that they were experiencing waves of deep sadness.
>
> They found the Saviour after sensing how great is God's mercy, which never ceases and is always there over them. One of the prisoners said, 'I belong to Jesus. I know my sins have been forgiven. I want to serve Jesus all my life. I want to give witness to my relations in my kampung that they should come to Jesus and be baptised.' These were the words of affirmation that came from the mouths of the detainees, to those who had already received God's freedom. We also said they had the opportunity to talk to the pastors after every worship every Sunday, or after the service for detainees. So I was sure that after many converted to Christianity, there would still be many more.
>
> Apart from that, we were also, to a certain extent, cheered by the witness given by three prisoners who had already been Christian for a long time. One of them was an old man from a tradition of polygamy, who liked gambling and wasting money, but he returned to God and his witness impressed us greatly. There were also two others who repented and were baptised. We were happy about this.[6]

The church, apart from issuing an encyclical that communism was in conflict with church beliefs, also imposed church discipline in the form of

---

6   Pastor Baarlink spoke in German. Following his earlier explanation about the three groups of prisoners (the first and second groups were killed, but not the third), this group of sixty they visited was the third group.

the requirement for anyone with communist connections to make a public confession.

Pastor Olde spoke about how a pastor from Sumba asked him to approach one of the children of the pastor who was an active member of the Communist Party, and ask him to make a confession.

> There was one day when one of his children had been asked to confess, but he refused because he had not been really involved. So they asked me to speak to him. He was open to me. He said, 'Yes, I know I have done wrong, but I do not want to confess, because if I do then the next day the police will come and arrest me and take me away to kill me.' And he refused. And he never did confess his sins.

Apart from Communist Party members or those suspected of being so, women considered to have been members of Gerwani were also urged to confess. Pastor Olde continued:

> It was different in Melolo, where Gerwani members confessed to a Sumbanese pastor because they had done wrong. [They] had been ordered to kill the children [of the people whose names were on the list]. At that time I did not realise they had intended to murder our children. At that time I did not yet understand because I could not yet understand the local Sumba and Sabu languages, but I still remember that those young women were about 19–20, they were Gerwani.

Church sanctions against Communist Party or Gerwani members, or people suspected of being so, continued for a long time after the events of 1965.

## Effects on the GKS in East Sumba

Having listened to Pastor Olde and Pastor Baarlink's stories about the church resolutions and the church care given to Communist Party and Gerwani members, our conversation moved on to talk in general about the effect of the 1965 Incident on the GKS.

One can say that the church did indeed 'benefit' from the 1965 incident. One example Pastor Baarlink gave was the village of Ramuk in East Sumba. This village had been a Communist Party stronghold, but then changed and the inhabitants converted to Christianity. Pastor Baarlink spoke about this:

> In my report, I talked about when, after the Kananggar Synod of 1966, we visited a village called Ramuk, which was the communist centre in that area. Some people had returned to the church, and the following

> year we decided that Ramuk would be the place to hold a conference for church workers, as we were working there as officers at the time. They [the villagers] were grateful and thanked us for not despising them… When we came there was a big celebration, a celebration of peace; there were services and a communal meal of about 100 people. When we first arrived, we were worried about whether we would be well received. But because they had confessed together, there were good developments after this in the village of Ramuk.

An account of the effect of the 1965 incident is also found in Pastor Baarlink's letter dated 3 January 1966 addressed to the leadership of the section in charge of missionaries of the Dutch Reformed church. The letter also reflects how the fear of Communist Party threats was commonly accepted as truth.

> On 1 October and the Sundays following, we already knew something was going on, but not much. However as time went by it became increasingly clear to us what had really happened, the communists and their cunning was revealed. Two days before Christmas, two top leaders of the Communist Party in Sumba, who had been tried for weeks and asked to give explanations, finally confessed. They had been planning the coup d'état and murders from May of the previous year.
> 
> According to the plan, once the planned attack in Jakarta succeeded, then the first action of the Communist Party in Sumba was to be the killing of regional heads, regional secretaries and the heads of police, and a few other high officials were to be kidnapped and taken to Wangga to be killed there in a massacre site called the crocodile hole. Then, in the second stage, church leaders and Muslim leaders were also to be killed, and lastly influential people in the government and political parties, anyone in opposition to Communist Party was to be exterminated. Churches and Christian organisations were to be razed to the ground. So if that plan had succeeded, we would all have fallen into an apocalypse as is written in Revelations 6:10. 'And they cried with a loud voice, saying, How long, O Lord, holy and true, dost thou not judge and avenge our blood on them that dwell on the earth?'
> 
> If that had happened, the Christian church in Sumba would have been destroyed, with no shepherd. But you should all know, that as is expected of us, we will remain upright and not budge, we will stand up, we will live by the Bible and die by the Bible.
> 
> We want to stress that we offer thanks to God whose great love is more powerful than those sinners. So we are truly protected and

respected by the Indonesian leaders, as we were before. We are also actively supporting them, and as a result the perpetrators have been arrested and put into prison, however no laws have been transgressed, even though the people just wanted to try them and crush them themselves.

Indeed, the people's attitude, anger and desire for revenge are evident, but have not erupted. Curfews have been operating since October, and they [are protected by the police and the army. We hope that God's rule and His word will stay powerful in Sumba. Then hatred and revenge have no power. In this, the government leaders in Sumba are giving a good example.

The power of God is truly evident in Sumba, one can sense this, for instance, in the thirst for truth, and everyone avoids sin. The church, through its sermons, is giving guidance to the people according to their various duties and responsibilities, both as part of government and as leaders of political parties. On 2 January last I gave a sermon on Sunday morning at Payeti and another later in the day at Kambaniru. My sermon was about Herod's killing of the baby boys in Bethlehem. Baby Jesus was going to be killed too, but it did not happen. This subject was fitting for our situation. God acts so that evil plans are not realised. Because of this, I told the congregation to continue to place their trust in God, like the statements by the prophets Elijah, Hosea, and Joseph, and we must all remain on the alert so that the Devil's plans will not eventuate in the nation or the church. I can also report that in Payeti, 34 adults and many children were baptised in 1965. I hear that one pastor has baptised many people, and perhaps we should give thanks that God crowned 1965 with His blessing.[7]

Both Pastor Olde and Pastor Baarlink acknowledged that attendance at Sunday service increased, and there was also an increase in conversions from the indigenous Sumba religion, Marapu. The story about the effect of the 1965 incident ended our conversation.

A final impression gained from these two missionaries was that they were touched that when the 1965 Incident occurred, security officers and the congregation ensured their safety and that of their families. Although they were foreigners, the people of Sumba protected them. They were both impressed by the solidarity between the different religions at that time.

---

7   Letter from Pastor Baarlink dated 3 January 1966, translated from the German. See *Buletin Zendingcentrum, Bulletin Situatie Indonesia No, 13* p. 1 which quotes from this letter.

Christians helped to guard mosques, and Muslims were active in guarding churches. This was a good model of solidarity.

## The 1965 Incident in the eyes of Pastor Hendricus van Oostrum

After listening to the stories told by two missionaries who had served in East Sumba, I became interested to listen to Pastor Hendricus van Oostrum, a missionary who had served in West Sumba. So, after spending a most enjoyable night with Pastor Olde's family in Zwolle, I continued my journey, accompanied by Mrs Corrie van der Ven, who works for Kerk in Actie, to Utrecht to meet Jeanette van Oostrum.

After meeting Jeanette and finding a comfortable place to chat, we began talking about West Sumba at the time of the 1965 Incident. Jeanette had brought with her a document that belonged to her father that could show her father's turmoil at that that time.

Pastor Hendricus van Oostrum was a Dutch evangelist who began his service in West Sumba in 1957. Back in 1954, the GKS in Waikabubak had sent an official request for a pastor, dated 15 December 1954. They asked for Pastor van Oostrum, who came and served in Sumba for 14 years, from 1956 to 1970.

Pastor van Oostrum seems to have had his own impressions about the 1965 Incident, so he tended to keep all stories about it to himself, and did not tell his children. Throughout his life, he never discussed the events of 1965. The one and only piece of information that he told his children was that the names of all the van Oostrum family were on the list the communists had drawn up of people they were going to kill. When I asked Jeanette why her father had chosen to remain silent, she said that he wanted to protect the identity of the victims.

It was only a few weeks before his death in 2010 that Pastor van Oostrum finally asked Jeanette to read his diary that related the 1965 events. But he asked her not to read it until after his death. It was from this diary that Jeanette learned about 1965.

When the 1965 Incident occurred, as a pastor, Pastor van Oostrum did not do nothing. He prayed for the victims, and accompanied them, even when they faced the firing squads. He wrote:

> On 5 May 1966, the death sentence was carried out against six Communist Party leaders in West Sumba. The death sentence was

carried out again against fifteen Communist Party members on 9 June. The local authorities allowed us full access to them from the time they were imprisoned until the time of their deaths, through Sunday service and through pastoral counselling to encourage them to repent and return to Jesus Christ. Through the power of the Holy Spirit, with only one exception, all of them offered themselves to Jesus Christ with true joy and faith. The one exception chose the path of the Prophet Mohammad. We give thanks that we brought them to God who gave us guidance and strength to carry out this heavy work.[8]

Those who were executed confronted death singing hymn no. 147 'Kuasamu, Ya Pengasihan' [Your Power, O Merciful One].

The other material Jeanette provided was a summary of a sermon that Pastor van Oostrum gave in Waikabubak and Payeti on 6 June 1965. In the sermon, he encouraged members of the congregation to care for each other; everyone must become a true person through caring for others. This plea was directed not only at individuals, but also at the church.

The church must fight for the liberation and renewal of man. They church must not hand that duty over to other organisations, like other beliefs or communist movements. The church's struggle for freedom must be grounded in the Word of God. This is no easy thing for the church, but it must be able to learn from Moses. When he endured difficult times in his struggle, Moses experienced and sensed God's guidance.

In his sermon, Pastor van Oostrum went on to encourage members of the congregation, not to just enjoy themselves in carrying out their service, but also to carry out their duty and their own struggles. Their duty was not easy, but God would always help. The church must not lose out to other movements in the struggle for liberation and renewal. Pastor van Oostrum finished the notes for his sermon with a very interesting sentence: 'I hope that all Christians become a kind of communist, but not atheist ones!'

In keeping with this sermon, something else he kept in his archives was an interview that was published in the Netherlands:

> When he was asked, 'Have there been changes in Sumba over the last fifteen years?' he answered, 'On the socio-political side, there has not been much change; on the spiritual side, yes.'

---

8   Quoted from a copy of a letter written by Pastor van Oostrum to the *Deputat Zending Sumba* dated 4 October 1966 (see also the report on West Sumba).

...In Sumba there was a lot of blood spilled. I spoke a lot with many communists. In my conversations with them, I was convinced that there is still much to be done. To come with just stories is no longer the way out.'

Because of this, over the last few years of his service in Sumba, he [Pastor van Oostrum] has been busy providing services for youth in the social and economic field, with a movement called Kuda Putih (White Horse). This movement aims to foster awareness about their potential as people of Sumba.

'Look, Indonesians live with the motto 'that's fate'. So their lives will never change. The Bible teaches them that change can and must take place. And the latter is the most important. Young people ask, 'What is going to happen?' And there are no changes. In this kind of situation, communism enters Indonesia. Their propaganda is action, and this immediately connects with the needs of youth. What I mean by this is that spreading the Good News of the Bible and making people aware is just not enough. There has to be something more direct [that's visible and answering needs].[9]

The church has to perform its social role, and can start from what it possesses. Emphasis on church involvement in problems of social development is also important.

Together with local church councils, we also conducted a Bible study of 2. Samuel 14:33 – 2 Samuel 19:8, and we talked about ways for the renewal of deaconical work in the Waikabubak congregation. Some of that work we are still doing now.[10]

This interesting conversation ended my meeting with Jeanette.

These are stories of the 1965 incident as seen by three missionaries, two Dutch and one German, who served in Sumba. Their views can enrich the various stories of the events of 1965. The multiplicity of views can help us not only understand, but also learn from the events of 1965 as part of the history of the Indonesian nation.

---

9   Original text in Dutch.
10  Copy of a letter from Pastor van Oostrum to the *Deputat Zending Sumba*, dated 4 October 1966. Original in Dutch.

# Epilogue

Start with the Victims: The meaning of the 1965 Tragedy for Contextual Theology and Pastoral Action in NTT

*Mery Kolimon*

Indonesia's history surrounding the 1965 Affair has long been told from the point of view of the victors in order to support the authorities and their power. In this history, the voices of the victims are muzzled; the victims are even blackened out. Their memories of the event they experienced have become forbidden memories. In the stories of the women victims and our analysis of them that we have set out in this book, readers are invited to look at this page of Indonesia's history from a different perspective; to uncover those forbidden memories. All the victims reject the official version, and particularly the women victims whose voices have been muzzled to date. The voices of all victims challenge the official version of the powers-that-be.

In the final section of this book, our aim is to continue the description and analysis we have carried out in the earlier chapters by doing two things; furthering contextual theological reflection from the narratives of the women who were victims of the 1965 Affair; and, based on these reflections, making recommendations for some pastoral action. It is not our intention to analyse everything in depth here, but only to raise some theological issues that could be developed further in the future. Whereas traditional theology is based on specific Biblical texts, the kind of theology we are proposing is a theology from below, from the reality of human life, and particularly from the way the women victims of the 1965 Affair in NTT coped with suffering and oppression.

## A. Learning from suffering and struggle

In the female victims' stories about their experiences of oppression and injustice, we discovered theological themes that demanded further exploration. In their oppression and in struggles to endure, the women reflected on God, the church, humanity and human relations, social (political) order, sin, suffering, truth and various other theological themes. Many of their questions and statements contained extremely meaningful theological reflection.

## 1. *Theology of suffering: Where is God when suffering occurs?*

> Where was God when I was suffering? Why did God let this happen? What part did God play?[1]

One theological question that arose forcefully in the stories of the women and children was: Where was God when they were suffering? Whose side was God on – on their side as victims of state tyranny, or on the side of the authoritarian state? Another question linked to this was: Did God really intend them to suffer? Did God really want to punish them with the lifelong suffering they experienced?[2] They lost husbands and fathers, who were tortured and killed without any legal process to prove their guilt. They were accused of being members of a banned political party that until March 1966 was a legal party officially recognised by the state.[3] Families who were left behind were humiliated in various ways. Women had their hair cut or shaved off and were forced to work. Some of them experienced sexual abuse in detention, and their children were branded as 'communist trash'.

The victims experienced suffering twice over after the 30th September Affair: suffering because of their treatment by the state, and social marginalisation. Family members had their civil rights curtailed; for instance, they no longer received salaries, and some of them found their children could not become civil servants. Their children and grandchildren were also

---

1 Maksi Talitai. This is part of Maksi's reaction when he watched the documentary 'Plantungan' which was shown at a meeting of victims in Liliba, Kupang, on 27 March 2011.
2 This is evident in some of the questions linked to the core question about evil and God's justice (theodicy), namely: How can we continue to believe in God in the midst of evil? On theodicy, see further, Zakaria J. Ngelow, 'Bianglala di atas Tsumani' in Teologi Bencana, ed. Zakaria Ngelow et. al (Makasar: Yayasan Oase Intim, 2006) pp 201–52. Also see Kenneth Cauthen 'Theodicy' at http://www.frontiernet.net/~kenc/theodicy.htm accessed 1 March 2012.
3 The Communist Party of Indonesia (PKI) and the mass organisations linked to it were disbanded and declared illegal in a document dated 12 March 1966. This decision was reinforced by the Special Presidential Decree MPRS No. 1/3/1966 dated 12 March 1966 and further enforced with the Presidential decree TAP MPRS No. XXV/MPRS/1966 dated 5 July 1966. According to this last decree, the Communist Party had to be forbidden because, amongst other things 'Communist/ Marxist-Leninist teaching are essentially in conflict with Pancasila' and because communists 'have been proven many times to have attempted to overthrow the legal government of the Republic of Indonesia using violent means.' See http://tatanusa.co.id/tapmpr/66TAPMPRS-XXV.pdf accessed on 10 December 2011.

discriminated against socially, branded as atheists and bad people best kept away from. Society, afraid of the state-implemented terror, kept quiet when the violence took place, and even participated in it. Even worse, the church made the victims publicly confess their sins in front of the congregation before they could take communion again. They were not permitted to join the congregation council and their children were rejected when they wanted to become pastors.

*Wrestling with non-understanding*

> Back then I was shocked... How could I be involved? I had done nothing wrong, I had not done anything bad to anyone, but I was taken to court... What was wrong with Gerwani? I never thought there was anything wrong with Gerwani. I never did anything bad to any other person, let alone to the government.[4]

> I could not talk... I could never tell my children about anything that happened. I just kept quiet because the suffering was too great.[5]

> Even though I had lost my husband, and after everything that had happened, what could I do about it? I had to accept that's how it was. Maybe these are the ways of God because my sins were so great. And as the Word of God says that the payment of sin is death, I had to be resolute.[6]

Some of the women still live with this confusion today. What did they do wrong? They feel they did no wrong, but are confused about their status, having been branded with a socio-political stigma as bad people in society. As a result, many of the victims were not prepared to talk. They chose to remain silent when we asked them to talk about their experience of violence. The trauma is still very real, and a psychological burden to this day.

At times when they felt under the greatest pressure, they also asked: Where was God when they were struck with injustice? Is God really the Almighty and All-Merciful? And if God is Almighty, then why did He not stop the incredible injustice? If He is All-Merciful, then why did he let the innocent become victims? They complained to God, in their confusion. And yet they did not desert God, and felt that God was with them.

---

4    Ibu Marsa, interview, 4 December 2010, Oeba, Kupang.
5    Ibu Bunga, interview 9 December 2010, Waikabubak, West Sumba.
6    Ibu Wila, interview 21 November 2010, Ledemanu, Sabu.

Jesus's cry on the cross at Golgotha, 'Eli, Eli, why hast thou forsaken me?' echoes the cry of those in deepest suffering, feeling that God has deserted them. At the same time, the suffering of Jesus, which is the suffering of God Himself, stresses that God does not desert humans in their suffering.

## *The suffering is not from God*

> Even though people might think what we did was not good, God is All-Just, so my children were able to pursue education... Because I know that I never did anything to undermine the unity of this nation.[7]

> I think that it was God's power that helped with Mama's release... I personally think that it was through the power of God defending us that we were saved.[8]

Other victims stressed that God was with them when they suffered oppression and injustice. It was because God was with them that they were able to endure it. Their emphasis that God was on their side was grounded in the belief that they had done no wrong, but were rather victims of violence and the overturning of truth. Their belief that God was on their side also allowed them to withstand the slander laid against them, helped them endure, and to find the strength to bring up their children to become people with self-respect knowing neither they nor their parents were criminals.

In theological terms, some of the victims stressed that the suffering they underwent was not God's will. It was not God who intended the oppression they suffered. In fact, the evil directed at them was actually a rebellion against God. Because of this, rather than being merely submissive in suffering, these women found ways to get out of it.

In these accounts of the women victims of the 1965 tragedy we find an understanding about God who is with the marginalised. He is not the God at the centre of history, but rather at the margins of history. He is the God who suffers with the oppressed. The crucified Christ is a sign of the presence of God with all victims in history, including the victims of the 1965 tragedy in NTT.

Further, the God who suffers alongside them is also the God who gives them the strength to go on and to find ways out of their suffering. The Christian faith in the resurrection of Jesus, is faith in God siding with the oppressed. The suffering and death on Good Friday is not the end of everything. Easter's dawn of victory has arisen. Suffering will be replaced by victory.

---

7    Ibu Wila, interview.
8    Ibu Neltji Kumar, interview 19 November 2010, SoE.

Like Hagar and Ismail in the desert after they were exiled by Sarah and Abraham (Genesis 21:8–21) so too will victims, in their suffering, find God is with them. Just as God prepared water for Hagar and Ismail when they were thirsty, and even led them to become a great nation, so too was He with the women victims and their children in the history of the 1965 tragedy in NTT, by providing what they needed and leading them through a treacherous life journey. He is not the God who is uncaring about the suffering of His people. He cries along with those who cry. He is wounded when violence and terror strike the weak. He has compassion for them. God is love: His Godhead is manifest in His love of them. It is this love that gives the victims strength to endure. It is this love that gives them the courage to persist so that their humanity is not completely destroyed. This love allowed them to hope that the time would come when the truth would come out. Some people in NTT share the belief of one of the women who was raped when she was detained at Kalabahi in Alor. As Mama Koba said of her rapist:

> they might think what they did was good, but the blood of the dead will take revenge.[9]

God will not let perpetrators go free of their deeds. At some time in their lives, they or their descendants will get their just desserts.

But at the same time, as a result of this kind of theological construction about God being on the side of the victims and His revenge on the perpetrators, coupled with the strong effects of social and political pressure, the victims have tended to remain silent and to reject aspects of social justice. They wrestle alone with their suffering and attempts to go on living, without any attempt at solidarity to protest against the social political reality that treated, and continues to treat, them so unjustly.

### *Suffering as a way of becoming close to God?*

In their suffering, many of the women victims of the 1965 tragedy in NTT found prayer groups helpful in supporting their efforts to endure. In these informal gatherings they felt they were accepted unconditionally. On the other hand, within the mainstream church fellowships (like the GMIT and the GKS) they felt rejected and given no place. Behind this reality we find different theological understandings of suffering.

In the prayer groups, the victims' suffering was viewed as a test that had made them mature in their faith. The more someone suffered, the more

---

9   Mama Koba, interview by the Alor research team on 15 November 2010 at Adagai, village of Kamot, Northeast Alor.

it was seen that God loved him or her. Suffering was seen as something coming from God with the intention of good. A person is 'beaten' by God because God loves them. Suffering is understood as God's process of forging a person to make him or her better as His child. Because of this, the prayer groups gave more positive value to the victims' suffering. A person is closer to God through his or her suffering, particularly if this suffering is not caused by their own misdeeds.

Unlike the mainstream church as the formal religious institution that directly interacted with the state, the prayer groups were freer to provide safe space to victims to develop their spirituality. Some of these victims also managed to develop their leadership within these non-formal channels.

As the GMIT and GKS saw it, the suffering of the victims was a sign of God's punishment. Here we see a kind of 'success theology' – success being the sign of God's blessing, whereas suffering is a sign of God's punishment. In this theological view, the victims of the 1965 tragedy suffered because they did not live according to God's will. This is why they had to confess their sins before they were allowed to join communion. Only when their lives had been restored (socially, economically and politically) could it be assumed that God had forgiven them. So they had to strive for economic, social and political restitution in order to prove that they had received God's forgiveness.

This theology of suffering in the mainspring churches shows that in fact the church had been coopted by the state. The theology the church developed about the victims' suffering affirmed the state's blackening of victims, and at the same time shows the church's attempts to protect itself from state terror. Any party seen to be siding with the victims was considered to be justifying the crimes attributed to them, and therefore also rebelling against the state. Thus, church theology was inconsistent with the principle of God siding with victims, as shown by Jesus. In developing the theology of success, the church went silent on injustice and tended to affirm tyranny for the sake of its own sense of security; and this is so even today. The church's theological explanations were and are, merely a mask to hide its fear and submission to the military throughout the 1965 Affair and the New Order regime that it issued in.

In the two kinds of theology of suffering described above – a person suffers because of God's punishment as a result of wrongdoing, versus a person suffers because of God's love – we do not find any strong theological understanding to support protest against injustice. The theologies developed by the mainstream church and by the prayer groups both strengthened the tendency of Christians to remain silent about state evil. A church that is silent about injustice is a sick church that needs healing.

In confronting suffering caused by oppressive social and political systems, an attitude of acceptance only perpetuates violence and oppression.[10] We can say that the sin of the oppressors is because they carry out violence on their fellows. On the other hand, the oppressed sin if they allow this violence and oppression to continue.

## 2. *Sin versus justice*

> They ordered me to confess my sins. So I said, what sins have I committed? It was people accusing, not me doing anything… I asked the pastor: 'What sins have I committed, maybe you have more sins'… but I joined confession, because of the church rules.[11]

> They said that I was a sinner. I said: 'Yes, thank you.'[12]

> They considered me not even human. They said that I was no more than their dirty rag.[13]

Some of the victims spoke about the demands the church made (especially the GKS) for them to make public confessions in front of the congregation before they would be allowed to join communion. In these stories we come across theological issues of sin and confession. What is sin?

The traditional Christian understanding of sin is that it is rebellion against God, the creator. According to the Bible, our ancestors rebelled against divine law, which led to their punishment (Genesis 3). Man's rebellion against God was manifest in the destruction of relations between people as well as between man and other creation. As a result, man is both a creature of good because he or she is created in God's likeness, and a creature that sins and easily falls into transgression against its Creator. According to Christian teaching, as a creature that sins, man needs God's forgiveness in order for

---

10 In their fight for liberation, the poor in South Korea, who call themselves *minjung*, stress that they are victims of the sins of others. In this kind of situation, suffering must not be accepted passively, The concept of *han* in Minjung theology stresses the importance of expressing anger and rejecting oppression and suffering as an effect of that oppression. See Volker Kuester, *Many Faces of Jesus Christ* (London: SCM Press, 2001).
11 Ibu Bunga, interview.
12 Ibu Marsa, interview.
13 Ibu Sina Manu-Loe, interview on 23 November 2010, Oesao.

relations between man and God to be restored. Without God's forgiveness, man can never be free of God's punishment for sin, namely death. God's forgiveness is given to those who confess their sins freely and sincerely. In every Sunday service, the congregation is invited to confess their sins and to ask for God's forgiveness.

In the destruction of the Communist Party movement in Indonesia, the church considered the members of the Party and those accused of being so as people who had sinned because they had followed communist teachings and were therefore atheist. As people seen to have sinned against God, they were required to confess their sins before God and the congregation. Even though, in fact the accusation of them being atheist had no strong basis because they were also active in the life of the church. In the GKS tradition, confession is a condition for receiving the sacraments, especially communion. Even so, the victims, especially those who had been unfairly accused of being members of the Communist Party, refused to accept that they were sinners. They saw that the demand for them to confess their sins was a form of injustice leveled against them.

Forgiveness of sin is an act of liberation that God carries out on the faithful who have rebelled against Him, and is also a restoration of harmonious relations between God and fellow beings. In fact, confession of the faithful within a community acknowledges openness to receiving God's blessing, liberation and restoration. The initiative for peace comes from God. God forgives us before we come to Him. Jesus's parable of the prodigal son (Luke 15:11–24) shows that God is always longing for His children to return from their feeling of loss. In this parable, God's forgiveness precedes the son's confession of loss. This is proven when the father orders the servants to celebrate the return of his son when he arrives at his father's house.

One can say that the practice of confession [in the wake of the 1965 Affair] was no longer an event where the gift and blessing of God's forgiveness was celebrated in submission to God. Because the church was co-opted by State power in the context of the 1965 tragedy, sin was no longer merely a theological concept, but also took on socio-political interest. Sin was viewed not merely as rebellion against God, but also as transgression of what is defined by the State. In other words, the concept of sin was exploited for socio-political interests and the State was given a status almost equal to God. In this way, the church itself sinned because it equated the State with God.

As a result, confession was no longer a moment for the gift of liberation and restoration, but rather a tool of oppression that punished victims in the church and society. It was as though the victims who confessed their sins accepted the accusations that had been made against them, which were never legally proven. Confessing sin meant that they internalised their branding as dirty people – as both Mama Karo in Alor and Gad'i in Sabu said, branded as trash, in their church and social lives for their entire lives.

When a woman refused to confess before the congregation, we see the clash between the victim's theology of sin and the church's theology that prioritised the concept of sin in understanding and giving meaning to the 1965 tragedy.

As we see in the report from West Sumba, what is needed here is an understanding of sin not only in the traditional way of individual rebellion against God the Creator, but also in connection to systems and structures that cause injustice and oppression. In the particular instance of the 1965 tragedy, where State violence was carried out against those involved with the Communist Party or accused of being so, this systematic violence must be viewed as a structural sin. This structural sin is related to social systems and structure, the law, and State politics that resulted in systemic mass murder, looting, and social exclusion.

The victims' grievances are a critical challenge of church teachings, which deliberately or not, were coopted by state authorities. Their grievances also invite us to rethink the meaning of sin and confession, and their relationship to the concept of justice. If confession is meant to be the making of peace, and the restoration of relations between man and God, and between fellowmen, then one must recall that in the Bible, the concept of peace (*shalom* in the Old Testament, and *eirene* in the New Testament), includes justice. There is no peace without justice. As long as the church remains unsympathetic and insensitive to the voices of victims of injustice and those who strive for justice, then the rite of confession for peace loses its meaning. On the other hand, although the GMIT, for instance, does not have a special liturgy for confession, in practice it is not free of the spirit of punishment of victims of 1965. The GMIT, therefore, also needs to be self-critical of its position and attitudes in this matter.

Another aspect of the refusal of some of the victims to confess their sins is the questioning of justice. One cannot deny that many parties stood to gain and felt they were 'victors' after the 1965 Affair. The church was even proud to see as its victory the crushing of the Communist Party and the killing of the victims. The rights of victims can begin to be upheld only when those parties who carried out bad deeds against them openly admit their wrongs. Indeed, without forgiveness there can be no future. But before we arrive at forgiveness, the perpetrators must be made to acknowledge their wrongdoing, because forgiveness can only be truly given to those who confess what they have done and ask forgiveness from the victims. It is only in this way that there can be a future, both for the victims and for the perpetrators, as well as for this nation.

The lack of any single, clear legal process for dealing with the perpetrators can only weaken the process of upholding the law in this country. Christian teaching about forgiveness does not mean allowing perpetrators of evil to be freed of their responsibility for their wrongdoing. We can indeed call the 1965 violence 'State' violence. But those who carried out that violence were individuals (State officials). If we do not want such violence to happen again, we need to analyse the wrong that was done. In this, the church needs to be at the forefront of the struggle for the upholding of the law and the rights of the victims.

## *3. Female spirituality*

> We had to report to authorities for five or six months, then our heads were shaved. Some were afraid. I said, 'Hey, we do not need to be afraid. We've done nothing wrong to be afraid of.' I told my other friends, 'After all, we know ourselves. We did not know anything [about PKI]. If we have hair, we will die. Somebody cuts it, we will also die. Or did you others know [about PKI]? I really didn't know.' I stood up and said, 'God knows [the truth], so just let it be. If someone wants to cut your hair really short, just let them.'[14]

> ...all that time no one paid me any attention. None of them ever asked any questions, not even whether things were hard. I had to bring up eight children... that's hard.[15]

> [During the food shortage and time of having to report to authorities] I would look for kapok seeds...I would eat them so that my milk would flow to feed the baby.[16]

Spirituality is connected to wholeness, sanctity, and a person's balancing of emotion, intelligence, body and soul. Female spirituality makes the female body and experience the source of expression of wholeness, sanctity, the balance of emotion, intellect, and the health of body and soul. Every woman

---

14  Mama Karo, interview.
15  Ibu Bunga, interview.
16  Ibu Karo Talitai, interview, 17 November 2010. Paliboo, Alor.

who menstruates, is pregnant, gives birth or enters menopause possesses within her the potential to become the place where the Holy Spirit resides and works. The work of the Holy Spirit within women allows them to value themselves and their bodies; also to value and enjoy sex as a divine gift; to give birth, nurse and protect life; to express anger and courage in rejecting oppression; to be actively involved in social life and leadership; to foster friendship with fellows and with nature; as well as to set aside time for rest and meditation.

In March 2011, a two-day meeting with elderly survivors of the 1965 tragedy and their children, gave us the opportunity to learn from these extraordinary women. They suffered injustice in their lives. Among them were women who, as former Gerwani office-bearers, were held for years as political prisoners far from their homes. They were separated from their children. Their careers were destroyed. During their detention they experienced various kinds of inhumane treatment. Some other women, from various regions, suffered the murder of their husbands, they themselves had their heads shaved or their hair cut short so as to humiliate them, and they were forced to work in the hot sun in public areas, watched by the crowd, as a form of punishment. From the endurance of these women, we learnt about keeping mental and spiritual health in the midst of pressure that was intended to destroy them.

Phyllis Tribble, a North American feminist theologian, wrote *Texts of Terror* about stories of violence against women found in the Bible.[17] The stories of the women victims of the 1965 violence in NTT can also be seen as 'texts of terror' in the history of this nation. But the women's stories are not only about violence. Their stories are also 'texts of survival'.

The women's determination to survive, using various ways, attracted many people's attention. They quietly found sources of strength within themselves and their surroundings so that they were not destroyed by the violence they experienced. Some of them entrusted their children with the family so they could go to school. All the mothers felt the pain of separation from their children, especially when the children were still small. However, for the sake of their futures, the women were prepared to entrust their children to others. Other women worked hard and developed skills to earn money to support the family and their children's education. They did embroidery, weaving, sewing, and made cakes to sell. They looked for ways for their children to

---

17   Phyllis Tribble, *Texts of Terror: Literary-Feminist Readings of Biblical Narratives* (Philadelphia: Fortress Press, 1984).

grow up with self-respect and to be good examples in their communities. Other women went back to nature to study traditional medicine, and as Mama Karo Talitai explained, even learnt how to treat poisonous plants to make them fit to eat when there was not enough food for their families.[18] Yet others were active in prayer groups as one way of deepening and nursing their spiritual strength.

In Christian teaching, Almighty God is experienced and understood in three manifestations: God the Father, His son the Saviour, and the Holy Spirit the One who consoles/ the One who renews. Whereas the first two manifestations of God are understood in masculine language (Father and Son), the Bible tends to use mixed language for God the Holy Spirit. In Hebrew, the Holy Spirit is called *ruah* (the word is feminine gender), in Greek, *pneuma* (the word is neutral), and in Latin, *spiritus* (masculine). Even so, many feminist theologians claim that in teaching about the Holy Spirit, we discover the work of God that consoles, revives and supports, like a mother.

The mothering Spirit of God fortified the spirits of the women victims of the 1965 tragedy, and enabled them to remain whole as human beings. The connection between the human spirits of these women who came from God, with the living Spirit of God, allowed them to survive the life tempest that was attempting to crush them. Spiritual strength, namely connection with the Divine Spirit, allowed these women to maintain a healthy mental and spiritual state, and this in turn prevented them from drowning in depression, but rather enabled them to rise up and become the actors of good in communal life. Led by Him, they stood erect and remained whole when confronting intimidation and tyrannical terror.

## *Women, Christianity and local culture*

> When the 1965 Incident (Gestok) happened, we had only mangoes to eat and water to drink. There were no men in the kampung. They were in hiding. We were alone. The hunger was dreadful. Only women and children were left in the kampung. For one whole month there were no men in the kampung.[19]

Different cultural communities have their own rules on the position and roles of women and men (gender construction). For example, in in South Central Timor, when a child is born it is welcomed with a rite called *Napoitan*

---

18   Mama Karo Talitahi, interview.
19   Ibu Yane Netomela, interview on 3 November, 2010 at SoE.

*Li Ana* that introduces the child to its traditional role.[20] Female children are welcomed as weavers who are responsible for clothing and nurturing communal identity through weaving motifs, whereas male children are introduced as tillers of the land and tappers of palm trees whose duty it is to provide food for the family. In other words, women are the nurturers of tradition. Through weaving, women not only nurture the identity of their communities, they also affirm their own identities as individuals within their communities.

The 1965 tragedy had an impact on local traditions and culture as well as on women's identity. Even though enmity between Christianity and local religions had been evident since the time of Christianity's arrival in Eastern Indonesia, the 1965 Affair marked a brutal attack. In the anti-communist pogroms, local religions were destroyed because of two things. Firstly, Christians who had formerly shown more tolerance of indigenous religious practices now took a sharp distance from them. Secondly, in order to avoid being branded as atheist, followers of local religions gave up their identities to become Christian. In traditional society, religion and culture are a unity. When local religions were attacked, so too were local cultures.

This brings us to the question: How did women, as those entrusted to uphold tradition, give meaning to the shift from local religion to Christianity? When women converted to Christianity, how did this affect their position and role? Where was the place for them in the church? A further question that should be asked is: How did women manage their old sources of spirituality (indigenous religion) that were being destroyed, and accommodate themselves to the new spirituality (Christianity) that was both a foreign religion and also the religion accepted in a situation of violence? Can we see the prayer groups as a space that helped them resolve that tension?

Further study is desperately needed to analyse these questions. When in 1614 Protestantism first arrived in the area that later became Nusa Tenggara Timor, Christian missionaries regarded local religions as competition. Later, during the Revival Movement of 1965–1966, which began in South Central Timor and later spread to other areas of Nusa Tenggara Timur, local religions and cultures were attacked. In many ways, Christianity in Sumba and Timor today have, to a certain degree, inherited this suspicion and hatred of local religions and cultures. Even so, the identity of Christian women in cultural communities today is shaped both by local religion and culture on

---

20  The term literally means 'bringing the baby out', in the sense of bringing the baby out of the roundhouse, which is the birthing space, to be welcomed by the entire family.

the one hand and Christianity on the other, within a tension. When the women from various cultural communities of East Nusa Tenggara Timur became Christian at an extremely violent time, they certainly did not discard their local cultural traditions. Secretly, they continued to nurture their local cultural traditions, for instance through safeguarding traditional weaving motifs, traditional healing, and various traditional rites.[21] Particularly at times of crisis, traditional rites become sources of spirituality from which they find strength to go on. Becoming Christian and becoming the church of today means to open oneself to celebrate the wealth of different spiritual sources that still exist within that tension, before they become extinct. This means that we need the courage to develop dialogic connections between Christianity and local cultures.

## *4. True to history*

It was shown that in the preceding two years Communism had gained considerable ground and that even Ministers and Members of Church Councils (elders) had joined the Party ... the increasing popularity of Communism [is] a natural result of the growing public disillusionment with the Government over the deteriorating economic situation coupled with an acceptance of the current PKI line that belief in God and Communism is not incompatible. (A recent PKI directive has urged Party members to be faithful to their religion whatever it might be and thus set an example to the rest of the community in this matter.)[22]

From this research project, the documentation gathered by various regional teams clearly shows that the number of members of GMIT and GKS who were attracted to and involved with activities of the Communist Party, Farmers' Front and Gerwani was considerable. The teachers in Sabu, the women of education in the city of Kupang, the village heads in Alor who were active in the church, even the members of the congregation councils, scripture teachers, and the members of the congregation all enjoyed finding

---

21   On the Christian response to traditional healing in West Timor see Mery Kolimon, *Theology of Empowerment. Reflections from a West Timorese Perspective*, Berlin: Lit. Verlag, 2008
22   'Communism and the Christian Church in Indonesian Timor', National Archives of Australia, series number A1838, Control Symbol: 3038/2/2/2, location, Canberra. Accessed via http://naa.gov.au/. This document is a letter from the Australian Consulate in East Timor sent to the Secretary of the Department of Foreign Affairs in Australia. The report was made based on a conversation with an Australian missionary working in Indonesian West Timor, about communism and its link to the church there. Accessed 26 January, 2012.

an outlet for their principles which they did not consider to be at odds with their own beliefs, for instance in distributing seeds and farming tools to the hungry. Many of them criticised imperialism. This was not very different to the discourse of today, namely the criticism of globalisation and neo-liberal economy.

This fact makes us reconsider the relationship between Christianity and Marxism/communism. One cannot deny that throughout history, the relationship between Marxism and Christianity has been more marked by hatred and suspicion.[23] Communism, which was born as a protest against capitalism in the early nineteenth century, views Christianity as the religion that throughout its history (except in its beginnings) has always been on the side of the oppressors by providing divine truth to social injustice.[24] Conversely, Christianity attacks communism because of the communists' atheism.

Christianity in Indonesia, specifically in East Nusa Tenggara, has inherited this hatred and suspicion from the many European missionaries who brought Christianity to this area. Most, but not all, of the missionaries were involved with anti-communist propaganda at the time. A report from the Australian Consulate in East Timor in 1961 reveals the attacks going on between an Australian missionary serving in the GMIT and the NTT leadership of the Communist Party. In one of his sermons, the pastor attacked the communists, and as a result he was attacked in turn in an open letter widely distributed in Kupang that accused the missionary with interfering with Indonesia's domestic affairs, and saying he was an agent of imperialism.[25]

Even so, not all European missionaries had a negative view of communism. As is evident in the report from the Sumba research team, Pastor Hendricus van Oostrum, in one of his sermons at the time said: 'I hope all Christians become kind of communists but: not atheists.' Implicit in this statement

---

23   See Dorothee Soelle, 'The Christian-Marxist dialogue of the 1960s", *Monthly Review* July-August 1984, pp 20–26 http://www.democraticunderground.com/discuss/duboard.php?az=view_all&address=214x117452 accessed on 24 November 2011.
24   See Karl Marx, 'Introduction to a Contribution to the Critique of Hegel's Philosophy of Right', in *Deutsch-Französische Jahrbucher* (Paris: 7& 10 February, 1844), http://www.angelfire.com/or/sociologyshop/marxrel.html accessed on 9 April 2012.
     See further Paulose, 'Encounter in Humanization: Insights for Christian-Marxist Dialogue and Cooperation', http://www.religion-online.org/cgi-bin/relsearchd.dll/showchapter?chapter_id=1516 (12 of 12), 80. Accessed 26 January, 2012.
25   'Communism and the Christian Church in Indonesian Timor', National Archives of Australia, series number A1838, Control Symbol: 3038/2/2/2, location, Canberra. Accessed via http://naa.gov.au/.

is appreciation of the activities the communists were carrying out at the time. He encouraged the congregation councils to strive for a ministry of liberation and renewal for the congregations as the communists were doing.

Institutionally, the GMIT and the GKS made strong statements rejecting the Communist Party. As the report in this book about the city of Kupang shows, the GMIT's position was clarified in a Synod meeting in SoE, Timor in 1960, and in the resolution of the extraordinary Synod meeting in 1965. The GKS also clearly rejected communism in the resolution on the dangers of communism made at Synod XI held at Tanggaba, Sumba in 1957, which was further affirmed in 1966 with the resolution of the Synod at Pameti Karata. The reasons given were that communism denied the existence of God, caused enmity between groups and despised all religion. Both churches tended to see the 1965 tragedy as a blessing because of the flood of converts when people were afraid of being branded as communist.[26]

However, in the wider sphere, since the 1970s there has been a new awareness among both Marxists and Christians in Europe and Latin America of the need to strive for dialogue between Christianity and Marxism, with the belief that both share a concern for humanity. Dorothee Soelle, a German feminist, points out that within Marxism a shift took place in its view of Christianity. Today, Christianity is understood as a contradiction: a defense and legitimation of the status quo and its culture of injustice on the one hand, and a tool of protest, change and liberation on the other.[27]

Marxists involved with the Marxist-Christian dialogue in Europe seriously re-examine Marx's teaching about why man needs to dream and create myths about religion. In this way, in the dialogue between Christianity and Marxism, Marxists who previously rejected the idea of transcendence can accept this concept in a new understanding as something that happens right here and now, not as something that will happen in the future.[28] Thus transcendence is understood not as a state but rather as an act, namely an ability to be creatively involved in a certain historical situation. This trans-

---

26 See 'Langkah Pertama: Suatu Tinjauan Terhadap Periode 25 Tahun GMIT, 31 Oktober 1947 – 31 Oktober 1972', 23. Also see *Buletin Zendingcentrum, Bulletin Situatie Indonesia No. 13*.

27 Soelle, op cit. Also see Terry Brown, "Marxism and Christianity", *Monthly Review*, October 1984: 42–44.

28 The issue of transcendence arises in Marx's criticism of Christianity in relation to Christian teaching about heaven and salvation after death. To Marx, the teachings about heaven make Christians unable to fully involve themselves in the struggle for justice in the present, and make them tend to accept injustice with the enticement of living happily in the afterlife. According to Marx, in this way Christianity supports injustice and helps oppress the poor.

cendence is something extremely profound because it is man's most creative self fulfilment in the endeavour to achieve humanisation. Thus through Marxist-Christian dialogue, Christians give a new language to Marxists. This new language is about transcendence to broaden their ideas about social and economic justice.

On the other hand, from Marxism Christians relearn the meaning of the event of incarnation (the Word of God made flesh). The meeting of Christianity and Marxism deepens Christians' understanding of the historical and social dimensions of man's existence. Traditionally, Christians believed that God relates only with the individual for the salvation of that individual. When Christians are confronted with the kind of emphasis on material things that Marxism prioritises, they are forced to consider material existence more seriously. Because of this, hunger, unemployment and industrial and military relations all develop as theological themes. Incarnation is no longer understood as a process that happens once and is over and done with, but rather as a process of God's self-revelation that is ongoing in history. Marx's criticism of Christianity that its understanding of humankind and human history is just abstract and fictional, is hereby answered with a new way of understanding the event of incarnation. The new way of understanding incarnation is connected to material and social matters. In this way, Marxists help Christians to better understand incarnation.

Latin American liberation theology is another example of how dialogue between Christian theology and Marxism is beneficial in the context of injustice and oppression.[29] Learning from Marxism can help sharpen the

---

29 'In its origins, liberation theology formed a part of a wider movement that marked a dramatic change within the church in Latin America. The Catholic Church, perceived over the centuries as a politically conservative force in Latin America, began to shift ground in the 1960s and 70s. Vatican II influenced this change, but social unrest within Latin America itself contributed significantly. As happened in the United States, student movements became radicalised and universities became centers of protest. But a new awareness of Latin American problems arose also from church efforts to evangelise the poor more effectively. Through a variety of contributing influences, a new generation of bishops, priests, religious, and laity became deeply concerned about the massive poverty that afflicted so much of Latin America. Many in this new generation took on apostolic work that involved living with and working with the poor directly, and this experience made them deeply conscious of both the misery and the hopes of the poor. They committed themselves to change, a change they believed would require a radical restructuring of Latin American society. A new group of Catholic theologians, joined from the outset by Protestant colleagues, gave voice to this new spirit in liberation theology. It set a new agenda for the church in Latin America, a call for the church to lend its power and influence to the cause of the poor.' Arthur F. McGovern, *Liberation Theology and Its Critics: Towards and Assessment* (Maryknoll, New York: Orbis Books, 1989) ix-x.

church's social analysis of the reality of oppression and help create a clear stand towards the oppressed.

It is high time that Christianity in Indonesia, and here specifically the GMIT and the GKS, think seriously about the possibilities of learning from Marxism rather than perpetuating hatred towards it. Openness to this will allow the church to become more sensitive to people's suffering and to show a clear attitude about where the church stands. Specifically, in the context of global capitalism today which tends to exploit the poor, the Church can take important lessons from Marxism which will help to enable it to carry out Jesus' teaching about serving those who are marginalised.

## 5. 'The truth will make you free'. Understanding historical truth from the victims' experience.

For a few decades after the 1965 tragedy, the Indonesian public was forced to believe the official version about what happened in this violent incident. The film *Penghianatan G30S/PKI* (Treachery of the 30th September Movement/PKI) screened every year and it was obligatory for school children to watch; it legitimised the annihilation of the Indonesian Communist Party and the oppression of Gerwani. In much writing on history, communists are branded as evil and Gerwani women as temptresses who sliced the Generals at the Crocodile Hole. This then became the reason to punish them without any trial and to crush the women's organisations and the women's movement.[30] For thirty-two years of the New Order, the people were fed lies about what really happened.

Given that the writing of Indonesian history has turned things around for the interests of the powerful, questions about truth become important: what really happened? This current research springs from concern about the 'amnesia' that will continue to inflict suffering on this nation if there is not courage to seek out and listen to the experiences of victims from this black hole of Indonesian history. We are motivated to write because history is one of the best teachers – people can learn from the good engraved in civilisation of the past and from the bad that must be corrected, to become wiser and better in the future.

This publication of victim's stories is an attempt at the truth of the marginalised. We are not claiming that their voices are the most true. Any real effort to straighten history must not lose a critical point of view, including

---

30  See Saskia Eleonora Wieringa, *Sexual politics in Indonesia*. New York: Palgrave Macmillan [Institute of Social Studies Series] 2002.

criticism of the victims' voices. Only in this way can we free ourselves from the need to accept forced truth.

'You will know the truth and the truth will make you free', Jesus said (John 8:32). There is a connection between truth and freedom. As long as people live with a slew of lies, they are not free. Deceit in history makes people servile. Deceit has also contributed to the loss of national solidarity between citizens. We have been taught to live with mutual suspicion, enmity and intrigue. Jesus also said, 'I am the way, the truth and the life' (John 14:6a). To know Jesus is to know the truth. Walking on the path of Jesus is to walk on the path of truth and justice and to side with those who became victims of the overturning of history. Those who walk on the path of truth will find life.

The church must be involved in efforts to express the truth, no matter how difficult this is. In Indonesia today there are many efforts to uncover human rights abuses in the history of the nation. The church, as a fellowship of disciples of Jesus, disciples of The Truth, has an inevitable duty to be involved in these efforts, because this truth will make us truly free. As long as the church does not declare truth because of fear of authorities, the church is not free. In this fear and lack of freedom, the church loses truth.

## B. Creating the future

The stories of the women victims and survivors of the 1965 tragedy in East Nusa Tenggara collected in this book, invite readers to reflect on their own suffering and to order their communal lives with more fairness and empathy. In particular, the churches in NTT are summoned to reconstruct their understanding and political roles in order to be involved in creating the nation's future.

### *1. Reconstruction of political theology*
The State's cooption of the church at the time of the mass violence in 1965 and the ongoing effects of that, bring us to theological questions about the church's teachings about politics, and what the church's role should be in politics, both organisationally and individually.

As a result of the 1965 Affair, teachers who participated in politics through a political party that was fully recognised by the State were considered to have committed a crime. Those who were critical of a social order that did not favour the common people, were silenced. Farmers who knew nothing at all about State politics, but whose names had been listed as recipients of aid in the form of food, seeds and agricultural tools, and who had been attracted to campaigns for land reform, were branded as members of a banned political party. The New Order was established on this silencing of critical voices and entrenched its power for more than 30 years. Even though the New Order has collapsed, to this day one still senses keenly a phobia about ordering Indonesia's political life. The church is still fearful of formulating its political role.

Theology is tightly linked to politics. To Christians, God is involved in history. He works in the world for the good of the universe (*mission Dei*). God's work is whole and cosmic. All God's work includes all fields of human life: social, economic, political, legal and cultural. The cosmic nature of God's work reveals God's mercy and good deeds to all creatures and to the entire world.

God involves the church in God's mission for the good of humankind and nature. The church's mission (*mission ecclesiae*) is therefore also whole and cosmic. The church, in its mission, cannot therefore neglect its political role. The Christian Evangelical Church in Timor (GMIT) formulates its mission as including five fields of ministry: fellowship (*koinonia*), witness (*marturia*), charity (*diakonia*), liturgy (*liturgia*), and stewardship (*oikonomia*). It is particularly in this last category that the church formulates its political role. The Greek term *oikonomia* comes from two root words – *oikos* (house) and *nomos* (order). The task of putting one's house in order includes the church ordering itself, the order life in society (social, economic and political) and the ordering of the environment (the church's ecological role). In the field of politics, the role of the church is to put its own house in order and to be involved in putting the house of the people, the nation, and nature in order also; so that it becomes an accommodative, prosperous house.[31] The church therefore has to be political in the sense of being involved in the ordering of life of society and the nation so that it is marked by values of God's commandments: love, truth, peace, justice, equality and wholeness of creation.[32] Fear of being branded communist led to the church's unclear position towards the poor and the marginalised in general – not only towards the 1965 victims – primarily because prioritising the poor was branded as

---

31  See further 'Pokok-Pokok Eklesiologi GMIT', unpublished, 2010.
32  The involvement of the church in politics means that the church advocates state policies, regulations and laws that guarantee values ordered by God, not that it should campaign for any candidate or particular political party.

communist, even though this is the Gospel message.³³ In this way, self-healing from the 1965 trauma would be the first step towards the church reclaiming what belongs to it: 'Good news for the poor'.

*The role of the church in empowerment of civil society*

In the discourse of democracy, the political arena is divided into three: the State, political society, and civil society.³⁴ What is meant by the State includes not only the government, but also all forms of bureaucracy and institutions of administration and the law. Political society involves individuals and groups who compete with each other to obtain power and public delegation in the ordering of State institutions, for instance, political parties. Civil society includes social movements and associations that organise themselves to clarify opinion, and struggle to obtain their ideals; for instance, critical groups among students, NGO activists and groups of religious background. They reject state tyranny and endeavour to be critical of power.

The church, in its political role, must make maximum use of the space for civil society. It is a well-known fact that for a very long time in the history of politics in Indonesia, civil society was extremely weak and weakened further, even becoming oppressed. During the New Order in particular, the bureaucratic machine and the military worked intensely to weaken the power of civil society and political society. Social movements and mass media critical of the government were crushed. Human rights activists who were critical were disappeared. Now, the tide of reformation offers hope for strengthening people, confronting the tendency towards cooption and excessive state violence towards society. The church must truly make good use of this space to shape its role in the field of politics.

In the current reformation era there is a trend for pastors to become candidates and members of the legislative assembly, or to compete in local elections for District Head and Deputy District Head. This is of course their civil right as citizens. However, in the interests of the church as an institution and in the execution of its mission, church employees would be better directed to strengthening civil society.

For this, there are two agenda of empowerment of civil society important for the church to implement. The first is to be involved in consciousness-

---

33 Throughout the New Order, for instance, authorities suspected liberation theology of being subversive, even though this theology motivates support for and involvement with the struggle of the poor for restoration of their rights.
34 See Alfred Stephan, *Rethinking Military Politics: Brazil and the Southern Cone* (Princeton, NJ): Princeton University Press, 1988), 3–4.

raising of citizens about their rights that have been thus far abused, and secondly, self-healing of the church itself from the political trauma that makes the church remain silent when injustice occurs.

*Consciousness-raising*

Consciousness-raising is intended to make people who are also members of the church understand their rights (political, civil, economic, social and cultural). First implemented by Paulo Freire and liberation theologists in Latin America, consciousness-raising encourages those who are oppressed to be aware of the fact of their oppression and of injustice in society, and to pursue the fight for change, justice and true peace in the church and society.[35]

In East Nusa Tenggara, the Sumba Christian Church (GKS) and the Christian Evangelical Church in Timor (GMIT) have well-organised structures of congregations as their base, and a wide-reaching synod. The GMIT's institutional structure is well organised from small groups or clusters of households within a congregation, each of which is coordinated by a small congregation council group, then spreading to the congregation, presbytery, and synod. Apart from this, both churches have their own categories of organisations for ministry, like children, teenagers, youth, women, men, the elderly and so on, in various areas. There are also functional groups like choirs and prayer groups in various levels of ministry from congregation to presbytery to synod. It is much to be regretted that this excellent organisational structure has not been used in a planned and systematic way for consciousness-raising of church members, even though it is an invaluable asset for the church to involve itself in empowering civil society in Indonesia.

Material for nurturing church members and for supplying church leaders in various fields and categories of ministry must include consciousness-raising of citizens sensitive to the realities of injustice that occur, and also building skills in advocacy for peace and justice. The youth groups' curricula, catechism, Bible Study and sermons all need to include the effort to raise the consciousness and astuteness of church members and church leaders. One hopes that this will provide them with the vision and skills to play the part of critical agents of civil society when confronting tyranny from any source, within or outside the church.

---

35   Paulo Freire is an influential Brazilian educator. He developed the concept of education of the oppressed based on his own experience of working alongside the poor in the slums in his literacy campaign. He then worked in the World Council of Churches for the program of renewal of education in former Portuguese colonies in Africa.

The theology curricula in the various theological colleges in NTT also require reform so that those studying to be pastors and theologians are provided with critical education that will allow them to become agents of renewal in society. This can occur when the theological campuses themselves become seminaries in the true sense, namely propagating values of equality, justice, peace and respect for human rights; not places where seniority, a culture of fear, and enmity are perpetuated.

*Women in politics*
One consequence for women of the 1965 tragedy was the shackling of their freedom to express their political rights in the public arena. The slandering of Gerwani and women's organisations at the time blackened the name of women's activism. The New Order then gave a new image to Indonesian women, which actually limited their participation: the good Indonesian woman was one who stayed at home, cared for her husband and children, and served without ambition. Woman's nature was depicted as soft, passive, obedient to the men in her family, self-sacrificing, and caring for the family. Politics was not her field. Politics was a man's affair. Men were responsible for organising the house of the nation: women organised the family household. Women were considered to know nothing about politics. The Five Principles of Women (Panca Dharma Wanita) in New Order politics emphasised the domestic roles of women: supporter of her husband; educator; home maker; worker, and member of society, especially of women's organisations which were also interpreted in a limited fashion.

Our research teams found that some of the women activists who were victims of the 1965 tragedy retreated from the hubbub of Indonesian politics. They became suspicious of any social organisation. The New Order regime that blackened their names made them apathetic to the role of women's politics. At the same time, the political reality of the organising of communal life for justice, peace and equality, shifted in meaning. Politics was depicted as a brutal, nasty, dirty power game. Because of this, good women – or such was the view in the gender arrangement of the New Order regime – do not participate in that political game. As a result, Indonesian women perpetuated the fear of politics that the New Order had created so successfully. Part of the effort for renewal that the current generation of women must carry out is to oppose terror and intimidation carried out against women, and also to restore political meaning as something important that requires the role of women.

One source for Christian women to rebuild women's political role is the Bible. The Bible tells us that men and women were created equal. Genesis 1 gives important witness to two things. The first is that men and women were created in God's image, and the second is that God gave power to them both (Genesis 1:26). Being created in God's image means that humans – women and men – were given the gift of mental and spiritual faculties that are also possessed by God. This divine gift is intended for humans to possess within themselves the ability and authority to order the world according to Divine will. Delegation as manager of God's house (*oikonomis*) was given not only to men or to women separately, but to women and men together. Because of this, acknowledgement of women's abilities in ordering national life is acknowledgement of the work of God in creating men and women with standing, position and abilities that are equal. Gender differences must not be seen as a reason to view women as inferior to men. Thus, the full involvement of women in the field of politics, in the sense of the ordering of the house of the nation, holds strong theological basis.

It is the task of the church today to create space for healing, nurturing and development of the political capabilities of women so that they can give maximum participation to the ordering of common life in the church and society. For this, the church itself needs to turn away from the tendency to favour male leadership, because actually women have the competence and talents to become leaders, but often are not given the same opportunities, skills and power as men to fulfill their potential. By creating space for raising the consciousness and political skills of women, the church will contribute to an equitable and fair national life. For this, the church needs to be on the alert against interpretations of the Bible that limit or oppress women. Apart from that, the church also needs to open a wider space for women to be involved in decision-making in all levels of ministry.

The involvement of women in politics is an attempt to reclaim their identity as citizens who actively pursue their rights. At the same time, it will restore political meaning that has been disgraced. In the fourth of Indonesia's five national principles, Pancasila (Democracy guided by the inner wisdom in the unanimity arising out of deliberations amongst representatives), the word for 'democracy', *kerakyatan*, includes both men and women. Women need to take part actively in discussions and deliberations to order the life of society, the people and the State. Their involvement in politics should thus be highlighted, with the clear vision that women's struggle in politics is for the good of all, for all the people of Indonesia, not only for their own interests or those of particular groups, and certainly not just to fill a certain quota.

## 2. Pastoral action: The healed and healing church

The church has a pastoral mission. Traditionally, pastoral is linked to the nurture and healing of souls, both of victims and perpetrators. In the church, various levels of ministry – including elders, deacons and pastors – are intended for this. Through pastoral ministry, weaker members of the congregation are strengthened, and those in mourning are consoled so that they can experience tranquility to help spread the Gospel as members of the church and society. This pastoral ministry should also include those who are strong and powerful.

In particular, in connection with the 1965 affair, churches in Indonesia, and specifically in Nusa Tenggara Timur, have the pastoral responsibility to put themselves in order as a fellowship that is wounded, and is serving its members who still live in trauma and suffering. These two things can go hand in hand and complement each other. The healing of members of the congregation (as individuals) will in turn contribute to the healing of the church as a fellowship. And conversely, the healing of the church as a fellowship is needed to give wider meaning to the healing of individuals in their communities. If this occurs, then the church will then be able to perform its pastoral role in society as the community that heals.

A study about healing from trauma conducted by Judith Herman, a lecturer at the Harvard Medical School, shows that trauma healing involves three stages: establishing safety, remembering and mourning terror/violence that occurred in the past, and creating a future.

### Building a sense of security

Establishing safety involves creating a safe environment. Trauma invades the victim's sense of power. The first step in healing must then be to build a sense of safety and a safe environment. The collapse of the Suharto regime and the beginning of the reformation era in Indonesia is contributing to this. The humanitarian tragedy occurred well over four decades ago. Around two generations have gone by. Reform is occurring in Indonesia through corrections to the law, the strengthening of democracy and social reform. But none of this will mean anything to the church, if the church does not actively take advantage of this opportunity to liberate itself. The church must be able to overcome the fear that has imprisoned it, because it is undeniable that the generations post 1965 have absorbed a secondary trauma in the form of willingness to submit to power, fear to oppose, fear to speak out and so forth. Today's generation of church members and leaders must become the generation able to confront that traumatic experience and to dare to overcome the fear that has imprisoned them and the church generations before them, so they can be healed.

Part of the duty of building a sense of security is also to make the church itself a safe space for victims to speak about the suffering and injustice they experienced. More than forty years after the tragedy occurred, the church today needs to provide healing, in various ways, to those victims who are still living, including listening to their stories.

We ourselves, in learning from the stories of the women victims of the 1965 tragedy in East Nusa Tenggara, have found that the need for a sense of security and a safe environment to speak perhaps differs for women and men. The experiences of men and women were not the same. Some of the female victims experienced sexual abuse and rape. Speaking about these experiences is not easy. The church needs to work alongside these women to create a sense of trust, so the victims do not think that telling their stories will lead to new violence, like being gossiped about, or blamed. For this the church needs skills in pastoral counseling in allowing victims to feel safe in sharing their experiences of violence.

Something else to be taken into consideration is the provision of proper graves for those killed in the aftermath of the 1965 affair. In our meetings with victims during our research, one of the things they planned was to hold commemorations and build memorials at the various execution sites. Our research has listed some of the sites where massacres occurred.[36] The church should be involved in this effort so that today's generation and future generations will come and learn about what happened, and will not repeat the same crime. This is also one way for us all to acknowledge the crimes done to them. Commemoration can be simple, like planting a tree or making stone cairns. It can also be the holding of a religious service at the sites, quiet moments during regular worship, special days commemorated in different ways, special prayers and so on. The form of commemoration can be adapted to local traditions, as has been done in Flores.[37]

Even today, many victims of the 1965 violence have not been fully accepted by the church. They participate in church services and are even active in the

---

36  See the appendix. Map of Massacre sites 1965–66 in NTT: Temporary findings.
37  In *Mematahkan Pewarisan Ingatan Wacana Anti-Komunis dan Politik rekonsiliasi Pasca-Soeharto* (Jakarta: Elsham, 2004, 14–15), Budiawan gives one such example of people in NTT. In his introduction to the book, Hersri Setiawan quotes Ita Nadya who speaks about commemoration by the people of Pantai Kewa in Flores who tend the mass grave of 1965 victims as part of everyday life.

ministry, but the church has still not really opened its ears and heart to the stories of violence and injustice they experienced.

### *Speak up, break the silence!*
Another stage of healing linked to the church giving its ears and heart to listen and respond to the victims' stories, is to remember and lament the terror and violence that happened in the past. In East Nusa Tenggara, even today when people speak of their traumatic experiences of 1965 they speak in a whisper. Or they refuse to talk about it at all.

The Gospel tells of how Jesus healed a mute man who was possessed by the devil (Matthew 9:32–34; Lucas 11:14–15). Traumatic memories, like the ghosts that continue to haunt this nation, produce paralysing fear. Fear is actually a basic mechanism to survive when one reacts to a particular stimulus like pain or the threat of danger. Fear can help people know danger and face it or avoid it. Even so, huge fear as a result of terror can paralyse. Becoming free of it, requires the courage to speak. The spirit of fear has to be driven out. As the Bible says: 'and after the devil was driven out, the man who had been mute spoke.' (Matthew 9:33a)

Once the church has reached a point where it feels safe, it needs to describe what happened and what the meaning of those events is for the church and its people. In this, the church must be prepared to face criticism – whether it is about the church's support of the victims or on the contrary, its marginalising of victims for the sake of its own sense of safety – both from outside parties as well as from inside the church.

As already stated in the prologue to this book, the Truth and Reconciliation Commission in South Africa is an example of how the church is challenged to give witness about its involvement, both in supporting and opposing human rights abuses in the past. The Christian Evangelical Church in Timor (GMIT) and the Sumba Christian Church (GKS) can form their own such commission for themselves.

The courage of the women victims in speaking up and in allowing us to publish their stories can be understood not only as giving witness about God who is on the side of the oppressed, but also as a challenge to history that has thus far slandered them. When the church is open to hearing their voices, and dares to speak about what really happened as well as its own role in that, then the shackles that have been binding it to date will break free, one by one. The victims, both in person and through their stories, can become sources for the younger generation to learn how to analyse fear. Healing the wounds of the victims and their descendants is also the beginning of healing the wounds of us all.

But when the church remains steadfastly silent, then it will remain in the binds that limit its role and prophetic action. At this stage, the church must have the courage to acknowledge that it did great wrong to humanity when it chose to remain silent at the time the tragedy occurred, or even forced victims to confess to the accusation of rebellion against the State, an accusation that was baseless. To make amends for demanding that the victims confess their sins, the church must confess its own sin that it failed to declare truth because it was afraid of the consequences.

As for the victims and survivors, not all of them wish to speak about what they experienced. There are various reasons for this. The choice of keeping their bitter stories to themselves should also be respected. But this might also be proof of the strength of the trauma, and that our society is still unable to produce a safe environment for victims to talk.

Another aspect of this stage is to mourn the loss that occurred as a result of the violence. We so often avoid lamenting the past, not because we are afraid, but because we want to maintain our self-respect. We must dare to mention things the violence stole from us. The church must dare to lament the fact that it lost its courage and its prophetic voice: it became fearful, and even today still tends to remain silent when violence and injustice occur. The church needs to mourn for those who were killed, those who experienced other forms of violence, and also mourn its own loss of courage and critical voice.

Something else the church needs to mourn is the fact that as a result of the 1965 tragedy, the church as a fellowship (*koinonia*) became sick. Relations between family members fractured, and even the church as a fellowship was broken. Fellowship as God's family, which should be marked by intimate and personal relations, was replaced by mutual suspicion and the loss of trust between people.[38] The church lost its internal solidarity and was unable to develop a pattern of reconciliation that healed the wounds of its fellowship. Management of internal conflict in the church was paralysed because the role of mediation was rarely implemented. This in turn led the church to fail to perform a role of reconciliation outside its own fellowship.

Apart from it being important for the church to open itself to listening to victims' stories, and to bearing witness to its own position when the 1965 tragedy occurred, another important thing is the restoration of the victims' rights. For almost 50 years, victims and their families have experienced all

---

38  The fracture of relations within the church was also caused by the weakening of national solidarity, as discussed earlier.

kinds of limitations of their civil, political, economic, social and cultural rights. It is not enough for the church and the nation just to listen to the victims' stories, they must also fight for restoration of their rights. Some of the victims we interviewed complained about the way they were summarily dismissed from their positions as civil servants, without any proof that they had been members of the Communist Party.[39] Others found their children were not accepted as civil servants. Restitution of the rights of victims can include medical needs, education, economy, re-acceptance and re-acknowledgement of their status as civil servants, payment of pensions to widows of civil servants who were murdered, and a just legal process for the evil that befell them.

## Creating the future

Creating the future is also one part of the healing process. After the church has mourned its past stolen from it by the traumatic experience, it needs to build a new picture of itself. At this stage, the church needs to be aware that it too is a victim and needs to learn to reclaim its power to heal. For this, the church needs to recognise the potential within itself to arise. Faith in Christ that liberates and heals is the most basic power the church has to correct itself. Like the lame man who was healed because of the healing power of Christ (Lucas 5:17–26), the church needs to claim the power that God gives to become healthy after traumatic experience. God always carries out the role of renewal in the church through the work of the Holy Spirit. But the church itself has to be open to God's work of renewal. The church, in creating a future for itself and for this nation, must clearly state its attitude towards real problems around it. Part of building a new self-image (new creation) is to clearly state its definitive siding with the oppressed in history.

Paul the apostle wrote that in Christ, those of faith become renewed (Ephesians 4:17–25). The mark of renewed people is to live in truth and the spirit (verse 25). As a fellowship of believers, the church must become a community that constantly renews itself within truth and the spirit. The church must dare to say yes to what is right and no to what is wrong. As a fellowship that is sanctified and entrusted to spread the good news, the identity of the church is tested by how far it is able to voice the truth. It is only in this way that the church becomes a fellowship that is renewed and that renews itself. The life stories shared with us by some of the women

---

39  See, for instance, the cases of Pak Derosari and Pak Ndili in Appendix 2.

victims, show that they confronted the challenges of life by attempting to manifest a new image. They rejected the branding of them by striving to bring up their children to be useful people. Their children's service in society overturned the bad stigma attached to them. The church can learn from this and strive to correct itself and manifest a new self-image fighting for truth and justice.

In the fight for truth and justice, the church is not alone. The church also needs to forge relations with other parties struggling for the same healing. Civil society groups outside the GMIT and GKS, and even those outside of Christianity, can become colleagues in the collective fight for a healed church and nation.

For the victims, it is extremely important to organise themselves into one organisation that enables them to share and find support in fostering a new self-image. In this, the church can consciously facilitate the formation of a victims' organisation. Of course, some of the victims who are better called survivors are already perfectly capable of developing a new self-image. However, not all of them are able to arise from depression. Victims' organisations can be a space for the building of solidarity between them, for communal healing. Further, those who have no voice can then express their hopes and needs, and fight for justice for themselves and for all others who experience marginalisation and oppression.

Related to this, organisations for the children of victims are also important. In our meetings with victims, we saw that widows whose husbands had been killed no longer had the physical strength for the fight for justice. Their children can commence the agenda of the restitution of victims' rights and the struggle for wider social justice.

In the victims' struggle, the church must stand firmly alongside them, as a new community that is healed and is healing, that fights alongside victims for justice, reconciliation, and the wiping of the stigma that has been attached to them all this while.

The victims have spoken. Take note, reflect on it, and act!

# Glossary

**ABRI** – Angkatan Bersenjata Republic Indonesia, Indonesian Armed Forces
**APIK** – Asosiasi Perempuan Indonesia untuk Keadilan, Association of Indonesian Women for Justice
**APMC** – Asia Pacific Christian Mission
**ATK** – Akademi Theologia Kupang (at Oesapa); Kupang Theological College
**Bakorstanas** – Badan Koordinasi Bantuan Pemantapan Stabilitas Nasional, Body for Coordination of Assistance for Consolidation of National Stability (renaming of Kopkamtib in 1988)
**Bappeda** – Badan Perencana Pembangunan Daerah, Regional Body for Planning and Development.
**BKN** – Badan Kepegawaian Negara – State Personnel Administration
**BODM** – Bintara Onder Distrik Militer, mid-ranking military at regional command
**BP** – Badan Pengurus, Executive Board
**BPC** – Badan Pengurus Cabang, Executive Board at branch level
**BTI** – Barisan Tani Indonesia, Indonesian Peasants' Front / Indonesian Farmers' Front
**Bupati** – Head of district or regency (kabupaten)
**BUTERPRA** – Bintara Urusan Teritorial dan Perlawanan Rakyat, (Non-Commissioned Officers for Territorial Affairs and People's Opposition) now known as KORAMIL, komando rayon Militer (Military district command at sub-district or kecamatan level
**BZG** – Badan Zending Belanda; Nederlandsche Zendeling Genootschap or NZG, Netherlands Missionary Society
**Camat** – (see also Kecamatan), Head of subdistrict, kecamatan
**CDB** – Comite Daerah Besar (PKI); Regional Committee of the Indonesian Communist Party
**CPM** – Military Police Corps
**CS** – Comite Seksi (PKI) Branch Committee
**Danden** – Komandan detasemen, Commander of a (military) detachment
**Dandim** – Komandan Distrik Militer, Commander of
**Dan Inrehab** – komandan instalasi rehabilitasi Commander of 'rehabilitation post' = detention camp
**DAN KDO OPS PEM Kam Tib NTT** – Komandan Komando Operasi Pemulihan Keamanan dan Ketertiban Nusa Tenggara Timur, Commander of the Command for the Operation to Restore Security and Order in East Nusa Tenggara
**Danrem** – Komandan Resort Militer, Commander of Military Area Command (i.e. the army command between Kodam and Kodim).
**Daswati** – daerah swatantra tingkat, autonomous region
**Deputat Zending Sumba**: Bureau for Mission in Sumba
**Desa** – village
**DGI** – Dewan Gereja-gereja di Indonesia, Council of Churches in Indonesia
**DPM** – Deputat Penjelidik Marxisme, (Delegation for the Investigation of Marxism [GKS established 1956])
**DPP** – Dewan Pimpinan Pusat, Council of Central Leadership
**DPR** – Dewan Perwakilan Rakyat, House of Representatives
**DPRD** – Dewan Perwakilan Rakyat Daerah, Regional House of Representatives

**DPRD-GR**; Dewan Perwakilan Rakyat Daerah-Gotong Royong) = Mutual Cooperation DRPD
**G30S** – Gerakan 30 Sepember, 30th September [1965] Movement
**Gerwani** – Gerakan Wanita Indonesia, Indonesian Women's Movement
**Gestapu** - Gerakan September Tiga Puluh, The 30th September [1965] Movement)
**Gestok** – Gerakan Satu Oktober, The 1st October [1965] Movement
**GKS** – Gereja Kristen Sumba, The Christian Church of Sumba
**GMIT** – Gereja Masehi Injil di Timor, The Christian Evangelical Church in Timor/ Timor Evangelical Christian Church
**GOP** – Gabungan Organisasi Perempuan, Affiliation of Women's Organizations
**GPIB** – Gereja Protestan Indonesia Barat, West Indonesian Protestant Church
**GSJA** – Gereja Jemaat Allah, Assemblies of God
**HAM** – hak asasi manusia, human rights
**Hansip** – pertahanan sipil, paramilitary civil defense corps
**ICTJ** – International Centre for Transitional Justice
**III** – Institut Injili Indonesia, Indonesian Evangelical Institute
**INREHAB** – Instalasi Rehabilitasi, 'rehabilitation post' = detention camp.
**ISSI** – Institut Sejarah Sosial Indonesia, Indonesian Institute for Social History
**JPIT**: Jaringan Perempuan Indonesia Timur untuk Studi Perempuan Agama dan Budaya, The Eastern Indonesia Women's Network for the Study of Women, Religion and Culture
**Kabupaten** – district, regency.
**Kampung** – an administrative unit, hamlet, neighbourhood, precinct.
**Kapolres** – Kepala Kepolisian Resort, regional police chief
**KA TEPERDA** – Kepala Tim Pemeriksa Daerah, Head of regional interrogation team
**Kasdam** - Kepala Staf Daerah Militer, (military) Head of Staff (regional level)
**Kastaf** – Kepala Staf, Head of Staff
**Kecamatan** – subdistrict (subdivision of kabupaten)
**Keppres** – keputusan presiden, presidential instruction
**KKR** – Kebaktian Kebangunan Rohani, Spiritual Awakening Service
**Kodam** – Komando Daerah Militer, Regional Military Command, army garrison
**Kodim** – Komando Distrik Militer, District Military Command
**Komop** – Komando Operasionil, Operational Command
**Komnas Perempuan** – Komite Nasional Perempuan, National Commission on Women
**KontraS** – Komisi untuk Orang Hilang dan Korban Tindak Kekerasan, Commission for the Disappeared and Victims of Violence
**Kopkamtib** – Komando Operasi Pemulihan Kemanan dan Ketertiban, Operations Command for the Restoration of Security and Order. [renamed as Bakorstanas in 1988]
**Koramil** – Komando Rayon Militer, Sub-District Military Command
**Korem** – Komando Resort Militer, Resort Military Command i.e. the army command between the Kodam and Kodim.
Kostrad – Komando Strategis Angkatan Darat, Army Strategic Reserve Command
KOTI Gabungan V – Komando Operasi Tertinggi Gabungan V: Commander of V Highest Joint Operation
**KPI** – Kebaktian Pekabaran Injil, Evangelization Service
**Laksus** – pelaksana khusus, special operations
**Laksusda** – pelaksana khusus daerah, regional special area operations
**LBH** – Lembaga Bantuan Hukum, Legal Aid

**Litsus** – penelitian khusus, special scrutiny
**LKK** – Lembaga Kreativitas Kemanusiaan, Institute for Human Creativity
**Masjumi/Masyumi** – Majelis Sjura Muslimin Indonesia, Consultative Council of Indonesian Muslims.
**MPR** – Majelis Permusyawaratan Rakyat. People's Consultative Assembly
**MS** – Majelis Synod, Synod Assembly
**Muspida** – Musyawarah Pempinan Daerah, Assembly of local leaders
**NTB** – Nusa Tenggara Barat, West Nusa Tenggara
**NTT** – Nusa Tenggara Timur, East Nusa Tenggara
**NU** – Nahdlatul Ulama – Revival of Islamic Scholars
**NUSRA** – Nusantara Tenggara, Eastern Indonesia (also called Lesser Sundas)
**NZG** – Nederlandsche Zendeling Genootschap, the Netherlands Missionary Society
**OPR** – Organisasi Pemuda Rakyat, Organization of People's Youth (in South Central Timor)
**P & K** – Pendidikan dan Kebudayaan, (Department of) Education and Culture
**Pancasila** – Five Guiding Pillars of Indonesian Republic
**Pangad** – Panglima Angkatan Darat, Army Commander
**Pangdam** – Panglima Daerah Militer, Military Region Commander
**Pangkopkamtib** – Panglima Komando Operasi Pemulihan Keamanan dan Ketertiban, Commander for the Restoration of Security and Order Operations
**Pangkopkamtibda** – Panglima Komando Operasi Pemulihan Keamanan dan Ketertiban Daerah, Commander for the Restoration of Security and Order Operations at regional level.
**Pangti** – Panglima Tertinggi, High Commander
**PAP** – Pengurus Am Persekolahan, General Board of Education
**Parkindo** – Partai Kristen Indonesia, Indonesian (Protestant) Christian Party
**Partindo** – Partai Indonesia, Indonesia Party
**Pertakin** – Perserikatan Tani Kristen, Christian Farmers Alliance
**Peruati** – Persekutuan Perempuan Berpendidikan Teologi di Indonesia, Association of Theologically Educated Women in Indonesia
**PDI** – Partai Demokrasi Indonesia, Indonesian Democratic Party
**PGI** – Persekutuan Gereja-gereja di Indonesia, Communion of Churches in Indonesia
**PKI** – Partai Komunis Indonesia, Indonesian Communist Party
**PKN** – Protestantse Kerk in Nederland
**PKTI** – Persaudaraan Kaum Tani Indonesia, Indonesian Farmers' League
**PKPI** – Partai Kesatuan dan Persatuan Indonesia, Party of Indonesian Union and Unity
**PNI** – Partai Nasional Indonesia, Indonesian National Party
**PNPS** – Penetapan Presiden, presidential decree
**PNS** – Pegawai Negeri Sipil, Government Civil Servant
**POM** – Polisi Militer, Military Police
**PPKI** – Persatuan Perempuan Kristen Indonesia, Union of Indonesian Christian Women) [this might be interviewee's mistake for PPWI, Trs].
**PRN** – Partai Rakyat Nasional, National People's Party
**PUTERPRA** – Perwira Urusan Teritorial dan Perlawanan Rakyat, Officers for Territorial Affairs and People's Opposition, (now KORAMIL) military district command at kabupaten level (cf Buterpra for kecamatan)
**PWKI** – Persatuan Wanita Kristen Indonesia, Union of Indonesian Christian Women)
**RPKAD** - Resimen Pasukan Khusus Angkatan Darat, Army's Special Forces

**RRI** – Radio Republik Indonesia, Indonesian national radio
**RT** – Rukun Tetangga, Neighbourhood organization
**SAAT** – Seminari Alkitab Asia Tenggara, Southeast Asian Bible Institute
**Sarbuksi** – Sarikat Buruh Kehutanan Seluruh Indonesia, The All Indonesia Union of Plantation/Forestry Workers.
**SGA** – Sekolah Guru Atas, vocational school for high school teachers
**SGB** – Sekolah Guru Bawah, vocational school for primary school teachers
**SGI** – Sekolah Guru Injili – School for Evangelists
**SKP** – Sekolah Kepandaian Puteri, Homecraft school for girls
**SKEP - SKEP LAKSUSDA NUSRA** – Surat Keputusan Pelaksana Khusus Daerah Nusa Tenggara, Executive Order by the Special Regional Executive of Nusantara Tenggara.
**SLTP** – Sekolah Lanjutan Tingkat Pertama, Junior High School
**SMA** – Sekolah Menengah Atas – Senior High School
**SMEA** – Sekolah Menengah Ekonomi Atas, Senior Economy High School
**SMEP** – Sekolah Menengah Ekonomi Pertama, Junior Economy High School
**SMP** – Sekolah Menengah Pertama, Junior High School
**SMPN** – Sekolah Menengah Pertama Negeri, State Junior High School
**SOBSI** – Sentral Organisasi Buruh Seluruh Indonesia, All Indonesia Trade Union Federation
**SPRIN LAKSUSDA NUSRA** – Surat Perintah LAKSUSDA NUSRA; Instruction of special area operations for Nusantara Tenggara
**SR** – Sekolah Rakyat, People's School (primary school)
**STTJ** – Sekolah Tinggi Teologi Jakarta, Jakarta Theology College
**STT** – Sekolah Tinggi Teologi, Theological College
**Swapraja** – autonomous area
**TAP MPRS** – Ketetapan Majelis Permusyawaratan Rakyat Sementara, Determination of Temporary Assembly for People's Deliberations
**TLM** – Tanaoba Lais Manekat, a GMIT foundation for micro credit
**TTS** – Timor Tengah Selatan, South Central Timor
**UKAW** – Universitas Kristen Artha Wacana, Artha Wacana Christian University
**Undana** – Universitas Nusa Cendana, Nusa Cendana University (State University for NTT)
**Yapmas** – Yayasan Pendidikan Masehi Sumba, Foundation for Evangelical Education (established by GKS in 1950)
**Yupenkris** – Yayasan Usaha Pendidikan Kristen, Christian Education Foundation (established by GMIT in 1966)

# *APPENDICES*

## Appendix 1

Chronology of Events in Selected Areas of NTT

In order to give a chronological picture of the 1965 tragedy in East Nusa Tenggara (Nusa Tenggara Timur, NTT), we have drawn up a time line presenting findings from field research and secondary data. Apart from the events in NTT we also include some events on a national scale which became the model for similar events in the regions. Even though Flores is not included in the field research for this book, we are including some information from Flores to show the wider pattern of violence that occurred in NTT. The information gathered here covers various categories, namely: politics, the military, customary groups, women, and religion or the church. Almost all names in the table below are not the informants' real names.

| Date | Location (locations outside NTT are in italics) | Incident |
|---|---|---|
| 1924 | *Java* | **Politics**: The Indonesian Communist Party (PKI) is established. (Farram, 2002) |
| 1925 | NTT | **Politics**: Christian Pandy, the first member of the PKI in Kupang, establishes the *Sarekat Rajat* (later *Sarekat Rakyat*) promising to get rid of taxes and system of forced labour. (Farram, 2002) |
| 18 Nov. 1945 | *Jakarta* | **Politics**: The (Protestant) Christian Party, Parkindo is established. (Y.B. Siswosoebroto, 'Siapa Sebenarnya Juru-selamat Dunia': http://media.isnet.org/antar/JuruSelamat/Kristenisasi-Politik.html) |
| 1947 | Adonara, Flores | **Politics**: The Dutch crush the opposition movement influenced by early communism in NTT. (Farram, 2002) |
| 1947 | Kupang | **Women**: The GMIT is established on 31 October 1947 with women's organisations in every parish, although they are not structured according to the synod. (Transcript of Ibu Maya, informant from the city of Kupang, in JPIT archives) |
| mid 1950s | Adonara, Flores | **Politics**: In the trial of leaders of the Indonesian Farmers' League (Persaudaraan Kaum Tani Indonesia, PKTI) some admit that they are communists, and say that PKTI means 'Branch of the Communist Party'. (Partai Komunis Tjabang Indonesia). (Farram, *Di-PKI-kan* 2002) |
| 1955 | NTT | **Politics**: Indonesia holds its first general elections. NTT is part of 'Lesser Sunda'. Parkindo wins 18% of the vote; PKI wins no seats in Lesser Sunda. (pemilu.asia;http://www.pemilu.asia/?opt=1&s=44&id=15) |
| mid 1957 | Sumba | **Church**: The GKS Synod XI makes a statement to all Christians in Sumba about communist/Marxist teachings. (*Sususan Keputusan-Keputusan Sinode GKS*; JPIT archives) |
| 1959 | East Kupang | **Customary group (masyarakat adat)**: The earlier 'kefetoran' administrative division is replaced by kecamatan (sub-district). (Pak Gaspar, informant from East Kupang, JPIT archives) |
| 1960s | Sabu | **Customary groups**: The authority of traditional leaders (*dewan adat*) is interfered with e.g. the people may no longer hear the *mone ama*. The PKI is accused of using the place for performing the *pedo' a* dances for cock fighting. (Transcript of Kitu, informant from Sabu, in JPIT archives) |
| 1960 | *Jakarta* | **Politics**: The National Front is formed as a vehicle to mobilise political forces under government supervision. The three primary goals are to complete the revolution, carry out development, and return West Irian to Indonesia. ('Perkembangan Kehidupan Politik & Pemerintahan Setelah Dekrit Presiden', accessed on 28 November 2011, http://klikbelajar.com/pelajaran-sekolah/pelajaran-sejarah/perkembangan-kehidupan-politik-dan-pemerintahan-setelah-dekrit-presiden/) |

| Date | Location (locations outside NTT are in italics) | Incident |
|---|---|---|
| 19 July 1950 | South Central Timor | **Politics**: PKI, OPR and BTI become members of the regional parliament DPRD-GR, Kabupaten Dati II, South Central Timor. (Rufus Ony Tunliu, *Kilas Balik DPRD TTS*; unpub. mss) |
| 1961 | Kupang | **Women**: Gerwani begins to recruit members. (Transcript of Ibu Marsa, informant from the city of Kupang, in JPIT archives) |
| 1961 | Kupang | **Politics**: The head of PKI for NTT becomes a member of the national People's Consultative Assembly (MPR). ('Communism and the Christian Church in Indonesia', National Archives of Australia) |
| 1962 | Sabu | **Politics**: PKI begins to flourish in Sabu. (Transcript of Yermi Mone Dami, informant from Sabu, in JPIT archives) |
| 1963 | Sabu | **Politics**: The PNI is established in Sabu. (Transcript of Yermi Mone Dami, informant from Sabu, in JPIT archives) |
| 1963 | West Timor | **Politics**: It is reported that BTI has more than 16,000 members. (*Memori Gubernur Kepala Daerah Propinsi NTT* quoted in Farram, 2002) |
| Sept 1963 | Maumere, Flores | **Military**: Regional Command (Kodim)1607 is established with Captain Hengki Ishak as commander. (Manuscript at Candraditya archives). |
| 1965 | NTT | **Women**: The GMIT women's organisation at synod level is named Wanita Masehi. |
| 3–4 July 1965 | Sabu | **Other**: Fire at Kota Seba. In 1966, during interrogation, some PKI members confess that PKI members were behind the fire. (Transcript of Yermi Mone Dami, informant from Sabu, in JPIT archives) |
| Early Aug. 1965 | Maumere, Flores | **Politics**: The Minister of Forestry visits Flores as head of the central committee of the Catholic Party and is warmly greeted by the local government and Sikka people. He stresses the absolute unity of the vision of the PNI and PKI in Maumere as 'unity based on Nasakom in the sense of sharing political seats between all groups'. (Manuscript held at Candraditya archives) |
| 25 Sept. 1965 | Maumere, Flores | **Military**: Lieutenant General Ahmad Yani visits Maumere and gives a talk at the Ledalero Seminary. He emphasises issues of Nasakom, competition of Manipol, Angkatan Ke-V, and other state matters. (Manuscript at Candraditya archives). |
| 26 Sept. 1965 | East Sumba | **Military**: Lieutenant General Ahmad Yani visits East Sumba. (Umbu Pura Woha, *Sejarah Pemerintahan di Pulau Sumba*) |
| 26 Sept. 1965 | South Central Timor | **Church**: Birth of the 'Revival Movement'. (*Gerakan Rch*). (Transcript of Dian Asnat, informant from South Central Timor, JPIT archives) |

| Date | Location (locations outside NTT are in italics) | Incident |
|---|---|---|
| 28 Sept. 1965 | Kupang | **Military**: El Tari (real name), writing in *Memori Gubernur Kepala Daerah Propinsi NTT*, about the period 1968–72, when he was Governor of NTT, and also about events before that, includes a photo of General A. Yani and Lt. Kol. Soetarmadjiin Kupangon 28 September 1965. (Farram, 2004) |
| 1 Oct. 1965 | *Jakarta* | **Politics**: Six generals and an officer are murdered. |
| Early Oct. 1965 | Alor | **Politics**: PKI officials in Alor are still recruiting members. (JPIT documentation of Apeles Tankalau, informant from Alor) |
| Early Oct. 1965 | *Jakarta* | **Politics**: Major General Soeharto is promoted to become leader of Kopkamtib. (Sumber:http://th1979.wordpress.com/2011/05/08/karir-militer-soeharto) |
| Oct. 1965 | Sabu | **Politics**: Beginning of arrests and detention of people accused of being PKI members. (Transcripts of Muji, Gad'i, and Mama Dina, three informants from Sabu, JPIT archives) **Customary groups**: Someone accused of being a PKI member runs and hides in a traditional house and the crowd threatens to burn down the house. (Transcript of Mama Dina, informant from Sabu, JPIT archives) |
| Oct.–Nov. 1965 | Namata, Sabu | **Customary groups**: War veteran officer (Bara Mata, aged 105) is burned with his house, the traditional Pulodo council house. (Transcript of Mama Dina, informant from Sabu, JPIT archives) |
| Oct.–Nov. 1965 | South Central Timor | **Politics**: People accused of being involved with the PKI begin to be summoned to the military office (Buterpra) for questioning about their involvement. (Transcript of Neltji Kumar, informant from South Central Timor, JPIT archives) |
| Nov.–Dec. 1965 | Kupang | **Politics**: The head of the Kupang branch of PKI, Nunhila, is murdered. (Farram, 2002). |
| Mid Nov. 1965 | Maumere, Flores | **Other**: The local government and other private bodies work together to combat the threat of famine. In November 1965, the Maumere branch of the Catholic Youth League puts on a fundraising performance. The funds raised, around one million rupiah, are given to the local military command, Dandim1607. (Manuscript at Candraditya Archives) |
| Dec. 1965 | East Kupang | **Politics**: First executions: massacres of people involved with the PKI. (Pak Charles, informant from East Kupang, JPIT archives) |

| Date | Location (locations outside NTT are in italics) | Incident |
|---|---|---|
| 6 Dec. 1965 | Koting and Maumere, Flores | **Politics:** A youth squad, working together with figures from Koting, goes to Nita on the night of 6 December to arrest a PKI figure and 'hand him over to the G30S Investigation Team for proper interrogation'. When they arrive in Nita, they find he has already been tortured by the mob. The Catholic Youth league takes two PKI figures to Koting, and '…there, under questioning, they freely admit they had planned PKI action at national and local level.' When the G30S Investigation Squad arrives from Maumere, the two PKI figures are handed over to them. During the night of 6–7 December, the G30S Investigation Team, led by the head of the Maumere State Court, arrests 37 members of PKI and 'their cover organisations throughout the jurisdiction of the local government' of Sikka. (Manuscript at Candraditya archives). **Church:** At the conclusion of the Second Vatican Council in Rome, the Archbishop of Ende, Henry Darius, sends a pastoral letter in which he responds to the issue of G30S. An extract of the letter shows that his interpretation follows the army line. (*Jurnal Ledalero*, Vol.5, No.2, December 2006, pp.93–94) |
| 10 Dec. 1965 | Maumere, Flores, and Kupang | **Military:** The Military Commander from 1607 Maumere headquarters goes to Kupang and returns on 12 December 1965. 'His trip was to seek clear information about methods and actions being carried out against PKI members.' (Manuscript at Candraditya archives) |
| 14 Dec. 1965 | Maumere, Flores | **Military:** 'The Military Commander of 1607 Maumere headquarters holds a briefing with all parties: civil, military, political parties, mass organisations, Golkar, schools, and Sikka figures about the organisational structure of the Operation for the Restoration of Security and Order as a result of the G30S movement. After the briefing, the tension decreased. Just before Christmas, the head of the G30S Investigation Team released the 37 PKI detainees who had not yet been interrogated, and they had to report in daily.' (Manuscript at Candraditya archives) |
| Late 1965 – early1966 | Kalabahi, Alor | **Women:** Women who were detained by or required to report regularly to the military (Buterpra) are sexually abused. (Transcript of Ibu Koba, informant from Alor, JPIT archives) |
| Late 1955 – 1970 | Sabu | **Church:** Many mass baptisms and confirmations are held. Many evangelists come from Batu, Malang (in Java) including Pastors Sarjito, Yahya, Lisias, and Sigalingging. The last mentioned died during a cleansing of customary altars at Gela Nalaluin Mesara. (Transcript of Kitu, informant from Sabu, JPIT archives) |
| 1966 | NTT | **Customary groups:** As many as 15% of those belonging to 'other religions' are followers of local traditional religion. (F. Cooley, *The Growing Seed*). |

| Date | Location (locations outside NTT are in italics) | Incident |
|---|---|---|
| Jan.–Feb. 1966 | South Central Timor (TTS) | **Politics**: Massacres in South Central Timor. Those already in detention are taken late at night by car to various execution sites in the sandalwood forests Nonohonis and Naismetan. (Bapak Beny, informant from South Central Timor, JPIT archives). |
| Early Jan. 1966 | Maumere, Flores | **Politics**: The head of the Central Committee of PKI in Maumere is taken by Larantuka police escort by motorboat to Maumere prison where he is imprisoned. (Manuscript at Candraditya archives) |
| 17 Jan. 1966 | Kupang | **Politics**: Further mass meetings of anti-PKI political parties demanding the disbanding of the PKI. (Farram, 2004) |
| 6 Feb. 1966 | Oesao, East Kupang | **Politics**: Eighteen men are killed (the last mass execution). (Transcript of Kobus Manu, informant from East Kupang, JPIT archives) |
| Mid Feb. 1966 | Maumere, Flores | **Politics**: All leaders of political parties, mass organisations, Golkar and other groups are summoned by the Head of Staff of the Operational Command (Kastafkomop) to attend a meeting at the house of the Commander of the 1607 Maumere army headquarters. The meeting is led by the Lieutenant Infantry, because the Commander of 1607 Maumere has been reassigned to Denpasar as of late Dec.1966. It is explained that 'there are instructions that all PKI figures and members, and sympathisers involved in the G30S affair must be 'secured' (*diamankan*). (Manuscript at Candraditya archives) |
| 16 Feb. 1966 | Maumere, Flores | **Politics**: Operation Command together with a Lieutenant Colonel brief religious brothers that the entire cleansing operation has meant many victims… 'at midnight a number of trucks left from Maumere to Koting'. (Manuscript at Candraditya archives). |
| 20 Feb. 1966 | Maumere, Flores | **Politics**: The first 'securing of suspects' is carried out at Wairita on the night of 20 February. Twenty PKI and PNI figures and sympathisers from Maumere are 'secured' by staff of the district military command (Kodim)1607 in Maumere. The transportation of prisoners and the preparation of mass graves is done by members of political parties, mass organisations and Golkar. (Manuscript at Candraditya archives) <br> **Church**: The previous day, a priest from the Maumere parish tries to give confession and spiritual counselling to those victims who are Catholic. Initially he is obstructed by the Staff of the Operation Command, but another priest succeeds in obtaining permission from the Head of Staff for some priests (including Father Dan) to go to the prison to carry out their pastoral duties. (Manuscript at Candraditya archives). |

Appendix 1 | 285

| Date | Location (locations outside NTT are in italics) | Incident |
|---|---|---|
| 27 Feb. 1966 | Maumere, Flores | **Politics**: 'In the evening there was a meeting in the rooms of the Sikka district local parliament (DPRD-GR) between the head of staff of Operations Command, the head of the G30S investigation team, and leaders of political parties, community organisations and Golkar. The leaders of the political parties, community organisations and Golkar were asked to determine who had to be "taken into security' in this second wave. That night, 24 PKI and PNI figures from Maumere who were classified as group A were "secured". Along with this resolution, were other missions of "securing": at Lela/Kuarwang eight people, at Nita eight people, and at Koting eight people.' (Manuscript at Candraditya archives). |
| 29 Feb. 1966 | Maumere, Flores | **Politics**: 'The news went around about the deaths of Wellem Neli and P.K. Siantar in the Maumere prison. Indeed, as a result of torture, the two men became weak and eventually died.' (Manuscript at Candraditya archives) |
| 10 Mar. 1966 | Bola, Sikka, Flores | **Politics**: The Regional Command indoctrination team goes to Bola to explain the 'Operation for the Restoration of Security and Order after the G30S affair' .(Manuscript at Candraditya archives)<br>**Church**: The Bishop issues a pastoral letter (Ndona, 10 March 1966) responding to the 'cleansing'. 'Like it or not, our attention is drawn to the cleansing acts that are now being carried out and have reached their peak. We give thanks that the venom that has been spreading in the body of society is being eliminated and wiped out. This elimination is from the state and nation that is under threat... and is essential to the duty to secure itself... we Catholics firmly adhere to the Catholic principle: Love – "love thy neighbour as you love yourself" (Mark 12:31)'. (*Jurnal Ledalero*, Vol.5 No.2, December 2006). |
| 11 Mar. 1966 | Sikka, Flores | **Politics**: At night, around 100 people from four kampungs (Dobo, Moro, Piring, Baobatung)are arrested and brought by car to Maumere. (Manuscript at Candraditya archives)<br>**Other**: 'That night there was something odd because there was no broadcast from the national radio in Jakarta.' (Manuscript at Candraditya archives). |
| 11–16 Mar. 1966 | Bola, Sikka, Flores | **Church**: 'At the insistence of... the pastor in Bola, Father Martin Dau, defended 64 (?) people (many of them from kampong Tadat, Wolokoli) who the district head had pointed out and who had been arrested. Fr. Dau went to defend them, going to Maumere. An argument took place, and the Operation Command (Komop) would not allow him to defend them further, and took the captives away to be "secured" at Wodong-Gabe/Nangalimang.' (Manuscript at Candraditya archives) |

| Date | Location (locations outside NTT are in italics) | Incident |
|---|---|---|
| 17 Mar. 1966 | Maumere, Flores | **Politics**: On 17 March, a general rollcall was held at the Kotabaru public square in Maumere. The Chief of Staff of Operation Command said that the action of Fr Dau had been incredibly stupid. A letter was also sent to the Archbishop in Ende demanding that Fr Dau be moved to another parish. (Manuscript at Candraditya archives) **Church**: The Archibishop moves Fr Dau temporarily to Ndona and after a few weeks he is made parish priest at Nelle. (Manuscript at Candraditya archives) |
| 29 Mar. 1966 | Sabu | **Politics**: Thirty-one PKI members or suspected members are executed. (Transcript of Kitu, informant from Sabu, JPIT archives) |
| 30 Mar. 1966 | Sabu | **Politics**: Three PKI members or suspected members are executed. (Transcript of Kitu, informant from Sabu, JPIT archives) |
| 20 Feb. – 29 Apr. 1966 | Paga, Sikka, Flores | **Politics**: Around 800 people (most from Kewapante, Talibura, and Bola with a few from towns like Maumere and Nelle) are 'secured' by Operation Command (Komop). Only 151 of all those arrested are grouped into 'classification C'. (Manuscript at Candraditya archives) **Women**: Two boys are killed because they do not have an identity card. Their mother 'threw away her identity card and asked the Operation Command officer to kill her too. She was also killed. 'There were 11 women killed, four of them were pregnant.' (Manuscript at Candraditya archives). |
| 29 Apr. 1966 | Maumere, Flores | **Customary groups**: After the 'securing operation' (*pengamanan*) is considered finished, a customary rite, called eba-goit, is held in front of the Sikka district offices to ward off evil spirits resulting from the 'pengamanan' carried out from February to April 1966. (Manuscript at Candraditya archives) |
| Early May 1966 | Maumere, Flores | **Other**: 'There is news that the National Front for the NTT province and the Staff of the NTT Military Area Command (Korem) 161 are coming to Maumere for a full report on the "security operation" carried out by Operation Command.' (Manuscript at Candraditya archives). |
| 5 May 1966 | West Sumba | **Politics**: Six PKI leaders are killed. (Copy of letter from Pastor H. van Oostrum to the Deputat Zending Sumba, JPIT archives) |
| Mid May 1966 | Maumere, Flores | **Military**: The Periodic Head (ketua periodik) of the NTT Front Nasional and officers from the Military Police Corps, Military Area Command 161 ask for an account from Operational Command (Komop) about the G30S 'security measures' taken in Maumere. A Lieutenant Colonel explains the entire policy of Komop in Maumere, and explicitly states that 'if anything done was wrong according to the assessment of his superiors, then he was prepared to be stood down and lose all this military ranks, or for other action to be taken against him. The meeting was concluded, and no further action was taken.' (Manuscript at Candraditya archives) |

| Date | Location (locations outside NTT are in italics) | Incident |
|---|---|---|
| Late May 1966 | NTT | **Military:** Komop Lieutenant Colonel in Maumere is moved to Kupang as Head of Staff of the Nusratim Military Area Command (Korem) 161. The regional military Head of Staff, Major Infantry, is promoted to Commander of Military District 1607 Maumere. With this changeover, 'all the work of Komop is declared concluded'. (Manuscript at Candraditya archives) |
| 9 June 1966 | West Sumba | **Politics:** Massacre of 15 members or suspected members of PKI. (Copy of letter from Pastor H. van Oostrum to Deputat Zending Sumba, JPIT archives) |
| 1966–67 | West Timor | **Politics:** Killings continue, causing the Protestant Party (Parkindo) to protest that those killed are Christians, not communists. (Transcript of Pak Edi Ihalau, informant from city of Kupang, JPIT archives) |
| 1968 | Kupang | **Women:** The GMIT forms its women's organisation. (Interview with Ibu Maya, informant from city of Kupang, JPIT archives) |
| 1969 | NTT | **Customary groups:** Thirteen percent of the [Christian] faithful have 'other religions'; most are adherents of traditional religion. (F. Cooley, *The Growing Seed*) |
| 1975–78 | *Bali* | **Women:** Three Gerwani officials from NTT are imprisoned in Bali for three years. (Transcript of interview with Ibu Marsa, informant from city of Kupang, JPIT archives). |
| 1980s | East Kupang | **Politics:** The requirement to regularly report to authorities begins to cease. (List compiled by Ben Laka and Pak Jack, two informants from East Kupang, JPIT archives) |
| 1983 | Sabu | **Politics:** The requirement to regularly report to authorities ends. (Gad'i, informant from Sabu, JPIT archives) |
| c. 2000 | West Sumba | **Politics:** Former political prisoners are freed from the requirement to report to authorities. (Transcript of Ibu Bunga, informant from West Sumba, JPIT archives) |

# Appendix 2

## Chronology of Two Cases

### *Chronology of the case of Pak Angga Derosari, from Waikabubak, West Sumba*

Pak Angga Derosari, Ibu Bunga's husband, having worked for years in a good job with a regular salary as a prison guard, suddenly lost everything as a result of the 1965 incident. Until his death in 2009, he never regained his status as a government civil servant (PNS). As can be seen in the following table, although documentation for his regular rise in salary is incomplete, there is enough to show the pattern of his salary as a civil servant from the late 1950s until the 1965 incident.

| Date | Issuer of Document | Contents of Document |
|---|---|---|
| 12 Jan. 1957 | Head of the Prison Service, Jakarta (Kepala Djawatan Kependjaraan, Djakarta) | Pak Derosari is given temporary employment at category B1 level with a monthly basic salary of Rp.105 |
| 28 Feb. 1958 | Head of the Prison Service, Jakarta | Commencing 1 March 1958, Pak Derosari is raised from status B2/I with a basic salary of Rp.117.50 to category B2/I with a basic salary of Rp.124 |
| 3 May 1958 | Head of the Prison Service, Jakarta | Commencing 1 February 1958, Pak Derosari's basic salary is raised from Rp.111 to Rp.117.50 |
| 31 Aug. 1959 | Head of the Prison Service, Jakarta | Document of 28 January 1959 about salary raise is cancelled (contents unknown) and replaced with salary raise from Rp.199 to Rp.211, commencing 1 February 1959 |
| 18 Jan. 1960 | Head of the Prison Service, Jakarta | Pak Derosari receives a raise in basic monthly salary from Rp.211 to Rp.223 commencing 1 February 1960 |
| 31 Jan. 1961 | Head of the Prison Service, Jakarta | Pak Derosari receives raise in basic salary from Rp.255 to Rp.259 commencing 1 Feb. 1961 |
| 27 June 1963 | Head of the Prison Division VII in Denpasar (Kepala Inspektorat Kependjaraan VII, Denpasar) | Commencing 1 January 1961, Pak Derosari is 'promoted to permanent/temporary civil servant' with his basic salary raised from Rp.293 to Rp.328[†] |

[†] There is a discrepancy in the basic salary between the official information from the document of 31 Jan. 1961 and the one dated 27 June 1963

| Date | Issuer of Document | Contents of Document |
| --- | --- | --- |
| 1 Oct. 1963 | Head of the Prison Division VII in Denpasar | Pak Derosari receives two salary raises, from Rp.382 to Rp.400, then from Rp.400 to Rp.418, but the dates are unclear. |
| 2 May 1964 | Head of the Prison Division VII in Denpasar | Pak Derosari is promoted from category BB/II with a basic salary of Rp.436 to category BB/III with a basic salary of Rp.496 |
| 7 May 1965 | Head of the Prison Division VII in Denpasar | Pak Derosari gets a raise in basic salary from Rp.496 to Rp.518 |
| 3 Dec. 1965 | Director for NTT region penitentiaries Kupang (Direktur Daerah Pemasjarakatan NTT, Kupang) | To implement instructions from Koti Gabungan V (dated 12 and 14 October 1965), the Head of the Directorate of Penitentiaries (18 and 19 October 1965) and the Head of the Inspectorate for the Penitentiary Territory VII (23 November 1965) '…to increase vigilance in relation to local conditions, it is necessary to issue a work ban for the time being for any staff of the Waikabubak penitentiary who are members of the Communist Party or any of its related organisations including the trade union for penitentiary officers and SOBSI (All Indonesia Trade Union Federation)' it is ordered that:<br>a. as of 30 November 1965, all staff named in the attached list are forbidden to work for the time being/ are stood down, until there is further repeal<br>b. every working day at 8 a.m. they are required to report to the Warden of the Waikabubak penitentiary in Waikabubak. |
| 26 Feb. 1966 | Director for NTT region penitentiaries Kupang | 'First: Dismissed from work for the time being… Commencing 22 January 1966'. 'Second:… commencing 1 February 1966 until further cancellation, you are given a dismissal payout of Rp.259 per month… namely 50% of last basic salary of Rp.518, with a minimum of Rp.45 and maximum of Rp.450 after being rounded up to the nearest full figure.' |
| 15 Nov. 1966 | Ministry of Justice, Republic of Indonesia | As of 1 October 1966, Pak Derosari is 'dishonorably dismissed from this Government position… because of carrying out dishonorable deeds in conflict with State and official interests…' |

| Date | Issuer of Document | Contents of Document |
| --- | --- | --- |
| 1 Dec. 1966 | Commander of Military District 1601, Sumba, acting as Commander for the Operation for Restoration of Security and Order in Sumba | 'First: Given that there has not been found information / indications / or facts that demonstratively show direct or indirect involvement in the counter-Revolutionary escapade of the 30th September movement; Second: therefore as of 1/12/1966 the person whose name is listed below is to be freed from detention. Third: the aforesaid person should be given indoctrination and reactivated in his previous position/work prior to the occurrence of the 30th September movement. Fourth: If this decision proves to have been made in error... it will be reassessed in future.' |
| 4 Dec. 2006 | Pak Derosari, Waikabubak, West Sumba (a letter to Minister for Efficient Use of State Apparatus (Menteri Pendayagunaan Aparatur Negara, Menpan), Jakarta) | 'Concerning: the fact that the rehabilitation of Pak Derosari's status as Government Civil Servant has not been realised since 1 December 1966 until the present, we humbly submit a detailed chronological outline of the matter as follows...' [summary of documentation above is then listed]. |

## *Chronology of the Case of Pak Nyongki Ndili, Kupang city*

*'I am sure someone's going to need this data one day.'*[1]

When the research team for the city of Kupang visited Pak Nyongki Ndili at his home in Oeba, Kupang on 25 November 2010, he greeted them with the statement above. Pak Ndili gladly handed over many documents about his status as a civil servant and his efforts to restore his status since his detention. As a result of the 1965 incident, Pak Nyongki Ndili lost his position as an official in a regional office in the province of NTT, and his right to a pension. After he was declared not to be involved with PKI activities he was freed, but he remained fired from his job. He, along with 11 of his colleagues, then fought for their rights via legal channels and asked for support from the Department of Internal Affairs. However, nothing changed, and to this day none of them has received their rightful pensions. Even though the correspondence presented in the matrix below is incomplete – obviously

---

1   Pak Nyongki Ndili, 2010.

there are holes here and there in the documentation – nonetheless it still shows how the case of Pak Ndili and his friends went around in endless circles and was never settled.

| Date | Issuer of Document | Contents |
| --- | --- | --- |
| 18 Mar. 1966 | Decision of Commander of Military Resort 161 for NTT | As of 18 March 1966, N Ndili is declared to be released from detention and cleared of accusations, and should be 'reactivated'. [some key words are illegible] |
| 22 Mar. 1966 (some parts of the letter are illegible) | From: Body for Research/ Evaluation/ Consideration in NTT To: illegible | Having read the interrogation report on Pak Ndili and heard the explanation, it is stated that he was 'not involved' and 'it is recommended that the aforesaid… return to society to carry out his normal duties'. |
| 29 Oct. 1966 | From: Commander of Military Resort 161 also in his capacity as Commander of the Operation for Restoration of Security and Order, NTT. | Statement that N Ndili and his colleagues are 'not involved' and that they should be freed from detention on 29 October 1966. |
| 9 Nov. 1967 | Letter from Commander of Kodim 1608 Cc: KODAM XVI UDAYANA & KODIM 1608 | Statement that 'Until the date of the writing of this letter, the above mentioned [N Ndili] was not involved, directly or indirectly, in the G 30S/PKI'. |
| 8 Sept. 1971 | From: Head of NTT branch office of the Department of Forestry To: Commander of Military Resort 161 also in his capacity as Commander of the Operation for Restoration of Security and Order, NTT. | Reporting follow up of the implementation of decisions regarding N Ndili and colleagues:<br>• because there is no information/indication/ facts that prove the involvement either directly or indirectly in the counter- revolutionary escapade of the 30th September movement, the aforementioned is released from detention and accusations and is to be 'reactivated' in his position/post prior to the movement…'<br>• 'While the aforementioned officials have worked under my care and supervision as leader, they have demonstrated excellent skills and have worked with great dedication; they can be entrusted with responsibility and can be expected to expedite official duties in building the nation of Indonesia.' |
| 30 May 1974 | From: Head of NTT branch office of the Department of Forestry To: Military Area Command (Korem) 161 | With reference to 'the results of the observation of N Ndili & co, that they were not involved with G30S/PKI and were released from detention/ accusation'… we request that the documents regarding the aforementioned be examined because their contribution is sorely needed.' |

| Date | Issuer of Document | Contents |
|---|---|---|
| 25 Aug. 1974 | From: Commander of Korem 161 Wirasakti To: Laksusda Nusra in Denpasar | Seventeen officials, including N Ndili 'are freed of all charges and may be given normal employment, but they must be under our supervision… [they] were truly… not involved in the G30S/PKI'. |
| Aug. 1974 (estimated, as date of document is illegible) | From: Commander Korem 161 Wirasakti To: Laksusda Nusra in Denpasar | Report of examination: Please note and settle, as per the decision that 17 officials, including N Ndili, were not involved in G30S/PKI and can be re-employed, under supervision. |
| 13 Feb. 1975 | From: ML Ishak (in a letter dated 22 March 1975, he was Head of administration for an NTT government office and also Secretary of the Screening Team for the same office) To: Handoyo (from a letter dated 12 August 1976, we know him as Commander of Military Police Corps in Kupang) | [referring to?] Request that eight people, including N Ndili, join the Board of NTT branch of Sarbuksi (The All Indonesia Union of Plantation Workers). '…IT IS IMPORTANT THAT YOU KEEP THESE PEOPLE OUT BECAUSE THEY ARE L. LELA'S LACKIES. REMEMBER THIS IS AN EXTREMELY SECRET MATTER AND MAKE SURE NO ONE ELSE KNOWS, THIS IS JUST AN INTERNAL MATTER BETWEEN US.[#] |
| 20 Feb. 1975 | Note from Handoyo to ML Ishak | I have read and understood the letter from Ismael dated 13 February… therefore, please complete the data about them as needed and send to me at the earliest opportunity. |
| 22 Mar. 1975 | From: Head of a Union of Kupang leaders (Kesatuan Pemangkuan Kupang) To: A [certain] minister via the head of a Directorate General | Request that the activities of the Screening Team for the NTT branch of the Department of Forestry be closely observed because what is being carried out conflicts with [a 1968 Kopkamtib guideline]… because the head of the NTT Department of Forestry is concurrently the Head of the Screening Team. |
| 15 Oct. 1975 | From: Governor of NTT To: Head of a Directorate of local government office | 1. It is requested that the activities of the Screening Team of one of the NTT Department offices be scrutinised because it is suspected that they are making false reports about your officials/staff who do not know and are being described as 'involved with G30S/PKI' 2. … make careful observation… taking into account that your officers/workers are known not to have been involved with G30S/PKI and already have a fixed verdict on this. 3. In your opinion as Head of the office, if you discover there has been irregularity by the Screening Team of a certain NTT regional office, then you are to immediately report to me at the first opportunity…' |

[#] It is not clear who "L. LELA" (a pseudonym) refers to; clearly he is considered so 'dangerous' that anyone accused of fraternising with him is also considered dangerous and has to be 'kept out'.

| Date | Issuer of Document | Contents |
|---|---|---|
| 12 Aug. 1976 | From: Head of the regional forestry office, NTT<br>To: Governor of NTT<br>Concerning: Report on irregularities of Dept of Forestry Screening Team | 'Further to your letter of 15 October 1975, we report that:<br>1. …the said officials have not been screened according to the guidelines… the screening data we found was dated 11 November 1974.<br>2. …we further discovered irregularities committed by ML Ishak as Secretary of the Screening Team of the regional office of the NTT Department of Forestry, together with Handoyo, Commander of the Military Police Corps, to destroy the staff of the Forestry Department office…by naming them as involved in G30S/PKI…<br>3. There was discord among the Screening Team and so the secret was leaked that one of the team members reported to the Minister of Agriculture on 22 March 1975.<br>4. Because of the Screening Team's fraudulent data, in agreement with Military Police Commander Handoyo, a recommendation was made for classification on 24 June 1976. Based on this recommendation for classification, the Litsus (Special investigative branch) issued a decision on 10 July 1976 concerning which staff were to be recommended for employment.' |
| 12 Nov. 1977 | From: Governor of NTT<br>To: Laksus Pangkopropkamtib NTT in Denpasar | I draw your attention to my earlier statement about the officers from the NTT regional branch of the Department of Forestry who were suspected of being G30S/PKI, that, as we have already pointed out to Laksus Pangkopkamtibda Nusra, we, as head of this region have never discovered any proof of their involvement, either directly or indirectly, with G30S/PKI…' |
| 19 Dec. 1977 | From: Head of Teperda Nusra<br>To:<br>1. Commander of Detachments 161 & 162<br>2. Commander of Inrehab Denpasar | Radiogram:<br>'Instruction dated 19 December 1977 the previously written house arrest is changed to release – repeat release. STOP.<br>Arrangements about the status of house arrest are to be considered wiped. STOP.<br>This radiogram is a correction. STOP. ENDS.' |
| 1 Aug. 1978 | Decision of the governor of NTT | Resolution:<br>'In anticipation of the decision by the Minister of Internal Affairs, [N Ndili and his colleagues] are hereby dishonorably dismissed as civil servants.' |

| Date | Issuer of Document | Contents |
|---|---|---|
| 19 Sept. 1978 | From: Pangkopkamtib in NTT, regional investigative team<br>To: Commander of detachment 161 | Based on the Instruction of special area operations for Eastern Indonesia (Nusra)… 15 September1978… hereby orders the Commander of the Military District (Dandim) 161:<br>1. On 20 September 1978… are freed from detention and all criminal charges against them [dropped] because there is no proof of wrongdoing<br>2. The aforementioned should be returned to work in their relevant departments as fitting |
| 12 Dec. 1978 | From: Laksus Pangkopkamtib, NTT | 1. 'The officials/workers whose names are listed in the attached document are declared to be not involved in the G30S/PKI treachery' [list includes name of N Ndili]<br>…<br>6. Head of Teperda Nusra must settle administrative matters in relation to current regulations |
| 24 Dec. 1978 | From: Pangkopkamtib in NTT, regional investigative team | '1. In relation to the fact no information/indications/facts have been found to indicate involvement either directly or indirectly in the counter revolution escapade of 30 September,<br>2. Therefore, with the issue of this document, those whose names are found in the attached list are declared FREE and can work as normal.' |
| 19 Feb. 1979 | From: Pangkopkamtib, NTT<br>To: Head of the regional office of the Department of Forestry, NTT | 'Concerning the written complaint made to us by your officials dated 28 January 1979 about… the implementation of Instruction 209/Taperda/II/78 and the fact that those officials have still not been returned to work as was stipulated in that decision, we see it necessary to tell you that upon receipt of this letter those officials whose names are listed below [N Ndili and friends] may be recalled to take up their positions as normal, and you should report to us the implementation of this at the first opportunity.' |
| 11 May 1979 | From: Kopkamtib Nusa Tenggara, regional investigative team<br>To: Governor of NTT | 'a. That the names of the officials from the NTT regional office of the Department of Forestry listed in this letter are declared to be FREE of the 30 September Movement/PKI, both directly and indirectly.' [The names include N Ndili and friends] |
| 4 Jan. 1982 | From: Governor of NTT<br>To: Head of a regional government office, NTT | 'With reference to the document dated 11 May 1979, with this letter we inform you that we hereby rescind the dishonorable dismissal [issued 1 Aug 1978] of… [names include N. Ndili] and that order is no longer valid, and we hope that you will re-employ those officers as is fitting and report to us according to existing guidelines.' |

| Date | Issuer of Document | Contents |
|---|---|---|
| 28 Dec. 1983 | From: Governor of NTT | Reactivation of Civil Servant status of several people, including N Ndili. |
| 8 May 1990 | From: Head of NTT regional office of Department of Forestry<br>To: Head of Kupang Police | 'Further to the letter from the Regional Chief of Police dated 30 April 1990… we inform you that we do not hold the original document of Executive Order by the Special Regional Executive of Eastern Indonesia (Nusra) dated 10 July 1976.'<br>Given that this is the case, we cannot assist the Regional Chief of Police in the matter of his letter. |
| 29 Oct. 1990 | From: Legal representation<br>To: Head of State Court Class 1, Kupang<br>Concerning: indictment | On behalf of 10 people, including N Ndlili, this legal counsel hereby indicts those involved with:<br>a. the restoration of the good name of those accused in Executive Order 28/Kamda/VII/1976<br>b. their dismissal from duties and positions as Government Civil Servants<br>c. the cessation of payment of their salaries as Government Civil Servants.<br>This document also serves as a kind of summary of the case. |
| 11 May 1991 | From: Head of the Pension Department, section D, Administrative Body for State Officials | Document about N Ndili's pension. |
| 26 Aug. 1991 | From: Head of Pension, section D, Administration Department, State Employees | Concerning:<br>a. the letter of the Governor of NTT dated 11 May 1991, Nyongki Ndili… was honorably retired as a State Civil Servant with pension rights as of 01 August 1990 TMT rates;<br>b. that in fact Nyongki Ndili… had previously been DISHONORABLY dismissed, as in the Governor of NTT's letter of 1 August 1990;<br>c. therefore, the Governor's letter of 11 May 1991 should be rescinded.<br>Decision: The Governor's decision of 11 May 1991 concerning N Ndili's pension was declared to be invalid. |
| 2 Apr. 1993 | From: Governor of NTT<br>To: Minister of Internal Affairs | 'Concerning our letter to the Minister of Internal Affairs…dated 19 January 1991 requesting the confirmation of the NTT Governor's decision… of 1 August 1978 [namely, the dishonorable dismissal], we retract that decision, because the officials concerned, having been examined, have the full documentation including:<br>1. decision of Kopkamtib dated 29 October 1966<br>2. decision of Teperda dated 24 December 1978 |

| Date | Issuer of Document | Contents |
|---|---|---|
| 2 Apr.1993 (cont'd) | | 3. letter from Kopkamtib to Governor of NTT dated 11 May 1979 about the retraction of the Decision of the Special Implementation Body (Laksus) dated 10 July 1976 which was declared invalid<br>4. letter from the Governor of NTT… of 4 January 1982 about the retraction of the Governor of NTT's decision of 1 August 1978 saying that the latter was no longer valid<br>5. decision of the Governor of NTT…dated 28 December 1983 about the re-installation of the officials… to their previous positions. That based on all the above data, we request that the Minister review the decision…' |
| 10 Mar. 1994 | From: Head of Bakorstanas [formerly Kopkamtib] in NTT<br>To: Governor of NTT | 1. With reference to the Governor of NTT's letter…of 24 January 1994 about the request for the affirmation of Civil Servant status within the NTT regional office of the Department of Forestry of those involved with G30S/PKI…<br>2. In order for there to be no further confusion among all parties, and having conducted investigations, we convey the following explanation:<br>   ◦ The decision of the Laksus Pangkopkamtibda Nusra, dated 10 July 1976, that SB Medina and colleagues were implicated remains in force.<br>   ◦ Whereas the [Teperda] decision of 24 December 1978 about the release of SB Medina and colleagues was not issued by Laksus Pangkopkamtibda Nusra. It is suspected this document is fraudulent and cannot be used as a basis for decision.<br>3. With reference to the letter from the head of Bakorstanas…of 12 January 1994 about the review of the classification of involvement in G30S/PKI which was directed to the Vice President of Indonesia and cc-ed to the Head of Bakorstanas for NTT, we re-emphasise the following:<br>   ◦ There will be no further investigation about the classification of those who were involved in G30S/PKI, because we consider sufficient time has been spent on this matter and sufficient time allowed for their complaints to be heard.<br>   ◦ Henceforth there is no need to answer further requests for review or changes to the classification that the people concerned were declared to have been involved. |

| Date | Issuer of Document | Contents |
|---|---|---|
| 8 May 1995 | From: Coordination of Personnel, General Administration, Head of the Personnel Bureau, Ministry of Internal Affairs To: Governor of NTT | 4. …based on the result that we have received only orally to date, it is found that the document issued by Teperda Nusra… dated 24 December 1978 [the declaration that N Ndili was free] has been found to have no valid legal basis. 5. The Governor of NTT's letter of 1 June 1994 about the validity of the decision of the Laksus Pangkopkamtibda Nusra ..dated 10 July 1976…has attached… the status of [various people's] involvement in G30S/PKI, but this list, it turns out, does not include the name of Nyongki Ndili. |
| 1 Nov. 2000 | From: Secretary to the Vice President, Deputy of Political Division. To: Head of State Personnel Administration (Badan Kepegawaian Negara, BKN) | '…we report that Madame Vice President has received the letter of Nyongki Ndili and colleagues (17 people) dated 12 September 2000 about the complaint that there has been no resolution to their personnel rights given that according to the decision of Laksusda Nusra… dated 12 December 1978 they were rehabilitated of the charges of being involved in banned organisations. Further, we note that following the decision of the Governor of NTT… dated 28 December 1983 in which the aforementioned are declared to be reactivated as State civil servants within the NTT regional government, this has still not been realised. 'Based on humanitarian considerations, and mindful of the fact that the State Personnel Administration is in charge of personnel matters, with this letter we forward copies of documentation for this matter to be handled as is proper in accordance with existing regulations.' |
| 26 Jan. 2002 | From: Head of legal bureau, NTT regional secretariat To: head of the NTT Personnel Bureau Secretariat | 'With reference to the letter of Nyongki Ndili… dated 15 December 2011… addressed to the Governor of NTT and Head of the Legal Bureau to resolve the personnel status of Nyongki Ndili and colleagues… we request that this issue be processed according to existing regulations.' |
| 23 Mar. 2002 | From: Governor of NTT To: Nyongki Ndili | '1. That based on the proof that you and your colleagues still have the status of being involved with G30S/PKI in the B2 classification according to the decision of Laksusda Nusra… dated 10 June 1976. 2. According to the decision of the coordinating meeting held at the NTT provincial level on 10 March 2002, it was concluded that the Governor of NTT, via the Personnel Bureau, make recommendations to the Minister of Internal Affairs about the dishonorable dismissal for reconsideration. |

| Date | Issuer of Document | Contents |
|---|---|---|
| 23 Mar. 2002 (cont'd) | | 3. That while awaiting clarification from the Minister of Internal Affairs, you and your colleagues are advised to submit a request for classification to the Udayana Regional Military Commander (Pangdam) in Denpasar, Bali, for decision. It is important that this is done for the process of review of your status as State Civil Servant.' |
| 8 Aug. 2002 | From: Secretary General of the Head of the Personnel Bureau<br>To: State Personnel Administration, Up. Deputi Bina Dakatsi | Concerning Nyongki Ndili's honorable dismissal as State Civil Servant with pension rights, the aforementioned requests that he be paid his pension without demanding personnel rights. Given this, and mindful of his letter of 16 May 2002 addressed to the President of Indonesia, with copies sent to the Minister of Internal Affairs and the Head of the State Personnel Administration, we request further consideration for resolution of Nyongki Ndili's case.' |
| 19 Aug. 2003 | From: Deputy State Secretary, Field of empowerment of resources (Bidang Pemberdayaan Sumber Daya)<br>To: Head of State Personnel Administration, Jakarta | '...we submit the letter from Nyongki Ndili and colleagues...dated 16 June 2003 addressed to the President of the Republic of Indonesia (copy attached) which in essence pleads for the restoration of personnel rights and his pension, because the aforementioned, in accordance with the decision of the NTT Governor dated 28 December 1983, was reactivated as a Government Civil Servant within the regional government of NTT, and was honorably dismissed with pension rights by the Head of State Personnel Administration (BKN) on 11 May 1991.<br>In relation to this matter, and mindful that this problem is related to the jurisdiction of BKN, we forward this request to you for further consideration.' |

# Appendix 3

## List of Human Rights Abuses

One step the JPIT research teams took during their research was training in transitional justice, human rights, and documentation (28 February to 1 March 2011). This training helped the researchers deepen their understanding of severe human rights abuse, especially murder, torture, disappearance, enslavement, and abuse of women, including sexual abuse. Discussion about human rights abuse and victims' rights including the right to truth, inspired the team members to draw up their findings of human rights abuse as a table. Although the table does not categorise the abuse into different types, a number of severe human rights abuses are listed including arbitrary arrest and detention, torture, murder, disappearance, and sexual abuse. On top of this, the destruction of possessions and the requirement to report to authorities, all without any due legal process, are also kinds of human rights abuses.[2]

---

2   Two publications from the National Commission on Women (Komnas Perempuan) are recommended as a basis for study about human rights abuse based on gender: *Hukum Pidana Internasional dan Perempuan: Sebuah Buku Acuan untuk Praktisi*, 4 volumes (Jakarta: Komnas Perempuan, 2006), and *Kejahatan terhadap Kemanusiaan Berbasis Jender: Mendengarkan Suara Perempuan Korban Peristiwa 1965* (Jakarta: Komnas Perempuan, 2007).

| No. | Human Rights Abuses in Alor | |
|---|---|---|
| 1 | INFORMANT | Witness: **APELES TANKALAU** (male, 63) customary law figure |
| | DATE, PLACE AND FORM OF ABUSE | *ca. 1965*<br>• people arrested and detained without any warrant<br>• people shot<br>• people made to do forced labour |
| | REASON GIVEN BY INFORMANT | The names of the people who were arrested and shot were on a list of people who received food aid from PKI and were branded as PKI members. In general they knew nothing at all about the PKI. |
| | NOTES | Customary leaders at the time were unable to resist the army; they could not do much.<br>The detainees were grouped into three categories:<br>a. officials/leaders of the PKI<br>b. still under suspicion<br>c. not directly involved with the PKI.<br>The church was protected from accusation of being PKI [however, according to other informants, many elders and deacons were accused of being PKI].<br>The PKI grew more quickly than other parties in the area (Parkindo, the Catholic Party and Islamic parties), even in remote inland areas.<br>After the Crocodile Hole incident in Jakarta, PKI recruitment was still going on in Alor. |
| 2 | INFORMANT | Witness: **DAKA LOMANG** (male) guard<br>Daka used to work in the Public Works Department as a guard of the equipment store. He gave out tools to those made to do forced labour. |
| | DATE, PLACE AND FORM OF ABUSE | **1965, Buterpra (Military District Command), Kalabahi**<br>'If there was any item of equipment missing or misplaced during forced labour, the worker has beaten by police and made to stand in the hot sun on the small Kalabahi sports field.'<br>'Some people were ill when they were forced to work, but this was ignored, so they died.' |
| | REASON GIVEN BY INFORMANT | Victims were beaten because they scattered the tools. |
| | NOTES | These comments add some information about political developments, including political parties, at the time. |
| 3 | INFORMANT | Victim: **ONFERO** (female, ±80)<br>Onfero's husband, **Tera Sekalau**, was a headman. |
| | DATE, PLACE AND FORM OF ABUSE | *ca. 1965*<br>Tera<br>• was arrested and detained without any warrant<br>• was tortured<br>• was made to do forced labour<br>• was required to regularly report to authorities. |

Appendix 3 – Alor | 301

| No. | Human Rights Abuses in Alor | |
|---|---|---|
| 3 (cont'd) | DATE, PLACE AND FORM OF ABUSE (cont'd) | Onfero<br>• was required to regularly report to authorities<br>• had her hair shaved<br>• was made to do forced labour (cleaning the office, officials' houses, ditches) when she reported in to authorities. |
| | REASON GIVEN BY INFORMANT | Tera was accused of being a member of the PKI.<br>Onfero was arrested and interrogated because her husband was accused of being a member of PKI and because she did not have a membership card for Parkindo. |
| | NOTES | Gerwani was operating there, but most of the members are no longer living. |
| 4 | INFORMANT | Witness: **FREDRIK PULINGGOMANG** (real name) (male, 79) Pastor emeritus, GMIT |
| | DATE, PLACE AND FORM OF ABUSE | *1965, at Buterpra headquarters and some temporary detention centres at North West Alor, Alor Kecil, Dulolong, and Kalabahi*<br>• detention<br>• torture<br>• massacre |
| | REASON GIVEN BY INFORMANT | Because they were accused of being PKI members and atheists. |
| | NOTES | • support given to a Bible teacher who was eventually released<br>• a meeting was held between all religious figures to formulate 'Nada Bhakti', a declaration that rejected the belief that the religion does not support PKI |
| 5 | INFORMANT | Victim: **KARO TALITAI** (female, 78). Karo's husband, **Kiel Talitai**, was headman and active in the church. Karo's sons were **Pastor Maksi** (also a victim), **Bastion** and **Ayub**. Karo's husband's older brother, Moses Talitai, was a soldier and perpetrator. |
| | DATE, PLACE AND FORM OF ABUSE | *ca. December 1965, barracks*<br>Kiel<br>• was picked up by paramilitary civil defence corps saying they were protecting the people, but arrested and then taken to army barracks (date unclear, but Karo said her baby was 20 days old at the time)<br>• was arrested/detained without a warrant<br>• had his head shaved<br>• was killed by his own older brother (location unknown).<br>*Puterpra, Kalabahi*<br>Karo<br>• was required to regularly report to authorities for about six months until her Parkindo card was issued<br>• was beaten, had her hair shaved, and was made to do forced labour (cleaning drains, offices, houses of worship, the homes of officials including the homes of church officials, and given no food or drink) when she went to report to authorities<br>• had to work while minding her baby<br>• was forbidden all communication with her family. |

| No. | Human Rights Abuses in Alor | | |
|---|---|---|---|
| 5 (cont'd) | REASON GIVEN BY INFORMANT | | Kiel was accused of being a communist because he helped distribute food aid (rice).<br>Karo was interrogated, detained and required to report to authorities because she was accused of being a member of Gerwani. |
| | NOTES | | • at the time, the church showed no concern for those accused of being communist and even viewed them with cynicism<br>• inter-family jealousies: Kiel was considered the tribal elder even though his brother Moses was actually older, but Moses had spent a long time away. All the village treasures were entrusted to Kiel, and Moses was jealous of this<br>• Karo participated in the meeting of victims held at Liliba, Kupang, 27–30 March, organised by the research team |
| 6 | INFORMANT | | Victim: **KOBA** (female, 70) weaver<br>Koba's husband, **Nani Pelotaka**, assisted in the church and led the choir. |
| | DATE, PLACE AND FORM OF ABUSE | | **1965, Kalabahi, Air Kenari**<br>Nani<br>• was arrested at Adagai and taken to Kalabahi<br>• was detained for one month<br>• was killed, allegedly at Air Kenari (date unknown).<br>**1965, Puterpra, Kalabahi**<br>Koba<br>• was arrested by the army, taken to Kalabahi and interrogated<br>• had her head shaved<br>• for four months was required to regularly report to authorities<br>• was made to do forced labour for four months (cleaning the army offices, drains, houses of worship and houses of officials including church officials, feed the pigs)<br>• was occasionally not allowed to return home and made to sleep outside in the yard of the military headquarters. |
| | REASON GIVEN BY INFORMANT | | Koba said that her husband, Nani, was a member of the PKI. At the time, he had just returned from evangelising and was immediately arrested. |
| | NOTES | | • Koba told a story of Mama Dora who was raped, became pregnant and gave birth. The sexual abuse happened at the Kalabahi military command. Others were also raped, but she does not remember their names. The rapists were soldiers. Koba knows about what happened to Mama Dora because she was with her when they were made to spend the night at the Kalabahi military command.<br>• information was provided about the failed harvest in 1964<br>• Koba was one of the women who participated in the meeting at Liliba, Kupang, organised by the research team |

| No. | Human Rights Abuses in Alor | |
|---|---|---|
| 7 | INFORMANT | Victim: **NETO** (female, ±78)<br>Neto's husband, **Mel Kelatanu**, was also a victim. |
| | DATE, PLACE AND FORM OF ABUSE | ***ca. 1965 (not sure of exact month)***<br>Mel<br>• was arrested.<br>NETO<br>• was arrested with no warrant<br>• had her hair shaved<br>• was made to report regularly to authorities. |
| 7 (cont'd) | REASON GIVEN BY INFORMANT | Mel was arrested because he was listed as a member of the Communist Party and he did not hold a membership card of Parkindo. |
| | NOTES | Gave Neto information that there were some women victims at Mataru. |
| 8 | INFORMANT | Victim: **RIBKA** (female, ±70) teacher for illiteracy program. Ribka's husband, **Titus Manitap**, was also a teacher. Her son was **Filus Manitapa**. |
| | DATE, PLACE AND FORM OF ABUSE | **1965**<br>Titus<br>• was arrested at Kakamauta, Kec. Pantar by police, with no warrant<br>• was detained first at Baranusa (Pantar) police headquarters, then taken to Kabir (Pantar), and herded to military headquarters at Kalabahi (Alor).<br>Ribka<br>• was required to regularly report at Baranusa and Kabir (Pantar), and then to military headquarters, Kalabahi, Alor. When she was away reporting, her family did not care for her children.<br>• had her hair shaved<br>• was made to do forced labour (cleaning the church, officials' houses, and ditches)<br>• at certain times was forced to remain overnight at the military headquarters. |
| | REASON GIVEN BY INFORMANT | Titus was arrested because he was a member of PKI. |
| | NOTES | • Information was provided about the famine of 1965<br>• Ribka denied that she had children in order to protect them from being arrested. |

| No. | Human rights abuses in the City of Kupang | |
|---|---|---|
| 1 | INFORMANT | Witness: **PAKADI** (male, 56) GMIT pastor<br>At the time he was 11 years old, in class five of primary school. |
| | DATE, PLACE AND FORM OF ABUSE | **Dec. 1965 – Feb. 1966, Oepura and Selam**<br>• his neighbour was killed at Oepura<br>• his father (a pastor) was arrested at his office by Petelrada (a kind of civilian militia) wearing military fatigues and detained at the old prison in Selam. Three days after his arrest, the family received a letter saying that he was in the old prison in Kupang.<br>• Pakadi was stigmatised as PKI for all the following years |
| | REASON GIVEN BY INFORMANT | • It was not clear why the neighbour, a carpenter, was killed.<br>• One of Pakadi's father's friends, a pastor, listed his father as a member of PKI. This pastor subsequently moved and admitted that it was he who had written this, even though Pakadi's father was not a communist. |
| | NOTES | • many political parties in the 1950s<br>• the people of NTT listened to the news on the radio and this was what formed public opinion to oppose the PKI because the PKI was considered to be atheist<br>• in 1965 there was rampant poverty<br>• the communists attracted members by distributing food<br>• at the time, Gerwani in NTT Kupang was stigmatised<br>• after the 1965 Incident, church membership increased but only because many people were afraid. The church itself was not strong, and did not do anything, out of fear. |
| 2 | INFORMANT | Witness: **EDI IHALAU** (male, 72) a Parkindo committee member and worker at a state-owned business |
| | DATE, PLACE AND FORM OF ABUSE | **1966**<br>• 20 young men suspected of being PKI members were arrested, but some were released because it was proven they were Parkindo members<br>• a dozen or more young men suspected of being PKI members were killed at Desa Tanah Merah, East Kupang |
| | REASON GIVEN BY INFORMANT | In 1965 there was an official instruction from the central government to 'secure' ['*mengamankan*'] members of PKI and associated organisations. |
| | NOTES | • Parkindo tracked its members through the church and by approaching pastors and members of the congregation<br>• according to Edi Ihalau, members of PKI were integrated in society and the life of the church at the time, and this caused anxiety within the church |

# Appendix 3 – City of Kupang | 305

| No. | Human rights abuses in the City of Kupang | |
|---|---|---|
| 3 | INFORMANT | Victim: **IBU MARSA** (female, 74) teacher at Piet primary school in Kuanino [Editor's note: The primary school is named after a former Bupati of Kupang, Piet Amalo.]<br>Ibu Marsa was a member of Gerwani from 1963 and replaced one of the Gerwani officials in Kupang. |
| | DATE, PLACE AND FORM OF ABUSE | **1967, Kodim (District Military Command) 1604, Merdeka Stadium, Public Hospital (RSU) Kupang**<br>• arbitrarily arrested at home<br>• taken to Kodim 1604 and interrogated by visiting army personnel (not from NTT)<br>• given no food for 24 hours<br>• after interrogation, taken to Merdeka Stadium and detained there (approx. 1 month)<br>• a few days after being taken to Merdeka Stadium, detainees were taken to the hospital, stripped naked, and examined for signs of 'hammer and sickle' tattoo<br>**1975–78, Pekambingan prison at Denpasar, Bali**<br>• detained<br>**since the1965 incident**<br>• loss of civil servant status<br>• unilateral decisions made about her employment<br>• received no pension<br>• received no identity card valid for life after turning 60 |
| | REASON GIVEN BY INFORMANT | Because she was listed as one of the Gerwani officials in Kupang replacing the former one. |
| | NOTES | • detained in Denpasar with two other women from Kupang<br>• information about the prison at Denpasar |
| 4 | INFORMANT | Victim: **IBU NONA** (female) worked in administration section of a school in Kupang.<br>Her husband was a Communist Party official in Kupang. |
| | DATE, PLACE AND FORM OF ABUSE | **Dec. 1965, Kupang**<br>• a mob surrounded the house threatening to destroy things, and said they were going to kill her husband<br>• her husband was detained at the old prison in Selam (in front of the old Kupang Bupati's office)<br>• her husband was murdered<br>• Ibu Nona was arrested and taken to the police station (carrying her two-month-old baby), then protected and taken to the home of her uncle (who was in the army)<br>• was fired from her position and received no pension |
| 4 (cont'd) | REASON GIVEN BY INFORMANT | Her husband was Head of PKI and, as his wife, Ibu Nona was suspected of being involved with the PKI. |
| | NOTES | • the majority of those arrested were teachers<br>• 'actually, communism is good, and it is not clear whether the people who carried out the violence engineered things because the PKI was a legal party at the time' |

| No. | Human rights abuses in the City of Kupang | |
|---|---|---|
| 5 | INFORMANT | Victim and witness: **NYONGKI NDILI** (male, 76) employee of a government regional office for NTT province; he became head of a union for government workers |
| | DATE, PLACE AND FORM OF ABUSE | • arbitrarily arrested and detained (together with Pakadi's father)<br>• saw Pakadi's father's head banged against the wall when he asked why they had been arrested<br>• fired from his job and did not receive any pension<br>• after he was granted permission to work again, his salary was stopped from August 1978 to 1990, even though he was working all that time |
| | REASON GIVEN BY INFORMANT | • he defended a neighbour (accused of being PKI)when they arrested him<br>• apart from that, some senior staff at his workplace did not like him and 12 others because they were all members of a union and therefore considered to be members of the PKI |
| | NOTES | A summary of Nyongki Ndili's case is given in Appendix 2. |
| 6 | INFORMANT | **TONY FAI** (male) emeritus pastor, GMIT |
| | DATE, PLACE AND FORM OF ABUSE | • confirmed the arrest of PKI members and the execution (shooting) of 13 PKI people from Baun |
| | REASON GIVEN BY INFORMANT | Because the military said that the G30S incident was instigated by the PKI |
| | NOTES | • the GMIT synod took a negative stand towards the G30S incident and towards PKI members<br>• the synod issued a circular to all GMIT congregations advising that they should not mix with or become members of political parties that did not have Christian ideology<br>• PKI members could not hold positions in the church: PKI members were considered to be trouble makers in the church and causing conflict everywhere |

## Appendix 3 – East Kupang

| No. | Human rights abuses in East Kupang | |
|---|---|---|
| 1 | INFORMANT | Witness: **BEN LAKA** (male, 62) farmer, customary figure<br>At the time he was a teenager. |
| | DATE, PLACE AND FORM OF ABUSE | People were:<br>• beaten<br>• taken at gunpoint<br>• murdered<br>• other detainees who were freed had to report until the 1980s |
| | REASON GIVEN BY INFORMANT | Of those murdered, some were PKI members and others just accused of being members. |
| | NOTES | • Spoke about a school friend, called Nona Asmi, suspected of being on the board of Gerwani<br>• Pak Ben quoted a government statement he remembers well: those released were 'non social' (tidak bermasyarakat), and therefore to be returned to society 'to be socialised'. |
| 2 | INFORMANT | Witness: **PAK CHARLES** (male, 62) customary figure<br>He was still a youth in 1965. |
| | DATE, PLACE AND FORM OF ABUSE | ***27 December 1965, Tanah Putih, Thie Island, Tarus, Lasiana and Kupang***<br><br>• confirmed the arrests and execution at Tanah Putih<br>• the army ordered the people to dig holes (graves); they also beat the detainees<br>• there were two large graves at Tanah Putih, Thie Island, behind Sasando<br>• at Tarus, the house behind the Bethesda meeting house was used for interrogating and beating victims<br>***1966, Tanah Putih***<br>• victims were beaten and made to run wearing placards |
| | NOTES | • additional information about how people from Rote became village chiefs in Babau<br>• gave the names of two PKI leaders from Merdeka (in the city of Kupang) who were killed |
| 3 | INFORMANT | Witness: **FANUS TEFA** (male)<br>His family's house was rented by the government as the district (camat) office and used in 1965 as a detention centre. |
| | DATE, PLACE AND FORM OF ABUSE | ***1966, Camat's office in Babau***<br>• witnessed the detainees beaten daily |
| | REASON GIVEN BY INFORMANT | They were PKI. |
| | NOTES | Fanus Tefa's family owned the first masonry house in Babau, which was why the government rented it as the district office from 1959. After the 1965 incident it was used as a detention centre. Now there is a new district office, but until today the government has never paid the six years' rent for the old office. |

| No. | Human rights abuses in East Kupang | |
|---|---|---|
| 4 | INFORMANT | Witness: **PAK GASPAR** (male, 50) Undana (university) lecturer, now a customary figure |
| | DATE, PLACE AND FORM OF ABUSE | **1965, Tanah Putih**<br>At that time there was still a gebang palm forest. In 1967 it was converted to a plantation and people began to build houses in the area.<br>• victims were killed without really knowing why<br>• execution victims who did not die were kicked into the mass grave and buried alive<br>• In the first grave there were about 24 people, and 16 in the second. It is not known how many were buried in the other graves but it is estimated that the total number of people buried in seven mass graves was about 100. |
| | REASON GIVEN BY INFORMANT | • most of the victims were killed because of personal vendettas; only some were really members and leaders of PKI<br>• before the 1965 incident, there was political conflict between the village heads and PKI leaders; when 1965 events happened, the village heads murdered the PKI leaders |
| | NOTES | In 1965 there were killings 'every night'. Near his house there are seven mass graves and there are many others in places unknown.<br>Pak Gaspar's uncle was appointed as one of the executioners (as a civilian, but having close relations with the village head). |
| 5 | INFORMANT | Witness and perpetrator: **PAK JACK** (male, 48)<br>In 1980 he worked as village official who helped organise those who had to regularly report to authorities. |
| | DATE, PLACE AND FORM OF ABUSE | **1965, Oesao village centre (Balai Desa Oesao), Camat office, Babau**<br>• confirmed that detainees were first held at Balai Desa, then taken to camat's office<br>**Tanah Putih, behind Oesao market**<br>• confirmed that some of the detainees were killed<br>**Oesao Village Office**<br>• former detainees had to report in until the 1980s<br>• Pak Jack, as village official, ordered the ex-detainees to clean up around the office |
| | REASON GIVEN BY INFORMANT | Some of the victims were PKI members but some were just accused of being members. |
| | NOTES | • provided some names of Gerwani and PKI members<br>• gave a chronology of implementation of requirement to report to authorities |

| No. | Human rights abuses in East Kupang | |
|---|---|---|
| 6 | INFORMANT | Victim and witness: **KOBUS MANU** (male, approx. 71) farmer |
| | DATE, PLACE AND FORM OF ABUSE | **Mid Dec. 1965, Oesao**<br>• arrested at home by the village head<br>• interrogated at the village centre (Balai Desa)<br>• detained at the Barnemeng house for about one month<br>• Pak Kobus and other detainees were made to run wearing placards hung around their necks with their names written on them, and made to sing the 'Nasakom' song<br>• during detention, made to do forced labour<br>**6 February 1966**<br>• witnessed the massacre behind the Oesao market which was also right behind his house<br>(This was the last massacre in East Kupang.) |
| | REASON GIVEN BY INFORMANT | Their names were on a list of people who received land from the government. |
| 7 | INFORMANT | Witness: **MARKUS OENAI** (male, approx. 70) emeritus pastor who served at Oesao |
| | DATE, PLACE AND FORM OF ABUSE | • confirmed the massacre behind the Oesao market<br>• was once asked to pray for the victims at the edge of the mass grave but fainted and was unable to do it |
| | NOTES | Pastor Markus provided information about:<br>• the chronology of events<br>• PKI programs<br>• the church's attitude at the time, not doing much to help the victims. |
| 8 | INFORMANT | Perpetrator and witness: **SAM MANDALI** (male, 69), teacher, a leader of Parkindo, customary figure and member of the Annihilate PKI committee |
| | DATE, PLACE AND FORM OF ABUSE | **1965 and early January 1966, Babau, Tanah Putih and Oesao**<br>• those suspected of being 'involved' were rounded up and taken to the Balai Desa where they were interrogated by the Annihilate PKI committee<br>• those proved to be members of PKI were taken to the camat's office in Babau and detained. They were taken from there to the execution site.<br>• he was asked to be one of the firing squad at the execution site but he refused because he was nervous<br>• the first killings in East Kupang were in early January 1966, at Tanah Putih, Babu<br>• the last massacre was behind Oesao market |
| | REASON GIVEN BY INFORMANT | Some of those killed were indeed members of the PKI but others only accused of being so. |
| | NOTES | After the 1965 events, the churches were full. He also spoke about<br>• the chronology of events<br>• the names of detainees who were 'involved'<br>• the names of detainees he released<br>• the political and economic situation. |

| No. | Human rights abuses in East Kupang | |
|---|---|---|
| 9 | INFORMANT | Victim: **SINA MANU-LOE** (female, approx 70) farmer |
| | DATE, PLACE AND FORM OF ABUSE | ***Mid Dec. 1965***<br>• summoned to the Balai Desa for interrogation a few weeks after giving birth<br>• was interrogated together with some other women accused of being communists, but she didn't mention their names. |
| | REASON GIVEN BY INFORMANT | Summoned because her husband, Pak Kobus, was accused of being a member of PKI. |
| | NOTES | Provided information about<br>• the names of people linked to G30S<br>• conditions at the detention centre (Balai Desa)<br>• the family situation after the 1965 incident. |

# Appendix 3 – Sabu

| No. | Human Rights abuses in Sabu | |
|---|---|---|
| 1 | INFORMANT | Witness: **DINA** (female, 58) weaver and teacher<br>Dina is an arts teacher, teacher of custom, traditional values and weaving, and a leadership trainer. She performed the gong for customary ceremonies.<br>Her Uncle **Rihi**, a Christian and a teacher, had a land dispute with the King of Sabu. Her Uncle **Bura** was an adherent of local religion, and member of the Customary Council. |
| | DATE, PLACE AND FORM OF ABUSE | *Early Oct. 1965, Kampung Lede Ana*<br>Uncle Bura<br>• was arrested in the middle of the day<br>• was chased by the mob from Kampung Lede Ana where he worked in the plantation and lived alone in his hostel. He ran to the Customary Village and hid in the house of the Customary head, Deo Rai. The mob then threatened Deo Rai that if he did not turn over Uncle Bura they would burn the customary house down. Eventually, encouraged by Deo Rai, Uncle Bura came down from the attic (but not to the ground) and was severely beaten by the mob.<br>Dina is not sure whether Uncle Bura was executed on the first day of the executions, 29 March 1966. |
| | REASON GIVEN BY INFORMANT | Uncle Bura and Uncle Rihi were suspected of being PKI. |
| | NOTES | According to the victim's widow, Rihi encouraged her husband to join the PKI in order to get land; she threatened to divorce him if he did not. |
| 2 | INFORMANT | Victim: **GAD'I** (female, 84) deputy head of Gerwani in Sabu.<br>Gad'i's husband was head of a government office at subdistrict level. |
| | DATE, PLACE AND FORM OF ABUSE | *Oct. 1965 – Mar. 1966, Seba*<br>Gad'i's husband<br>• was taken from his house by the mob which included the head of PNI<br>• was held without warrant at the Seba prison<br>• was released (an order for his release came as he was about to be taken for execution).<br>Gad'i<br>• was taken by the mob, dragged, beaten and kicked (she fainted many times because she was pregnant)<br>• had to leave her baby, under one year old, at home<br>• had all communication devices (aerial, radio, etc) looted from the house<br>• was detained at the Village Head complex in Manu, Seba<br>• had her hair shaved<br>• had to report regularly to authorities from 1966–1983<br>• was discriminated against and stigmatised (not respected). |
| | REASON GIVEN BY INFORMANT | Gad'i's husband was accused of being a member of the PKI. Gad'i was accused of being a member of Gerwani. |
| | NOTES | Gad'i was renowned as a cook.<br>She was chosen to demonstrate Sabu traditional cloth weaving when President Soeharto visited Kupang but she fainted when she saw the soldiers and could not greet Soeharto |

| No. | Human Rights abuses in Sabu | |
|---|---|---|
| 3 | INFORMANT | Victim: **GAJA** (male, 69) literacy teacher and member of PKI |
| | DATE, PLACE AND FORM OF ABUSE | **30 September – 30 March 1966, Tali Miri, Raijua**<br>• arrested and detained without warrant at a large house that held many people, but did not experience physical abuse<br>• had to report regularly to authorities (forgets for how long)<br>• had to do forced labour at Raijua, including clearing the roads |
| | REASON GIVEN BY INFORMANT | His name was on a list of PKI members. |
| | NOTES | • PKI was well known in Raijua – it paid attention to land and education issues.<br>• The head of PKI, Rabo Lana, was a teacher at Raijua at that time, so many of the locals, including many women, joined the PKI (the membership was almost evenly divided between men and women).<br>• Pak Rabo Lana used teachers and local figures as a way to get close to the people.<br>• It was the PKI that took notice of the people's needs (land issues, illiteracy, food supplies) and therefore the PKI was the closest to the people.<br>• The PKI distributed rice, and he felt that the PKI really answered their needs.<br>• The people were given literacy classes – for both children and adults.<br>• His niece and her husband (who were both schoolteachers) joined the PKI. The husband was detained along with Gaja, and was in the group that was executed on the first day.<br>• At that time almost everyone in Raijua, especially Desa Ledeka, was a member of PKI but no one was executed apart from three of the five male teachers who were taken to Seba. Two were released: one stayed in Seba and became the husband of NPL (Mr N), and the other one, N, became a teacher in Raijua. |
| 4 | INFORMANT | Witness: **PAK KANIS** (male, 86) local king's messenger and local government [swapraja] leader<br>Dealt with tax issues, administration, social issues and registration and salaries. Retired from the camat office of West Sabu. |
| | DATE, PLACE AND FORM OF ABUSE | His house was located beside one of the places where Gerwani women were detained. (After the 30 September event he also once stayed in a detention house located about 300 meters from the prison.) |
| | NOTES | • information about the change in government system from Dutch times to the swapraja system (1947) and from swapraja to Everyday Governing Council (Majelis Pemerintahan Harian, MPH) and Regional Government Emissaries (Utusan Pemerintahan Daerah, UPD). Subdistrict of West Sabu was created in 1965.<br>• information about the history of the church in Sabu (1901, 1918). |

| No. | Human Rights abuses in Sabu | |
|---|---|---|
| 5 | INFORMANT | Witness: **KATI** (female, 82) weaver and teacher of weaving and genealogy through weaving colours and motifs, leader of women's rites of the customary house (*tegid'a*) |
| | DATE, PLACE AND FORM OF ABUSE | **Late 1965, Dina's Uncle Rihi's house in Rae Loro**<br>• heard the victims being beaten and their cries, sobs, and groans. Also heard the yelling of the mob (could be heard from the summit of the hills, but not from below).<br>• Rihi's house in Rae Loro and the people inside were attacked by the mob |
| 6 | INFORMANT | Perpetrator: **KITU** (male, 70) former teacher, secretary of PNI Panting Ligu Mesara, member of the team for annihilation of PKI |
| | DATE, PLACE AND FORM OF ABUSE | **29 and 30 March 1966**<br>• on the night of 29 March 31 people were executed<br>• early on the morning of 30 March three people were executed<br>• Kitu prayed for the victims where they had been gathered, tied their thumbs together and went with them from the prison, walking to the execution site at the Loki Pad'ae stream<br>• victims walked blindfolded, thumbs tied with mattress thread behind their backs, each victim led by one official<br>• officials were forbidden to speak, cry, show any sympathy, or look behind them<br>• on the first night, Kitu was beside the lamp about 1 metre from the execution site and was sprayed with blood and brains from the victims<br>• on the second night, two victims were beheaded with machetes, not shot<br>• after the execution, the officials returned to the site and locals (including Kitu) had to bury the bodies. The prepared grave was too small so they had to dig some more. The graves were covered with earth, grass and stones so as not to be dug up by dogs and pigs. |
| | NOTES | • On the night of the first executions, the government showed a film about development at the house beside the police station, to distract peoples' attention.<br>• The government announced that the Gerwani women would not be executed, they would just have their heads shaved.<br>• On the first night there was only one shooter (a man from Sabu who was a policeman). One victim who was shot did not die, and he ran back to the police station. When he was called he said, 'enough'. The Commander took over the duty of the police [executioner] and shot the victim, but he still did not die. In the end he was buried alive.<br>• Information about the church and poverty: the church was not able to protect its flock. The church was confused.<br>• The head of the PKI in Sabu and Mama Dina's Uncle Rihi were already involved in a dispute because cock fighting had been linked to prayer (*pedo'a*) by having them at the same place (in Rae Loro) which contravened Sabu custom. |

| No. | Human Rights abuses in Sabu | |
|---|---|---|
| 7 | INFORMANT | Witness: **MADI LOBA** (female, 58) housewife and weaver |
| | DATE, PLACE AND FORM OF ABUSE | *Seba (not sure about the time)*<br>• saw her husband arrested and detained<br>• her husband was required to regularly report to authorities |
| | REASON GIVEN BY INFORMANT | Her husband was accused of being a member of the PKI. |
| | NOTES | • when she converted to Christianity (she cannot remember the exact year), she gave up her role as a teacher of local culture<br>• her husband asked for early retirement (according to others this was probably because he was exhausted with the stigma and having to report to authorities). |
| 8 | INFORMANT | Witness: **MAHE** (female, 85) weaver, housewife |
| | DATE, PLACE AND FORM OF ABUSE | *1965–66, house of village chief (fetor) Jariwala, Seba*<br>• saw Mama Dina's Uncle Bura chased and kicked and taken away by the mob |
| | REASON GIVEN BY INFORMANT | Bura was a member of the PKI. |
| | NOTES | One of Mahe's younger siblings was a literacy teacher and often gave extra-curricular literacy classes called 'night packets'. This was also the name of a PKI program, but according to Mahe, her sibling's one was a government program. |
| 9 | INFORMANT | Witness: **MALI** (female, 67) weaver, farmer, housewife<br>Mali's husband **Rohi** is informant 12 below. |
| | DATE, PLACE AND FORM OF ABUSE | *29 March 1966*<br>• that night she was gathering sea worms at the beach and heard gunshots |
| 10 | INFORMANT | Victim: **MUJI** (female, 69) teacher SGB<br>Muji's husband, **Kepe**, was a key PKI committee member in Sabu. |
| | DATE, PLACE AND FORM OF ABUSE | *Early October 1965, Seba*<br>• taken by force from her house with her newborn baby by the Police Chief; her older child was left at home with the grandmother<br>• taken to the police station and held for two weeks at a house beside the police station together with two other teachers (one unmarried, one the wife of a policeman from Sumba)<br>• while in detention climbed over the gate and went home to breastfeed the baby who was left at home<br>• fired from her teaching position without any official letter, just summarily dismissed |
| | REASON GIVEN BY INFORMANT | The Police Chief for Sabu, Mas, a Kiser person, came and asked whether she was a member of Gerwani, even though she had no idea what Gerwani was. |

| No. | Human Rights abuses in Sabu | |
|---|---|---|
| | NOTES | • Kepe was missing for about two months before the 30th September incident when he went to Kupang to defend the people's rights regarding land. (A teaching colleague, Mama Dina's Uncle Rihi, had a land dispute with the King of Seba).<br>• 1 Jan. 1961: began teaching (in Seba)<br>• 1968: went to Yupenkris (Kupang), and received salary for 1966–68 (but not 1965) and obtained a letter of authorisation to teach<br>• 1969: began teaching again in Seba and was moved to a primary school<br>• The head of Yupenkris in Sabu moved her from the primary school to the Yupenkris office to an administrative position managing salaries and rice of GMIT teachers<br>• 1994: authorisation for early pension (she asked to retire at 50 because she was exhausted) |
| 11 | INFORMANT | Witness: **RAI MORI** (male, 83) farmer, leader of Customary Council |
| | DATE, PLACE AND FORM OF ABUSE | ***Kampung Lede Manu, near the (former) village of Railoro***<br>• saw the mob herding many people<br>• there was a 'cross' system, namely that people from one area were arrested by people from another area |
| | NOTES | Information about history: Sabu forces once assisted the Sumba people in a war with Ende, Flores (the people of Ende sold Sumbanese people to Batavia as slaves). |
| 12 | INFORMANT | Perpetrator: **ROHI** (male, 69) farmer and maker of alcoholic drink tuak<br>Asked by the head of Parkindo to head the Annihilation of PKI team. Accompanied those executed at the time of their execution.<br>Rohi's wife, **Mali**, is informant 9 above. |
| | DATE, PLACE AND FORM OF ABUSE | ***29 and 30 March 1966***<br>• Rohi accompanied one of the victims who was executed, but he was not sprayed with blood and brains when the victim was shot, because he managed to get a distance away |
| 13 | INFORMANT | Victim: **TENGA** (female, 75) a committee member of PWKI |
| | DATE, PLACE AND FORM OF ABUSE | Does not remember the date<br>• arrested by authorities<br>• detained at the complex of the Seba village head (fetor)<br>• required to report regularly to authorities<br>• forced labour:<br>  ◦ road sweeping<br>  ◦ cleaning offices, homes of officials including an official in the subdistrict of West Sabu<br>  ◦ cleaning the Ledemanu primary school yard |
| | REASON GIVEN BY INFORMANT | Tenga once gave a public speech for Labour Day. Someone did not agree with this at the time and, as result, later, when people who were suspected of being communists and Gerwani were arrested, she was also arrested, for no reason at all. |

| No. | Human Rights abuses in Sabu | |
|---|---|---|
| 14 | INFORMANT | Victim: **WILA** (female, 76) teacher, head of Gerwani in Sabu |
| | DATE, PLACE AND FORM OF ABUSE | Wila's husband, **Huki**, was detained without any warrant, together with a pastor, at a house near the police station and was executed in March 1966.<br>**Dec. 1965, Seba harbour** *(as Wila arrived by boat from Kupang)*<br>• a mob attacked a man who got off the boat. Does not know where he was taken.<br>• after getting off the boat, she was interrogated by police at the harbour who were going to arrest her, but when she asked the Camat how she would give birth, they let her go<br>**March 1966**<br>• taken by authorities from her home to the old Dutch hospital, now prison. Family members accompanied her, with her newborn baby<br>• had her hair shaved<br>• was required to regularly report until late 1966, then again in the 1980s<br>• had to do forced labour: cleaning the Jeruwel Church in the town of Seba, and high school (SMP)<br>• insulted by the Camat of East Sabu (a former student of hers)<br>• fired from her job with no official letter of dismissal<br>• children stigmatised and younger sibling discriminated against at work |
| | REASON GIVEN BY INFORMANT | She was head of Gerwani |
| | NOTES | Went to Kupang three times trying to organise her letter of authorisation to teach again, because other teaching colleagues had recommenced teaching. One of the officials in the P & K provincial office said the letter had been sent to Sabu, but even so Wila was not permitted to teach again. |
| 15 | INFORMANT | Victim (pre-1965) and perpetrator (with relation to 1965): **YERMI MONE DAMI** (male, 72) primary and junior high school teacher (moved to Sabuin 1963), an official for PNI |
| | DATE, PLACE AND FORM OF ABUSE | **3 and 4 June 1965, Seba**<br>• his house was raided, burned down. Yermi suspects that the perpetrator was an SMP teacher who was also suspected of being a member of PKI.<br>• the fire spread and engulfed about 100 houses in Seba<br>• Yermi was accused of being the arsonist in the town of Seba (and PKI members), and was taken by Sabu District Police from his house to the police station and forced to confess<br>• together with a man who lived at his house, he was held without any warrant for 21 days at the police station, sleeping on a mat<br>• conflict arose around the issue of the fire: one side defended Yermi, others accused him |

| No. | Human Rights abuses in Sabu | |
|---|---|---|
| 15 (cont'd) | DATE, PLACE AND FORM OF ABUSE (cont'd) | • Gad'i explained that Yermi led the crowd that attacked and destroyed her house, taking all communication equipment in the house |
| | NOTES | **LAND CONFLICT** (ca. 1965 prior to the 30th September affair)<br>• PKI was said to defend the rights of the people, but it also stirred up violence. For instance, the PKI led people to rebel, demanding that the king's lands be returned to the people.<br>• At Seba square, the people demonstrated demanding land rights. According to Yermi, the PKI was behind this disturbance. After the demonstration, the PNI tried to mediate between the king and the people, but the Camat would not allow the king to attend. Because of the role he took at this time, Yermi was accused of being a PKI sympathiser.<br><br>**CONFLICT BETWEEN POLITICAL PARTIES**<br>• PNI became extremely fearful when it heard that the PKI had murdered generals in Jakarta.<br>• political parties, including the PNI, were agitated because the PKI was distributing rice at the time of famine (they did not know where the PKI got the rice from).<br>• The National Front (Fron Nasional) supported the government because, according to Yermi, it was in disorder after the 30th September affair and as a result many civil servants, like teachers, were not working well.<br>• Yermi bought the house formerly owned by the Head of PKI.<br><br>**BURNING OF SCHOOLS**<br>• THE GMIT primary school in Mesara and a few other schools were burned down.<br>• Many houses and primary schools (including the GMIT primary school at Lederae Mawide, Mesara) were burnt down in the hot season of 1965 because, according to Yermi, '[teachers] were working more for the party [PKI] than fulfilling their duty as teachers'.<br>• Yermi was chosen to be a member of the Annihilation [of PKI] Team from his kampung, and could not refuse. |

| No. | Human rights abuses in Sumba | |
|---|---|---|
| 1 | INFORMANT | Victim: **IBU BUNGA** (female, 71) housewife, member of Parkindo, member of PWKI in the 1960s, one of the founders of orphanage at Waikabubak, a founder of SKP<br>Ibu Bunga's husband, **Bapak Angga**, was an official involved with the labour union, a branch of SOBSI based in Waikabubak. |
| | DATE, PLACE AND FORM OF ABUSE | ***1966, West Sumba***<br>Bakap Angga was<br>• arrested by the mob who raided their house in January or February (everything taken out of the cupboards and thrown on the ground; a soldier picked up a ring that fell and returned it to Ibu Bunga)<br>• detained at Waikabubak prison for about eight months<br>• tortured: strung up, beaten<br>• threatened with execution in April 1966 (and was in the group ready to be taken to Memboro to be executed but for an unknown reason – perhaps the quota was filled or perhaps someone from another family was killed in his place – he was ordered to get off the truck)<br>• required to report daily to the head of Lapas Waikabubak<br>• given a letter of dismissal from his job as prison officer on 15 November 1966 (as of 1 October 1966).<br>***Apr.–May 1966, West Sumba***<br>Ibu Bunga was<br>• arrested by the mob when her baby was only four months old and still breast feeding<br>• held in prison for two nights and two days (ordered home on the morning of the second day).<br>Feb.–Sept. 1966<br>Ibu Bunga's mother was<br>• held in prison for about eight months<br>• tortured: strung up, beaten<br>• required to report to authorities until Gus Dur became president.. |
| | REASON GIVEN BY INFORMANT | Her husband was a member of a labour union.<br>Her mother was active in PWKI and accused of being Gerwani. Those who arrested her called PWKI [deliberately incorrectly] 'Perseketuan Wanita *Komunis* di Indonesia'. |
| | NOTES | • When Ibu Bunga was arrested her baby was sick, but those who arrested her said this was no concern of theirs.<br>• A summary of Pak Angga's case is tabulated and presented in Appendix 2. |

| No. | Human rights abuses in Sumba | |
|---|---|---|
| 2 | INFORMANT | Victim: **IBU INA** (female, 78) housewife<br>Ibu Ina's husband, **Bapak Ama**, was an official from a government office, not a member of any labour union. |
| | DATE, PLACE, AND FORM OF ABUSE | ***16 or 17 January 1966, West Sumba***<br>• people went to her mother-in-law's house. beside her own house (Pak Ama's sister lived there) and opened all cupboards, threw down the contents from the attic until they found a list of names, but that list was the names of those who had given donations at the death of their mother in late 1965<br>***18 January 1966, West Sumba***<br>At about 10.00am Bapak Ama was<br>• arrested by the mob (one of them was a civil servant whom he knew)<br>• interrogated at the judge's house until 8.00 at night<br>• held at Waingapu jail from then until May 1967 (one year, four months)<br>• executed at Rua Beach in September 1966 during the second wave of executions. |
| | REASON GIVEN BY INFORMANT | Bapak Ama was probably arrested and murdered because his older brother was a PKI official in East Sumba. |
| | NOTES | The person leading the mob that ransacked the house and arrested Bapak Ama was renowned as a heavy drinker who was angry and brutal. |
| 3 | INFORMANT | Victim: **WIDOW (JANDA) MBULU-DIMA** (female) housewife<br>Janda's husband was a member of the PKI organising committee in East Sumba and also member of parliament |
| | DATE, PLACE AND FORM OF ABUSE | ***January 1966, East Sumba***<br>Janda<br>• her house was ransacked and looted<br>• after her husband's arrest, she was interrogated at Waingapu police station but not beaten<br>• while held in detention at police station she never met her husband who was being held at the same place<br>• under town arrest until 1978.<br>Janda's husband was<br>• arrested by the regional military late at night<br>• held in prison for several months and the family was not allowed to visit him<br>• was executed on 1 March 1966 at Waingapu harbour |
| | REASON GIVEN BY INFORMANT | Her husband was executed because he was on a PKI committee.<br>She was detained because of her husband's PKI position. |

| No. | Human rights abuses in Sumba | |
|---|---|---|
| 4 | INFORMANT | Witness: **IBU MELATI** (female, 65) staff member at Waikabubak prison |
| | DATE, PLACE AND FORM OF ABUSE | ***Jan.–Sept. 1966, West Sumba***<br>• witnessed the torture of victims in the prison: they were strung up by their feet, then pulled up and then dropped to the ground. Some were beaten while in this position, some were beaten with barbed sticks, also burnt with cigarettes.<br>• anyone who showed the slightest pity would be arrested and given the same treatment<br>• once joined in beating a victim. She did not want to do this, but could not escape the demands of the perpetrators (other prison guards) that she join in. If they did not beat the prisoners, they themselves were beaten.<br>• A PNS person once slapped the prison warden, probably teaching him a lesson as the person in charge of arrests. |
| | REASON GIVEN BY INFORMANT | Because the detainees were members of the PKI. However, there were also other prisoners who were not PKI who were mixed together with them. About 20 people were thieves and robbers (not political prisoners). |
| | NOTES | • Ibu Melati seemed to be reticent still about giving information.<br>• Ibu Melati's husband is a policeman. He was asked to join the execution squad, but declined. |
| 5 | INFORMANT | Victim: **IBU RIA** (female, 68) primary school teacher<br>Ibu Ria's father was member of the PKI organising committee in East Sumba. Her mother was a member of the organising committee of Gerwani. |
| | DATE, PLACE AND FORM OF ABUSE | ***Early 1966, Melolo, East Sumba***<br>Ibu Ria's parents<br>• had their house burned down by a group of youths<br>• were arrested and taken to the police station in Waingapu (60km from Melolo)<br>• at the police station, her father had a pestle forced into his mouth, smashing his teeth, and he had to be taken to hospital. He was executed on 1 March 1966, in a mangrove swamp at Padadita.<br>Ibu Ria was<br>• 'secured' from the teacher's hostel before a group of youths arrived to kill her<br>• detained at the police station for one month where she<br>  ◦ slept under the table of the office watchman<br>  ◦ was not permitted to leave the station<br>  ◦ saw many other detainees who were Christians<br>  ◦ was interrogated, asked about her activities<br>  ◦ was forced into labour: cleaning floors, washing, cutting grass (those who refused were punished, but she did manage to escape forced labour). |

| No. | Human rights abuses in Sumba | |
|---|---|---|
| 5 (cont'd) | DATE, PLACE AND FORM OF ABUSE (cont'd) | • sexual abuse. Late at night in October 1966, taken to the Judge's office **(Kantor Jaksa) in Waingapu**; there was an interrogation team from Kupang (the judge, military commander, police and members of Muspida (Assembly of local leaders);IBU RIA was not interrogated but left alone with the head of the team who attempted to rape her.<br>• after her release, she could not resume her teaching because her certificates had all been burnt when her house was looted and burnt.<br>• was subject to Church sanctions and ostracized in the church, society, and even within her own family.<br>• Her children were not accepted as Civil Servants until a close member of family intervened. One of her children is now a civil servant. |
| | REASON GIVEN BY INFORMANT | Her father was on the organising committee for PKI in East Sumba. Her mother was on the organising committee of Gerwani. |
| | NOTES | • The younger children who were at home when her parents were arrested, moved and lived with their grandmother in Waingapu<br>• In 1967, Ibu Ria married a policeman (a widower with three children) who was one of the interrogation team who interrogated her and who guarded her while in detention. She was widowed in 1979. |
| 6 | INFORMANT | Witness: **IBU RINA** (female, ±76) housewife, church activist, former leader of PWKI, Waikabubak |
| | DATE, PLACE AND FORM OF ABUSE | ***West Sumba***<br>• confirmed that Ibu Bunga was detained as a member of PWKI |
| | REASON GIVEN BY INFORMANT | Ibu Rina is not sure whether Ibu Bunga and her own mother, Mama Nel, were arrested because they were suspected of being members of Gerwani or whether it was because a member of their family was a PKI leader in West Sumba. |
| 7 | INFORMANT | Victim and witness: **UMBU DANGU** (male, 71) village official at the time |
| | DATE, PLACE AND FORM OF ABUSE | ***1966, West Sumba***<br>• detained at the Mamboro kecamatan office for a few weeks.<br>***April 1966, Mananga Kiau Beach, West Sumba (approximately 4.00–5.00 am)***<br>• Everyone involved in village administration was required to witness the executions. He saw seven people executed (people living nearby also witnessed this).<br>• The victims were blindfolded with black cloth, their hands tied behind their backs, and they stood side by side on the shore. The firing squad, three people (one policeman and two soldiers, or the other way around), shot them from a distance of about 10m. |

| No. | Human rights abuses in Sumba | |
|---|---|---|
| 7 (cont'd) | DATE, PLACE AND FORM OF ABUSE (cont'd) | • After the victims were shot, they were put into sacks, one person per sack. The sacks had weights tied to them; they were taken by boat to sea and were sunk.<br>• Two people did not die immediately, and had to be shot a few times. |
| | REASON GIVEN BY INFORMANT | The seven people were executed because they were PKI members, and accused of being PKI.<br>Umbu was once detained because he was accused of being PKI. |
| 8 | INFORMANT | Witness: **PAK YAKOB** (male, 62) SMP student at the time |
| | DATE, PLACE AND FORM OF ABUSE | **1966, Waikabubak, West Sumba**<br>• witnessed torture at the old prison and at the Sobawari village office (3 km from the prison)<br>• witnessed victims being taken by truck to Mamboro (Apr.) and to Rua (Sept.) to be executed |
| | REASON GIVEN BY INFORMANT | Victims were tortured and executed because they were PKI members and also as a warning to thieves and criminals. |
| | NOTES | Pak Yakob remembered the names of the victims and referred the researchers to people who could be approached. |

| No. | Human rights abuses in South Central Timor | |
|---|---|---|
| 1 | INFORMANT | Witness: **ANTON META** (male, 67) teacher |
| | DATE, PLACE AND FORM OF ABUSE | **Jan. or Feb. 1966, Naismetan forest, Kecamatan Mollo Utara**<br>Bapak Anton witnessed three victims, whom he recognised, made to kneel. Then a solider stood behind them and shot them in the nape of the neck. Before they were shot they were asked if they wanted to pray or have someone pray for them. One of the victims prayed 'God, forgive me my sins…' After they were shot, the victims were immediately kicked into the hole in Naismetan Forest. |
| 2 | INFORMANT | Witness: **ANITA BESI** (female, ±70), housewife. |
| | DATE, PLACE AND FORM OF ABUSE | **October 1967, Boti, Kecamatan KiE**<br>• witnessed her husband, **Miu Besi**, and some other men beaten then left outside in the sun until sunset, their heads shaven; the king of the customary people (raja masyarakat adat) was kicked by the soldier Pello<br>**1969, Boti**<br>• the soldier Pello returned. The king escaped, but several others were arrested and threatened with execution including Miu Besi. He was released because he agreed to convert to Christianity. The others were beaten. |
| | REASON GIVEN BY INFORMANT | The customary group did not want to convert to Christianity. |
| 3 | INFORMANT | Witness: **BENDALINA PUAI** (female)<br>Victim: **OBED NAKAMNANU** (male) Bendalina's husband |
| | DATE, PLACE AND FORM OF ABUSE | **1966, Amanuban Timur**<br>• Bapak Obed was arrested and taken to Niki-niki, Central Amanuban<br>• detained without warrant at Niki-niki for two years |
| | REASON GIVEN BY INFORMANT | Unknown to Bapak Obed, his name had been listed as a member of PKI |
| 4 | INFORMANT | Perpetrator: **BENY SANO** (male, 68) retired policeman |
| | DATE, PLACE AND FORM OF ABUSE | **1965–66, various locations in South Central Timor**<br>• executed victims |
| | REASON GIVEN BY IN | They were executed as members of PKI, but not all those killed were members of PKI. |
| | NOTES | • Pak Beny's story can be read in full in *Breaking the Silence* (original Indonesian *Memecah Pembisuan*) ed. Putu Oka Sukanta, Melbourne: Monash University Publishing, 2014, pp 19–33. |

| No. | Human rights abuses in South Central Timor | |
|---|---|---|
| 5 | INFORMANT | Victim: **FERI TAINANU** (male) farmer |
| | DATE, PLACE AND FORM OF ABUSE | **1965, Naip, Panite and Bena, South Amanuban**<br>• arrested in Naip, then taken to Panite<br>• interrogated at Panite<br>• forced labour (clearing land for farming) in Bena |
| | REASON GIVEN BY INFORMANT | His name was listed among recipients of aid from BTI. |
| 6 | INFORMANT | Perpetrator: **FESTOR LAISNEPA** (male, 84) retired public servant |
| | DATE, PLACE AND FORM OF ABUSE | **1965–66, Kecamatan of North Amanutan**<br>• as a government employee he was ordered to take part in arresting and eradicating PKI |
| 7 | INFORMANT | Perpetrator: **LENI TOPA** (male, age unknown, but born during Japanese occupation) member of OPR |
| | DATE, PLACE AND FORM OF ABUSE | **1965, Naip, Kecamatan of South Amanuban**<br>• members of OPR were given the right to arrest victims and take them from Naip to Panite<br>• victims were then murdered and discarded in Kolbebe |
| | REASON GIVEN BY INFORMANT | PKI and especially BTI members often stole people's goats and cattle for their parties and sinful activities. |
| 8 | INFORMANT | Witness: **MATAN TONLAKA** (male, 60) farmer |
| | DATE, PLACE AND FORM OF ABUSE | *Imanuel Church, Desa Kombaki, Kecamatan Polen*<br>• Pak Matan witnessed torture at the Kombaki church. There were as many as 36 victims together (he doesn't remember the date) who were beaten by the army, then taken to some unknown place (people said it was SoE) and they never returned. After a few months someone brought back some cloth belonging to the victims to be given to their wives. This was done with a ceremony at Kombaki village. |
| 9 | INFORMANT | Victims:<br>**MELDA SARKIN** (female, ±74) housewife<br>**TEOFILUS KIUBANI** (Melda's husband) prominent in BTI at Amanuban Sel<br>**SIPORA NABUASA** (wife of Yan Fandu)<br>**YAN FANDU** (husband of Sipora Nabusa) prominent BTI/PKI figure in South Amanuban<br>**FRITS NOMLENI** (Melda's son)<br>**EFRAIM TUFLAKA** (Malda's second husband, married after Teofilus disappeared). |
| | DATE, PLACE AND FORM OF ABUSE | *Early 1966* (the corn was still young), *various locations in South Amanuban and SoE*<br>Mama Melda and Sipora Nabuasa were<br>• picked up from their houses by OPR youth from their village of Naip<br>• made to join the arresting party heading for Oe'usapi to arrest their husbands |

| No. | Human rights abuses in South Central Timor | | |
|---|---|---|---|
| 9 (cont'd) | DATE, PLACE AND FORM OF ABUSE (cont'd) | | • taken from Oe'usapi to Oe'mofa, Bena, and Noemuki, and finally to Basmuti, where their husbands had been taken (Mama Sipora complained she wanted to go home)<br>• taken from Basmuti on to SoE to 'face the judge'<br>• summoned to SoE barracks (where their husbands were held) for interrogation until the 'last day' when the officer ordered them home and told them not to return.<br>Teofilus Kiubani and Yan Fandu<br>• were arrested at a village by a fully-armed official (they could hear gunshots at the time).<br>• were beaten and tortured in front of Mama Melda ('their hands and bodies were crushed until they went black')<br>• had their heads shaved<br>• were detained for two months at the SoE barracks<br>• were never seen again after they were detained. |
| | REASON GIVEN BY INFORMANT | | Teofilus Kiubani used to list the names of people in the village who would become members of BTI and Gerwani (most of them were people with good education). Yan Fandu was a BTI/PKI figure in South Amanuban. |
| | NOTES | | When she saw her partner arrested, Mama Melda did not want to cry because she was afraid of being called a PKI sympathiser and then tortured. |
| 10 | INFORMANT | | **NANSI KANIS** (female) housewife |
| | DATE, PLACE AND FORM OF ABUSE | | **SoE**<br>• her relative was detained at the Puterpra in SoE and Mama Nansi visited her there |
| | REASON GIVEN BY INFORMANT | | Her relative was detained because she was accused of being a member of PKI/ Gerwani. |
| 11 | INFORMANT | | Victim: **NELTJI KUMAR** (female, 63) former public servant (finance section) in a government office at Kabupaten level |
| | DATE, PLACE AND FORM OF ABUSE | | **Oct. 1965, Puterpra, SoE**<br>• immediately on her return from Jakarta was arrested and taken to the SoE military command office<br>• arrested without any warrant<br>• suspended from her position<br>• received a promotion, but was never paid any salary |
| | REASON GIVEN BY INFORMANT | | Accused of being a member of Gerwani because the head of the office where she worked was a member of the organising committee of PKI in South Central Timor. |

| No. | Human rights abuses in South Central Timor | |
|---|---|---|
| 12 | INFORMANT | **PAK OENASI** (male, 67) retired public servant |
| | DATE, PLACE AND FORM OF ABUSE | *1965, Puterpra, SoE*<br>• Pak Oenasi used to visit his girlfriend (now wife) when she was held at Puterpra in SoE |
| | REASON GIVEN BY INFORMANT | His girlfriend was detained because she was accused of being a member of Gerwani. |
| | NOTES | He gave information about the miracle of water turning to wine in front of his house. |
| 13 | INFORMANT | Victim: **S.Y. NAILIU** (male, 76) farmer |
| | DATE, PLACE AND FORM OF ABUSE | *1965, Nunusunu and Panite, in South Amanuban*<br>• arrested in Nunusunu then taken to Panite<br>• in Panite, detained and suffered physical abuse |
| | REASON GIVEN BY INFORMANT | In 1964 he had already been accused of belonging to PKI but had denied this by sending a letter to the Bupati of South Central Timor and the Governor of NTT. |
| | NOTES | Pak Nailiu gave information about PKI and some information about Gerwani. |
| 14 | INFORMANT | Victim: **SALMUN TANU** (male, 71) teacher |
| | DATE, PLACE AND FORM OF ABUSE | *January 1966, SoE*<br>• summoned<br>• interrogated and detained at the army barracks<br>• after his release he returned to teach at the Fafinisin primary school (5 km from SoE)<br>*1983*<br>• fired from his position. Re-employed then fired again.<br>• promoted, but given no commensurate rise in salary |
| | REASON GIVEN BY INFORMANT | Accused of being a member of PKI. |
| 15 | INFORMANT | Witness: **SANCE NELO** (female, 77) housewife |
| | DATE, PLACE AND FORM OF ABUSE | *Oct. 1967, Boti, in the kecamatan of KiE*<br>• her husband beaten by a soldier called Pello with a rattan stick edged with brass. The soldier wore a uniform and carried a gun.<br>• her husband was beaten for a full day<br>• other men were also beaten and left out in the hot sun; the king was kicked, had his hair shaved, and was left out in the hot sun |
| | REASON GIVEN BY INFORMANT | Because the people of Boti had not converted to Christianity. |
| | NOTES | Some of the people of the customary group decided to convert to Christianity, rather than have their king killed. |

# Appendix 3 – South Central Timor | 327

| No. | Human rights abuses in South Central Timor | |
|---|---|---|
| 16 | INFORMANT | **STEF BANI** (male) farmer (his father was a victim)<br>**TEDA SANAP** (female) housewife<br>**MAMA STEF BANI** (her husband was a victim) |
| | DATE, PLACE AND FORM OF ABUSE | *February 1966, Taum market, Panite, South Amanuban, SoE*<br>• Pak Stef's father was shot at by police, then taken to SoE for medical treatment and to be 'processed'<br>• Pak Stef's father disappeared |
| | REASON GIVEN BY INFORMANT | Pak Stef's father was shot because he was suspected of being PKI when he refused to accept some banknotes that were torn and dirty. |
| 17 | INFORMANT | Perpetrator: **YABES FANI** (male) farmer, member of OPR |
| | DATE, PLACE AND FORM OF ABUSE | *1965, Naip, South Amanuban*<br>• OPR members were given the right to arrest victims in Naip and take them to Panite<br>• victims were then murdered and discarded at Kolbebe |
| | REASON GIVEN BY INFORMANT | According to Pak Yabes, PKI members, and especially BTI members, often stole the people's goats and cattle for parties and sinful activities. |
| 18 | INFORMANT | Victims:<br>**YANE NETOMELA** (female, 74) housewife<br>**YOSUA NETOMELA** (male) GMIT primary school teacher<br>**YUSAK BEI** (male) PKI figure in Babuin |
| | DATE, PLACE AND FORM OF ABUSE | *1965, Babuin, Niki-niki, SoE*<br>Yosua Netomela was<br>• arrested, with some others, in Babuin by the army with no warrant<br>• taken to Niki-niki police station, then to SoE police station<br>• interrogated in SoE (some were beaten and had teeth and finger/toenails pulled out)<br>• forced into labor at the police station<br>  ◦ digging<br>  ◦ cleaning bathrooms and toilets (having to use only their hands)<br>  ◦ laying stones on the road to the police station (the road was not yet paved)<br>• released after about three months (but the others were not).<br>Yusak Bei received the same treatment as Yosua Netomela except that he was taken away and disappeared (believed killed). |
| | REASON GIVEN BY INFORMANT | As a teacher, Pak Yosua could read and write and therefore was asked by the local head (*usif*) to write the names of BTI members. (Many people of Babuin were attracted to join BTI because of promises of release from tax requirements and promises of food). Because Pak Yosua wrote the list, he himself was said to be a member of PKI. |

| No. | Human rights abuses in South Central Timor | |
|---|---|---|
| 19 | INFORMANT | **YULIANTI MENO** (female) housewife |
| | DATE, PLACE AND FORM OF ABUSE | **Feb. 1966, Puterpra, SoE**<br>Yulianto's husband, **Kristofel Meno** was<br>• arrested and detained<br>• required to report daily for around three months.<br>**1983**<br>• Kristofel was dishonorably dismissed from his position as public servant and given no salary or pension. |
| | REASON GIVEN BY INFORMANT | Accused of being a member of PKI. |
| | NOTES | When he was freed of the requirement to report regularly to authorities, he was ordered to return to teaching at a junior high school in SoE. |

# Appendix 4

## Efforts to Source Secondary Data

| No. | Institution / Type of data | Approach (date) | Results |
|---|---|---|---|
| 1 | Undana Library | **Visit to library** (11 Nov. 2010) Research team received a positive response from Undana Library Chief Librarian. | **DEAD END** The search for historical material of the period 1960–70 revealed there was virtually no material and what was there was irrelevant. |
| 2 | Regional Museum NTT | **Visit to museum library** (2 Nov. 2010) Kupang city research team, with letter of introduction from JPIT, were well received by museum staff. | **DOCUMENTS NOTED** Information about the arrival of the PKI in NTT was included in 'Periodisation of the history of the 1928 PKI Rebellion and its influence on NTT' (Periodisasi Sejarah Pemberontakan PKI Tahun 1928 dan pengaruhnya di NTT') in a collection of articles entitled *Regional History with the Theme of National Awakening in the region of Nusa Tenggara Timur 1900–1942* (*Sejarah Daerah Tematis Zaman Kebangkitan Nasional di Daerah Nusa Tenggara Timur Tahun 1900–1942*). |
| 3 | Badan Arsip Daerah (Regional Archives) | **Visit to the office** (24 Nov. 2010) Secretariat Team presented a letter of request to carry out research in archives. Letter accepted by female staff member. | **OBSTRUCTION** Told to come back and check in two days. |
| | | **Return visit to the office** (26 Nov. 2010) | The Secretariat Team was given a letter from the Regional Archives saying they were prepared to assist with the intended research. |
| | | **Return visit to the office** (29 Nov. 2010) The Secretariat Team explains the purpose of the research and presents the 26 Nov. 2010 letter of agreement from the archives to the official in charge of archive management. | In spite of the letter, the Secretariat Team is not permitted to look for the archives themselves. The staff member says she will look for the required material. She gives her mobile phone number to the team. |
| | | **Telephone contact** The team contacts the archives manager various times by phone. | The official always says she has had no time to check for the material. |
| | | **Visit to the office** (2 Dec. 2010) The Secretariat Team visits the office again and meet the archives manager in person. | Archives manager says she is still too busy and the researchers should wait until she contacts them. |

| No. | Institution / Type of data | Approach (date) | Results |
|---|---|---|---|
| 4 | RRI (Indonesian National Radio) Kupang | **Visit to office** (20 Nov. 2010) The Secretariat Team explains the purpose of their research to head of RRI Kupang, then goes to look at the collection of recordings of news at RRI. | **DEAD END** Conclusion: probably extremely difficult to find material. Official explains that recordings for the 1960–1970 period no longer exist. RRI has wiped them following their internal policy of wiping tapes after 2 years, 5 years, 10 years and 20 years, depending on type. |
| 5 | STTJ (Jakarta Theology College) | **Email to part-time lecturer** (26 Jan. 2011) Does the STTJ and/or PGI possibly hold relevant church archives and, if so, is it possible to photocopy them? | **INFORMATION** **Reply to 26 Jan. 2011 email** (27 Jan. 2011) 'The Centre for Documentation of the History of the Indonesian Church, under STTJ, holds very little information about the period 1960–1970, namely: <br>• acknowledgment of the 1965 political turmoil <br>• massacres. <br>The church was forced to be involved in the massacres, many of the religious leaders remained silent. The number of Christians dramatically increased because members of organisations considered to be affiliated to PKI had to choose one of the five 'official' religions.' 'Other archives held relate to the period before this.' <br><br>**Response to another email** (27 Jan. 2011) 'Actually there is a lot of material about NTT, especially about the period prior to 1960 and after 1970. However… don't get your hopes up… for source material about women… There is one relatively thick book about the sources of missions to Sumba, but virtually no stories about women…' <br>\* Team members have not had the opportunity to go to Jakarta to follow up this information. |
| 6 | PGI (Communion of Churches in Indonesia) | **Email to PGI Chairman** (27 Jan. 2011) Does the PGI library hold any relevant archives, for instance correspondence between PGI with GMIT or GKS, or non-formal archives about the 1965 incident? | **DEAD END** **Email reply** (27 Jan. 2011) 'Greetings. It seems as though the PGI archives have experienced the same fate.' |

| No. | Institution / Type of data | Approach (date) | Results |
|---|---|---|---|
| 7 | Informant, Rote | **Email to a contact in Rote** (28 Jan. 2011)<br>1. 1. Request for suggestions and advice about search for archives and relevant secondary sources.<br>2. If the research team were to do some extra 'mini lightning research' in Rote, are there any suggestions for good informants? | **SOME LEADS**<br>**Reply to email** (28 Jan. 2011)<br>1. Access to information can be difficult; try Ben Mboi library, also try KITLV publications.<br>2. Recommends postponing research in Rote.<br>3. Suggests some informants in the Kupang area. |
| 8 | Documents held by victims/ informants | **Field research** (Nov. 2010 – Feb. 2011)<br>Some researchers obtained access to documents held by informants. | **DOCUMENTS PHOTOCOPIED**<br>**From Pak Nyongki** (via research team for Kupang): photocopied all the official correspondence about his dismissal as a civil servant, and his efforts to reclaim his rights.<br>**From Ibu Bunga** (via the Sumba research team): case chronology and correspondence about her husband's, Pak Angga's, salary and linked to his dismissal. |
| 9 | GMIT Archives 'Pembersihan Tubuh GMIT dari Unsur2 G30S', ['Cleansing of the Body of GMIT from G30S elements] Synod pastoral letters etc (from Indonesia) | **Face-to-face and telephone conversations** (24 Oct. 2010)<br>Discussion between Team Coordinator and a former General Secretary of the GMIT Synod at the Synod office and also via telephone. | **A LEAD WITHOUT DOCUMENTATION**<br>Heard from a former Deputy Head of the Synod Assembly that the 1960 Synod in SoE made a resolution about the position of GMIT towards the PKI, but this documentation is not held at the synod office. Suggestion that the researchers approach other pastors in Kupang and SoE – they might have this material in their private papers. |
| | | **Mobile phone conversation** (24 Oct. 2010)<br>Discussion between the Team Coordinator and a member of the Synod via mobile phone. | **DEAD END**<br>The Synod Assembly for the period 2007–2011 tried to sort out its documentation, but this did not include the correspondence the researchers were looking for, including the pastoral letters. There are no other documents from the 1965 period. |
| | | **Library search** (Nov. 2010)<br>Research team supporters look for material in the library. | **DATA FOUND**<br>**Document (Nov. 2010)**<br>An unpublished document, *Sejarah Gereja Jemaat Wilayah Netpa'a* [TTS] by Pdt. P. Bani STh. (1997), was photocopied and deposited in JPIT library. |

| No. | Institution / Type of data | Approach (date) | Results |
|---|---|---|---|
| 9 (cont'd) | GMIT Archives 'Pembersihan Tubuh GMIT dari Unsur2 G30S', ['Cleansing of the Body of GMIT from G30S elements] Synod pastoral letters etc (from Indonesia) (cont'd) | **Visit** (Dec. 2010) The Secretariat Team visits a former General Secretary of the GMIT Synod. | **DEAD END** He says that he holds no material relating to the position of the church towards the 30th September Movement or PKI. |
| | | **Visit** (8 Jan. 2011) The East Kupang team meets with a former Secretary General of the GMIT synod at his house. | **DEAD END** He says that he has no archives from that period and does not think that such archives are still at the Synod Office. |
| | | **Request** (Apr. 2011) The Secretariat Team asks for assistance from the Theology Commission of the GMIT Synod to search for archives. | **OBSTRUCTION** Team told that they have checked with a colleague in Alor, but not found anything. |
| | | **Telephone contact** (12 Feb.2012) Team Coordinator phones various contacts in Alor searching for a document entitled 'Nada Bhakti' drawn up by church leaders in Alor in May 1966. | **DATA FOUND** Reply (12 Feb. 2012) from the child of an emeritus GMIT pastor in Alor. 'Nada Bhakti' is scanned and sent, but is incomplete (has no signatures). The original document is not found. |
| 10 | Archives about GMIT (from sister churches and GMIT missionaries) | **Email** (2–3 March 2011) One of the team supporters sends an email to staff of the Uniting Church of Australia (UCA): Does the UCA possibly hold relevant archives that can be accessed? | **OBSTRUCTION** Reply to email (18 March 2011) The archives are in storage and they do not know about GMIT; they will check and get back to us. Meanwhile, the former missionaries are ageing; will contact again shortly. *There was no more contact. |
| | | **Email** (11 June 2011) A team supporter sents an email to the Common Global Ministries Board (USA) and former staff of the Board: Do they hold archives about GMIT in the period 1960–70 that would be open to access for research? Also requests contact information for former missionaries. | **LIMITED INFORMATION** Reply to email (12 June 2011) from former staff member. Staff member recalls there was a lot of information about developments of the church in Sumatra over the period 1960–70, but little linked to developments in the GMIT and the 30th September movement. The current staff hold archives from that time. Regarding the missionaries, contact information can be found: a telephone number and an address are given, but no email account. *There is no response from current CGMB staff. |

Appendix 4 | 333

| No. | Institution / Type of data | Approach (date) | Results |
|---|---|---|---|
| 10 (cont'd) | Archives about GMIT (from sister churches and GMIT missionaries) (cont'd) | **Email to missionaries in Holland who served the GMIT in the 1970s** (1 Dec. 2011) Team coordinator sends email asking: Do they hold any relevant notes? Do they have any contact information for other GMIT missionaries before them (in the 1960s)? | **LIMITED INFORMATION** **Reply to email** (1 Dec. 2011) • arrived in Timor in 1973 • once held closed discussion about this with a lecturer friend; the wife of an Undana lecturer was detained • a student from Sumba escaped from Java to Sumba and studied at the Kupang Theological College (ATK) in Oesapa to 'purify' himself. |
| | | **Email to former missionary in Holland who taught at the ATK in Oesapa, from 1959 to 1967** (8 Dec. 2011) Team Coordinator sends an email asking: Does he have any information to share with the research team? We want to collect the perspectives and experiences of women victims, and also want to know the GMIT's position at the time. | **LIMITED INFORMATION** **Reply to email** (29 Dec. 2011) He does not know much, only heard general things. The communists were imprisoned, and then, as a result of pressure from Jakarta, they – especially the leaders and secretaries – were executed. The pastors gave the spiritual ministry. Members of the PKI were usually imprisoned for long periods and then released. |
| | | **Archive search** (26 Dec. 2011) Team supporters find some relevant information at the National Archives of Australia <http://www.naa.gov.au/>. | **DATA FOUND** **Letter** (26 Dec. 2011) A letter downloaded: 'Communism and the Christian Church in Indonesian Timor' (written on 2 Feb. 1961 by Luscombe, Australian Consul in Dili). |
| 11 | Archives about the Catholic Church in NTT | **Visit to Ledalero, Flores** (10–13 Nov. 2010) The Secretariat Team visits the Candraditya Research Centre, the Catholic College of Philosophy (STFK) library, the provincial office of the Society of the Divine Word (SVD) and had discussions with STFK lecturers. | **LIMITED DATA FOUND AND POTENTIAL FOR FURTHER ACTION** **Candraditya Research Centre**: Found material from a priest who shared information about the 1965–1966 events in Sikka, Flores. **STFK Library**: Most information held relates to the national level rather than local. **STFK lecturers and priests**: 'Sedjarah Geredja Protestan di Timor' (translated from German) in a journal entitled *Pastoralia* (Ende: Pertjetakan Arnoldus, unknown date). The article describes the history of the GMIT including some reference to events in 1965 and the GMIT's response. Important information about what happened at Sikka, Flores: the event itself, and before and after it, as well as the position and attitude of the Catholic Church. One of the priests also provided valuable information about key contacts in Ende. |

| No. | Institution / Type of data | Approach (date) | Results |
|---|---|---|---|
| 11 (cont'd) | Archives about the Catholic Church in NTT (cont'd) | (cont'd) | **SVD provincial office**: attempted to find Maumere deaconate records at this office, but the staff were busy with a change of staffing, and said they would not have time to devote to this search until July 2011. |
| | | **Visit to Ende, Flores** (14–16 Nov. 2010) The Secretariat Team visited the Bishop of Ende's office at Ndona, Ende Parish Centre, Nusa Indah Publishing and Syalom Ende Church (GMIT). | **DEAD END**<br>• **Bishop of Ende's office at Ndona**: Search for pastoral letter related to the 1965 event, but the staff were in mourning (a recent death) and could not be approached.<br>• **Ende parish centre**: archives bad, nothing found.<br>• **Nusa Indah publishers**: archives bad, nothing found<br>• **Syalom Ende Church (GMIT)**: according to the pastor and an elderly member of the church council, the church archives are bad and many documents are lost. |
| | | **Visit to Soeverdi Monastery (SVD) in Kupang** (20 Nov. 2010) The Secretariat Team visits two priests at the monastery and discuss with them the possibility of finding relevant information at the SVD library at Nenuk, Belu. | **DEAD END** The two priests explain that the archives from Nenuk have been brought to the SVD library in Kupang (where they are) but there is no information relating to 1965. One of the priests helps the team to search for old material about this period, but their search is unsuccessful. He says he has never seen any such material in the library. |
| | | **Return visit to Candraditya Research Centre** (12–14 Jan. 2011) The Secretariat Team returns to the centre in Ledelero, Flores, to meet a priest who carried out research about 1965. | **LIMITED INFORMATION (contacts for victims)** The priest is not prepared to share the information he has gathered as he is preparing it for publication, but he is prepared to facilitate meetings between the Secretariat Team and some victims in Maumere. Because of limited time, the team does not take up this offer. |

Appendix 4 | 335

| No. | Institution / Type of data | Approach (date) | Results |
|---|---|---|---|
| 12 | Archives about GKS (from Indonesia) | **Archive search** (late Dec. 2010) The head of the research team for Sumba requests the team members in Sumba to search for relevant GKS documents. | **DATA FOUND** **Key GKS documents photocopied and sent** (second week of Jan. 2011) Team members of the Sumba field research team succeed in photocopying some key documents from the GKS Office, PajetiVII/ 93Pos: Waingapu, Sumba emeritus GKS pastor. <br>• List of resolutions of the GKS Synod, Synod no.–I (1947) – Synod no.–XX (1966) <br>• Notes from various Synod Meetings of the GKS and attachments: <br>   ◦ Meeting 20; 20–28 July 1966 at Kananggaru <br>   ◦ Meeting 21; 26 July – 4 August 1967 at Ede <br>   ◦ Meeting 22; 23 July – 2 August 1968 at Mamboru |
| 13 | Archives about GKS (from sister churches and GKS missionaries) | **Email to former missionary's daughter** (24 Feb. 2011) Email sent to the daughter of a former Dutch missionary, who served the GKS at the time, requesting access to any relevant writing by her father. | **LIMITED INFORMATION** **Reply to email** (25 Feb. 2011) Explanation that her father had tried to save as many people as possible, even praying for them on the beach when they were executed, but had not written much for fear of reprisals against the church and victims' families. **POTENTIAL FOR FURTHER ACTION** The daughter will search the material that exists. |
| | | **Visit to former missionaries** (11–12 Nov. 2011) Research supporters visited some former missionaries who served the GKS in Sumba over the 1960–70 period, and their families living in Holland and Germany. | **DATA FOUND: DOCUMENTS PHOTOCOPIED, INTERVIEWS RECORDED** <br>• interviews with two former missionaries who spoke about their experience of the 1965 incident when they were in Sumba (recorded on video) <br>• some official church reports and articles in church journals (in German) <br>• some obligatory three monthly church reports (in Dutch) <br>• various computer files printed <br>• various photos <br>• letters to Paul Webb (one in English, one in Dutch) <br>• hymns sung at execution of victims |

| No. | Institution / Type of data | Approach (date) | Results |
|---|---|---|---|
| 13 (cont'd) | Archives about GKS (from sister churches and GKS missionaries) (cont'd) | (cont'd) | • chapter from book *De zending voorbij* (in Dutch)<br>• 'Surat Panggilan Pendeta Utusan' [Letter of Instruction to Pastors]<br>• 'Ringkasan Chotbah, 6 Djuni 1965 di: Waikabubak dan di Pajeti'. [summary of sermon given on 6 June 1965 at Waikabubak and Pajeti (in Indonesian)]<br>• newspaper clippings (in Dutch) |

# Appendix 5

## Tools for 1965 Victims' Advocacy

## In Indonesian

### 1. HAK ATAS PENGADILAN
UU 26/2000: PENGADILAN HAM
[RIGHT TO JUSTICE: LAW 26/200: HUMAN RIGHTS JUSTICE]

The text of the law and its explanation:

http://www.hukumonline.com/pusatdata/detail/17499/nprt/541/uu-no-26-tahun-2000-pengadilan-hak-asasi-manusia

### 2. HAK ATAS KEBENARAN
TAP MPR V/2000 TENTANG PEMANTAPAN PERSATUAN DAN KESATUAN NASIONAL
[RIGHT TO THE TRUTH: Parliamentary ruling V/2000 on National Union and Unity]

Mandates the process of expression of truth about human rights abuses of the past, achievement of justice and restoration of victims' rights:

http://ebookbrowsee.net/gdoc.php?id=27144564&url=ff581edab1539dc007d63cf26333adab

### 3. KOMNAS PEREMPUAN TENTANG HAK PEREMPUAN
[National Commission on Women on the rights of women]

http://www.komnasperempuan.or.id/?s=HAK+PEREMPUAN+ATAS+KEBENARAN+ ATAS KEBENARAN

### 4. HARI HAK KORBAN UNTUK KEBENARAN DAN KEADILAN
[Day for the Rights of Victims to Truth and Justice]

An appeal to make 24 March the Day for the Rights of Victims to Truth and Justice.

Text can be downloaded via the National Commission on Women at:
http://www.komnasperempuan.or.id/?s=HARI+HAK+KORBAN+UNTUK+KEBENARAN+DAN+KEADILAN

# In English

### 5. RIGHT TO A REMEDY AND REPARATION
United Nations General Assembly (UNGA) Resolution 60/147: Basic Principles and Guidelines on the Right to a Remedy and Reparation for Victims of Gross Violations of International Human Rights Law and Serious Violations of International Humanitarian Law

http://legal.un.org/avl/pdf/ha/ga_60-147/ga_60-147_e.pdf

### 6. NAIROBI DECLARATION ON THE RIGHTS OF WOMEN AND GIRLS TO REMEDY AND REPARATION

http://www.womensrightscoalition.org/site/reparation/sig nature_en.php

### 7. RIGHT TO THE TRUTH
United Nations Human Rights Council (UNHRC) Resolution 12/12: Right to the Truth

http://daccess-dds-ny.un.org/doc/RESOLUTION/GEN/G09/165/99/PDF/G0916599.pdf?OpenElement

Report by the Office of the High Commissioner for Human Rights on Rights to the Truth.

http://www2.ohchr.org/ english/bodies/hrcouncil/docs/12session/A-HRC-12-19.pdf

# Appendix 6

## Biodata of Research Team Members

### Alor Team

***Pastor Dorkas Sir*** was born in Kalabahi on 22 December 1963 as the fifth of nine children. She attended primary school at Kalabahi, and went on to study junior high school (SLTP) and high school (SLTA) in Kupang. In 1983, Dorkas entered the Kupang Theological College (Sekolah Tinggi Teologi) and graduated in 1989. Her pre-ordination pastoral training was in 1990 with the Lus Congregation, North Central Alor Presbytery, and in 1991 she was placed as pastor of the Balunggada Region Congregation, Pantar Presbytery, where she also served as Vice Moderator of the Pantar Presbytery. In 1994, she was moved to the Nule congregation, Pantar Presbytery, and in 2002 was elected as Moderator of the East Pantar Presbytery. In 2002 she pursued a master's degree in sociology of religion at Satya Wacana Christian University (Universitas Kristen Satya Wacana) graduating in 2004. In 2005 she was placed as the pastor with the Ichtus Puildon Kalabahi Congregation, and then in 2011 she was transferred to the Pola Tribuana Kalabahi Congregation, north-west Alor Presbytery where she is at present. Apart from carrying out her duties as pastor, Dorkas was also head of the Affiliation of Women's Organisations (Gabungan Organisasi Perempuan) in Alor from 2000 to 2002, head of the Union of Indonesian Christian Women (Persatuan Wanita Kristen Indonesia) from 2011 to 2015, and Chair of the Tribuana Women's Prayer Group from 2010 to 2015.

***Pastor Adriana Tiluata (Ina)*** was born in Kupang on 21 October 1973. She completed primary school in Kupang in 1985, graduated from junior high school in 1988 and high school in 1991. Ina began further study at the Agricultural Institute in Bogor (Institut Pertanian Bogor) in 1991, and joined the Association of Christian Students there. She was also a Bible Study Leader in villages in West Java based with the Sebaoth Ministry Post of the West Indonesian Protestant Church. In 1994, Ina began study at the Theological College in Jakarta and graduated in 1999. She carried out her period of student ministry with the Ichtus Puildon Kalabahi Congregation from 1999 to 2001 and was ordained as a minister on 21 October 2001 with the Christian Evangelical Church in Timor (Gereja Masehi Injil di Timor, GMIT). From 2001 to 2004, Ina ministered at the Oelunggu Congregation, Lobalain Presbytery. She was then transferred to the Padakika Diaspora Congregation in the pastoral area of Mahuting Timur, Central North Alor Presbytery and served there from 2004 to 2009. She was transferred again to the Fanating Congregation in North Central Alor Presbytery in 2009 where she is at present.

***Erna Hinadang*** was born on 28 March 1982, the eldest of six children. She completed her primary schooling at the GMIT primary school at Kabola Kalabahi in 1995, then graduated from junior high school (SMP Negeri 2) in Kalabahi in 1998, and high school (SMA Negeri 1) in Kalabahi in 2001. She went on to study at the Faculty of Theology at Artha Wacana Christian University (UKAW) in Kupang. Erna also did a period of field work study with the Ponain Congregation, East Amarasi Presbytery, and in 2005 pursued her student internship with the Getsemani Congregation in Tarus Timur. She graduated with her bachelor's degree in 2009. On 1 June 2009 Erna commenced serving as a candidate for student ministry with the Ichtus Puildon Kalabahi Congregation.

## City of Kupang Team

***Pastor Petronela Loy Bhoga (Nela)*** was born in Bajawa, Flores on 13 June 1965. She is the youngest of eight children. She completed her primary and high schooling at Bajawa, graduating in 1982, and then did further Bachelor's study at the Faculty of Theology at UKAW in Kupang from 1984 to 1989. She did her student ministry in Alor from 1989 to 1990 and was ordained as a pastor with the GMIT on 18 November 1990. Nela is now serving as minister with the congregation of the city of Kupang.

***Martha Bire (Ata)*** was born in Kupang on 8 April 1987 as the second of five children. She did her primary and high schooling in Kupang. In 2005, she was accepted as a student in the Faculty of Theology at UKAW in Kupang and graduated as top student of that faculty in February 2011. During her study, she was a member of the Student Senate of the Faculty of Theology. She is currently a candidate for student ministry with the GMIT Congregation of Efata di Liliba, Central Kupang Presbytery. In November 2010, she participated in the workshop on transitional justice organised by the Indonesian branch of the International Center for Transitional Justice (ICTJ) in Bali.

*Golda ME Sooai* was born in the city of Kupang on 30 January 1988, the eldest of three children, and raised in Oebufu. Golda did her primary and secondary schooling in Kupang and became a student in the Theology Department at UKAW in 2005. In 2010, she graduated *cum laude*. In 2011, Golda was made Language Ambassador for the Eastern Indonesia province (NTT) and participated in a national competition in Jakarta. Golda is now doing her student ministry in Rote.

## East Kupang Team

*Pastor Welys Hawu Haba-TaEdini* was born in the city of Kupang on 8 February 1966 as the eldest of four children. Her father was a pastor and her mother a midwife. When Welys was five years old, she accompanied her parents to South Kalimantan while they were on an evangelical mission with the Dayak people. When she was 12, her family moved to Papua and her father served with the Dani people. Welys studied at the Indonesian Biblical College (Institut Injil Indonesia) in Malang and graduated in 1992. In the same year, she began serving in the Papua interior as a team member for the Asia Pacific Christian Mission, which is based in Australia. This missionary team assists Dani women and children with spiritual guidance, health care and education. In 1996, Welys returned to Eastern Indonesia (NTT) to do her period of student ministry with the Musafir Inggorea Congregation (GMIT), North Biboki Presbytery, North Central Timor. She was ordained as pastor in Seba, Sabu in 1997 and married Pastor D. Hawu-Leba in 1998. Welys served for eight years in Sabu, then from 2003 to 2006 she joined her husband who was studying in Jakarta. In April 2006, she began serving the Imanuel Oesao Congregation, East Kupang Presbytery, and commenced the research for this book. In June 2011, Welys was transferred to the Pniel Sikumana Congregation, West Kupang Presbytery.

*Elfrantin J de Haan (Fanty)* was born in Kapan, South Central Timor on 18 December 1987, the second of three children. Her parents are also pastors. She completed her theological studies at UKAW in Kupang in February 2010 and assisted ministering with the Nazareth Congregation in East Oesapa. Now she is doing her student ministry in North Amfoang. In December 2010, Fanty was selected by the Eastern Indonesia Women's Network for the Study of Women, Religion and Culture (Jaringan Perempuan Indonesia Timur, JPIT) to join a workshop in Bali, *Healing of Memories*. Together with members of the JPIT research team, Fanty wrote the stories of the families of victims in East Kupang, which are included in the volume *Memecah Pembisuan* edited by Putu Oka Sukanta (published in English translation as *Breaking the Silence*, Melbourne: Monash University Publishing, 2014).

***Fransina Rissi (Rani)*** was born in Maeoe-Rote on 6 February, 1986 and is the youngest of five children. She completed her primary schooling at SD16 Inpres Maeoe in 1998. She attended junior high school at SLTP Negeri 8 in Kupang and graduated in 2002. In 2005 she graduated from high school (SMA Negeri 3) in Kupang and went to pursue further study at the UKAW in the Christianity Study Program of the Faculty of Theology. In September 2010 Rani obtained her bachelor's degree in Theology. She joined the JPIT in October 2010 and had a period of student ministry was with the Silo Congregation in Naikoten I, Kupang. Now she is doing her student ministry in Belu, West Timor. In October 2010 Rani represented JPIT in Jakarta at the launching of *Memecah Pembisuan* (*Breaking the Silence*) which was organised by the Institute for Human Creativity (Lembaga Kreativitas Kemanusiaan, LKK). JPIT contributed to this book, and Fransina was part of the team that contributed to the chapter 'Niko: Clarity at Last'.

## Sabu Team

***Pastor Paoina Bara Pa (Ina)*** was born in Kampung Ligu, Sabu on 16 February 1964 as an only child. Both her parents were primary school teachers. She did her primary and junior high schooling in Sabu and her high schooling in Kupang (SMA Kristen 2), graduating in 1983. She then pursued further study in the Faculty of Theology at UKAW in Kupang and graduated in 1989. She is now a GMIT minister with the Elim Congregation in Lasiana, Kupang. She was a founding member of JPIT, when it was established in Belo, Kupang in 2009. She was part of the research team that contributed to the book *Memecah Pembisan* (*Breaking the Silence*), particularly the chapter 'Nadue: Always Loyal to My Country'.

***Dorkas Nyake Wiwi (Doa)***, the fifth of six children, was born on 20 December 1985 in the village of Ledeke, Sabu where she was raised. She attended primary school and junior high school in Raijua, and then attended the Catholic junior high school (St. Gabriel) in Maumere, Flores. She did further study at the Faculty of Theology at UKAW in Kupang, becoming an alumna in 2010. From June 2011, she served as candidate for student ministry with the Gethsemani Congregation in East Tarus. She is now doing her student ministry on the island of Raijua.

*Petrus Chanisius Bara Pa (Mabara)* was born in Sabu on 2 April 1942. He lives in Kampung Eikepaka, Desa Rae Loro, in West Sabu. He is now retired, but used to be a primary school teacher in Sabu-Raijua. He joined the Sabu-Raijua research team in November 2010 as a local Sabu resident.

## Sumba team

*Pastor Yetty Leyloh* was born on 6 January 1962 in Waikabubak, West Sumba Barat and completed her primary and high school there. In 1982 she entered the Theology College (Sekolah Tinggi Theologia, STT) in Kupang and completed her studies there in1988. In August of that year she became a student minister with the Christian Church of Sumba (Gereja Kristen Sumba, GKS) Melolo Congregation in East Sumba, and in February 1989 student minister with the GKS Tanggaba Congregation in West Sumba. She was ordained as the GKS's first woman pastor on 20 December 1990. In January 1991 she was sent to lecture in the Faculty of Theology at UKAW in Kupang, where she is now. Her focus is traditional religion and theology, and communication. Yetty graduated with a master's degree from Sanata Dharma University in Yogyakarta in the Religion and Culture program in 2007. Since 2009, she has been the JPIT coordinator for the territory of Eastern Indonesia (NTT).

*Pastor Irene Umbu Lolo* was born in Lewa, East Sumba on 4 May 1975 and is the third of four children. Both her father and younger sister are GKS pastors. Her primary and junior high schooling was in Lewa, and her high schooling in Waingapu (SMAN 2) where she graduated in 1993. She did further study in the Faculty of Theology at UKAW in Kupang and graduated in 1999. After doing her student ministry with the GKS, she did her master's degree at the STT in Jakarta, in the field of Practical Theology, and graduated in 2007. She was ordained minister in the GKS at Wai Wei in 2009 and was sent to teach at the GKS STT. She is currently Head of this college for the period 2011–2015.

## South Central Timor Team

*Pastor Dina Penpada* was born in SoE, South Central Timor on 15 November 1966. She completed her bachelor's degree at the Faculty of Theology at UKAW in Kupang in 1989, and on 11 November 1990 was ordained as GMIT pastor. From 1998 to 2001, Dina pursued a master's degree in Yogyakarta at Duta Wacana University, graduating in July 2001. From November 2001 to March 2008 she was a staff member of the GMIT

Synod Council at the GMIT Synod office, working as Secretary of Personnel Development and Education. She also worked as Secretary of the Research and Development section for the Synod from 2002 to 2006. On 1 April 2011, Dina moved to Elfafa Congregation in Liliba, where she still serves. Apart from her pastoral duties, Dia is also a member of JPIT and a member of Peruati (Persekutuan Perempuan Berpendidikan Teologi di Indonesia, Alliance of Women Educated in Theology in Indonesia).

*Pastor Ivonne Peka* was born in SoE, South Central Timor on 2 April 1984 as the oldest of four children. Her primary and high schooling was in SoE. In 2002 Ivonne began studying in the Faculty of Theology at Satya Wacana Christian University (UKSW) in Salatiga and obtained her bachelor's degree in Theology in 2007. In 2009, Ivonne commenced her GMIT student ministry with the Congregation at Efata Liliba, at the Presbytery of Kupang, Central Kupang, where she was until 8 May 2001. She was ordained GMIT pastor at the Elim Bolok Congregation on 21 August 2011 and in February 2012 was placed with the congregation in Tobin region, the Presbytery of North Amanatun.

*Pastor Anna Salukhfeto* was born in Kapan on 24 December 1967, the second of seven children. She completed primary school (SD GMIT) and junior high school (SMP Kristen) at Kapan, and her high schooling at SoE (SMAN). She studied in the Faculty of Theology at UKAW in Kupang and graduated 1993. While writing her thesis, Anna's focus of interest was the attitude of the Church towards those accused of being involved with the 30 September Movement. Anna has been doing her student ministry serving four GMIT congregations in Babuin Village since 1997. In December 2010, the GMIT sent her to Bali to participate in a workshop on healing for victims.

## Editorial Team

*Pastor Mery Kolimon* was born on 2 June 1972 in SoE, South Central Timor. She began serving with the congregation in the area of Bijeli, East Mollo Presbytery, South Central Timor (1997–99). After completing her doctoral studies at the Protestant Theological University in Holland in 2008, she worked in Kupang at her alma mater, UKAW, in the Faculty of Theology as a lecturer in missiology. Apart from acting as Director of the Postgraduate program at UKAW, Mery is also coordinator of the Women's Network of East Indonesia (Jaringan Perempuan Indonesia Timur, JPIT). Mery wrote the story of her father's role as a perpetrator in the book *Memecah Pembisuan*

(*Breaking the Silence*, published in English in 2014 by Monash University Publishing). The chapter on her father is 'The Search for Healing'.

**Desy Aris Santi** was born in Jombang, East Java on 14 December 1986. She completed her high schooling at SMU Negeri I in Kupang in 2005. In the same year, she began further study in the Faculty of Theology at UKAW Kupang. Desy undertook field study with the GMI Congregation at Lelakapa Meoain, the Presbytery of South West Rote, and her candidature for GMIT student ministry in the area of Sungkaen, Central Kupang Presbytery. She participated in a capacity-building course run by the Dian Interfidei Institute in Menado (2010) and Banjarmasin (2011). Desy worked as JPIT secretary in 2010, and she joined the research team for this project in October 2010.

**Elia Maggang** was born in Kabir, Pantar on 12 March 1987. She undertook her primary and high schooling in Kupang. In 2010 she graduated from the Faculty of Theology at UKAW. She now serves with the Emaus Liliba Congregation. Elia worked for a period at the Faculty of Theology as hostel staff. She joined JPIT in 2010 and began to participate in research. In June 2011, she joined a training course in Bali on community video run by Asia Justice and Rights (AJAR).

**Josua LN Tamu Ama (Yos)** was born in Kalabahi, Alor on 11 June 1987. He graduated from the GMIT Imanuel Pepura primary school in Kupang in 2001. In 2003, he graduated from SMP 3 junior high school in Kupang, and in 2005 from SMKN I high school in Kupang. In the same year, he entered the Faculty of Theology at UKAW to undertake further study. In 2010, Yos was awarded his bachelor's degree from the Faculty of Theology, and in October 2010 joined the research team. In June 2011, he began his candidature for student ministry with the Betesda Congregration in Central Tarus.

**Liliya Wetangterah (Lia)** was born to a modest family in Kupang on 7 February 1984. She spent her childhood in Kupang, and completed her theological studies there at the Faculty of Theology at UKAW in 2007. In the same year, Lia served with the Ebenhezer-Oeba Congregation. The following year, she began further study of church law at the Jakarta Theology College (Sekolah Tinggi Teologi Jakarta, STTJ), and graduated in March 2011. In November 2011, Lia joined the JPIT research team, assisting in particular with editing. In the same month she had the opportunity to attend a conference on church law in Holland. While she was there she carried out some interviews to assist the report of the Sumba research team, and also managed to gather some relevant documentation.

# Bibliography

'African National Congress', http://en.wikipedia.org/wiki/African_National_Congress.
*Alor dalam Angka 2009*, Badan Pusat Statistik Kabupaten Alor, Katalog BPS: 1403.5307,160.
Aritonang, Jan Sihar & Karel Steenbrink, eds. *A History of Christianity in Indonesia.* (Leiden, the Netherlands: Koninklijke Brill NV, 2008.
Bani, Pdt. P. STh. 'Sejarah Gereja Jemaat Wilayah Netpala.' Unpublished manuscript, 1997.
'Bayang-bayang teologi pembebasan.' *Gatra,* Nomor 42, Tahun II, 31 August 1996; http://media.isnet.org/islam/Etc/TeologiPembebasan.html.
Baum, Gregory and Harold Wells eds. *The Reconciliation of Peoples: Challenge to the Churches* (Geneva: WCC Publications, 1997).
Bevans, Stephen B. *Model-Model Teologi Kontekstual.* (translated into Indonesian by Yosef Maria Florisan). Maumere: Penerbit Ledalero, 2002. [Original, *Models of Contextual Theology,* Orbit Books 2002].
Boden, Ragna. 'Cold War Economics: Soviet Aid to Indonesia', *Journal of Cold War Studies* 10:3 (Summer 2008).
Bria, Florens Maxi Un. *Introduction to the Wonders of the Canary Island,* a bilingual publication, Indonesian title is *Mengenal Keajaiban Pulau Kenari: Pluralisme dan Paradigma Pembangunan Kabupaten Alor Memasuki Otonomi Daerah dan Indonesia Baru Era Millenium III.* Kupang: Yayasan Parahita Widya Bhakti and Caritas Publishing House: 2001.
Bronkshort, Daan. *Menguak Masa Lalu, Merenda Hari Depan: Komisi Kebenaran di Berbagai Negara,* translated into Indonesian by Elsam translation team).Jakarta: ELSAM, 2002. Indonesian translation of *Truth and Reconciliation: Obstacles and Opportunities* for Human Rights: Amsterdam: Amnesty International Dutch Session, 1995.
Brown, Terry. 'Marxism and Christianity.' *Monthly Review* 36:5 (October 1984): 42–44.
Budiawan. *Mematahkan Pewarisan Ingatan: Wacana Anti-Komunis dan Politik Rekonsiliasi Pasca-Soeharto* (Translated into Indonesian by the Elsam Translation Team). Jakarta: ELSAM, 2004.
*Buku Peringatan 30 Tahun Kesatuan Pergerakan Wanita Indonesia, 22 Desember 1928–22 Desember 1958.* Jakarta: Kementerian Penerangan RI, 1958.
Bustam, Mia *Dari Kamp ke Kamp: Cerita Seorang Perempuan.* Jakarta: Spasi & VHR Book, 2008.
Campbell-Nelson, John and Corrie van der Ven. *Pedoman Penggunaan Metode Studi Kasus* at http://www.oaseonline.org/artikel/corrie-johnMSK.htm.
Chamim, Mardiyah, ed. *Saatnya Korban Bicara: Menata Derap Merajut Langkah.* Jakarta: Yayasan Tifa, Jaringan Relawan Kemanusiaan, and Jaringan Korban untuk Keadilan, 2009.
'Communism and the Christian Church in Indonesian Timor' National Archives of Australia: series number: A1838, Control Symbol: 3038/2/2/2, Location: Canberra. http:// www.naa.gov.au/.
Cooley, Frank L. *Benih Yang Tumbuh XI: Memperkenalkan Gereja Masehi Injili Timor.* Jakarta: Lembaga Penelitian dan Studi Dewan Gereja-gereja di Indonesia, 1976.
*The Growing Seed,* Jakarta: Christian Publishing House BPK, Gunung Mulia, 1982.

Cribbs, Robert. 'Unresolved Problems in the Killings of 1965–1966', *Asian Survey* 42:4 (July/August 2002), 550–63.
Cribbs, Robert ed. *The Indonesian Killings: Pembantaian PKI di Jawa dan di Bali 1965–1966*, translated into Indonesian by Erika S. Alkhattab and Narulita Rusli. Yogyakarta: Mata Bangsa, 2003.
Cribbs, Robert ed. *The Indonesian Killings of 1965–1966: studies from Java and Bali*. Clayton, Vic: Centre of Southeast Asian Studies.
Dorkas, Sir. 'Pengorganisasian Pelayanan', (S1 [BA] thesis, Faculty of Theology, UKAW Kupang, 1990.
Duggan, Genevieve. *Bunga Palem dari Sabu*. Jakarta: Himpunan Wastraprema, 2010.
Eka Darmaputera. 'Religiositas Meningkat, Tapi ke Mana?' *Penuntun: Jurnal Teologi dan Gereja* 2:5 (October-December 1995; Sinode GKI Jawa Barat).
El Tari. *Memori Gubernur Kepala Daerah Propinsi NTT.*
'Faith Communities and Apartheid', Report Prepared for the Truth and Reconciliation Commission. Research Institute on Christianity in South Africa (March 1998). http://web.uct.ac.za/depts/ricsa/commiss/trc/trcout.htm.
Farid, Hilmar. 'Indonesia's Original Sin: Mass Killings and Capitalist Expansion 1965–1966', *Penebar e-News*, No. 9 (January 2006).
Farram, Steven. 'From 'Timor Koepang' to 'Timor NTT': A Political History of West Timor, 1901–1967.' A thesis submitted for the degree of Doctor of Philosophy, Charles Darwin University, 2004 http://espace.cdu.edu.au/eserv/cdu:6450/Thesis_CDU_6450_Farram_S.pdf.
Farram, Steven. 'Revolution, Religion and Magic: The PKI in West Timor, 1924–1966.' *Bijdragen tot de Taal-, Land- en Volkenkunde*, 158 (2002), 21–48.
Fransisca Ria Susanti. *Kembang-kembang Genjer*. Yogyakarta: Jejak 2007.
Gereja Kristen Sumba. 'Susunan Keputusan-Keputusan Synode Geredja Keristen Sumba, Synode ke-I (1947) s/d Synode ke-XX (1966),' selected sections. Unpublished GKS document.
Gereja Kristen Sumba. 'Tjatatan dari Sidang Synode ke 20 Geredja Keristen Sumba jang terhimpun di Kananggaru pada tanggal 20 s/d 28 Djuli 1966', selected sections. Unpublished GKS document.
Gereja Kristen Sumba. 'Tjatatan dari Sidang Synode ke 21 Geredja Keristen Sumba jang terhimpun di Ede pada tanggal 26 Djuli s/d 4 Agustus 1967', selected sections. Unpublished GKS document.
Gereja Kristen Sumba. 'Tjatatan dari Sidang Synode ke 22 Geredja Keristen Sumba jang terhimpun di Mamboru pada tanggal 23 Djuli s/d 2 Agustus 1968', selected sections. Unpublished GKS document.
Gogali, Lian. *Konflik Poso: Suara Perempuan dan Anak Menuju Rekonsiliasi Ingatan*. Yogyakarta: Galangpress, 2009.
Grimes, Charles E, Tom Therik, Barbara Dix Grimes and Max Jacob. *A guide to the people and languages of Nusa Tenggara*. Kupang: Artha Wacana Press, 1997.
Gultom, Samuel. *Mengadili Korban: Praktek Pembenaran Terhadap Kekerasan Negara*. Jakarta: ELSAM, 2003.
Hasse, J. 'Kebijakan Negara terhadap Agama Lokal 'Towani Tolotang' si Kabupaten Sidrap, Sulawesi Selatan' in *Jurnal Studi Pemerintahan* 1:1 (August 2010).
Hayner, Pricilla B. *Kebenaran Tak Terbahasakan: Refleksi Pengalaman Komisi-komisi Kebenaran, Kenyataan dan Harapan*, (translated into Indonesian by the ELSHAM translation team). Jakarta: ELSAM, 2004. Original publication *Unspeakable Truth: Facing the Challenge of Truth Commissions*. New York and London: Routledge, 2002.

Herman, Judith. *Trauma and Recovery. The Aftermath of Violence: From Domestic Abuse to Political Terror.* New York: Basic Books, 1992.
*Hukum Pidana Internasional dan Perempuan: Sebuah Buku Acuan untuk Praktisi*, 4 jilid. Jakarta: Komnas Perempuan, 2006. http://komnasperempuan.or.id/2009/01/hukum-pidana-internasional-dan-perempuan-2/.
'Internal resistance to South African apartheid'. http://en.wikipedia.org/wiki/Internal_resistance_to_South_African_apartheid.
Itta, Hans ed. *Timor Tengah Selatan dalam Jangkauan Zaman* (SoE: Pemerintah Daerah Kabupaten TTS, 2006.
Jacob, June and Charles E. Grimes. *Kamus Pengantar Bahasa Kupang.* Kupang: Artha Wacana Press, 2003.
'Juan Luis Segundo (1925–1996),' entry in *Boston Collaborative Encyclopedia of Western Theology.* http://people.bu.edu/wwildman/bce/segundo.htm.
Kaligis, O.C. and Rum Aly, eds. *Simtom Politik 1965: PKI dalam Perspektif Pembalasan dan Pengampunan.* Jakarta: Kata Hasta Pustaka, 2007.
Kasim, Ifdhal and Eddie Riyadi Terre, eds. *Pencarian Keadilan di Masa Transisi.* Jakarta: ELSAM, 2003.
*Kejahatan terhadap Kemanusiaan Berbasis Jender: Mendengarkan Suara Perempuan Korban Peristiwa 1965.* Jakarta: Komnas Perempuan, 2007.
*Keluar Jalur: Keadilan Transisi di Indonesia Setelah Jatuhnya Soeharto.* Jakarta: ICTJ and KontraS, 2011.
Kolimon, Mery. *Theology of Empowerment. Reflections from a West Timorese Perspective.* Berlin: Lit. Verlag, 2008.
Kroef, Justus, M. van der. 'Indonesian Communism's Expansionist Role in Southeast Asia', *International Journal* 20:2 (Spring 1965).
Kuester, Volker. *Many Faces of Jesus Christ.* London: SCM Press, 2001.
'Langkah Pertama: Suatu Tinjauan terhadap Periode 25 Tahun G.M.I.T. 31 Oktober 1974–31 Oktober 1972.' Kupang: Majelis Sinode G.M.I.T., 1972. Unpublished GMIT document.
Martin, Stephen William. 'Civic Sacrament and Social Imaginaries in Transition: The Case of the South African Churches and the Truth and Reconciliation Commission.' *Political Theology* 12:3 (2011). http://www.politicaltheology.com/PT/article/view/6399.
Marx, Karl. 'Introduction to a Contribution to the Critique of Hegel's Philosophy of Right', *Deutsch-Französische Jahrbucher.* Paris: 7 & 10 February, 1844.
McGovern, Arthur F. *Liberation Theology and Its Critics: Toward an Assessment.* Maryknoll, New York: Orbis Books, 1989.
McGregor, Katherine E. *History in Uniform: Military Ideology and the Construction of Indonesia's Past,* NUS Press, 2007.
Merta, Dyah, Fati Soewandi, Gde Aryantha Soetama, et al. *Antologi Cerita Pendek Lobakan: Kesenyapan Gemuruh Bali '65.* Jakarta: Koekoesan dan Lembaga Kreatifitas Kemanusiaan, 2009.
Middelkoop, Pieter. *Curse-Retribution-Enmity: As Data in Natural Religion, Especially in Timor, Confronted with the Scripture.* Amsterdam: Drukkeerij en Uitgeverij Jacob van Campen, 1960.
Middelkoop, P. *Atoni Pah Meto: Pertemuan Injil dan Kebudayaan di Kalangan Suku Timor Asli.* Jakarta: BPK Gunung Mulia, 1982.
Moh, Mahfud MD. 'Kebebasan Beragama dalam Perspektif Konstitusi', http://law.uii.ac.id/dokumentasi/task,doc_download/gid,62/.

Moore, Mary Elizabeth. *Teaching from the Heart: Theology and Educational Method.* Harrisburg PA: Trinity Press International, 1998.
Muhammad Farid. 'How the Cold War influences US-Indonesia relations', *The Jakarta Post*, 9 February 2007.
Munawar-Rachman, Budhy. 'Teologi Pembebasan: Komentar terhadap artikel di majalah *Gatra*.' http://media.isnet.org/ islam/Etc/TanggapPembebasan.html.
Nadia, Ita F. *Suara Perempuan Korban Tragedi '65'.* Yogyakarta: Galang Press, 2009.
Ngelow, Zakaria J. 'Bianglala di atas Tsumani' in *Teologi Bencana*, ed. Zakaria Ngelow et. al Makassar: Yayasan Oase Intim, 2006.
Nordholt, Henk Schulte, Bambang Purwanto, and Ratna Saptari, eds. *Perspektif Baru Penulisan Sejarah Indonesia.* Jakarta: Yayasan Obor Indonesia, KITLV-Jakarta, and Denpasar: Pustaka Larasan, 2008.
Nugroho, Singgih. *Menyintas dan Menyebrang: Perpindahan Massal Keagamaan Pasca 1965 di Pedesaan Jawa.* Yogyakarta: Syarikat Indonesia, 2008.
Nurhabsyah. 'Penerapan Sejarah Lisan dalam Sejarah Lokal.' Fakultas Sastra, Jurusan Sejarah, Universitas Sumatera Utara.
'Old and New Christianity in the Southeastern Islands.' Ch. 7 in *A History of Christianity in Indonesia*, eds. Jan Sihar Aritonang and Karel Steenbrink. Leiden, The Netherlands: Koninklijke Brill NV, 2008, 229–344.
Pada, Maria Regina A. 'Praktek Pengakuan Dosa Pribadi di Hadapan Jemaat dalam Gereja Kristen Sumba (GKS): Suatu Tinjauan Dogmatis,' (BA thesis, Faculty of Theology UKAW, Kupang.
Paulose, Mar. Paulose. *Encounter in Humanity: Insights for Christian-Marxist Dialogue and Cooperation.* Formerly available online from http://www.religion-online.org/ cgi-bin/relsearchd.dll/ showchapter? chapter_ id=1516(12 of 12).
'Peristiwa 1965' in *Kita Bersikap: Empat Dasawarsa Kekerasan terhadap Perempuan dalam Perjlanan Berbangsa* (174–80). Jakarta: Komnas Perempuan, 2009.
Pokok-Pokok Eklesiologi GMIT' (2010) unpublished.
Prior, John. 'The Silent Scream of a Silenced History: The Maumere Massacre of 1966,' *Exchange* 40 (2011), 117–43, 311–21.
'Provinsi Nusa Tenggara Timur'. Kementerian Dalam Negeri Republik Indonesia. http://www.depdagri.go.id/pages/profil-daerah/provinsi/detail/53/nusa-tenggara-timur.
Roosa, John. *Pretext for Mass Murder: The September 30th Movement and Suharto's Coup d'État in Indonesia.* Madison: University of Wisconsin Press, 2006.
'Dictionary of a Disaster', *Inside Indonesia* 99 (January–March 2010).
Roosa, John, Ayu Ratih and Hilmar Farid, eds. *Tahun yang Tak Pernah Berakhir.* Jakarta: Lembaga Studi Masyarakat, 2004.
Roosa, John and Ayu Ratih. 'Catatan Singkat tentang Fungsi Sejarah Lisan.' Unpublished manuscript.
Rubio-Marin, Ruth, ed. *Perempuan Menggugat: Masalah Gender dan Reparasi dalam Kejahatan Hak Asasi Manusia.* (Translated into Indonesian by Alda Milasari.) Jakarta: ELSAM, 2008.
Rufus Ony Tunliu. *Kilas Balik DPRD TTS.* Unpublished manuscript.
Salukhfeto, Anna Ch. 'Perhatian Gereja terhadap Anggota Jemaat yang Terlibat PKI di Mollo Utara: Sebuah Tinjauan Kritis Theologis terhadap Cara Gereja di Mollo Utara Member lakukan Disiplin Gerejawi bagi Anggota Jemaatnya yang Terlibat PKI.' Unpublished S1 [BA] thesis, Fakultas Teologi UKAW Kupang, 1993.

Samsoeri, Danielle. 'Pentingnya Keterlibatan Komnas Perempuan dalam Judicial Review UU Penodaan Agama,' unpublished and undated manuscript. http://www.komnasperempuan.or.id/2010/03/pentingny a-keterlibatan-komnas-perempuan-dalam-judicial-review- uu-penodaan-agama/.
Scott, Peter Dale. 'The United States and the Overthrow of Soekarno, 1965–1967', *Pacific Affairs* 58 (Summer 1985), 239–64.
Segundo, Juan Luis. *Signs of the Times: Theological Reflection*. Edited by Alfred T. Hennelly and translated by Robert R. Barr. Maryknoll, New York: Orbis Books, 1993.
*Seri Studi Kasus Pastoral I-III*, SEAGST Institute of Advanced Pastoral Studies, Jakarta: BPK 1985, 1990.
Setiawan, Hersri. *Aku Eks Tapol*. Yogyakarta: Galang Press, 2003.
Setwilda TTS. *Kenang-Kenangan: Dewan Perwakilan Rakyat Daerah Tingkat II Timor Tengah Selatan Periode 1971–1977*. Soe: Setwilda TTS (no year of publication given).
Siwirni C, Sumiyarsi. *Plantungan: Pembuangan Tapol Perempuan*. Yogyakarta: Pusdep Univ. Sanata Dharma, 2010.
Soelle, Dorothee. 'The Christian-Marxist dialogue of the 1960s,' *Monthly Review* 36:3 (July-August 1984): 20–26.
Stephan, Alfred. *Rethinking Military Politics: Brazil and the Southern Cone*. Princeton, NJ: Princeton University Press, 1988.
*Studi Kasus Pastoral II: Nusa Tenggara Timur* [Pastoral Case Studies II: East Nusatenggara].Team Penulis: Panitia Metode Studi Kasus GMIT/GKS. Jakarta: BPK Gunung Mulia, 1990.
Sukanta, Putu Oka, ed. *Memecah Pembisuan: Tuturan Penyintas Tragedi '65–'66*. Jakarta: Lembaga Kreatifitas Kemanusiaan, ICTJ, TIFA, 2011. *Breaking the Silence: Survivors speak about 1965–66 violence in Indonesia* [English translation of *Memecah Pembisuan*, translator Jennifer Lindsay] Melbourne: Monash University Publishing 2014.
Susanti, Fransisca Ria. *Kembang-kembang Genjer*. Yogyakarta: Jejak, 2007.
Syukur, Abdul. 'Sejarah Lisan Orang Biasa: Sebuah Pengalaman Penelitian.' Paper presented at the National History Conference VIII, 14–17 November 2006, Jakarta.
Taufik. *Kamp Pengasingan Moncongloe*. Jakarta: Desantara, 2009.
Teitel, Ruti G. *Keadilan Transisional: Sebuah Tinjauan Komperhensif*. (Indonesian translation by the ELSAM translaton team). Jakarta: ELSAM, 2004.
Tere, Eddie R, and Betty Yolanda, eds.
*Pedoman Perlindungan Terhadap Saksi dan Pekerja HAM*. (Indonesian translation by ELSAM translation team.) Jakarta: ELSAM, 2006.
Therik, W. 'Perkembangan Pers di Nusa Tenggara Timur' in *The World of Wilson Therik*, http://wilson-therik.blogspot.com/2010/11/perkembangan-pers-di-nusa-tenggara.html.
Thich Nhat Hanh. *Jesus and Buddha as Brothers*. New York: The Penguin Group, 1999.
Tillich, Paul. 'The Marks of Man's Estrangement and the Concept of Sin', *Systematic Theology*, II.
Tribble, Phyllis. *Texts of Terror: Literary-Feminist Readings of Biblical Narratives* (Philadelphia: Fortress Press, 1984.
Umbu Pura Woha. *Sejarah Pemerintahan di Pulau Sumba*, Kupang: Undana Press, 2008.

Van Boven, Theo and Ifdhal Kasim. *Mereka Yang Menjadi Korban: Hak Korban atas Restitusi, Kompensasi, dan Rehabilitasi.* Jakarta: Elsam, 2002.
Webb, R.A.F. Paul and Steven Farram. *Di-PKI-kan: Tragedi 1965 dan Kaum Nasrani di Indonesia Timur.* Indonesian language translation by Chandra Utama. Yogyakarta: Syarikat Indonesia, 2005. [Translation of R.A.F. Webb 'The Sickle and the Cross', and Steven Farram 'Revolution, religion and magic'].
Webb, R.A.F. 'The Sickle and the Cross: Christians and Communists in Bali, Flores, Sumba and Timor, 1965–67,' *Journal of Southeast Asian Studies* XVII:1 (March 1986), 94–112.
Wellem, F.D. *Injil & Marapu* (Jakarta: BPK Gunung Mulia 2004). 'Old and New Christianity in the Southeastern Islands', in *A History of Christianity in Indonesia*, eds. Jan Sihar Aritonang and Karel Sttenbrink (Leiden, The Netherlands: Koninklijke Brill NV, 2008, 229–344).
'What is Transitional Justice?' International Center for Transitional Justice. http://ictj.org/about/transitional-justice.
Wieringa, Saskia Eleonora. *Penghancuran Gerakan Perempuan di Indonesia.* Jakarta: Garba Budaya dan Kalyanamitra, 1999.
Wieringa, Saskia. *Sexual politics in Indonesia.* New York: Palgrave Macmillan [Institute of Social Studies Series] 2002.
Yewangoe, A. A. *Tidak Ada Penumpang Gelap, Warga Gereja Warga Bangsa.* Jakarta: BPK Gunung Mulia 2009.
Yunus, Ahmad. 'Seanandung Bisu 1965.' May 2010. http://indoprogress.blogspot.com/2010/06/senandung-bisu-1965.html.

www.ingramcontent.com/pod-product-compliance
Ingram Content Group Australia Pty Ltd
76 Discovery Rd, Dandenong South VIC 3175, AU
AUHW020941240125
406045AU00002B/17